South Africa in the Twentieth Century

HISTORY OF THE CONTEMPORARY WORLD

Consultant Editors: Dr Peter Catterall and Professor Lawrence Freedman

This series aims to provide students of contemporary history, politics and international relations with concise, critical overviews of the major themes and the development of key geographical regions that have dominated discussion of world events in the twentieth century. The emphasis in the regional histories will be on the period since the Second World War, but coverage will extend to the earlier twentieth century wherever necessary. The books will assume little or no prior knowledge of the subject, and are intended to be used by students as their point of entry into a wide range of topics in contemporary international history.

Published

South Africa in the Twentieth Century
James Barber

The Causes of the Second World War
Andrew J. Crozier

The West and the Third World
D. K. Fieldhouse

The Communist Movement since 1945
Willie Thompson

Forthcoming

Decolonization and its Impact
Martin Shipway

South Africa in the Twentieth Century

A Political History – In Search of a Nation State

James Barber

First published 1999

2 4 6 8 10 9 7 5 3 1

Blackwell Publishers Ltd
108 Cowley Road
Oxford OX4 1JF
UK

Blackwell Publishers Inc.
350 Main Street
Malden, Massachusetts 02148
USA

British Library Cataloguing in Publication Data

A CIP catalogue record for this book is available from the British Library.

Library of Congress Cataloging-in-Publication Data

Barber, James.
    South Africa in the twentieth century : a political history in
search of a nation state / James Barber.
        p.   cm. — (History of the contemporary world)
    Includes bibliographical references and index.
    ISBN 0–631–19101–1 (alk. paper). — ISBN 0–631–19102–X
(pbk. : alk. paper)
    1. South Africa—Politics and government—20th century. 2. South
Africa—Ethnic relations—Political aspects—History—20th century.
I. Title. II. Series.
DT1945.B37   1999
968.082—dc21   99–11161
                                                                                      CIP

Typeset in Bembo 10pt. on 11½pt.
by Grahame & Grahame Editorial, Brighton
Printed in Great Britain by TJ International Ltd, Padstow, Cornwall

Contents

Illustrations

PLATES

MAPS

TABLES

Acknowledgements

I would like to record my thanks to the following for their help and support: Professor Hermann Giliomee, Professor David Welsh, Professor Nigel Worden, Christopher Hill, Kathy Viljeon, Elizabeth Barratt, Tessa Harvey and Louise Spencely of Blackwell Publishers, and my wife.

Cambridge, April 1999

Abbreviations

AAC	All African Convention
ANC	African National Congress
AWB	Afrikaner Weerstands Beweging
AFV	Afrikaner Volksfront
AP	Afrikaner Party
APLA	Azanian People's Liberation Army
Azapo	Azanian People's Organisation
BC	Black Consciousness
BPC	Black People's Convention
CCB	Civil Co-operation Bureau
Codesa	Convention for a Democratic South Africa
COSAG	Concerned South Africans Group
COSATU	Congress of South African Trade Unions
CP	Conservative Party
CPSA	Communist Party of South Africa
CYL	Congress Youth League
DP	Democratic Party
EPG	Eminent Persons Group (Commonwealth)
FA	Freedom Alliance
FF	Freedom Front
HNP	Herstigte Nasionale Party
ICU	Industrial and Commercial [Workers'] Union
IDASA	Institute for Democratic Alternatives for South Africa
IEC	Independent Electoral Commission
IFP	Inkatha Freedom Party
IRR	South African Institute of Race Relations
MDM	Mass Democratic Movement
MK	Umkhonto we Sizwe (ANC's armed wing)
MUFC	Mandela United Football Club
NCP	National Conservative Party
NF	National Forum
NNC	Native National Congress
NP	National Party

NRC	Native Representative Council
NRP	New Republican Party
NSMS	National Security Management Scheme
OAU	Organisation of African Unity
OFS	Orange Free State
ORC	Orange River Colony
PAC	Pan Africanist Congress
PFP	Progressive Federal Party
PP	Progressive Party
RDP	Reconstruction and Development Programme
SACP	South African Communist Party
SADCC	Southern African Development Co-ordination Conference
SADF	South African Defence Force
SAP	South African (National) Party
SASO	South African Students Organisation
SSC	State Security Council
SWAPO	South West African People's Organisation
TRC	Truth and Reconciliation Commission
UDF	United Democratic Front
UNIA	United Negro Improvement Association
UP	Unionist Party (Disbanded 1921)
UP	United Party (Formed 1934)
ZANU	Zimbabwe African National Union
ZAPU	Zimbabwe African People's Union

For my friend John Barratt
and for Sarah, Kate, Katherine,
Alice, Georgie and Emma

Introduction

In 1987 I was invited by the South African Institute of International Affairs to give the Jan Smuts Memorial Lecture. It was a time of deep gloom in the Republic. The apartheid government was in power, led by the authoritarian figure of P. W. Botha. The country was reeling from the bitter clashes between the government forces and black urban dwellers who had risen against the oppressive regime; some black townships were ungovernable; emergency regulations were in operation; many African leaders were in prison or exile; small units from the armed wing of the African National Congress (ANC) had infiltrated the country but there was no prospect of a clear-cut military victory either for them or for the government; international sanctions were biting into the economy without destroying it; South African forces were raiding and destabilizing neighbouring states. All was darkness.

I took as the title for my lecture: 'Is there a South African Nation?' In answer I argued that the way to end the terrible conflict was for the peoples of South Africa to come together, to establish a sense of common identity, to forge a nation. But I was pessimistic. I finished by saying that remarkable changes do take place, 'but you have to be an extreme optimist to believe that the degree of change I am suggesting is possible here [in South Africa]'. 'As an outsider,' I continued, 'I sometimes feel like a member of a theatre audience. On the stage are the various South African actors . . . At first we in the audience are confused about the nature of the play. Is it a farce or a tragedy? As it unfolds it soon becomes clear that it is a tragedy, and one of potentially immense proportions. Yet those on the stage either do not understand what is happening, or are not prepared to do anything about it. By now we in the audience have become so engrossed that we call out, trying to attract the attention of the players, to point out the dangers; but they are so wrapped in fear and suspicion of each other that they can absorb nothing else. They don't hear us as we shout: "Come together; work together; make a nation"' (Barber 1987: 16).

My pessimism was misplaced. Remarkable changes have taken place – apartheid is no more, and under the leadership of President Nelson Mandela most South Africans are working to form a single nation – 'the rainbow nation'. This is not to suggest that all people support the new order, or that all the old problems have disappeared (they have not and serious new ones have arisen). However, a bold start has been made. Now there is hope, where previously there was only despair. One way to appreciate the scale and significance of the change is to examine the efforts throughout the country's twentieth-century history to establish a dominant nationalism and to shape the South African state in the interests of that nationalism. The century has been characterized, cursed even, by conflicting interpretations of nationalism; by assertions of who are 'the true South Africans', and dependent on that who has the right to shape and control the state. Never has South Africa been free from clashing claims and counter claims. This book seeks to examine them.

At the turn of the century South Africa did not exist as a single political entity. Instead there were two British colonies (Cape Colony, and Natal), and two Afrikaner/Boer republics (The South African Republic or Transvaal, and the Orange Free State). That was the setting for a great drama to unfold: a drama of conflict about fundamental political issues concerning the rights of individuals and groups; about who should control the state; and about the nature of society and government. It is not a debate which has been conducted within a broad consensus, with differences only over particular policies or the detailed allocation of resources. Rather it has been a struggle over basic issues of power and rights. The scene across the century was never still. It changed as economic and social circumstances changed, as old assumptions proved false, as different groups gained power only to face new challenges, as new leaders and ideas emerged, and as external factors intruded to alter the political setting. That led to tragic conflicts, but it also produced leaders with powerful ideas and ideals. Whether those leaders are regarded as heroes or villains, saints or sinners, has changed over time and will continue to change as new judgements are made.

The central theme of this study is the relationship between 'nation' and 'state' in South Africa. I have approached this as a political issue, in which the main concentration is upon political leaders, their parties and the structure and functioning of the state. It is, therefore, 'top down history'. Such an approach does not imply that social and economic developments at various levels were unimportant. They were not – either in their own right or in the context of this study. In relation to this study they influenced the views of politicians; they helped to shape the policies they pursued; and political leaders used economic and social rewards as a means of recruiting and retaining support. However, my approach does imply that political leadership and political debate play a major part in shaping the society and the power relationships within it. It further implies that the interaction between the ideas and aims of politicians and their efforts to realize these is central to understanding the development of the state.

Hans Kohn wrote: 'Nationalism is a state of mind . . . which fills man's brain and heart with new thoughts and new sentiments, and drives him to translate his consciousness into deeds of organised action. Nationality is therefore not only a group held together and animated by common consciousness, but it is also a group seeking to find its expression in what it regards as the highest form of organized activity, a sovereign state . . . Nationalism demands the nation state' (Kohn 1965: 5).

Kohn rightly recognized a relationship between 'nationalism' and 'the state', but how are those concepts to be understood? Here, in thumbnail terms, I have identified 'the state' by four characteristics. First it occupies and seeks to control a geographical area; second, it has a government and formal institutions – manned by ministers and officials, and backed by armed forces; third, the government claims sovereignty (i.e. the right to make final decisions); and finally, it is recognized as sovereign by other states which make up the international community.

'Nationalism' is a powerful but elusive and disputed concept. While the state is associated with a geographical area and its government, nationalism is associated with people. As with all social groups, it is not static. Here there is no attempt to establish a definitive position. Nationalism is treated as a self-defining concept. If a person says that he or she is part of a particular nation, that is accepted. National identity has many sources – ethnic pride, shared history, common culture and language, economic and social factors, possession of territory and so on. To take but one example in South Africa's case, Shula Marks and Stanley Trapido have stated that 'both black and white nationalism can in large part be seen as responses to later nineteenth century industrialisation; imperialism and British "race patriotism"' (Marks and Trapido 1987: 2). However, in this study I have laid less stress on the sources of national self-identification than the way it has affected political behaviour.

In retrospect nationalism can often seem confused and misplaced. Yet, that has made it no less compelling for those who believed in it at the time. It can generate great loyalty and faith. Scattered across South Africa are memorials to those who gave their lives for causes which now appear pointless or misguided, but the fact that people were prepared to die for them shows the strength of the commitment. Nationalism provides its adherents with a legitimizing claim or myth for control of the state. As Henry Tudor wrote, the aim of the myth 'is either to advocate a certain course of action or to justify an existing state of affairs. Myths are therefore believed to be true, not because the historical evidence is compelling, but because they make sense of men's present experience' (Tudor 1972: 124). That has been the case in South Africa.

The relationship between nation and state has long been recognized, but is often disputed. After the First World War, US President Woodrow Wilson swept into Europe confident that he could ensure future peace by identifying distinctive European nations and drawing clear state boundaries around them. For him the nation would create the state, based on 'ethnic nationalism', exclusive to those belonging to readily identifiable national group. However, as well as the practical difficulties Wilson encountered – because national groups do not live in neat geographical packages – experience shows that the relationship between nation and state is often reversed. Instead of a nation creating a state, the state – through the activities of its political leaders – creates a nation. Massimo D'Azeglio declared in 1860: 'Now we have made Italy, we must set to work to make the Italians.' Wilson's own state – the USA – illustrates the same point, as waves of immigrants have become 'Americans'. In such cases the state builds the nation, through a 'civic nationalism', which is inclusive of all who live in the state irrespective of their origins.

The new South African Government is committed to a form of civic national-ism. It seeks to build a nation from all who live in the Republic, irrespective of colour, creed or status. It preaches a single overriding identity for all. Yet, for most of the twentieth century, nationalism in South Africa was promoted in its narrower, ethnic form. The result was a persistent struggle to impose a dominant nationalism. This study examines that struggle. It investigates the way in which political leaders promoted their aims and ideas in a competition for power. In doing so, it recog-nizes that politicians, like everybody else, change their minds and are not always consistent; that they have to respond to changing circumstances, and are surrounded by constraints. There were periods when a particular form of nationalism appeared to have entrenched itself in control of the state only to be undermined by its own weaknesses and contradictions and by outside challenges. None of the efforts, there-fore, had fully succeeded before Mandela came to power preaching 'the rainbow nation', and it is too early to judge that.

There are many pitfalls in writing about twentieth-century South Africa. Among them is that of political vocabulary. Some words have changed their meaning, and others, which were employed at one time, have fallen into disuse or become pejorative. For example, in the early part of the century 'race relations' was used to describe relations between whites (Afrikaans and English speakers), while the position of Africans was described as 'the Native question' or 'the Native problem'. Also, various names have been used for the country's indigenous inhabitants, including 'Kaffir', 'Native', 'Bantu', 'African' and 'Black'. A further difficulty is that several of the names – like 'Coloured', 'English speaker', 'black', 'Afrikaner' and 'African' – are portmanteau terms embracing a variety of peoples. The 'Coloureds', for example, are people of mixed race – whose origins include Indonesians, Europeans, Malaysians and African (from West Africa as well as South Africa); and mixed religions (Islam and Christianity). 'English-speaking whites' include not only those born in South Africa of British stock or who have emigrated from Britain, but other Europeans who use English as a main language. 'Afrikaner' has also been a fluid term. Hermann Giliomee noted that before the twentieth century it was often used 'for whites whose loyalty was to the region rather than the Dutch or British metropole'. To a more limited extent that continued into the early twen-tieth century, and some politicians, in their search for votes in the Cape, extended the name 'Afrikaner' to embrace Coloureds (Giliomee 1995: 204–5). Finally, 'black' is sometimes applied solely to Africans, whereas at other times it includes Coloureds and Indians. Doubtless with so many linguistic pitfalls I have fallen into some of them. Yet, despite such problems, generalizations have to be made in a study of this nature. My aim has been to be as clear as possible.

Another area of uncertainty is the relationship between white and black political activity. For most of the century the state was controlled by whites. Blacks, and especially Africans, were a matter of constant concern for the government, but they had no direct part in managing the state. Yet, they had to react to its policies and actions, in responding to a government imposed agenda. In doing so the nature of black reaction changed during the century. While before the Second World War African/black leaders were mainly concerned to gain a place in the existing government structure, from the 1940s they increasingly aimed to overthrow it and form a state based on majority rule. At first the challenge came in protests, demonstrations and peaceful political activities, but, from the early 1960s, it took the form of a liberation movement with an armed wing. After decades of conflict a democratic system was finally achieved by negotiation, embracing blacks and whites, in a new South Africa. This book seeks to tell that story.

Part I

The Clash of British Imperialism
and Afrikaner Nationalism

1

Prelude to War: Afrikaner and British Imperial Nationalism

In the early hours of 12 October 1899 a column 'of silent misty figures, horsemen, artillery, and wagons' filed past the dark shoulder of Majuba mountain (Packenham 1982: 107). They were the forces of the Transvaal (the South African Republic) invading the British colony of Natal. It was the start of a war, known to the British as 'the Boer War' and to Afrikaners (or Boers) as 'The Second War of Liberation'. Two days before the invasion Paul Kruger, the Transvaal's President, had issued an ultimatum to the British, which brought to an end prolonged negotiations between the two governments. Two days after the invasion, a large enthusiastic crowd lined Southampton docks to wave off Sir Redvers Buller with British reinforcements for South Africa. As with most wars both sides anticipated a quick clear victory, and, as with many, they were proved wrong. The fighting extended over three and a half years – first in set battles and later in guerilla warfare – and claimed tens of thousands of lives. Eventually the British gained a military victory but the political outcome was far from clear.

The war was fuelled by two deeply held faiths: British imperialism and Afrikaner republicanism. In 1899 what is now South Africa consisted of two British Colonies (Cape Colony and Natal) and two Boer Republics (The Orange Free State and the Transvaal). The British 'imperial factor' had entered South Africa during the Napoleonic wars when Britain occupied the old Dutch Cape Colony to secure her communications with the East and to deny the French. In absorbing the Cape the British inherited a mixed population of Africans, Coloureds (mixed race) and whites. The whites were a mixture of Dutch, French and Germans – mainly of Protestant stock – who called themselves 'Boers' (Farmers) or Afrikaners. Some came to accept British rule; others did not. In 1835 substantial numbers of Boers trekked north in an endeavour to throw off the imperial yoke, not least because of British liberalism towards blacks, including the abolition of slavery. Fortified by their Calvinist faith, their sense of identity and their success in adapting to the harsh life, the Voortrekkers established themselves in the lands north of the Cape Colony. Sometimes they settled in peace; often they occupied and conquered territory at the expense of its African inhabitants. It was a fragile tenure; beset by natural hazards and conflicts with African peoples. The trekkers did not set out to establish a single

Afrikaner state. Initially they created a number of small political units, but eventually they formed their two republics. Even so, the government structures were sparse and weak, especially in the Transvaal. 'The truth was,' wrote Geoffrey Wheatcroft, 'that the Transvaal was not really a "state" at all, scarcely more so than the neighbouring African kingdoms' (Wheatcroft 1993: 160).

The British Government's reaction to Boer expansion was ambivalent. Sometimes it was ignored, but when British interests were perceived to be threatened – and the perception depended on the view from London as well as South Africa – attempts were made to exercise control. Despite British vacillation, there was a broad consensus that all southern Africa was a British sphere of influence. Therefore, what the Boers saw as a search for independence could be seen by the British as a threat to their imperial paramountcy. The perceived threat took two forms: first, that imperial rivals would establish footholds via the republics; and second that conflict over land and cattle between Africans and Boers would destabilize the sub-continent. To preserve and extend their stake the British fought a series of wars against African peoples, most notably against the Xhosa on the eastern frontiers of the Cape and the Zulu in Natal.

The result was that the British were always snapping at the heels of the Boers and their republics. In 1877 they took over the administration of the Transvaal, claiming that it was insolvent and inefficient; that it created instability by its clashes with Africans; and that it flirted with imperial rivals. Confident of the imperial cause Sir Garnet Wolseley declared: 'So long as the sun shines, the Transvaal will be British territory; and the Vaal River shall flow back on its sources before the Transvaal is again independent' (Fisher 1975: 91). He was a poor prophet. Two years later the British attacked the Zulu whom they saw as a threat to Natal. Although the British were eventually victorious, it was only after the Zulu had inflicted a major defeat on them at Isandlwana. That defeat temporarily made London cautious of further South African adventures. In 1880 Lord Kimberley, the Colonial Secretary, lamented: 'We have more than fifty colonies and South Africa gives more trouble than all the rest together' (Lehmann 1985: 296). At the same time the Boers took heart because the final British victory over the Zulu removed that threat from the Transvaal's flank. Ironically it had opened up an opportunity for the Boers to challenge the British.

In 1881 the Transvaal Boers seized that opportunity. They rose and defeated a British force at Majuba in what the Boers called 'the First War of Liberation' (known in Britain as 'The Transvaal War'). In London, despite the humiliation, which was keenly felt in the army, Gladstone's Liberal Government decided against an attempt to avenge the defeat by seeking to reimpose direct rule. Instead both parties signed the Pretoria Convention of 1881, which gave the Transvaal internal self-government, while the British retained veto powers in foreign policy and Native affairs, and claimed 'suzerainty' – a grand but elusive concept. A second Convention, signed at London in 1884, made concessions to the Transvaal. It made no mention of 'suzerainty', it removed the veto over Native legislation, but stated that the Transvaal must gain British approval for agreements with African peoples or with other states (except the Orange Free State).

Despite the setbacks in the Transvaal British imperialism gained a new momentum in the late nineteenth century, both from a growing confidence in the imperial mission and from increasing rivalry among European powers. In southern Africa this received a great boost through changing economic circumstances. In the late 1860s, a rich diamond field was discovered at Kimberley in Griqua territory on the northern borders of the Cape. Despite claims to the area from the Boer republics, the British absorbed the territory into the Cape Colony. A surge of prospectors and labour arrived in that arid, remote region to mine the diamonds and create a new wave of economic activity. Then, only two years after the signing of the 1884 London Convention, gold was discovered on the Witwatersrand in the Transvaal. The scene was transformed, and it was transformed with remarkable speed. The Transvaal, which had been a rural backwater, now housed a major mining/industrial complex. Capital and labour flooded in to exploit and develop the world's largest deposits of the precious metal. In terms of world production the Rand contributed 0.16 per cent in 1886 (the year gold was discovered); while by 1898 it was the largest single source of gold, producing 27 per cent of the total (Van Onselen 1982: 1). As the currencies of the industrialized world were based on the gold standard, and as Britain was the leading industrial and financial state, the

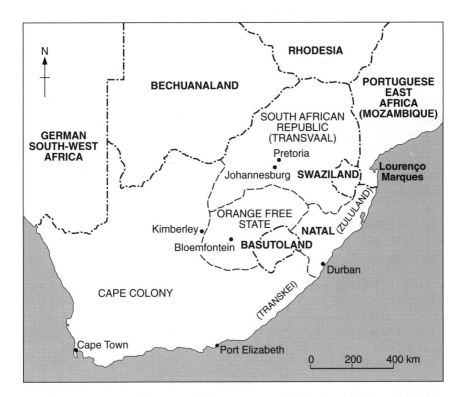

Map 1.1 South Africa at the time of the South African/Boer War (adapted from K. Shillington, *History of Southern Africa* [London: Longman, 1987, 137])

transformation added substantially to British interests in the region, and invigorated its claims to suzerainty.

In South Africa the mineral discoveries reshaped the economy and society, not least for Africans. In the earliest days of the diamond workings at Kimberley blacks and whites joined the rush to stake out claims to the diggings, but soon whites were demanding that blacks be controlled. With the growth of larger mining companies Africans were increasingly viewed as migrant workers and accommodated in compounds, which was a convenient way of controlling the work force. It was also a means of segregating African workers from the rest of society (Worden 1995: 38). The compound system was later used at the gold mines, where there was less chance of theft, but it was attractive to the mine owners as a way of imposing discipline and co-operation in a dangerous industry; and to whites generally as a means of segregation (Lipton 1985: 125). Alongside the gold mines of the Rand an industrialized, urban society grew up. The Rand's gold had the virtue of being in regular and reliable seams, but it suffered from being low grade – and so it required expensive, sophisticated processes to extract and had to be mined at increasing depths. It was therefore both capital and labour intensive. Nor could the new industries escape rapid changes of fortune; which, in the case of gold, was exacerbated by a fixed world price, so that the main tool in the hands of mine owners to balance the books was labour costs. From its earliest years the mining industries experienced periods of boom and bust.

Yet, despite the uncertainties, people were drawn to the mines and the towns which grew up around them – in search of work, fortune and adventure. They included skilled white workers from abroad, Afrikaners drawn off the land and an increasing number of blacks. While many worked directly in the mining industries, others found a variety of jobs in the new urban setting – as clerks, house servants, brick makers, washermen, transport drivers, brewers, prostitutes and so on (Van Onselen 1982). The new industrial/urban development also introduced social patterns that were to persist and spread across the whole country. Most Africans who were drawn or driven to the new towns were migrant workers, whose roots remained in the rural areas. Therefore provision – whether inside or outside the compounds – was made mainly for single men, on the assumption that they were there on a temporary basis and had a rural base to which they could retreat. Thus from the earliest days attempts were made to gain the economic advantages of employing African labour without the full social costs and implications of urbanization. The experience of whites also varied, ranging from those who became wealthy capitalists to unskilled rural Afrikaners drawn into a world dominated by urbanized Europeans, the English language and capitalist institutions, and where they had often to compete with Africans for jobs.

The economic and social implications of the new developments were not confined to the immediate vicinity of the mines, but spread across the whole country. The impact varied in intensity and timing. In some places the effects were immediate, as, for example, along the lines of rail that stretched out from the ports of the Cape, Durban and Lorenco Marques to the mines and industrial complexes, opening up new areas for development. Elsewhere, such as the Transkei, changes 'seeped in rather than swept through the communities' (Beinart and Bundy

1987: 3). Yet in other parts agriculture was transformed for both whites and blacks. White farmers expanded their production to meet demands, and as they did so the price of land rose, with the result that tenants and squatters were driven out. Africa peasant farming also had diverse experiences. Colin Bundy, outlining the changes between 1890 and 1913 in the Cape, noted that some African peasant farmers were able to consolidate their holdings, and others to make profits; but, at the same time there was increased pressure on the peasants because of the increased commercialization of agriculture. Access to land became more difficult, taxes and rents were raised, control of squatting intensified and the demand for labour increased. As a result many peasants lost their economic independence and ability even to meet their subsistence needs. Bundy concluded that by 1914 a growing number of peasants 'had become proletarianized, most commonly as migrant labour', and peasant agriculture became increasingly less self reliant (Bundy 1979: 110).

Relations between Britain and the Transvaal changed radically with the new economic circumstances. The bulk of the capital and the majority of the new white immigrants (known to the Boers as 'Uitlanders' or 'Outsiders') came from Britain or from British stock in South Africa. They included skilled workers, freebooters and capitalists. In Boer eyes imperialism and capitalism soon merged; while in London the newly enriched Transvaal was seen as an increasing threat to British paramountcy. The British came to regret signing the conventions, as they saw the balance of power in the sub-continent shift towards the Transvaal. At the same time the Uitlanders complained about Pretoria's corruption and inefficiency, its discriminatory policies, and their own lack of political rights. Although they protested to Pretoria, their hopes were pinned on Cape Town and London. In Pretoria President Paul Kruger's government was torn between delight at the burgeoning revenue from the mines – in 1886 state revenue was £196,000; by 1896 it had risen to £4,000,000 – its fear of losing control of the situation, and its contempt for the Uitlanders' life-style. Kruger predicted that 'every ounce of gold taken from the bowels of our soil will have to be weighed up with rivers of tears' (Wheatcroft 1993: 160). Later he claimed that without gold there would have been no war.

The scene was set for war between conflicting interests and competing creeds: Afrikaner nationalism and British imperialism – for what is imperialism but nationalism writ large? When the fighting started both sides proclaimed it as 'a white man's war'. At best that was a partial truth. It was true in the sense that it was fought to decide which white group would be dominant. It was also true that blacks had little or no political say. The old African kingdoms and tribal states had been conquered; and the Coloureds of Cape Colony and the Indians (who had been brought to Natal by the British mainly as indentured labour) were subordinate to the whites. Black political activity had existed before the war, but it was fragile, intermittent and fragmented. It suffered from problems which were to plague it persistently – lack of resources, poor communications, a vast country to cover, few educated people, hostile white governments, and a diversity of peoples and languages. Most activity was localized, and there were clear differences of political setting – notably between the Cape Colony, with its relatively liberal regime (including a colour blind franchise), and elsewhere where racial discrimination was openly acknowledged and practised.

Yet, despite the difficulties, black political activity and a press existed. In 1882, for example, 'Ibumba Yama Nyama' was formed in the Eastern Cape, which 'aimed to unite Africans in political matters so they could band together in fighting for national rights' (Marks and Trapido 1987: 6). In 1884 John Tengo Jabavu, a strong advocate of the liberal Cape tradition, launched his newspaper *Imvo Zabantusundu* (African Opinion); and ten years later the Natal Indian Congress was formed by a young lawyer, Mahatma Gandhi. Among Africans two main approaches to politics can be traced at that time – first a claim to the rights of British citizenship exemplified in the Cape system; and second 'Ethiopianism', which emphasized exclusive African activity, apart from whites. For many years to come, however, blacks were in the wings of the political stage.

Yet, in many ways the claim of a white man's war was unfounded. Most of South Africa's inhabitants were black, and it was inevitable that their lives would be affected by such a fierce and widespread conflict. Some were recruited to support the armies; and many died fighting. African farmers were driven from their land; miners lost their jobs; some gained new occupations; others settled on land deserted by Boer farmers; and, as the British sought to counter Boer guerilla tactics in the later stages of the war, more than 100,000 Africans were herded into concentration camps. Of those about 14,000 died (Warwick 1983: 4). The black involvement in the war often came in local settings in which racial divisions played their part. Bill Nasson writes of the Cape countryside becoming 'a cradle of civil conflict' between blacks and Boer farmers. 'Away from the battlefields and set piece sieges of Stormberg, Makefing and Kimberley . . . a kind of irregular civil war was being played out, with continued, muffled skirmishing over alternative sets of rights and assumptions. The atmosphere in white farming districts thus became clouded by smouldering enmities . . . between angry Boers and equally rancorous black labourers, servants and tenants' (Nasson 1991: 142).

The Coloured and African elite of the Cape had an immediate stake in the war. The Cape system offered them not only a qualified franchise, but an 'ideological package which stressed the virtues of free wage labour, secure property rights linked to a free market in land and individual tenure, equality before the law . . . "Progress and improvements", were its watchwords' (Marks and Trapido 1987: 5). Although in practice that package was often abused, many Cape blacks saw the conflict in terms of preserving their rights under the British crown and their hopes of extending those rights to blacks in the north. They held to Cecil Rhodes' dictum of 'equal rights for all civilised men south of the Zambezi' (although Rhodes had had political gain rather than liberal sentiment in mind when he made the statement during the Cape's 1898 election campaign). In January 1900 a petition to the British High Commissioner from leading Coloureds assured him of their loyalty, and their hopes of extending liberty to all civilized people in the north, as 'only under the British flag and protection can the Coloured people obtain justice, equality and freedom' (Nasson 1991: 33).

Afrikaner Nationalism: the Cape

Afrikaner nationalism has been shaped and reshaped by changing circumstances, ideas and experience. During much of the nineteenth century it had little coherence because of the different settings in which it developed. Although many Afrikaners trekked north a majority remained in the Cape, where they outnumbered the British by two to one. Whenever disputes arose between the British and the Boer Republics the Cape Afrikaners walked a tight rope between their loyalty to the crown as British subjects, and sympathy with their fellow Afrikaners to the north. While most in the Cape accepted British rule and opposed intervention by other colonial powers, they also supported the independence of the Boer Republics. This delicate balance bred suspicion from the committed on both sides. The jingoes among the British distrusted them; but so did the most militant Transvaalers, who regarded them as 'disguised enemies of our independence' (Marais 1961: 16).

The British had granted 'responsible government' (local self-government) to the Cape in 1872. Within that framework the Afrikaner Bond – a movement with a mainly rural, conservative base – emerged as the main political group. Led by J. H. (Jan) Hofmeyr the Bond set out to revive Afrikaners' self-esteem, not in opposition to the British but by fulfilling their own potential. Hofmeyr was a man of patience and compromise, who preferred to work by influence rather than through public office. He sought language equality between Dutch and English, at a time when English was the official language. (Although Dutch was the language of literature and the church for Afrikaners, Afrikaans – a local mixed language including a simplified Dutch – was also widely spoken.) In 1882 it was agreed that Dutch could be used in Parliament, after which its use was extended to the courts and public services. Alongside language and farming interests the Bond had three main concerns: Native affairs, a South African union, and imperial relations. In Native affairs the Bond rejected the rigid inequality of the Transvaal, but was cautious about the Cape's 'colour blind' franchise, emphasizing the need to restrict the number of Native voters. Towards a South Africa union (bringing together the British colonies and Boer republics) it had a gradualist approach, believing it was best developed indirectly by economic co-operation, such as a customs union and shared railway systems. In imperial affairs the Bond was content to live under the crown, accepting that with responsible government its interests could more easily be achieved within the empire than outside it. In 1899 Hofmeyr stated: 'I was born under Her Majesty's Government and I am content to remain under it' (Hancock 1962: 27).

In 1890 the Bond further demonstrated its acceptance of the imperial link by supporting Cecil Rhodes as Prime Minister of the Cape. It backed him because he favoured responsible government, because many of his local interests coincided with those of the Bond, and because he advocated economic expansion to the north from the Cape. My ambition, said Rhodes, is 'to bring South Africa into one system as to its railways, as to its customs, and as to its trade in the various products of the country'. The Cape, he declared, must not abandon the north. 'If your ambition is a union of South Africa, then the Cape . . . must keep as many cards as it may possess' (Rotberg 1988: 352). On the Native question Rhodes, by endorsing the

Bond's position, subordinated any concern he may have had for African rights to the aim of closer white unity. He demonstrated this in the Franchise Act of 1892, which, without breaching the principle of non-racialism, cut out many Africans by raising voters' qualifications, and, at the same time, disqualified tribal land as property which could be used for qualification. Finally, Rhodes seemed close to the Bond on Afrikaner–British relations. He endorsed Hofmeyr's call to bridge the gap between Boer and Briton, and readily accepted the Bond's claims for the Dutch language.

While most Cape Afrikaners followed the Bond, a more militant group existed. At first its members concentrated on cultural matters, especially the Afrikaans language. Afrikaans had developed since the seventeenth century as a spoken rather than a written language, used by whites, Coloureds and Khoikhoi. While it had a strong element of Dutch it was a mixture of tongues, and had varied 'by region, dialect and social class' (Hofmeyr 1987: 96). In the late nineteenth century, however, culture and politics were mixed together, as men like Rev S. J. du Toit sought to develop Afrikaans as a 'European' language of white Afrikaners. In 1875 du Toit and his colleagues formed the 'Genootskap van Regte Afrikaners' (Society of True Afrikaners), whose manifesto identified three types of Afrikaners: 'Afrikaners with "English" hearts . . . Afrikaners with "Dutch" hearts . . . true Afrikaners with "Afrikaans" hearts' (D'Oliveira 1977: 15). Du Toit proclaimed the need to stand for our language, nation and religion. He rejected British domination and argued for a united South Africa under a Republican flag. He wrote a history relating Afrikaners' heroic deeds, their suffering at the hands of Africans and the British, and he used Old Testament analogies to create a picture of them as a chosen people purified by suffering (Thompson 1985: 30). Du Toit gained some followers in the Cape but he found more fertile soil in the Transvaal, where he moved to become Superintendent of Education.

The difference between the Bond and du Toit was captured in their use of the name 'Afrikaner'. Du Toit employed it exclusively, to distinguish 'the volk' from other whites. In contrast, the Bond gave 'Afrikaner' an inclusive meaning. Its constitution stated: 'The Bond knows no nationality whatsoever, except that of the Afrikaners, and considers as belonging to it anyone [white] no matter of what descent, who seeks the welfare of South Africa' (Adam and Giliomee 1979: 102). For some the Rhodes/Bond alliance was an ideal, merging whites into a single nation. Among these was a young Cape Afrikaner lawyer, Jan Smuts, recently returned from Cambridge. At a Bond meeting in October 1895, Smuts called for the consolidation of the two 'Teutonic peoples'. He claimed a special role for whites in Africa: a continent of 100 million 'barbarians', but where, in the south, a quarter million whites were 'not only working for their own destiny, but also using their position as a basis for lifting up and opening up that vast dead weight of immemorial barbarism and animal savagery to the light and blessing of ordered civilization'. To achieve that, he argued, required more than material forces. It needed a 'sentiment of nationality'. This, Smuts declared, had found its highest form in the Rhodes/Bond alliance: bringing Boer and Briton together, bridging the gulf between capitalists and farmers, and keeping out foreign rivalry (Hancock 1962: 57, 8).

Afrikaner Nationalism: the Transvaal

In the Transvaal Afrikaner sentiment was shaped by a different experience: that of a dispersed, predominantly pastoral people whose lives were characterized by struggle – against African peoples; against a harsh environment in which many Boers were no more than subsistence farmers, and against British imperialism. Until the discovery of gold the Transvaalers lived in a backward country, their cultural life bounded by the 'taal' (Afrikaans) and the Dutch Reformed Church with its Calvinistic message. They were a tough, tenacious people, whose independence and isolation made them difficult to govern, whoever had the responsibility. Their intimate community, with interlocking ties of family, friendship and obligation, fostered personalized authority, as exemplified by President Paul Kruger sitting on his stoep dispensing justice and advice to all. Kruger himself symbolized their strengths and limitations. After trekking north in 1835 as a boy of ten, he later gained a reputation as a warrior and leader. He had crude manners, little formal education,

Paul Kruger
(courtesy of
the South
African High
Commission)

bigoted views and was physically unattractive; but he had a powerful personality, great courage and determination, a pride in his people, and he was a skilled negotiator. He flourished in his ramshackle state as a populist leader. On four occasions his fellow Afrikaners elected him as their President.

Kruger's tenacity was built on religious faith. God, he believed, who shaped the destinies of nations, had chosen the Afrikaners to mould and be moulded by Africa; but their lot involved suffering, in which tragedies and failures were purifying experiences. 'It was necessary,' said Kruger, 'that the vine be pruned to the stem so that it could bear good fruit'. In contrast Africans were not of the elect – they were the sons of Ham, destined to be hewers of wood and drawers of water. Kruger's core political aim was to maintain an independent Afrikaner republic. When reelected in 1898 he declared: 'I shall particularly ensure that the independence of the land is not in the least endangered; not the least right which will undermine the independence of the land shall be given over . . . which God's hand gave us' (Moodie 1975: 26/32). The 'independence of the land' was built on two assumptions. First that the Boers/Afrikaners ('the volk'), who had fought for, settled and developed the land, were the true citizens of the republic, and that neither Africans nor British could make similar claims. Kruger dismissed Africans as an inferior race; while the British, who had only settled in numbers since the discovery of gold, were birds of passage, who regarded Britain as their home. Second, Kruger believed that the government of the republic must be responsible to 'the volk'. That was achieved through the election by Afrikaners of their President and their Volksraad: an Assembly of 25 members, based on a franchise which excluded Africans and offered little to the Uitlanders.

Inevitably Kruger evoked strong reactions. While far away in London Joseph Chamberlain (the British Colonial Secretary) dismissed him as 'an ignorant, cunning, dirty and obstinate man'; Edmund Garrett, an English traveller, who was aware of the Transvaal's limitations and Kruger's bizarre views, concluded that, despite his 'gross peasant ways . . . I never doubted that I had before me one of the few really significant personalities of our time' (Fisher 1975: 226). Two major obstacles lay in Kruger's path – the British and the Africans. The British were the more immediate and powerful, and Kruger always suspected their advances. When in 1880 Sir Garnet Wolseley had offered the Transvaal self-government under the British flag Kruger retorted: 'They say to you, "First put your head quietly in the noose, so that I can hang you up: then you may kick your legs about as much as you please".' Although Kruger recognized British strength, he reasoned that 'England is mighty but do not lose sight of our goal. It is a sacred course and God will help us' (Fisher 1975: 92–5). By the end of the nineteenth century the British challenge came from the combined threat of the Uitlanders; and imperial demands via the conventions, which shackled the Transvaal's claim to independence.

The Uitlanders, who were concentrated in the urban/mining areas in the Transvaal's heartland, were seen by Kruger as a potential Trojan horse. An 1896 census of Johannesburg recorded a white population of 50,907, of which only 6,205 were Afrikaners (Marais 1961: 1). No overall Transvaal census was taken at that time and the number of Burghers to Uitlanders in the whole Republic was probably evenly balanced. However, Kruger, eager to underline the dangers to the

Afrikaners, claimed that a majority were aliens. He compared the Uitlanders to squatters on a farm whose owner, having won it by blood and toil, was now asked to share it with the squatters. He reasoned that by granting the Uitlanders full political rights the Boers would lose control of their state. 'If we give them the franchise tomorrow,' he said, 'we might as well give them the Republic.' They would never be satisfied. 'If you give them a finger they will want the whole hand, then an arm, then a head, and then they want the whole body bit by bit' (Packenham 1982: 66–7).

To counter the British threat Kruger looked to other European powers. In 1884 Germany had moved into southern Africa by occupying the vast, arid territory of South West Africa. In the same year, immediately after negotiating the London Convention, Kruger visited Germany, where he was warmly received by the Kaiser and the Society for the Promotion of German Colonisation. They complimented the Boers on their 'heroic struggle with England for their independence', and spoke of working together to carry forward civilization and colonization. In response Kruger compared the Transvaal to a child who would look for 'protection from its strong and mighty mother country Germany'. On his return home Kruger stated: 'If one nation tries to enthral us, the other will try to prevent this' (Fisher 1975: 131–203). The Transvaal also concluded commercial, friendship and extradition treaties with other European states, thereby stretching the Conventions to their limits and beyond. At the same time it sought European capital to build a railway to Delagoa Bay in Mozambique and thereby break its dependence for transport on the British colonies.

The Jameson Raid and Afrikaner Nationalism

In 1895 the strands of Afrikaner nationalism were drawn together and radicalized in reaction to the Jameson Raid. The Raid was planned by Cecil Rhodes (with covert support from Joseph Chamberlain) and led by Rhodes's hot-headed lieutenant, Dr Leander Starr Jameson. The plan was that Jameson would lead a force of horsemen from the neighbouring British Protectorate of Bechuanaland to support a rising of Uitlanders, who had been secretly armed by Rhodes. Jameson waited impatiently on the border, but the rising failed to take place. Despite Rhodes's last-minute recognition of this and his attempts to abort the operation, Jameson rode – falsely believing that his raid into the Transvaal would prompt the rising and topple Kruger's administration. It was a disastrous miscalculation leading to ignominious defeat.

In military terms the Raid was a small affair, but it had a major political impact – undermining co-operation between Boer and Briton, giving 'birth to a new form of self conscious Afrikaner nationalism, at once self critical and self congratulatory . . . in which outsiders could not share', and souring relations between Britain and Germany (Davenport 1966: 167). Although Jameson's small force had easily been defeated, the Raid also alerted Pretoria to its relative military weakness. The government decided to remedy that with the help of external powers, employing revenue from the gold fields to purchase modern weapons, which were often superior to those used by the British. In terms of Afrikaner identity the Raid promoted sympathy for Kruger both in the Cape and in the Orange Free State. In the Cape the loyalty of Bond members to the crown was tested to breaking point. It came as a hammer blow to those like Smuts who had put their trust in the Rhodes/Bond alliance. Rhodes was forced to resign as Premier, and abandon his bridging role between Boer and Briton. A disillusioned Smuts condemned Britain in a brilliant polemic: *A Century of Wrong*. Later he reflected: 'The Dutch set aside all considerations of blood and nationality and loved him [Rhodes] and trusted him and served him because they believed he was the man to carry out that great idea of an internally sovereign and united South Africa in which the white race would be supreme . . . Here at last our Moses had appeared – and it made no difference that he was an Egyptian in blood' (Hancock 1962: 59). His vision shattered, Smuts moved to the Transvaal in 1897, where a year later, at the age of 28, he became State Attorney. The arrival of Du Toit and even more Smuts in the Transvaal, symbolized stages in the development of Afrikaner nationalism, bringing together those who had earlier trekked north and those who had stayed behind. As Allister Sparks commented: 'It was the headstrong critics who went forth and experienced the grievances, but it was those milder cousins who stayed at home and got educated who articulated those grievances and gave them ideological shape' (Sparks 1990: 116).

The sense of common Afrikaner identity and destiny was further demonstrated by the reaction of the other Boer republic, the Orange Free State (OFS). The OFS was better administered and had an easier relationship with Britain than the Transvaal, but following the Raid a pro-Kruger party came to power under President M. T. Steyn. In 1897 it signed a military pact with the Transvaal, and it too undertook a rearmament programme. Outside South Africa the British were condemned as bullies. The Kaiser telegraphed Kruger sending 'sincere congratulations that without calling on the aid of friendly powers you . . . have succeeded in . . . defending the independence of the country against attacks from without' (Kruger 1964: 41). That infuriated the British. The telegram implied an acceptance of the Transvaal's 'independence' and that Germany was willing to come to Pretoria's aid against the British. On the wave of indignation which followed the Kaiser's telegram Chamberlain and Rhodes rode out the storm. Chamberlain was suspected of complicity, but despite a parliamentary inquiry, he covered up his tracks. 'It was,' wrote Jay, 'a superb, if disgraceful, exercise in political survival' (Jay 1981: 207).

British Imperial Nationalism

Throughout the nineteenth century British attitudes towards the Empire ranged from jingoism to scepticism. However, the end of the century saw a surge of imperial activity, as ambition was sharpened by European rivalry in the scramble for Africa. In southern Africa, Britain was defending an area of established influence against potential rivals. Lord Ripon wrote that 'to have the Germans meddling at Pretoria and Johannesburg would be fatal to our position and influence'. Lord

Kimberley, the Foreign Secretary, concluded that the Cape was of even greater importance than Malta or Gibraltar because it secured communications with India (Robinson and Gallagher 1961: 419). Their concerns also included British investments in the mining industry and the future potential of that industry. Seen in this light the continued independence of the Transvaal was an anomaly, endangering Britain's position. London had assumed that it could exclude European rivals, and create a loyal South Africa indirectly by building on the foundations of the colonies surrounding the Boer Republics. The Raid had undermined that assumption, and strengthened the Transvaal's position.

'How,' asked the British 'can we retrieve the situation and forward our interests?' Three main influences shaped Britain's response to that question: the government in London, British officials in South Africa, and British settlers in southern Africa. All were committed to a prosperous and vigorous Empire, but their perceptions and interests varied according to the contexts in which they operated. In London, South Africa could not be isolated from a vast range of international and domestic concerns; nor could public opinion, parliament and the press be ignored. Often London's ambition was simply to have a quiet and cheap life; whereas British officials working in South Africa were less concerned about the broader setting or overall imperial expenditure. Usually they were eager to promote initiatives and extend frontiers. Inevitably, these 'men on the spot' believed that they knew the situation better than London, and were frustrated if their proposals were blocked. In terms of public opinion they were more conscious of local views (which usually meant white views) than attitudes at home. Finally, there were the British settlers, who were eager to remain under the crown, to have protection against foreign enemies, and to enjoy the rights of British citizens (including local self-government). Often they accused London and the officials of failing to understand their needs and of being soft on the Natives.

At the turn of the century these imperial currents were epitomized by three powerful figures: Joseph Chamberlain, the Colonial Secretary in London; Alfred Milner, the British High Commissioner in Cape Town; and Cecil Rhodes, the mining magnate and politician. All were advocates of a 'forward' policy, involving pressure on the Transvaal. Yet, they all faced internal opposition. Chamberlain was confronted by doubts and scepticism in the cabinet and parliament, where sections of the Liberal Party were strongly opposed to an aggressive South African policy. Some officials in South Africa, unlike Milner, favoured a pacific approach to the Transvaal. These included Sir William Butler, Commander in Chief of the British Troops in South Africa and who acted as High Commissioner in Milner's absence. Butler regarded the Uitlanders as 'trouble-makers', and 'Rhodes as a menace to the peace of the country'. He was convinced that South Africa needed conciliation, not surgery (Smith 1996: 224). In the Cape, Rhodes faced opposition not only from Afrikaners, but Englishmen like John X. Merriman who accused him of jingoism. At the turn of the century, therefore, imperialism was both a prominent and a disputed issue for the British. For a time, however, it was the advocates of an aggressive imperialism who carried the day.

The View from London: Chamberlain

In June 1895 a coalition of Conservatives and Liberal Unionists won a resounding election victory in Britain. The Liberal Unionists were led by Joseph Chamberlain, a man of great political determination and skill. When the Prime Minister, Lord Salisbury, asked Chamberlain to name a cabinet post he chose the Colonial Office. It was a surprising decision to select what previously had been a political backwater, but Chamberlain realized that the office gave him a degree of autonomy which cemented his authority in the government, demonstrated his Unionist credentials to sceptical Tories, and kept him in the public eye as the 'New Imperialism' became fashionable and prominent. He served in the office for eight years.

In opposition Chamberlain had already revealed his belief in vigorous imperialism. He favoured a British federation spanning the globe – founded on economic, military and political co-operation. For him it was not enough simply to control territory; it must be developed, and so he proposed an imperial free trade area. 'We are landlords,' he said, 'of a great estate: it is the duty of the landlord to develop his estate . . . improving the property, in making communications, in making outlets for the products of his land' (Jay 1981: 195). He never doubted that imperial expansion was beneficial; 'that this great Empire of ours, powerful as it is, is nothing to what it will become in the course of ages when it will be in permanence, a guarantee for the peace and civilization of the world' (Marais 1961: 68). To achieve that the Empire must embrace 'Great Britain beyond the seas – the young and vigorous nations carrying everywhere a knowledge of the English tongue and English love of liberty and law' (Jay 1981: 187).

Within this broad context Chamberlain wanted the Transvaal's wealth employed to further the imperial cause. The failure of the Jameson Raid was a setback, and London's immediate reaction was retrenchment, but that did not last. With imperial rivalry increasing, the lesson drawn from the failure was that the informal 'hands off' approach was no longer tenable. When Chamberlain speculated on whether it might be best to stand back, Lord Selborne (the Parliamentary Under Secretary) predicted that within a generation the Transvaal would dominate South Africa. As the chief market for the agricultural produce of the Cape and Natal and the main user of their transport systems, the Transvaal's commercial pull was such that a union of South Africa was inevitable. The only question said Selborne, 'is whether that Union will be inside or outside the British empire' (Judd 1977: 214). For Chamberlain there could only be one answer. To that end he pursued a strict interpretation of the Transvaal conventions, emphasizing Britain's claim to suzerainty. He approached the conventions not as agreements between separate states, but as documents in which Britain, as paramount power, had the final say.

Chamberlain anticipated that by exerting constant pressure Kruger could be brought to heel short of war, but he did not rule out the use of arms. 'What is now at stake,' he wrote, 'is the position of Great Britain in South Africa and with it the estimate formed of our power and influence in our colonies and throughout the world.' Further he was determined that policy should be shaped by the government in London and not the locally elected government of the Cape. He favoured 'a bold policy fully recognising imperial responsibilities and duties [and] it should be the policy of the Imperial and not the Cape Government, and should be carried out by officials taking their instructions from the former' (Marais 1961: 123, 318). Early in 1897, with that in mind, Chamberlain appointed Sir Alfred Milner as Governor of the Cape Colony and High Commissioner to South Africa. It was a fateful decision.

The Man on the Spot: Milner

Milner was already an experienced civil servant when he was appointed to South Africa. He had previously served under Lord Cromer in Egypt, and was currently Chairman of the Board of Inland Revenue. He shared Chamberlain's imperial passion. On the eve of his departure to the Cape Milner described himself as 'a civilian soldier of the Empire'. Imperialism, for him, was a 'great movement of the human spirit'. I am, he wrote, 'a British (indeed primarily an English) Nationalist. If I am also an Imperialist it is because the destiny of the English race . . . has been to strike fresh roots in distant parts of the world'. It is, he continued, 'the British race which had built the Empire, and it is the undivided British race which can uphold it'. He spoke of a force 'deeper, stronger, more primordial than material ties . . . the common bond of blood, a common language, common history and traditions' (Marais 1961: 172, 174).

Milner was an outstanding administrator, who dismissed pragmatism and empiricism as 'drift'. For him imperialism was justified by its achievements. The aim was not to strip peoples of their culture and character, but to open up opportunities and build on them. The white man in Africa, he argued, could only justify his rule over blacks by using it for the benefit of the subject races and not for his own advancement and convenience (Thornton 1966: 213). Whether in Britain or the Cape, his emphasis on efficiency and order made him sceptical of the political process of parliamentary democracy, with its compromises and vacillations. He felt frustrated by the way the home government blew hot and cold, and was held back by public opinion.

In South Africa Milner pursued his faith with great determination. His ambition was to make it a pillar of the Empire, whereas currently it was 'the weakest link in the imperial chain'. To achieve that the Transvaal was critical – if things went well there South Africa would become a source of strength; if badly it could threaten the whole Empire. Fail there, he reasoned, and the rest could come tumbling down. Milner therefore set out to establish a united South Africa – loyal to the crown; based on a self-governing white community with a British majority; supported by well treated and justly governed blacks; and with a vigorous economy driven by the gold of the Rand. In seeking these ends Milner assumed that Afrikaners, even in the Cape, could not be fully trusted. In March 1898 when the Afrikaner Bond assured him of their loyalty he responded acidly. 'What reason could there be for disloyalty? . . . Of course you are loyal. It would be monstrous if you were not.' He went on to criticize Bond members who in relation to the Transvaal 'espouse the side of the Republic' (O'Brien 1979: 133, 147). Milner therefore concluded that it would be madness to offer self-government before a British majority was established through a vigorous immigration policy.

Milner accepted that Britain had a responsibility towards blacks. In November 1897 he wrote that one of his aims was to 'secure for the Natives . . . adequate and sufficient protection against oppression and wrong' (Le May 1965: 11). However, as with everything else, he judged this in relation to imperial interests. His first priority was to ensure British supremacy, and he knew that any attempt to improve the lot of blacks would be opposed by most whites (British and Afrikaner alike) and that could weaken Britain's position. His focus, therefore, was not on Native affairs but on the Transvaal and its Afrikaner rulers. For him South Africa was the setting for a power struggle between two very different societies. He spoke of 'the great game between ourselves and the Transvaal': of 'two wholly antagonistic systems: a medieval race oligarchy [Transvaal], and a modern industrial state' [Britain] which was beneficial to all. He reasoned that the two 'cannot live side by side in what is after all "one country". The race oligarchy has to go and I see no signs of its removing itself' (Marais 1961: 205, 331).

At first, conscious of Chamberlain's instructions to proceed with caution, and hoping that steady pressure would bring its rewards, Milner negotiated with

Alfred, First Viscount Milner (courtesy of Mary Evans Picture Library)

Pretoria. He concentrated on two issues: the conventions and the Uitlanders' claims. The conventions involved quasi-legal debates in which Milner played the suzerainty card for all it was worth and more. When Kruger claimed that the conventions must be interpreted by 'the accepted principles of the law of nations' and suggested independent arbitration, Milner countered by saying that arbitration would be incompatible with Britain's position as suzerain power, and that her interpretation must prevail. When Milner turned to the Uitlanders he relied not on legal points but emotional appeals about the rights of British subjects, their immense contribution to the Transvaal and the injustice of their treatment. In fact the Uitlanders were not a monolithic body, but a motley collection 'of diverse nationalities, divided by class and disunited', many of whom were more concerned with making money than 'whether Queen Victoria or President Kruger rules over them' (Smith 1996: 47, 83). However, there was a committed imperial group among them, who had grievances – heavy taxes without adequate services, limited franchise rights, inefficient police and judiciary, the threat of military service for the Transvaal, and government monopolies which frustrated investment. Milner used these to fan the flames of discontent. In May 1899, as the pressure for war increased, the British Government published Milner's notorious 'helots dispatch', in which he claimed that 'the spectacle of thousands of British subjects kept permanently in the position of helots . . . calling vainly to Her Majesty's Government for redress, does steadily undermine the influence and reputation of Great Britain and respect for the British Government within the Queen's dominions' (Marais 1961: 267).

In Milner's eyes the chance that British aims could be achieved by negotiation had largely disappeared when Kruger was re-elected President of the Transvaal in 1898. In February 1898 he had concluded: 'There is no way out of the political troubles of S. Africa except reform of the Transvaal or war . . . The question which line to take cannot therefore be settled exclusively with reference to S. Africa. It depends on the imperial outlook as a whole' (Smith 1996: 185). Milner's own outlook was to drive forward in the hope that Kruger would 'bluff up to the cannon's mouth', but if necessary to accept war. Thus while in 1899 the Cape and OFS politicians continued to work for compromise Milner prepared for war. Chamberlain was more constrained. He was more hopeful of achieving a peaceful outcome, but was also prepared to use force as the ultimate step. The negotiations ended at Bloemfontein in May 1899, when Milner rejected compromises offered by Kruger. He had come to believe in war, and in the end was firmly supported by Chamberlain. Even in retrospect Milner had no regrets. 'Certainly,' he stated in 1905, 'I engaged in that struggle with all my might, because I was from head to foot, one glowing mass of conviction of the rightness of our cause' (Worsfold 1906: 129).

The British Settler: Rhodes

People of British stock had settled in South Africa since the early nineteenth century, but not in the numbers that emigrated to Australia, Canada and the USA. From the 1870s onwards, the mining discoveries drew in a new wave of immigrants. They included Cecil Rhodes, a man of extraordinary vitality, drive, self-confidence, obstinacy and eventually wealth. He played many roles – Kimberley diamond magnate, Randlord, Cape politician, and imperialist – and as an imperialist he used his British South Africa Company to conquer and occupy Southern and Northern Rhodesia for Britain. Rhodes engendered strong reactions. His admirers were dazzled and prepared to follow wherever he led. One later recalled that when listening to him 'you remembered only that you were in the presence of a man dominated by an inspiring faith, and an ambition in which there was nothing narrow or selfish' (Rotberg: 1988: 343). However, he had opponents among the British, both in South Africa and Britain, who challenged his imperial ambitions and ruthlessness. Among them was John Merriman, who became Prime Minister of the Cape; while in London the Liberal politician, Sir William Harcourt, described the government's support for Rhodes as 'imperialism on the cheap', which had developed into 'privateering degenerating into piracy' (Smith 1996: 120).

Although Rhodes acquired great wealth his financial ambition was subordinate

Cecil Rhodes
(courtesy of
The Star)

to his imperial vision. 'If I forfeit my flag,' he asked, 'what have I left?' The core of Rhodes's faith was formed as early as the 1870s, in his days as a mature student at Oxford. There he told a friend: 'The object of which I intend to devote my life is the defence and the extension of the British Empire.' In a private 'Confession of Faith', he reasoned that since the British 'are the finest race in the world . . . the more of the world we inhabit the better for the human race'; and that was particularly true of Africa which 'is still lying ready for us, it is our duty to take it' (Rotberg 1988: 100, 103, 682). As a Cape politician he sought to unite a self-governing community of British and Afrikaner within an imperial framework, and to use the Cape as a base for expansion to the north. In that ambition Rhodes, like Chamberlain and Milner, saw Kruger's Republic standing in his path. By the mid-1890s he had concluded that he must act, that delay would only benefit the Transvaal, and so he initiated the Jameson Raid. In explaining why he took such a risk, he said: 'I want to see it [Transvaal] a friendly member of a community of South African States. I want equal rights for the English language, a Customs Union, a common railway policy, a common Native policy, a central South African Court of Appeal, British coast protection. I have tried to deal with the old man Kruger and I have failed. I shall never bring him into line . . . What I want to do is lay the foundations of a united South Africa. I want men to associate my name with it after I have gone' (Rotberg 1988: 531).

Rhodes never fully trusted the Uitlanders as a body, even before the Raid. He understood their grievances but he knew they were a mixed bag, in which few shared his vision. He feared that if they overthrew Kruger themselves, they might set up an independent Republic. To counter that he wanted his own hand on the tiller. Although the Raid temporarily undermined his position he re-entered Cape politics within two years, but never again as the reconciler of Boer and Briton. Instead he declared: 'One section of the people want to make a Republic in South Africa, and another section wants to make a united South Africa under our flag . . . These are the politics of South Africa' (Marais 1961: 224).

In the Cape the Bond continued to retain the bulk of Afrikaner support, while two mainly English-speaking parties emerged. The first, the South Africa Party, with Merriman among its leaders, opposed Rhodes, and was prepared to work with the Bond. In contrast the Progressive Party, led by Rhodes, was dedicated to British supremacy. 'During the next five years,' Rhodes declared, 'the States of South Africa will crystallise one way or the other', and in his view it must do so as a closer union under 'our flag' (Rotberg 1988: 58). In the 1898 Cape election Rhodes attacked the Bond, claiming that Afrikaner interests were best served by following his wider vision, and that by backing the Bond the Cape's interests in the north would be undermined. He told electors that he was not the source of trouble. 'It is the Transvaal's position that is causing unrest in Africa', and trouble would continue until the 'new people' received the same treatment as the old. He claimed that through the Bond the Cape was in danger of falling under the domination of Krugerism (Rotberg 1988: 605). In a close run election, in which his party gained a majority of votes but not of seats, Rhodes became leader of the opposition. He was not Prime Minister, but he was back in business.

2

War, Peace and Reconstruction

In Britain the outbreak of war was greeted by an outburst of imperial fervour. Crowds waved the flags, cheered and sang patriotic songs as the troops marched away to fight; the royal family gave its blessing; offers of help poured in from around the Empire; and Rudyard Kipling urged support 'For a gentleman in khaki ordered South.' (Kruger 1964: 57) Most of the leading politicians and the press were infected by the national enthusiasm, and the determination to put Kruger in his place. However, some critical voices were raised. The Liberal Party was divided between the Liberal imperialists, who supported the war, and those like David Lloyd-George, Sir William Harcourt and John Morley who opposed it. A month before the fighting started Morley told a London audience: 'You may make thousands of women widows and thousands of children fatherless. It will be wrong. You may add a new province to your Empire. It will still be wrong . . . You may send the price of Mr Rhodes's Chartereds up to a point beyond the dreams of avarice. Yes, even that will be wrong' (Taylor 1996: 38).

There was also press critics. While the jingo papers lauded Chamberlain, Milner and Rhodes, J. A. Hobson, of the *Manchester Guardian*, wrote of an ignoble conspiracy, based on capitalist financial power and a bought press. War, he concluded was a disaster for everyone except the mine owners, for whom it means 'an increase in profits' (Wheatcroft 1993; 204). Doubters were found even in the government. They included Lord Salisbury, the Prime Minister, who thought that Milner had lost all sense of proportion, but concluded that the situation had gained such a momentum that it was impossible to stop. In Salisbury's eyes Britain was being drawn into a conflict 'all for a people we despise and for a territory which will bring no power to Britain' (Packenham 1982: 94). In public he masked his doubts, but, with world weary resignation, wrote: 'What he has done cannot be effaced. We have to act upon moral ground prepared for us by him and his jingo supporters.'

Nor in South Africa could Milner rely on the Cape Government. W. P. Schreiner's ministry of moderates, which was in power at the time, was eager to reach agreement by compromise. It petitioned Queen Victoria pointing to the 'ties of blood relationships, intermarriage and friendship' between the Cape and the Republics. It remained loyal but passive; eager to avoid war, and, if conflict came, to play as little part as possible. That did not suit Milner, who concluded: 'If it comes to a fight we shall have to rely on British forces alone' (Marais 1961: 205). Once the fighting started Schreiner summoned volunteers, but only to protect the colony's borders, and took no further war-like steps, warning Milner: 'More men will fight for the Boers than will fight for you' (Worsfold 1906: 281). The Bond passed a resolution disapproving of the Imperial Government's policies, which had led to 'the bloody and unjust war'. Milner dismissed these protests as 'frankly nationalistic [wanting] a South Africa united under the Dutch flag' (Davenport 1966: 221).

The fighting started with a series of spectacular Boer victories, but they soon gave way to British successes, as the sheer weight of numbers and fire power of the imperial forces was made to count. By September 1900 Kruger had fled; the British controlled the main lines of communication and the towns; most of the Boer forces had surrendered; and the Transvaal and the Orange Free State (renamed the Orange River Colony) had been annexed as British colonies. In December 1900, Lord Roberts, Commander of the imperial forces, left South Africa confident of final victory. He had miscalculated. Even before he left the war had assumed a new face, as set piece battles were replaced by a determined Boer guerilla campaign which spread across the country. The imperial army, now led by General Kitchener, had the greatest difficulty in countering these tactics, and the army's activities more and more 'assumed the characteristics of a punitive expedition' (Le May 1965: 86). It swept across the country, burning farms and crops to deny them to the guerillas, rounding up and slaughtering stock, deporting prisoners, and confining Boer women, children and old men to concentration camps. Badly administered by people with no experience and sometimes little compassion, disease ran through the camps, leading to appalling death rates, not least among children. Some Boers came to believe that there was a deliberate attempt to exterminate them as a people, with false rumours that camp food had been poisoned or contaminated with ground glass. When the army handed over the camps to Milner's civil administration, conditions improved greatly, but in all more than 20,000 Afrikaners died in them. The camps left a legacy of hatred. The criticism spread to Britain where Emily Hobhouse waged a vigorous campaign against them, and Campbell Bannerman, the Liberal leader, referred to 'methods of barbarism in South Africa.'

Initially the British said they would not arm blacks. Chamberlain explained this not as a moral issue (for native troops were used throughout the Empire) but as a sensible policy in South Africa, where white opinion – both Boer and British – was opposed to it. However, that did not last. From early days Coloureds in the Cape were armed in defence of local communities – especially when the loyalty of local Afrikaners was in doubt – and, as the war dragged on more blacks were recruited. From abroad the British brought in small contingents of Indian and Egyptian troops to act in support roles, and increasingly local blacks were used for combat as well as non-combat duties. Schreiner objected strongly. He wrote to Milner: 'I do not hesitate to say that the idea of approving of any violence by natives to whites in South Africa is abhorrent to me.' Such objections reflected the deep fears that would threaten the security of white society. The *Scottish Review* of April 1990, spoke of 'the dangers of their [the natives] getting out of hand and committing the atrocities of barbarous warfare'. However, at least some liberal whites favoured arming blacks, not only for their value in the field but because they would then have a stake in the outcome of the struggle (Nasson 1991: 14–16). By the end of the war it was estimated that about 20,000 blacks were under arms on the imperial side, and many more – up to 100,000 – were employed in ancillary services; such as transport, scouting, construction works and domestic service (Warwick 1983: 4–5).

The Boers accused the British of bad faith, and stated that they would kill any blacks they found under arms. It was a threat they carried out, at least on some occasions. For example, in March and April 1901 the Boers were reported to have treated their white prisoners well at Pearston, Klipfontein and Concordia, but to have executed the blacks (Nasson 1991: 57). Yet the Boers also employed Africans and Coloureds in preparing defences, in transport work and in spying, and some were given arms. However, the numbers were much smaller than on the British side, and most blacks were reluctant to aid the Boers, unless they were long-standing family servants. Louis Botha admitted: 'The Kaffirs turned against us and we not only had to fight against the English but against the Natives as well' (Plaatje 1982: 287).

From War to Negotiation and Peace

As the guerilla campaign dragged on differences arose on both sides between those who were prepared to negotiate a settlement and those committed to fighting on. Among the British Kitchener favoured negotiation; whereas Milner wanted to fight until the Boers accepted unconditional surrender. He dismissed Kitchener's approach as short-sighted, because it failed to recognize the broader picture, of reinforcing imperial power by subordinating the Boers. There is, Milner claimed, 'no room for compromise in South Africa'. He suspected Kitchener of seeking a quick end so that he could move on to command the army in India. How ironic, said Milner, 'that the army had defeated the Boers and now Kitchener was dead set on chucking it away' (Packenham 1982: 551–3). On his side Kitchener commented that 'Milner's views may be strictly just, but they are in my mind vindictive' (Le May 1965: 98).

Milner increasingly feared a 'wobble' in London. His concern was well founded, for the tide had started to run against him. With the heavy cost in lives and money and public weariness and disillusionment of a long war, pressure increased for a settlement. Initially the British Government had estimated that the war would cost £10m. and require up to 75,000 troops. In the event it cost £230m. and drew in 450,000 troops. The loss of life was heavy: 22,000 on the British side (many from disease); 34,000 Boers including those in the camps; and probably 15,000 blacks (although they were not accurately recorded) (Smith 1996: 2). There was also a shift of public opinion in Britain. Imperialism as experienced in a major bloody war seemed far removed from the excitement of waving off 'the boys in khaki' and the glamour of Queen Victoria's 1887 Golden Jubilee.

The change was reflected in political attitudes, especially in the Liberal Party. As the fighting dragged on even the Liberal imperialists withdrew their support. Lord Rosebery, their leader, saw that internationally the Boers occupied the high moral ground: they were perceived as a small people seeking to preserve their independence against an imperial bully. In December 1901 he said of the war: 'In the first place it is an open sore through which is oozing much of our strength. In the next place it weakens our international position and reduces us to a stand point in international politics very different from that we are accustomed to occupy. In the third place it stops domestic reform, and in the fourth place it adjourns and embitters the ultimate settlement of South Africa' (Le May 1965: 128). The overall result was a call for compromise, based on the belief that the way forward lay in working with, not against the Boer; and that the alternative was a permanent standing army in South Africa.

Divisions were also found among the Boers. While the most committed had turned to guerilla tactics, many more had abandoned the struggle. In mid-1900, when Lord Roberts offered amnesty and the return of farms to those who took an oath of neutrality, 13,900 Boers (a quarter of the fighting strength) became 'Hendsoppers' (hands uppers) and eventually more than 5,000 fought on the British side (Smith 1996: 7). By 1902, even those who had continued to fight were split. The line of fissure was broadly between the Transvaal Boers on one side and the Free Staters on the other. The OFS, led by President Steyn, had joined the war as a matter of principle, to support its sister republic, and it remained committed to fighting. Steyn stated that if independence were taken away from Afrikaners they would be degraded, and 'a grievance would arise which would necessarily lead to a condition of things similar to that in Ireland . . . [that of] a conquered country' (Le May 1965: 11). The Transvaalers were no less concerned about Afrikaner rights but their circumstances were different. Milner had already established his administration in Johannesburg, and as his grip tightened, as the economy recovered, and as the Uitlanders returned in greater numbers than ever, so the threat of British domination grew. While the OFS had a secure Afrikaner majority the Transvaalers feared they would be swamped and favoured negotiating a settlement while they still retained some leverage.

The appeal which finally carried the day among the fighters was not based on the military situation, but the preservation of Afrikaners as a people. Smuts voiced that view. He accepted that they were still unbeaten in the field, but declared: 'We are not here as an army, but as a people; we have not only a military question but also a national matter to deal with.' It was right, he said, to struggle and make sacrifices for independence, 'but we may not sacrifice the Afrikaner people for that' (Hancock 1962: 159). Schalk Burger, Vice President of the Transvaal, reinforced this view with a belief in God's will and acceptance of purification through suffering. The Boers, he said, had arrived at the stage of history when they must pray: 'Thy will be done . . . Perhaps it is God's will that the English nation should suppress us, in order that our pride may be subdued, and that we may come through the fires of our trouble purified' (Le May 1965: 11). The Afrikaners made peace to preserve the nation.

★   ★   ★

Peace terms were agreed in May 1902. The original document had no heading. Kitchener called it 'Terms of Peace', Milner 'Terms of Surrender'; the Boers spoke of 'The Treaty of Vereeniging', and that was the name that stuck. The treaty was a compromise. The Afrikaners accepted that the old republics would become British colonies, but would eventually gain responsible self-government. Among the peace terms Boer prisoners were to be repatriated and given freedom, but initially they were denied the vote; English was to be the official language, but Dutch could be used in court and taught in schools when parents chose it, and Britain agreed to grant £3m. for restoration work.

The issue that raised most controversy in London was the Native franchise. In the negotiations the British agreed a rewording of the treaty. Originally it had read: 'The franchise will not be given to Natives until after the introduction of self-government.' That was changed to 'The question of granting the franchise to Natives will not be decided until after the introduction of self-government.' The implications of that were immense, for nobody doubted that no concessions would be made by white representative governments. In 1897 Milner had written that Britain should aim 'to secure for the Natives . . . adequate and sufficient protection against oppression and wrong'. Lord Salisbury had spoken of the need 'for the kindly and improving treatment of those countless indigenous races of whose destiny I fear we have been too forgetful' (Willan 1984: 104). In 1902, when the fighting was over, Chamberlain assured the Barolong of Mafeking that Native rights would be protected. Such claims led black leaders to hope, even believe, that the war had been fought to establish justice for all. They were mistaken. The British had fought to establish their paramountcy. It had become clear that to achieve that meant subordinating British concerns over African rights to an agreement with the Boers. In British eyes that was fully justified by the need for peace within the Empire, but it ran against the claim that the imperial order offered equality before the law and protection for Native peoples.

Milner and Reconstruction

All South Africa was now under British control, but it was still divided into four separate entities: two colonies with responsible government (The Cape and Natal), and two crown colonies (The Transvaal and Orange River Colony) directly administrated by the British. A census taken in April 1904 recorded 5.1 million people living in the four colonies. Of these nearly 3.5 million were Africans, 1.1 million whites, 445,000 Coloureds and 122,000 Indians. In terms of the individual colonies the Cape had 2.4 million people, the Transvaal 1.2 million, Natal 1.1 million (of whom less than 100,000 were white), and the ORC 400,000. Milner remained High Commissioner for all South Africa, and added the Governorships of the Transvaal and the ORC. He therefore became the major player in British policy making, partly because of his immense formal power, but also because of changes in circumstances and personnel. For one thing the British settler element was less prominent. In March 1902 Rhodes died, having spent a frustrating war at first holed up in the siege of Mafeking and then suffering from increasing ill health. The imperialists among the settlers who remained gave their support to Milner, but they had neither the driving force nor the conditions to emulate the mighty Rhodes. Equally, although London retained overall control, Britain's intense political concern with South Africa faded in the aftermath of war, leaving the 'man on the spot' with greater discretion. In September 1903 Chamberlain resigned after a clash over imperial preferences. He was replaced by Lord Lyttleton, who was deferential to Milner both as a person and as the 'man on the spot'.

Milner set out to use his position to reconstruct the economy and society and to shape South Africa in an imperial mould. For him reconstruction was not an end in itself – it was the means to achieve a 'British' South Africa. 'It is,' said Milner, 'no longer war with bullets, but it is war. Still . . . we now hold the winning cards, but it is not true that we have won the game, and we cannot afford to lose a single trick. We are fighting something immensely big' (O'Brien 1979: 205). His plans involved major social and economic engineering, with the intention of creating a loyal dominion of the crown. Early in the war Milner had set out his long-term objectives. 'The ultimate end,' he wrote, 'is a self governing white Community, supported by well treated and justly governed black labour from Cape Town to the Zambezi. There must be one flag, the Union Jack, but under it an equality of races [i.e. between the whites] and languages. Given equality all round English must prevail, though . . . I do not wish that Dutch should altogether die out. I think though that all South Africa should be one Dominion, with a common government dealing with Customs, Railways, and Defence, perhaps also with Native Policy, a considerable amount of freedom should be left to the several States. But though this is the ultimate end, it would be madness to attempt it at once. There must be an interval, to allow the British population of the Transvaal to return and increase, and the mess to be cleared up' (Lavin 1995: 34). There was no doubting Milner's commitment. When Chamberlain resigned from office Milner was offered his post in the British government, but he chose to soldier on in South Africa, explaining 'I do not think I ought to abandon the work to which I have devoted so many years at its present necessarily very uncomplete state' (O'Brien 1979: 205).

Although his long-term aim was a self-governing community Milner was in no hurry. By instinct he was an autocrat. During the war he had recommended the suspension of the Cape constitution in favour of direct government, but London had vetoed that. He believed that his job was to govern; that efficiency took precedence over representation. He set out to build 'an administration so competent and so imposing as to enforce an unwilling respect: a system which self government when it comes, is not likely altogether to destroy' (Le May 1965: 157). He was suspicious of politicians, whether British or South African, believing that in their desire to gain party advantage they were willing to pursue short-sighted policies which could damage the Empire. In his view a permanent settlement required 'years of strong, patient policy', without interference from British party politics. Those years were needed to bring in more British settlers and to reverse Afrikaner attitudes. It was, in Milner's view, the Afrikaners who had to change. 'Either,' he wrote, 'they must accept our flag and membership of the British Empire in good faith . . . or we shall have to keep up a system of autocratic rule till their opposition to the new order of things is completely broken' (Le May 1995: 130). Later he confided to his successor, Lord Selborne, that no Afrikaner politician could be trusted.

In practical terms Milner believed that his aims could be achieved in three ways. The first was to increase the British population by a vigorous immigration policy. 'If,' he reasoned, 'ten years hence there are three men of British race to two of Dutch, the country will be safe and prosperous' (Thompson 1960: 7). The second was to retain control in the hands of British officials while the changes were taking place. To help him with this Milner appointed a group of young Oxford graduates, who, known as 'the Kindergarten', included Lionel Curtis, Philip Kerr, Richard Feetham, Geoffrey Dawson and Patrick Duncan. These young men combined burning idealism with practical efficiency. 'By day they built storm water drains and pergolas,' wrote Deborah Lavin, 'in the evenings there were long debates about closer union and empire' (Lavin 1995: 64). Milner's third route to his ends was through cultural imperialism; in particular the use of education to anglicize the Boers. 'I do not think,' he said, 'that there is any class of man so likely to influence the future generations for good or evil, loyalty or the reverse, as the teachers' (Le May 1995: 127). He recruited British staff who were prepared to support the government in making Afrikaners into British citizens. In the schools Dutch would only be used to teach English, and English to teach everything else. A similar approach was used in higher education. 'In the new colonies,' wrote Milner, 'the case will be easier to deal with [than the Cape] provided we make English the language of all higher education . . . Language is important, but the tone and spirit of the teaching conveyed is even more important . . . I attach especial importance to school history books' (Muller 1969: 320).

Although he was in no hurry, Milner soon realized that time was not on his side, that British politicians were under pressure to grant self-government to the colonies and then merge them into a South African federation. Personally he was opposed to such change 'until we are sure that it cannot fall into the hands of men opposed to the Imperial connection. I do not see how a Federal Government in the hands of the Afrikaner party could lead to any other result except separation or another war' (Le May 1965: 165). Instead he wanted to retain the old republics as crown colonies until British dominance was secure. The Transvaal was critical. In political terms Milner assumed that Natal and the Orange River Colony would cancel each other out; that no reliance could be placed on the Cape with its Afrikaner majority; and therefore the Transvaal was the hinge on which the future turned. 'If we make the Transvaal what it ought to be,' he wrote, 'the Colony [Cape] will matter less, and in the long run with the heart sound the whole body will be saved' (O'Brien 1979: 178).

To succeed Milner needed an economic revival both to provide resources for his administration and to attract British immigrants. However, in the immediate post-war period the economy slumped with the departure of the troops and a prolonged drought. Again Milner recognized that the Transvaal was the key to the future. The recovery of the mines was essential to revive the economy, and so he set out to harmonize the efforts of the government and mine owners by providing an efficient administration sympathetic to mining capitalism. The main brake on a mining revival was a shortage of labour. Milner, therefore, appointed a commission which reported in November 1903 stating that 120,000 extra men were required. In his attempts to provide them Milner improved local recruiting and made labour agreements with Mozambique, Basutoland and Swaziland, but there was still a gap. Anxious to push ahead, he persuaded a reluctant British Government to fill it by importing indentured Chinese labourers. They started to arrive in 1904 and eventually more than 60,000 Chinese worked in the mines. At the same time Milner gave Lionel Curtis the task of transforming Johannesburg from a boom town into a modern city, because, said Milner: 'A great Johannesburg, great in intelligence, in cultivation, in public spirit – means a British Transvaal' (Nimocks 1970: 30).

In physical terms Milner's reconstruction programme was a success. When he left South Africa in April 1905 he could look with satisfaction at the financial and material achievements. Immediately before the war gold production had been worth £15.4m.; by 1901 it had fallen to £1.1m. Under Milner's guidance it recovered, so that by 1903 it was £12.6m. and by 1906 £24.6m. Milner also resisted London's initial plan to impose a war debt on South Africa of £72m. Instead he obtained substantial British funds for reconstruction; including £16.5m. for postwar reparations and resettlement; a £2.5m. loan to buy land for British settlers; and a loan of £35m. for railways and public works. He further created a strong framework for the country's future – in administration, transport, communications, education and its industrial base. He promoted joint action among the four colonies – through a united transport system, a common customs service, the creation of an Intercolonial Council and he also initiated a comprehensive investigation of Native Policy. These were solid achievements. In his farewell speech, Milner appealed to his supporters: 'If you believe in me defend my works when I am gone . . . I should prefer to be remembered for the tremendous effort, wise or unwise in various particulars, made after the war, not only to repair the ravages, but also to start the new colonies on a far higher plane than they had previously attained' (Thompson 1960: 16).

The Balance Moves against Milner

Despite the material progress Milner was well aware of the political opposition that faced him. In the Cape he was never at ease with parliament and responsible government. Although the people of the Cape were British citizens many did not fit Milner's imperial model. He pointed to those Afrikaners who had failed to support Britain in the war. The Bond leaders responded by emphasizing that despite their torn loyalties most Afrikaners had refused to take up arms against the crown. But that failed to persuade Milner. 'If,' he wrote 'when our troops have withdrawn, the government remains in the old hands, the Colony will be part of the British Empire only in name.' He was convinced that 'the Dutch will try to recover by politics what they have lost in arms, and the Cape Colony will be their base of operations' (O'Brien 1979: 176). Meanwhile Merriman continued to warn of the dangers of 'Downing St meddling'. However, in the short term, Milner's fears for the Cape were unfounded. In the 1904 election (in which war rebels had forfeited the right to vote) the Progressive Party came to power with Jameson, the arch imperialist of the notorious Raid, as Prime Minister.

In the two new crown colonies (Transvaal and Orange River Colony) Milner worked with constitutions in which members of the legislative and executive councils were nominated. He accepted that the ORC had a permanent Afrikaner majority. In the Transvaal he tried to gain legitimacy by appointing Afrikaner representatives to the legislative assembly, while retaining executive power in official hands. This was the aim behind the Lyttleton Constitution of 1905, but leading Afrikaners refused to participate. As in the Cape so in the Transvaal Milner met a mixed response from the British population. By 1904 two English-speaking parties had emerged: the Progressives, and Responsibles. The Progressives, backed by the mine owners, supported Milner. They concentrated on the economy, feared Afrikaner control and opposed early self-government. Echoing Milner, Sir Percy Fitzpatrick, their leader, stated that self-government should come only when there is 'a loyal majority', and that the British Government should not 'yield to the ballot what they have held from the rifle'. Such views were not shared by the Responsibles, who were mainly drawn from professional and commercial classes. They disliked crown colony government, demanded representative institutions leading to self-government and declared that Afrikaners must be trusted. When Chamberlain visited South Africa in December 1902 they pleaded for 'a little less "Crown" and a little more "Colony"'. However, on one issue the Transvaal English-speaking parties, like their Afrikaner colleagues, were united: they opposed the extension of the franchise to blacks.

In seeking his ends Milner was never without allies but the balance of forces steadily moved against him – crucially in London. There he could rely on broad support from Chamberlain and his successor, Lord Lyttleton, but to Milner's despair, even they were subject to the vagaries of democracy and public opinion, and in Britain the political mood had changed. Never again would it be glad, confident imperial morn. Confidence and arrogance had been subdued beneath the reality of war: its length, conduct and cost (in lives and material). By its end political leaders were eager to direct their attention elsewhere; the public mood was less assertive and the critics' voices were louder. The claims of a special imperial mission were attacked by those who pointed to the failure to protect black interests; who associated imperialism with capitalism; who accused the government of denying Afrikaners their rights as a small nation; and who asserted that principle had been abandoned for power.

Opposition became focused on particular policies, of which Chinese labour was the most explosive. The Chinese improved output in the mines, but the policy was a political disaster and seriously undermined Milner's prestige. Opposition came from sources as different as British humanitarians who were repelled by 'Chinese slavery', and white miners in South Africa who feared that 'coolie labour' would undermine their jobs. Milner dismissed such criticism. 'There is,' he said, 'an immense amount of cant about the "moral" evils attending Chinese immigration . . . It is the pro Boers and the little Englanders who are really at the bottom of the whole business' (Nimocks 1970: 167). For Milner the 'pro Boers and the little Englanders' became associated with the Liberal Party. Increasingly he feared that the Liberals would gain power in Britain and undo his work by offering early self-government to the new colonies, thereby enabling the Boers to gain political power. He became reluctant to send despatches which might fall into Liberal hands. 'I regard the Opposition,' he said, 'as wreckers in so far as South Africa is concerned; and inside information supplied to them simply would be material supplied to the Powers of Darkness' (Le May 1965: 167). On his return to London in 1905 Milner told the Lords that 'a prosperous and loyal Transvaal is the key to the whole situation,' and urged that self-government should not be rushed. In response Sir Henry Campbell-Bannerman, the Liberal leader, said that Liberals regarded self-government 'not as an odious necessity, not as a foolish theory to which unfortunately the British Empire is committed. We treat it as a blessing' (Thornton 1966: 135).

For all his achievements Milner left South Africa knowing that his overriding ambition was unfulfilled. He had not established a securely British-dominated state. The settlement scheme had only produced 2,500 immigrants, the political future was uncertain, and he could not rely upon London to continue to pursue his policies. Publicly he put on a brave face but privately he was gloomy fearing that Afrikaners would return to power. Yet he never lost his commitment to the imperial cause. In his farewell speech in Johannesburg he claimed that Boer and Briton could unite without any loss of dignity through loyalty to the Empire. 'And so you see,' he reasoned, 'the true Imperialist is also the best South African.'

3

Afrikaners, Blacks
and Reconstruction

The war had left Afrikaners a dispirited, divided people. However, a new breed of leaders emerged who had gained their spurs in battle and were more efficient than 'the older generation of patriarchs and incompetents' (Giliomee 1987). Among the new men were Louis Botha and Jan Smuts in the Transvaal, and J. B. M. Hertzog in the Free State – all Boer generals in the war, and all bitter opponents of Milner and his imperialism. For a time they had no formal position in the new colonies. Botha and Smuts refused to be nominated to the Transvaal Legislative Council – 'Milner's Debating Society' as they called it – because, they argued, the British administration must take the praise or blame for what happened until there was responsible government. Yet the continuing strength of Afrikaner identity was demonstrated by the vast crowd that attended Paul Kruger's funeral in Pretoria on 16 December 1904. The dominee who conducted the service called on the mourners to pray to the God of Kruger and not to let national feeling die.

Early stirrings of Afrikaner political revival soon came; not in Milner's formal bodies, but in interest groups – such as agricultural societies, women's groups and cultural and religious movements – where school teachers and dominees of the Dutch Reformed Church were prominent in promoting Afrikaner culture as a reaction to Milner's anglicization policy. In response to an Ordinance of 1903, which stipulated the use of English in state schools, private Christian National Schools were established that taught in Dutch and Afrikaans. Attendance at these schools took on a form of patriotic resistance. By 1905 Afrikaner journalists were using Afrikaans extensively in their newspapers, helping to make it a more sophisticated, written language, and to break its association with poverty and 'colouredness' (Hofmeyr 1987: 103). Political activity gained further momentum from the controversy over Chinese labour. Botha called a meeting in Pretoria at which he denounced the recruitment of the Chinese as a capitalist plot, and went on to demand equality between Dutch and English, local control of education, and no debt payment without the consent of elected representatives. When Lord Lyttelton in London disputed Botha's and Smuts' claims to represent Afrikaner opinion in the Transvaal, they responded by forming 'Het Volk' (The People) in January 1905. A year later J. B. M. Hertzog formed the 'Orangia Unie' in the ORC.

As leaders of Het Volk, Botha and Smuts were a formidable team: Botha with his common touch and Smuts the intellectual and man of vision. Both had proved themselves in war, now they were to do so in peace. Their immediate aim was to overturn the Lyttelton constitution and gain self-government for the old republics, but their long-term objective was reconciliation. At first they directed their attention to reconciling Afrikaners in the Transvaal, seeking to bring them together by rekindling hope and healing the deep wounds that had arisen between 'bitter-enders' (who had fought to the end), 'hands-uppers' (who had surrendered), and National Scouts (who had fought for the British). Later Botha and Smuts were to extend reconciliation to embrace all whites, so that a single, self-governing white nation could develop. Smuts had contemplated this even during the war. 'The war,' he wrote, 'between the white races will run its course and pass away and may, if followed by a statesmanlike settlement, one day be remembered as a great thunderstorm which purified the atmosphere of the sub continent.' With the war over he returned to his old Cape theme of common white interests and identity. He wrote: 'In a generous spirit of forgive and forget let us try to found a stable Commonwealth in South Africa, in which both Boer and Briton will be proud to be partners; let it be clearly understood that England shall meddle as little with the internal concerns of this Commonwealth as with those of Canada or Australia.' If Britain failed to do that, he warned that 'the ghost of the murdered Boer people will haunt the British Empire to its grave.' As Milner left South Africa he was probably astonished to receive a generous note from Smuts, his old enemy. 'History,' wrote Smuts, 'writes the word "Reconciliation" over all her quarrels' (Hancock 1962: 148, 198).

Botha and Smuts believed that self-government was the key to the future. They accepted that they were now subjects of the British crown, but while Milner favoured crown colony government – so that British officials could exercise control – they wanted self-government, so that local whites could govern through their own representatives. Smuts wrote: 'An army of occupation won't keep the Boers down', whereas 'honest, real "bona fide" self-government will satisfy them and make them really contented' (Hancock 1962: 187). At that time Smuts believed that future divisions among whites would be linked to economic, not ethnic, factors – based on 'the distribution of political power between the mine owners and the permanent population of the land, English as well as Dutch'; and on the tension between 'the liberties of the people as against the encroachment of money power' (Hancock 1962: 207–9).

Like Milner the Het Volk leaders realized that to gain their ends political change must come in London; that early self-government rested on the Liberals gaining power in Britain.

Blacks: Reconstruction and Political Activity

On his return to Britain Milner admitted only one major error: the abandonment of the principle of 'equal rights for every civilised man' (Le May 1965: 177). One of the expressed aims of war had been to improve the position of blacks. In March

1901, Chamberlain had told Milner that he should endeavour to extend the franchise to qualified Africans in the old republics, not to undermine white predominance but to recognize the importance of civilization. Following the war Milner urged a Johannesburg audience to take a stand 'on the firm and inexpungable ground of civilization against the rotten and indefensible ground of colour' (Pyrah 1955: 99). However, he faced the dilemma that if he were liberal towards blacks he would unite whites against him. He therefore tried to steer a middle course, based on the assumption that while whites must continue to rule because of their superior civilization, they had a duty to help blacks to achieve the same standards, and, when they did, to grant them equal rights. Yet, although he argued that it would be dangerous for whites to abandon the principle of 'equal rights for every civilized man', whenever Britain's position was threatened by a white backlash he retreated from that position. Like others on the British side he was not prepared to endanger a settlement with the Afrikaners for the sake of race equality. Therefore instead of promoting equal rights he floated the idea of creating Native Councils in each colony, to discuss matters of concern to Africans, before they were referred to the white assemblies. Overall Milner made little progress. He did change some aspects of the daily life of Africans by improving the pass laws and standards of living in the townships, but on the bigger issues he made no headway.

Black Political Activity

Despite the absence of progress (or perhaps because of it) black political activity developed in the post-war period. For example, Sol Plaatje launched a newspaper (*Koranta ea Becoana*) which was first published in 1901, with articles in Tswana and English; and in 1903 Coloureds in Cape Town founded the African People's Organisation, demanding equality for all. Within black politics various factors were at work, which did not always complement each other. They included religious influences (often linked to Christian schools); loyalty to the imperial idea; increased urbanization leading to economic but not social integration; respect for traditional authority; and the impact of external ideas (in particular British liberalism and American black rights movements). From these influences four broad if ill-defined streams can be detected. The first emphasized the imperial link, looked to 'the mother country' for support, and claimed the rights of British citizens, as exemplified in the Cape franchise. The second was influenced by pan-African movements which were opposed to white rule. The third had strong traditional roots and was linked to separate African peoples and tribal groups. Finally there was growing class consciousness, loosely related to the global struggle against capitalism (Rich 1996: 10).

Yet, black activity was still relatively weak and immature. It was too early to speak of a distinctive African nationalism. Black leaders of the time were predominantly moderate men, who aimed to keep their activities within legal and constitutional boundaries. They were not in a position to dictate terms, and had little choice but to respond to agendas set by the white authorities. Inevitably their activity was largely reactive, and constrained by the context in which they operated. In that context, when the choice was between the policies of the Afrikaner republics or British imperialism, the imperial route seemed much the better option. In the Transvaal and the ORC race relations had been based on the principle of no equality in church or state, and Africans had been regarded as a lower race who carried the mark of Cain upon them. Sol Plaatje wrote: 'The history of the treatment of blacks north of the Orange River is one long and uninterrupted record of rapine and greed' (Plaatje 1982: 155).

While fear of the extension of republican policies was a negative factor encouraging support for British imperialism, there were also positive factors. The appeal of imperial nationalism was not confined to one state, but rather offered an identity and set of rights associated with a world empire. It had within it the lure that drew earlier generations to claim citizenship of Rome. Often with a background of British mission education, many black leaders built up an idealized picture of British imperialism. They pinned their hopes on an Empire governed on non-racial lines, with equality before the law, fair play and representation through parliamentary institutions. For them politics was less the messy compromises and fudged decisions of day-to-day government, than a set of moral principles. 'Imperial lines are benevolent,' wrote Plaatje in 1902, 'while South African lines are cruel.' He claimed that 'under the Union Jack every person is his neighbour's equal – race or colour is no bar' (Willan 1984: 111). Some black leaders, however, were more pragmatic and supported the imperial order, not because it offered genuine equality, but because it was the best they could expect at the time. Dr Abdurahman (a Coloured leader, a Cape Town Councillor, and President of the African People's Organisation) recognized that there was inequality in the Cape, but accepted that blacks were treated with theoretical justice. 'Justice and equity are our demands,' he said, 'as inherent rights of every man, especially a free-born British subject, even in South Africa' (Plaatje 1982: 153).

Far from challenging the imperial government, therefore, most blacks regarded it as the legitimate authority – a source of rights, and a potential protector against local white exploitation. In 1903 the Native Congress wrote to Chamberlain stating: 'The natives of South Africa are naturally Imperialistic in their sympathies . . . Throughout the severe trials which our race has undergone in the past nothing has impressed us more than the high sense of fairness, justice and humanity displayed by Governors of British birth' (Karis and Carter 1972: 21). They praised Milner and referred to Cecil Rhodes's dictum of 'equal rights for all civilized men'. Yet, while they hoped for justice, they realized that white control, whether by imperial officials or Boer Presidents, was based on the oldest rule in the book – the right of conquest. There was no immediate prospect of changing that, but they trusted the British to recognize their responsibilities towards their black subjects. Later, in July 1914, an African petition to King George V spoke of their love and respect for him as 'father and protector', and described themselves as 'descendants of a race which, when their forebears were conquered by your Majesty's might . . . loyally and cheerfully submitted to your Majesty's sway in the full belief that they would be allowed to possess their land as British subjects, and would be given the full benefits of British rule' (Karis and Carter 1972: 21).

In claiming rights by peaceful means within the imperial setting African leaders had an inspiring example on their door step in the person of Mahatma Gandhi. When he helped form the Natal Indian Congress, Gandhi claimed the rights and duties of a citizen of the Empire. He served the British as a stretcher-bearer during the South Africa war and again in the Bambatha rising of 1906, and it was in South Africa that he first developed the principle of 'Satyagraha' (non-violent force) to resist unjust legislation against Asians. However, at the time there was little co-operation across racial lines. Rather than looking to Indians of Natal and the Transvaal, Africans and Coloureds pinned their hopes on preserving and even extending the Cape system across South Africa. Tengo Jabavu claimed that the situation in the Cape is 'ethically moral because it places a premium on merit rather than colour. It is Christian, indicating the white man's humanitarian duty towards the black. It is economically sound for it confers equality of opportunity on all who rise freely on the scale of civilization' (Karis and Carter 1972: 207). Loyalty to the imperial connection in the Cape had been enhanced by the war, and by the danger that the republican racial policies could have been extended there. The overriding sentiment was relief at what had been saved, rather than appreciation of the trials that lay ahead. What had been at stake was 'the survival of a colonial system with known structures habits and order, against the perceived threat of its authoritarian dismemberment'. The war had meant the survival in the Cape of 'the liberal synthesis of citizenship, rights and limited political freedoms' (Nasson 1991: 187).

However, alongside hopes of imperial justice – built on experience in the Cape – was concern about the situation in Natal. That presented a model of imperial injustice. As a British colony it formally offered equality between the races, but practised discrimination against blacks, who in Natal were mainly Zulus and Indians. The colony's record of Native administration was poor, and its franchise qualifications were so loaded against Africans that at the turn of the century only six of them had the vote. In 1906, a combination of the colony's harsh administration, the steady encroachment of white farming and the demands of cheap labour, led to a Zulu rising – the Poll tax or Bambatha rising (named after the chief who defied the government). Many of those who rebelled behaved recklessly because they believed that a ritual ceremony had made them invulnerable to bullets. It had not. The rising was suppressed by overwhelming force, in which between 3,000 and 4,000 Zulus were killed compared with 24 whites. When, even after Bambatha's death, the disturbances continued, the Natal authorities accused Dinuzulu, the head of the Zulu royal house, of promoting the troubles. At his trial, Dinuzulu was defended by W. P. Schreiner, the former Premier of the Cape, and was acquitted on the more serious charges, but sentenced to five years' imprisonment for harbouring rebels. The Natal Government was criticized for the harsh and hysterical way it dealt with the rebellion and more generally its native policy, but a brutal lesson had been handed out to Africans across the whole country. The rebellion, wrote Shula Marks, was 'the last armed resistance to poletarianization on the part of Africans. After this, Africans did not need to be reminded of the white man's power' (Marks 1986: 29).

Despite Natal's poor record, the greatest fear for blacks was that the policies and values of the old Boer republics would come to predominate. With that in mind,

African representatives from the four colonies attended a Native Convention in 1902. They claimed that the imperial government was 'bound by both fundamental and specific obligations towards the Native and Coloured races of South Africa to extend to them the same measures of equitable justice and consideration as is extended to those of European descent' (Thompson 1960: 326). Later a delegation visited London to plead the Africans' cause, as they became increasingly concerned about the progress of events. The delegates received sympathy from some MPs, sections of the press and the churches, but little from the government. The blunt fact was that if the British wanted peace they had to satisfy the Boers not the blacks. One way to gain that was to ignore black claims. Milner had long recognized that most whites were opposed to a liberal Native policy. 'You have the singular situation,' he wrote, 'that you might indeed unite Dutch and English by protecting the black man, but you would unite them against your policy of protection. There is the whole core of the South African situation' (O'Brien 1979: 149). That did not change. On another occasion Milner encapsulated the situation when he wrote: 'You have only to sacrifice "the nigger" and the game is easy' (Le May 1965: 11). That the sacrifice was being made became clear as early as the Treaty of Vereeniging. Later an African delegation concluded that the 1902 treaty was 'when the British after hundreds of years of fighting for the maintenance of these ideals [liberty and justice] departed from the path of justice and compromised with tyranny' (Walshe 1987: 63).

The period of reconstruction underlined the message. Milner was aware of African aspirations, but was less concerned about them than building a thriving economy, creating an effective British administration and avoiding a white back-lash. In seeking his ends he never lost faith in the flag or the need for 'a self governing white community supported by well treated and justly governed black labour', but he became increasingly hesitant both about the 'self governing white community' (without a British majority), and about 'justly governed black labour' if that implied equal political rights. He could see the fairness of extending the Cape franchise, but concluded that 'for the sake of a theory it would be unwise to start a conflict with the whites' (Le May 1965: 77). Similar sentiments were found in the kindergarten. Lionel Curtis concluded that although whites would eventually have to be given self-government, blacks could be ruled autocratically. Curtis doubted, however, that local whites could be trusted to handle Native affairs, and favoured retaining the responsibility in imperial hands.

To achieve an economic revival Milner was again confronted by the challenge of race, especially in the mines. The mine owners were opposed to increasing the number of white workers because of their high costs and the threat of militancy from white trade unions. Milner supported that view and added that the quality of whites was at least as important as quantity. Bluntly he concluded: 'We do not want a white proletariat in this country' (Wheatcroft 1993: 220). Yet, at the same time, Africans were difficult to recruit because mine work was hard, alien to them and the wages were low – much lower than for whites. It was when his efforts and those of the mine owners failed to produce the required numbers of blacks that he took the unpopular decision – with blacks as well as whites – to recruit Chinese labour.

In terms of general native policy Milner also envisaged a long haul. In 1903 he told a Johannesburg audience: 'The white man must rule because he is elevated by many, many steps above the black man . . . which it will take the latter centuries to climb and which . . . the vast bulk of the black population may never be able to climb at all' (Marks and Trapido 1987: 7). To help shape policy he set up a Native Affairs Commission, to investigate and make recommendations. Between 1903 and 1905 it toured the four colonies taking evidence from a wide range of people, including many Africans. It reported shortly before Milner left the country and so it is uncertain how he would have responded to its recommendations. However, it helps to identify the thrust of official opinion at the time, and that thrust 'provided the first clear articulation of segregationist ideals' (Worden 1995: 73). The commission proposed racial separation of land ownership, the establishment of native locations in towns; the regulation of labour into urban areas; differential racial wage levels; and separation in education. It stated that initially at least 'the rational policy . . . is to facilitate the development of the aboriginal on lines which do not merge too closely into European life, lest it lead to enmity and stem the tide of healthy progress.' Yet complete separation was not recommended. Although Africans were to be kept socially and politically apart, they were to be employed in mining and industrial development. 'It could not', commented the commission, 'be deemed of advantage for an inferior race struggling upwards, to be brought up in the notion that its only means of subsistence must be the land . . . success in the struggle for existence lies in learning handicrafts and in pursuing callings which offer a ready and comfortable return for industry. Advance cannot be stayed, but must be conducted under civilised guidance.' (Legassick 1972: 47, 49). In that light it regarded the Cape franchise as intolerable because it gave blacks power to influence elections and even policy. It therefore recommended replacing the Cape franchise with a separate Native voters' roll for all the colonies, by which a set number of white MPs would be returned to represent black views. The message was clear – the Commission saw the future in terms of separation not integration. It was a far cry from the common citizenship for which black leaders pleaded.

Part II

The White Union and Black Reaction

4

Responsible Government and the Union

Within a year of Milner's return to London the Liberal Party was returned to power. Botha and Smuts were delighted, but they feared that in office the Liberals might back track on the bold claims they had made in opposition; that caution would prevail. Would, they asked, the new government listen to them or to Milner? And what would it do about black claims? Smuts therefore hurried to London to press their case. He believed he was making an audacious request: that a people who had been defeated in war only five years before should now be trusted to govern themselves. On his arrival he stressed that the Transvaal Afrikaners fully accepted loyalty to the crown, and argued that for the future consent would be a more enduring bond than constraint. The central issue, he said, was no longer Boer against Briton but the distribution of power between the mine owners and the general population in the Transvaal. In an interview with Henry Campbell-Bannerman, the Liberal Prime Minister, Smuts posed the question: 'Do you want friends or enemies? . . . You can make them [the Boers] enemies and possibly have another Ireland on your hands.' Like the Liberals, said Smuts, Afrikaners had faith in liberty (Hancock 1962: 215).

In response Campbell-Bannerman emphasized that the Liberal government was committed to retaining British supremacy, but intended to do so by influence and liberality, not direct rule. Political supremacy, he said, could only be maintained 'by conciliation and friendship; it will never be by domination and ascendancy because the British power cannot . . . rest securely unless it rests on the willing consent of a sympathetic and contented people' (Le May 1965: 188). From Botha's and Smuts's viewpoint Campbell-Bannerman's response was magnificent and magnanimous. 'Was it possible for the Boers ever to forget such generosity?' asked Botha (Le May 1965: 212). Yet, even for Liberals the 'contented people', to whom Campbell-Bannerman referred, were the whites – Boer and Briton alike. Winston Churchill, the Under Secretary for the Colonies, underlined this when he said that the previous government had tried to stand British authority on one leg, whereas it must stand on two (Afrikaner and British). 'We on this side know that if British dominion is to endure in South Africa it must endure with the assent of the Dutch' (Le May 1965: 86).

Yet what for Botha and Smuts was generosity was to imperialists like Milner irresponsibility. The imperialists feared that instead of fostering loyalty the policy would undermine the Empire by showing weakness in the face of militant Afrikaner nationalism. Arthur Balfour, the Conservative leader, described it as 'the most reckless experiment ever tried in the development of a great colonial policy' (Le May 1965: 189). In South Africa many English speakers accused the Liberals of betraying the imperial cause. Yet, despite the protests London moved quickly to implement its commitment to self-government for the two former republics. It withdrew the Lytellton Constitution and appointed a commission, under Sir Joseph Ridgeway, which recommended the grant of responsible government for the two colonies, with executive power exercised by ministries responsible to local legislatures, elected by white males.

Renewed White Politics in the Transvaal and Orange Free State

Within the Transvaal the Ridgeway Commission had gained the trust of Het Volk, but it did not regard its proposals as biased towards Afrikaners. It estimated that its proposal for the distribution of seats – 33 to the Witwatersrand, 6 to Pretoria, and 30 to the rest – would produce an English-speaking majority if the English speakers were united (Le May 1965: 206). In the longer term the Commissioners said that British interests would best be served by increased British settlement; by a South African federation on similar principles to those in Canada and Australia; and by a contented white population using Dutch as well as English in government. On such terms responsible government was granted to the Transvaal in December 1906 and in February 1907 to the Orange River Colony (which regained its name 'Orange Free State' – OFS).

Attention then turned to the elections. In the OFS, as expected, the predominantly Afrikaner 'Orangia Unie' scored a runaway victory, gaining 30 of the 38 seats in the Legislative Assembly. Inevitably, however, the main political battlefield was the Transvaal. The Ridgeway Commission's calculations had assumed that voting would follow language lines (English and Afrikaans). In broad terms that was correct, but it was not straightforward. Botha and Smuts were seeking reconciliation. Their first aim was to bring together Afrikaners through the vehicle of Het Volk, and in that they largely succeeded. Then they took a further step by forming an electoral alliance with the predominantly English-speaking Responsibles, who supported self-government. Before the election it was agreed that if the alliance won a majority the Premiership would go to Sir Richard Solomon, leader of the Responsibles, and Botha and Smuts would serve under him. In contrast, the Progressives, again predominantly English speaking, opposed responsible government, and sent a 41,000 signature petition to London to say so. Nevertheless they decided to fight the election. The English-speaking vote was therefore divided, and other English-speaking candidates stood for the Labour Party and as Independents.

In the event Het Volk gained an overall majority of seats, but not votes, while the Responsibles did badly. The results – seats, with votes in brackets – were: Het Volk 37 (24,123); Progressives 21 (17,635); Responsibles 6(6,025); Labour

5(5,216); and Independents 2(8,255). The result surprised and delighted Botha and Smuts. Success had come from party efficiency. Afrikaner solidarity and the divided English vote. As for the Responsibles, even Solomon was defeated, and in the new situation the original agreement was revised so that Louis Botha became Prime Minister, with a cabinet of four Het Volk and two Responsibles. Therefore, partly by astute management and partly by chance, Botha and Smuts had achieved their political ambitions more quickly than they had dared to hope. Not only had they gained responsible government; they had been voted into power, and started along the road of reconciliation. The Transvaal was now controlled by a government led by Afrikaners with some English-speaking support. It was Milner's nightmare come to life and a pattern that was to repeat itself in South Africa's future. On assuming office Botha immediately promised to care for the interests of English speakers as well as Afrikaners, and looking to the future spoke of creating a new white identity built on co-operation between the two white language groups.

While the whites of the Transvaal and OFS seized their new opportunities there was no consolation for blacks. Churchill had spoken of the need to stand British authority on two legs. He made no mention of a third (black) leg, because the British Government was fully aware that it could not woo the Boers if it departed 'one iota from the political colour bar' (Thompson 1960: 27). Although it was clear that in the Transvaal Africans had been excluded from the franchise as 'Natives', there was uncertainty about the position of the Coloureds. Were they 'Natives' or would they have the vote? That was soon cleared up in London by Churchill. In response to a question in the Commons he stated: 'I believe the precise meaning attached to the word "native" is native of any country other than a European country' (Le May 1965: 205). Therefore responsible government, which was generous towards the whites, and the Afrikaners in particular, was repressive towards blacks. But the Ridgeway Commission did not see it that way when they had recommended exclusion of blacks from the political equation. Although they noted that Native taxation had increased substantially (in the Transvaal from £110,000 in 1898 to £653,000 in 1905) and that 'little or nothing has been done for the amelioration of the Native population', the commissioners claimed that responsible government would favour blacks as well as whites. The basis of the claim was that any attempt to enact specific protection for blacks, or to operate Native policy and/or safeguards from London would only unite whites against the blacks as well as the British Government.

Self-Government in the Four Colonies

Following the grant of responsible government to the Transvaal and the Free State, power in domestic affairs now lay in the hands of the four colonial governments. London remained the hub of the imperial wheel, but there would be no more dominant local British officials – no more Milners. In time this led to a reshaping of attitudes towards nationalism and the structure of the state, but the immediate concerns of the colonial governments were the day-to-day issues of administration and domestic politics. The Transvaal retained centre stage because of its wealth, its broadly balanced white population (Afrikaner and British), and the quality of its political leadership. Among the problems it inherited was that of labour for the mines. Botha was determined that the Chinese must go, but who would replace them? Should an attempt be made to recruit an all-white labour force, or should it be a mixture of Africans and whites, and if so what mixture? In its response the new government moved closer to the mine owners. Within a month of taking office Smuts, the old critic of the Randlords, found that their case had 'a sound substratum of fact' (Hancock 1962: 237). In 1907 when white (mainly English-speaking) miners went on strike the owners broke it by employing out of work Afrikaners, while Smuts summoned imperial troops to help keep order. Lionel Phillips commented: 'The whole business is getting topsy turvy: a Boer government calling out British troops to keep English miners in order, while Dutchmen are replacing them in the mines' (Liebenberg and Spies 1993: 42).

On another front controversy arose over Smuts's 1907 Education Act. Botha and Smuts saw it as part of a broader policy in which they sought to marry together the strength and loyalty of both British and Afrikaners. The act provided free compulsory education for whites at primary level, based on Christian foundations. In Smuts's eyes this removed the need for the separate Afrikaner Christian National Schools; a view not shared by Afrikaner nationalists. However, the most controversial aspects of the legislation concerned the language to be used in state schools. Pupils were to receive mother tongue instruction in the early years, but after Standard IV English would be obligatory, while Dutch would be taught as a subject, although, by parental choice, it could be used for two other subjects.

On the broader front Botha and Smuts worked for a new white unity and identity. Having consolidated their Afrikaner support in Het Volk, their aim was to draw a line across past divisions, to create a single white nation. Botha prayed: 'That it might please the Almighty Father to inspire all whites of South Africa with likemindedness, that thence one nation may be born' (Thompson 1960: 31). Reconciliation was both an ideal and a practical step. It made sense politically, because Botha and Smuts needed English-speaking support to underpin their position; constitutionally they accepted the crown and responsible government; and in the administration they steadily recruited Afrikaners without alienating the more experienced British civil servants. If they had been exclusively minded Afrikaner nationalists, seeking to recover by politics what had been lost in war, they might well have stopped there, restricting themselves to the Transvaal, but their broader vision led them to consider South Africa as a whole. They saw reconciliation leading to a new state – a self-governing and united white South Africa. They declared that the future lay within the Empire, but they saw it as an evolving Empire which would offer increasing autonomy to self-governing communities. At the 1907 Colonial Conference, which Botha attended as Transvaal representative, an early step was taken along the road to equality of status. In future the self-governing colonies were to be called 'Dominions' not 'Colonies'. An Australian call for greater imperial centralization failed because of strong opposition from Botha, among others.

Botha and Smuts faced opposition from both sides of the old divide: from imperial jingoes and Afrikaner militants who could not or would not forget the past, who did not share the vision of an inclusive white nation. From the Afrikaner side Botha was criticized for attending the imperial conference and presenting the magnificent Cullinan diamond to Edward VII as a symbol of allegiance. Smuts was attacked for his education policy and both men were criticized for failing to support Afrikaner cultural bodies. Botha complained that 'Hollanders, Krugerites and a large section of the Predikants were engaged in a desperate intrigue against him and his policy of closer union and reconciliation' (Muller 1969: 327). Exclusive Afrikaner nationalism was also strong in the Free State, where ex President Steyn, although too ill to return to office, retained his republican sympathies and accused Botha and Smuts of laying 'on the loyalty butter too thick' (Hancock 1962: 234). He supported Christian National Education; suspected foreign influences; and urged parents to teach their children about the concentration camps. For him Afrikaners remained a distinctive people with a divine mission. And, if Steyn's was a voice from the past, the Free State had a voice for the future – that of General J. B. M. Hertzog. Like Botha and Smuts, Hertzog had fought with distinction against the British, and like them he accepted that Afrikaners and English speakers must live and work together. In doing so, he gave a distinctive stamp to the meaning of 'Afrikaner' by including any whites who were committed to South Africa, irrespective of their origins. Yet, while Botha and Smuts favoured merging Boer and Briton into a single white nation, Hertzog's solution was to develop parallel streams, which would co-operate but retain separate identities; and while Botha and Smuts sought to conciliate the imperialists Hertzog sought to discredit them.

Hertzog's two-stream approach was reflected in his 1908 Free State Education Bill. He proposed that in their early years children would be educated in their mother tongue, while the other language (English or Dutch) would be taught as a subject. At senior level children from both streams would attend the same schools, where subjects would be taught equally between the two languages. Hertzog had a double purpose behind the legislation – first to ensure the preservation of Afrikaner culture, and second to encourage English speakers to become true South Africans by learning Dutch/Afrikaans. For him 'bilingualism was the test of sincerity' (Le May 1995: 142). Hertzog's proposals were opposed by most English speakers. There were several reasons for this. Many of them (including teachers) did not speak Dutch or Afrikaans, and as citizens of the British Empire they thought it was an imposition to have bilingualism thrust on them. Further, Hertzog's style and presentation undermined his message. He tended to be impatient and emotional, and to present his ideas in a confrontational and confused style. 'Hertzogism' therefore became a hostile creed for English speakers.

While these issues unfolded in the Transvaal and the Free State, the old colonies were also in the throes of post-war reorganization. In the Cape Jameson's Progressive Party was defeated in 1908 by the South African Party, led by John Merriman and backed by the Bond (an alliance similar to Het Volk and the Responsibles in the Transvaal). Merriman never questioned loyalty to the crown, but like the Bond he favoured colonial devolution and retained his suspicions of interference from London. Although the Transvaal and the Cape were similar in that respect, in terms of Native policy and the franchise major divergences persisted.

The Cape remained the bastion of liberal hopes. The same could not be said of Natal. It remained on the periphery, renowned neither for its efficiency nor its liberalism. There the least attractive parts of the imperial embers burnt on. These weaknesses were underlined not only by the 1906 Bambatha rebellion, but by persistent confrontation with the Indian community led by M. K. Gandhi.

By 1908, therefore, with Het Volk in power in the Transvaal, the SAP/Bond alliance in the Cape and Orangia Unie in the OFS the political balance across South Africa had swung against the old imperialism. It looked, said Leo Amery, 'as if the Boers had regained at the ballot box all that they had lost on the field and conceded at Vereeniging' (Nimocks 1970: 72).

Attitudes to Union

In addition to their own immediate concerns, the colonial governments were confronted by the issue of greater unity. Should they support or oppose it? If they supported it what form should it take? All earlier proposals for unity had favoured a federation with considerable powers devolved to the provinces (the old Colonies) and that approach had strong support in the immediate post-war years. Yet, it was clear that if a single South African state were adopted, whatever its form, it would be a step in the dark. Because the implications were so uncertain politicians with very different backgrounds and aims found themselves supporting the same cause. Despite Milner's doubts about early union the imperialists who remained in South Africa (including the kindergarten, the Progressives, and Lord Selborne the High Commissioner) came to support the movement. This was partly on pragmatic grounds, that the four colonies would have no choice but to work together, in such areas as transport, customs, taxation and Native affairs. They also feared that without union London would be drawn into interminable disputes between the colonies. Finally, the imperialists believed that in the changed circumstance (following responsible government) union would enhance British influence by stimulating the economy, attracting settlers and capital, lead to greater efficiency and encourage 'qualities of British government and idealism as opposed to the ignorance, reaction and selfishness of Boerdom'. The present situation of four separate colonies, wrote Richard Feetham, 'makes for a South Africa which will be Dutch rather than British in sentiment and character. Disunion in South Africa means a weakening of the Imperial tie' (Thompson 1960: 60–2).

These latter-day imperialists were hoping to realize Milner's dream by different means. They accepted that initially the union government might be led by Afrikaners, but they did not regard that as fatal in the long term. They assumed that as unity would bring prosperity, so British industry, capital and settlers would follow; and political parties would be formed which were bound together by common interests rather than language ties. To further the cause kindergarten members produced *The State*, a weekly magazine, which advocated union and fostered the concept of 'being South African'. Lionel Curtis resigned his official post to devote himself to the campaign. He drafted 'A Review of the Present Mutual Relations of the British South Africa Colonies', which Selborne revised and then circulated as a memorandum. The memo called on the four colonies to unite in their own interests, arguing that with common railways, a customs union, and a single Native policy the country would prosper – attracting capital and settlers, and overcoming labour problems. 'Three choices lie before the people of South Africa,' wrote Selborne, 'the makeshift regime of the High Commissioner; the jarring separatism of the states of South America; the noble union of the States of North America' (Thompson 1960: 68). He left no doubt which he favoured.

In the following year Selborne, who was regarded as a 'liberal', sent a further memo to Botha and Smuts, this time about Native policy. In it he reiterated support for union leading to a common Native policy, which, he argued, by promoting peace, Christianity and civilization, would eventually destroy tribalism. He saw economic advance as the vehicle by which Africans would move 'from tribalism into an atmosphere of civilization', and so he opposed restrictions on labour movement such as the pass laws. However, Selborne did not advocate political equality. He was prepared to make exceptions for those Natives who could prove their civilized credentials before a panel of judges; but otherwise he regarded Native participation in elections as 'absurd, futile and dangerous'. 'No one,' he wrote, 'can have any experience of the two races without feeling the intrinsic superiority of the white man.' He favoured retaining the franchise for Coloureds, because it would be a mistake to classify them with Africans and so make common cause. For Africans he advocated separate arrangements with responsibility falling on a Department of Native Affairs advised by Native Councils (Hancock 1962: 317).

Ironically, many of Milner's old opponents also came to advocate union. Now that Afrikaners could expect to dominate a united state and shape its constitution they were willing – even eager – for unification. They included Steyn in the OFS, who saw an opportunity to counter British influence by uniting Afrikaners in a single state which in time would regain independence as a republic. Botha and Smuts also advocated union. At first Smuts saw it as a means of countering Milnerism. In May 1904 he claimed that a united South Africa 'has always been a deeply felt political aspiration [for Afrikaners] and it might profitably be substituted for the imperialism which imports Chinese, a foreign bureaucracy and a foreign standing army' (Thompson 1960: 71). He also argued strongly that unity would help to counter capitalism by keeping 'Hoggenheimer' (the cartoon capitalist figure) in place.

Following responsible government Botha and Smuts came to see union in more positive terms – with idealism as well as power considerations behind their approach. They saw it as a means of transforming the memory of war from a nightmare to an ideal. 'I was fighting,' Smuts wrote later, 'for a United South Africa in which there would be the greatest possible freedom, but from which the disturbing influence of Downing Street would have been finally eliminated. I was not fighting for "Dutch" supremacy or predominance over [the] English . . . Let us try to arrange our politics, our administration and our legislation that a compact South African nationality may be built up with the best elements of both parts of the colonial population so that [we shall] be united within and present a united front to the outside world' (Hancock 1962: 199). Within that framework Botha and Smuts believed that a united state would bring together the two white groups into a single nation within the Empire; it would reduce interference from London; and place responsibility for Native affairs in local hands.

Union had its opponents. Inevitably, in the aftermath of a bitter war, there were those who resisted attempts to harness them to past enemies. The British in Natal feared it would lead to Afrikaner dominance. In the Cape Merriman suspected it might sow new imperial seeds. He feared that South Africa might be 'dragged at the wheels of the Imperial Chariot or the mine owners' mud cart' (Thompson 1960: 75). Alongside the fears were clashing economic interests. Some farmers and manufacturers demanded protection from their neighbours. Many Transvaalers were so convinced that they would be a milch cow for others that Smuts wrote anxiously of 'a movement for separatism similar to that which existed before the war' (Hancock 1962: 251).

Among the major issues to be settled by the colonial governments were customs disputes and railway rivalry. The two coastal colonies relied on customs and railway receipts for their revenue; whereas the two landlocked colonies (the old republics) benefited by keeping the charges as low as possible. As the coastal colonies competed for business for their ports, the inland colonies used the competition to drive a hard bargain. The situation was exacerbated by the Transvaal's economic importance. The Cape and Natal ports wanted its trade, but to their consternation an increasing proportion followed the shortest route to Lorenco Marques in Mozambique. By 1908 that port had 63 per cent of the Rand's traffic, compared with 24 per cent for Durban, and only 13 per cent for the Cape ports. In July 1907, after several unsuccessful attempts to reach an agreement, the Transvaal threw down the gauntlet by giving notice of its withdrawal from the existing customs union. That prompted an Intercolonial Customs Conference in May 1908, with an agenda, drafted by Smuts, which was much wider than an economic brief. The conference concluded that the economic problems could only be overcome by bold political measures, and it accepted six resolutions, again prepared by Smuts, including proposals that the four colonies should be united under the British crown, and that a national convention be called to draft a constitution.

The National Convention

By 1908 a situation had been reached whereby, with different long-term aims in mind, the Afrikaner leaders of the Transvaal and OFS, and Milner's old supporters were working for union. To address that task an all-white National Convention was convened, with twelve representatives from the Cape, eight from the Transvaal, and five each from Natal and the Free State. They faced a series of thorny problems both of principle and practice. Should a single state be formed at all? If so should it be federal or unitary? What should be the franchise arrangements? Should blacks have the vote and if so on what terms? How should constituency boundaries be drawn and should proportional representation be introduced? What should be the official language? Who should control the railways and harbours? Where should the capital be sited? The answer to such questions would determine the future form of the state and the sense of national identity.

In their deliberations the representatives had to balance the thrust towards union with their separate agendas. The Cape wanted to preserve its colour blind franchise; Natal feared centralized Afrikaner domination; the Transvaal wanted to protect its commercial interests; and the Free State stood firm on language equality. Most delegates arrived believing that union was the best option, but during the negotiations there were moments when it appeared that all would be lost. Steyn of the Free State, looking to the future from the shadows of the past, reminded them that: 'For as long as the one [white] race considers itself in ever so slight a way placed in an inferior position to the other, there will never be that harmonious cooperation which is so necessary and desired by us all' (Thompson 1960: 137). But the drive for union steadily gained momentum, not least because most representatives believed that it would bring increased wealth and economic stability. It was, for example, eventually accepted that all railways and harbours would become Union property, and agreement was reached on the division of Rand traffic – Lourenzo Marques (50/55 per cent), Durban (30 per cent) and the Cape ports (15/20 per cent).

Blacks were not directly represented at the convention, and so were obliged to try to make their voices heard through petitions, press articles, public meetings and contact with sympathetic whites. They were only prepared to support a union if the imperial power would ensure that the spirit and letter of the Cape constitution spread across South Africa. The Coloureds through the African People's Organisation petitioned to retain their Cape rights and to extend them elsewhere for all who were 'fully civilized' irrespective of race. Yet lack of unity reduced the impact of black demands. At the time they had no co-ordinating body. Some African politicians in the Cape decided to lie low for fear of losing their existing rights, which was no consolation to those further north. The Transvaal National Native Union sent a petition urging a non-racial franchise throughout the country, but it arrived after the decisions had been made. Black claims were not entirely ignored. From sympathy or fear some delegates advocated moves towards racial equality. Merriman favoured a qualified colour blind franchise, and warned that to deprive blacks of rights would be 'building a volcano' for the future. 'How,' he asked, 'can you without blushing talk of manhood suffrage and exclude of design two thirds of the population?' (Thompson 1960: 118, 119). Colonel W. E. D. Stanford, a retired Native Administrator, proposed that all British subjects should have equal franchise rights, for without a just policy 'the white man would go under in South Africa . . . It is impossible to govern fairly unless the people themselves are represented in government' (Thompson 1960: 215–16).

But these were voices crying in the wilderness. Their proposals were rejected by a large majority of the delegates. Smuts argued that politics would unsettle the Natives, and spoke mystically of looking into 'the shadow and darkness'. He favoured leaving matters to future generations. Hertzog stated that the Native was a child 'thousands of years behind the white man'. It was Botha who had the greatest impact. Replying to Stanford he said that the first duty of the delegates was to gain the unity of the whites and only after that it would be possible to turn to the Natives. With that in mind, and unable to reach agreement on black rights, the Convention decided to retain the existing franchise in each province, but stipulated that only whites could sit in parliament. Further, the imperial factor disappeared when it was agreed that Native policy should be placed in the hands of the 'Governor in Council', who would act on the advice of the local white government.

The Structure of the Union

In terms of structure a federation had its advocates. Some argued that it would reflect the distinctive qualities and experience of the separate colonies; a number of liberals wanted to disperse power to counter authoritarianism, and suspected that blacks would be treated harshly by a strong central government; while the Natal delegates feared Afrikaner dominance of a centralized government. However, Merriman dismissed federalism as complicated and extravagant; Curtis wanted to avoid disputes and ensure uniform treatment of natives; and crucially Smuts, the dominant figure at the conference, argued against a federation. He claimed that it would cause friction between the provinces and between them and the centre; that the system was rigid and would leave the last word with a constitutional court rather than elected representatives; that it would lead to conflicting native policies; and it would hold back economic development. Instead Smuts supported a unitary government with an executive drawn from parliament on the British model. 'What we want,' he said, 'is a supreme national authority to give expression to the national will of South Africa, and the rest is really subordinate' (Thompson 1960: 308). That appeal won the day; a large majority supported a centralized unitary state.

It was agreed, therefore, that there should be a unitary government, with the Governor General representing the crown, and power in the hand of a bicameral parliament (the House of Assembly and the Senate) from which the executive would be drawn. That still left a number of issues in dispute – including the franchise, the division of parliamentary seats among the provinces, and the delimitation of constituencies. Eventually all those issues were resolved by various compromises, which attempted to ensure 'equal rights' between British and Afrikaners. Until late in the day a form of proportional representation was favoured but it was dropped in the final discussions, to the advantage of Afrikaner rural constituencies. Parliament was to consist of a House of Assembly, initially of 121 elected white members (51 from the Cape, 36 the Transvaal and 17 each from Natal and the Free State); and a 40-strong, all-white Senate, each province returning eight indirectly elected members, plus eight members nominated by the government of whom four were to have extensive experience/knowledge of blacks. The constitution contained entrenched clauses – including the two official languages and the Cape franchise – which to amend required a two-thirds majority of both houses.

Before the proposals were sent to Westminster they had to gain the approval of each colonial parliament. That proved easy in the Transvaal and the Free State where it was accepted unanimously, and even in the Cape where there were only two dissenters. The main challenge came in Natal where the matter was put to a referendum of the electorate. The Natal Government, despite its continuing doubts about centralization, campaigned for union because it recognized its economic dependence on the Transvaal, and the danger of isolation for its relatively small number of whites. To gain support it not only underlined the economic advantages but played the imperial card. Union, said the Natal Government, would be 'in the interests of England . . . and in that grand Empire that we are so proud'. Through Union a white nation can be built 'which will be one of the brightest jewels in the British Crown'. There would be no Dutch or British domination, for 'we are all Britishers alike now'. We have all accepted the British flag to form one nation 'to the glory of the British Empire' (Thompson 1960: 349, 50). The appeal worked, and three-quarters of those who voted supported Union.

Delegates from all four colonies signed the draft South Africa Act on 11 May 1909, before forwarding it to London. For most whites it was a moment of high hope. There was rejoicing on both sides of the old divide. General De Wet, a former Boer commander, stated: 'Today it does not matter what race we belong to . . . as long as we are South Africans'. Sir Percy Fitzpatrick, a Randlord and imperialist, spoke of 'a final peace' between Boer and Briton. Smuts saw the opportunity to weld 'the various sections of its white people into a compact nationality inspired by one common pervading national spirit'. Botha called on Transvaalers not to be 'little Transvaalers but great South Africans' (Thompson 1960: 307–10). In contrast, African leaders protested vigorously. In a last ditch effort to influence the Imperial Parliament a South African Native Convention met at Bloemfontein in March 1909. It condemned the draft constitution as 'illiberal and short sighted' (Warwick 1983: 178). The newspaper *Imvo* protested that: 'To alienate the Africans at the very onset of the Union is dangerous and bad indeed' (Thompson 1960: 325–6). In a final effort to challenge the proposals W. P. Schreiner led a predominantly black delegation to London, and it was soon followed by Gandhi and an Indian group. They received tea and sympathy but nothing else. In retrospect it is clear that their protests, however persuasive, could not change the fundamental situation. Blacks had a strong moral case but no political power.

Westminster's Approval

When the draft legislation came before the Imperial Parliament South Africa was no longer a burning public issue. The British were eager to settle the business and put behind them the cost and anxiety of the war and the post-war settlement. The main debate concerned Native policy and the franchise. Schreiner's delegation gained support from the more radical wing of the Liberal Party, led by Sir Charles Dilke. Even the Prime Minister, H. H. Asquith, expressed concern about the position of the Natives, and hoped that the restrictive franchise might be modified. However, he then added that the bill would not be delayed to achieve that. Initially the British Government had favoured a non-racial franchise on the Cape model, but Smuts correctly calculated that London would not endanger a union settlement by holding out for that.

The British objective was to achieve a long-term settlement, which would establish a stable, prosperous and loyal dominion. With that in mind, the view that prevailed was that Native policy was best left to the local whites. The Liberal

Government rested its case on three points. First, that it was bound by the Treaty of Vereeniging; second, that it could not give self-government to the whites with one hand and try to take it away with the other; and third, the hope that a more liberal attitude would permeate north from the Cape. Churchill, hoped that the 'new charity which may come from that feeling of unity may lead them [whites] to unite, not for the purposes of crushing the native by force, but in the nobler and wiser policy of raising the native to his proper position' (Pyrah 1955: 103). It was a false hope. The British government had been faced by what it saw as clashing liberal aims — to accept the implications of self-government for whites, or to seek equal treatment for blacks. Once again racial equality was given a lower priority than white reconciliation. The furthest the British were prepared to go was to suspend incorporation of the three Protectorates of Bechuanaland, Basutoland and Swaziland into the new union, until conditions were met which satisfied London.

It was a thin and low key House of Commons that considered the Union Bill. Dilkes reminded members that an avowed aim of the war had been to implement the principle of equal rights for all civilized men. He warned of the difficulties ahead if that were abandoned. When it came to voting some Liberals opposed their own government, but amendments proposing improvements in African rights were easily voted down, and the legislation went through unamended. The *Daily News* commented that one of the reasons given for fighting had been 'to liberate the native in the Transvaal. One result of it is that we have practically less opportunity to inter-vene than we had under the Convention' (Plaatje 1982: 256). From the Colonial Office Lord Crewe explained that although no change had been made in the fran-chise in South Africa itself, the government had listened to the Africans of the Protectorates, who had begged not to be transferred to the Union at this stage. Therefore Britain would remain as their trustee for the present.

Milner sulked in the wings. He admitted that given the circumstances the overall constitution was not too bad, but he believed that union had come too early, and his frustration boiled over when he wrote privately to a friend about the concept of 'equal rights' between the white language groups. 'The British attitude on the whole question is so astounding, to my mind so absolutely idiotic,' he stated, 'it really is amazing that anybody should think that, after we had conquered S. A. at so immense a cost, it is something wonderful and to be thankful for, and to exude with gratitude and satisfaction over, that British people should be allowed equal rights — just think of it, actually equal rights, with the people whom they have only recently conquered. Of course there is no real equality. All power is with the Boers, and will remain with them' (Lavin 1995: 97). Yet, despite Milner's gloom, the union settlement had considerable long-term advantages for Britain. The cost and strain of controlling South Africa was transferred into local hands; Britain retained and greatly expanded her economic links; the Union remained a member of the Empire and Commonwealth for the next fifty years; cultural ties were strong; and the Union fought alongside Britain in two world wars.

5

The New Union:
White and Black Political Activity

With union, South Africa became a single country. (Whether it was 'a state' was a matter of controversy because of its membership of the British Empire.) The old colonies were transformed into provinces, and the framework of the constitution was to serve for more than seventy years. Yet, although a new country had been born, the issues it faced were rooted in the past. Three themes were to dominate its future: the relationship with Britain; the search for conciliation among the whites; and race relations. The imperial factor persisted through economic links, membership of the Empire and Commonwealth, and the continued loyalty of many to the crown. The new country, while giving white political leaders the opportunity to pursue their aims, did not resolve the white nationalist issue. Although the situation was helpful to those who sought to build a single white nation, based on loyalty to the new country, many whites clung to their old identities. The position was much bleaker for blacks. They had few political opportunities. The failure to extend the Cape franchise to the north, and the establishment of an all-white parliament left them powerless in constitutional terms.

White Political Developments

At the start of the Union's life an interim government was formed while the first country-wide election was being organized. When Louis Botha was asked to lead that interim government he at first flirted with the idea of creating a 'best man' cabinet by selecting people irrespective of party. Eventually, however, he settled for one drawn from the ruling parties of the four provinces, with four members from the Cape and two each from the other provinces. Like all Union cabinets until 1948 it contained both Afrikaans and English speakers.

To fight the election Union-wide parties emerged, mainly by merging the old provincial parties. Three political groupings were formed. The first, which supported Botha and his interim government, was an amalgam of the South African Party of the Cape, Orangia Unie from the OFS, and the Transvaal's Het Volk/Responsibles. It was only after the election, in November 1911, that they formally joined together in the South African Party (SAP). It was a broad, diffuse group from which Botha and Smuts hoped to build a white nation, bound together by race and not split by class. It accepted the Union's position in the Empire; supported European immigration; proposed that native policy should be handled on a non-party basis; criticized the power of capitalism; and opposed further Asian immigration. The second grouping was the Unionist Party, led by Jameson. It combined the Transvaal Progressives, the Cape Unionists, the Free State Constitutional Party and had support in Natal. It was mainly English speaking; was backed by urban capitalists; and favoured strong links with Britain. Third was the Labour Party, which was formed in January 1910, under Colonel F. H. P. Creswell's leadership. It too was mainly English speaking, with an emphasis on white working-class/artisan solidarity.

When the election was held in September 1910 Botha's SAP won easily. It gained the support of most Afrikaners and a substantial number of English speakers. In terms of seats it won 67, to the Unionists' 39, Labour's 4 and there were 11 Independents. Yet, despite the SAP's overall success, Botha personally lost to Sir Percy Fitzpatrick (Unionist) in Pretoria East. Botha was soon found a safe seat and resumed the Premiership, but he attributed his loss, and that of five other Transvaal seats, to English-speaking voters' reaction against 'Hertzogism'.

Tension in the South African Party (SAP)

The first Union Parliament met in November 1910. Ahead lay the task of establishing a new political order by knitting together the old colonies and republics; balancing central and provincial powers; creating a new administration; and shaping relations both within the white community and between blacks and whites. In seeking these ends Botha's and Smuts's top priority was white conciliation. This was partly from expediency, to cement their political power; but it also reflected their commitment of principle to a single white nationalism within the Empire. The SAP cabinet, which was designed for that purpose, was drawn from the four provinces and both main language groups, with Afrikaners in the majority. Never had such unity been achieved, but it was fragile.

Inevitably in such a broad based party as the SAP divisions appeared, and they extended into the cabinet. The most prominent was that between Hertzog on one side and Botha and Smuts on the other. Hertzog came to represent those Afrikaners who were suspicious of Britain and British capitalism, and were intent on emphasizing their own culture. They suspected that Smuts and even Botha had become creatures of the Empire. Hertzog, who saw danger in being too subservient to Britain, and too generous to the Unionists, wrote to Steyn: 'If the old trend of ignoring and sacrificing the people's [Afrikaner] interests in order to gain popularity with the opposition continues, I shall soon have to refuse to be a party member any longer' (Muller 1969: 245). With regard to the state Hertzog accepted the new constitution, but was concerned about Britain's power in relation to the Union, and inside the administration he wanted to ensure that Afrikaners were recruited to senior posts and that Dutch/Afrikaans was used. Hertzog's 'two stream'

(Afrikaner/English) approach emerged naturally for him from past history. 'Each,' he wrote, 'has the right to honour, to protect and to maintain its own. But it is our duty to help develop a more exalted national life wherein we may enter together notwithstanding the difference of language' (Kruger 1969: 67). He never supported an exclusive Afrikaner nationalism confined to Afrikaans speakers. His 'Afrikaners' could come from either stream but their first loyalty must be to South Africa. At the SAP's 1912 congress he seconded a motion to delete 'national' from the party's name, because it was associated with Afrikaners as a separate group. 'Our wish,' he said, 'is to form a party which will embrace all white people in South Africa' (Stultz 1974: 11).

Yet, he could and did sound extreme in English ears. For him 'conciliation' was an empty word, because it tried to embrace those who remained loyal to Britain. In a famous/notorious speech in October 1912 he claimed that 'only one person has the right to be "boss" in South Africa, namely the Afrikaner . . . Afrikaners and not strangers should rule the country'. He excluded those who looked to Britain as their national home; he denounced 'foreign fortune hunters, and adventurers', who were committed to the Empire rather than South Africa; and he accused some English speakers, including members of the Union Party, of being among the fortune hunters. There was uproar. Sir Thomas Smartt, the UP leader, asserted that he did place the interests of the Empire before the narrow interests of South Africa. To that Hertzog retorted: 'Imperialism in my view is only good as it is useful to South Africa. Where it conflicts I oppose it unequivocally' (Moodie 1975: 77). What, asked Alan Paton later, 'was one to make of a man who spoke of national unity at the same time that he spoke of separate language, religion and customs. And a man who . . . reserved all his fire and warmth and passion for the Afrikaner cause?' (Paton 1964: 51). Hertzog, therefore, intentionally, or unintentionally, came to symbolize those Afrikaners (some of them republicans) who still carried the scars of war, who wanted to redefine the relationship with Britain, to protect Afrikaner culture and language, to ensure that power was in Afrikaner hands, and who accused Botha and Smuts of becoming Empire men.

Hertzog ran into two groups of opponents. The first were English–speaking Unionists, who regarded him as a fanatic. For them there was no clash of loyalty between the Empire and the Union, because the interests of one nurtured and fostered the interests of the other. Loyalty to the Empire was loyalty to South Africa; whereas they saw Hertzog's views as implying separate paths, based on different loyalties and interests, and the decision of which path to follow was to be left to self-defined 'Afrikaners'. The UP also opposed Hertzog's education policy, and were delighted when a government committee found against compulsory bilingualism. Hertzog's other opponents were in the SAP itself. The party's English speakers were so resentful of his 1912 speeches that Sir George Leuchars of Natal resigned from the cabinet. Botha and Smuts also attacked Hertzog. Their appeal was to a common white nationalism built on loyalty to the new state; Hertzog's was to past culture, language and history. 'For Botha,' wrote D. W. Kruger, 'the republics had lost the war forever and the Afrikaners had to find a new future completely merged in a new nationhood. For Hertzog the past was not dead in that sense, and he was resolved that Afrikanerdom should regain the substance of what it had lost while surrendering the shadow' (Kruger 1969: 63). Botha declared that 'under our free constitution within the Empire, the South African nation can fully develop its local patriotism and national instincts'. To which Hertzog replied: 'I am a Minister of South Africa and not of the Empire, and as a Minister I am called to attend to the interests of South Africa and not those of the Empire' (Pirow: 60).

The Formation of the National Party

Differences within the government became so acute that Botha asked Hertzog to resign. He refused. Botha therefore resigned himself, and was immediately re-appointed by the Governor General. When he formed a new cabinet he excluded both Hertzog and Leuchars (the most imperialistic minded minister). Botha appeared to have scored a knock out blow when only five members of the House of Assembly supported Hertzog. However, that was misleading. Outside Parliament Hertzog had considerable support. At the SAP's Free State Congress 47 members backed him and only one opposed. At Pretoria in December 1912, a mass meeting was held in honour of Hertzog and the Afrikaans language. Emotions ran high. General De Wet declared that 'he would rather live with his own people on a dunghill than stay in the palaces of the British Empire' (Kruger 1969: 67). Early in 1913 Hertzog, still a SAP member, took his case to the party's Central Congress, and, although he was defeated, he gained 90 votes to Botha's 131. After that there was no way back. Hertzog led his followers out of the SAP, and in January 1914 formed the National Party (NP).

The formation of the NP was a defining point in white politics. From the start it was an Afrikaner party. Its constitution said that it represented the national aspirations of 'the South African people', and although it claimed to favour one nation formed by Afrikaner and English peoples together, its orientation was always towards Afrikaners. It was committed to development on Christian National lines, and said that white unity 'need not be more than a social and spiritual unity, with full preservation of our respective national riches, consisting of language, history, religion and morals'. The constitution placed the interests of South Africa above all others and called for autonomy. Good relations with Britain were dependent on the avoidance of action that would inhibit the freedom of the Union (Pirow n.d.: 64). However, the differences between the SAP and the NP were not confined to nationalist fervour. Economic and provincial interests also came into play – for 'confronted with the economic domination of English speakers, the Afrikaner objective came to be the capture of the state through ethnic mobilisation' (Marks and Trapido 1987: 3). The NP appealed to smaller white farmers, and the language issue had economic implications in that bilingualism benefited Afrikaners, as few English spoke Afrikaans. There were also different attitudes to the mining industry, where Hertzog's South Africa first policy in relation to foreign capital implied 'a greater share of the mining surplus [being] appropriated for national interests, particularly farming' (Lipton 1985: 259). In provincial terms the NP initially had greater strength in the Cape and the OFS, than the Transvaal. Economic interests played a part in this. The Cape NP led by Dr D. F. Malan, brought together the interests of wine and fruit farmers of the Western Cape, the wool farmers of the Karoo, and Afrikaner business interests. In the OFS the party looked to support from the maize farmers, whereas initially in the Transvaal the NP had to rely on support from petty bourgeoisie and poor whites. Dan O'Meara concluded that these economic and provincial differences for the NP 'were expressed through different ideological emphases, political styles and priorities' (O'Meara 1983: 32).

The issues at stake between the NP and SAP were, therefore, not concerned with relations between black and white. Both were committed to white supremacy, but divided by a combination of economic interests and nationalist aspirations – whether to build a white single stream nation or retain separate streams, and, directly linked to that, was the question of the Union's relation with Britain. Previously the great bulk of Afrikaners had supported the SAP alliance. Now they split along political battle lines, which were to shape white perceptions of nation and state for decades to come. In broad terms the division was between those who committed themselves to conciliation between the white groups and those who supported an exclusive Afrikaner nationalism. This was partly masked, even confused, by Hertzog's personal position. He never lost faith in his two-stream approach to nationalism, but the NP attracted support from those who favoured a separate, exclusive and dominant Afrikaner nation. Among this latter group was Dr D. F. Malan, the leading NP figure in the Cape.

The NP's formation coincided with and in part stimulated a vigorous language movement. Afrikaans was promoted in churches, schools, and homes (where Afrikaner women played a prominent role) to become a symbol of Afrikaner national identity. The determination to avoid subordination to English was given militant expression by Steyn. 'The language,' he said, 'of the conqueror in the mouth of the conquered is the language of slaves' (Kruger 1969: 57). Malan was less militant but equally clear about the importance of language. 'Raise the Afrikaans language to a written language,' he had said in 1908, 'let it become the vehicle of our culture, our history, our national identity and you will also raise the people who speak it' (Adam and Giliomee 1979: 203).

NP suspicion of the imperial link led it to draw a distinction between 'autonomy' and 'independence', claiming that the Union had the former but not the latter. Although Hertzog personally was sincere in wanting to embrace both white streams, his speeches were characterized by passion not clarity, and took colour from the audiences he addressed. As the audiences were usually Afrikaners, most of his supporters, as well as his opponents, came to believe that by 'nation' he meant 'volk', that by 'independence' he meant 'republican independence'. Many NP followers did indeed hold such beliefs, convinced that Afrikaners were a people chosen by God. In 1911 Malan declared: 'We are Afrikaners and so ought we always to be, because any nationality, formed by God through history and the environment, has itself a right to existence . . . My feeling of nationalism thus rests finally upon a religious foundation' (Moodie 1975: 73). Based upon bitter memory and present discontent the NP quickly recruited substantial support. Initially it came from the Free State, but the NP's message soon spread among Afrikaners elsewhere. It had a wider appeal than that of nationalism and culture. It drew support from Afrikaners who suffered from a sense of group deprivation in relation to English speakers, and nursed economic and social fears as blacks moved into urban areas and competed for jobs. Newly urbanized Afrikaners, wrote Newell Stultz, 'felt embattled by English speaking whites with their powerful urban culture, as well as by non-whites, with whom they were now often in economic competition' (Stultz 1974: 17). As support for the NP grew so Botha and his SAP government had to place more reliance on English-speaking supporters, thereby reinforcing the prejudices of both sides, and deepening the gap between the parties and language groups. In NP eyes, Botha and Smuts had been seduced by the English and their Empire, and they were accused of failing to appreciate the depth of Afrikaner feeling. The NP criticized the Union's financial contribution to the British navy, the gift of the Cullinan diamond to the monarch, the encouragement of British immigration, Botha's unveiling of Rhodes's statute, his fraternizing with the Unionists and his indifference to the Afrikaans language movement.

The government (mainly in the person of Smuts who acted while others vacillated) was also drawn into problems with white labour. In 1913 the setting was the Witwatersrand, where an attempt by mine owners to introduce new working practices led to a major strike by the unionized white miners, which the owners tried to break by employing non-unionized labour. The strike reached a climax early in July, when the strikers burnt buildings and destroyed property. The government, ill prepared for such a situation, retaliated by calling out the police and imperial troops (in the absence of a Union Defence Force). In the ensuing clashes 25 people were killed. Botha and Smuts subsequently met the union leaders, several of whom had been born in Britain, and to regain order agreed that all the strikers would be reinstated and an enquiry set up. For the moment white labour had gained a victory, but for the longer term the government had learnt a lesson. When in January 1914 a railwaymen's strike threatened to lead to a general strike Martial Law was proclaimed, and units of a newly formed Citizen Force were summoned to support the police. Many strikers were arrested, and, by Smuts's orders, nine of the foreign born strike leaders were deported without trial. He covered himself legally by persuading parliament later to pass an indemnity act, but he was not forgotten or forgiven by white labour.

Black Political Activity: the Formation of the Native National Congress (NNC)

The Union settlement changed the face of black as well as white politics. What can be recognized as 'African nationalism' began as a reaction to the Union's racially inspired constitution, which offered little or nothing to blacks. The Native National Congress passed a resolution stating that the constitution gave Africans no protection or privilege, 'no legal safeguard of their interests and vested rights as subjects of the British Empire . . . no recognised means whereby they can effectively make their legitimate objections felt by the Union Parliament' (Karis and Carter 1972: 87). The same sentiments were expressed by J. T. Gumede, to a committee of white MPs. 'It is,' said Gumede, 'all so confused to us. The white man makes the law, and the Native is not consulted. The white man is represented in parliament and his parliament can restrict him, but parliament is also restricting me without consulting me, and taking away my freedom and liberty – restricting me against my will' (Karis and Carter 1972: 96). African leaders who previously had sought a colour blind franchise and favoured non-racial parties were now obliged to form their own racial organization because, excluded by the constitution, they had no other means of forwarding their interests. A few tried to hold out, to retain the idealized Cape tradition, such as Tengo Jabavu, who refused to join the Native National Congress because it was not open to all races. But he was whistling in the wind.

African political aims moved slowly but steadily from seeking rights as British citizens within an imperial order to struggling to promote their interests in a white dominated state. The failure to achieve a non-racial franchise across the Union was a major blow. Even the loyal Plaatje came to realize they could no longer rest their hopes on the imperial/Cape ideal. 'While we sing the funeral dirge of Cape ideals,' he said, 'the republicans sing songs of gladness' (Plaatje 1982: 189). On another occasion he wrote: 'Now the natives know that annexation to the Union will mean the elimination of the Imperial factor, and that Cape Town, like Pretoria, has ceased to represent British ideas of fair play and justice' (Plaatje 1982: 245). The harsh reality of the constitutional position for blacks was soon made clear. In 1913 when Lord Harcourt (British Colonial Secretary) was asked to intervene against the Union's Land Act because it discriminated against blacks, he replied: 'If General Botha breaks his word I have no power to enforce it. I cannot bind his successors. If the Government of South Africa is not to be trusted in this matter they are to be trusted in nothing' (Plaatje 1982: 233).

The African response to the new situation was given concrete shape in January 1912 when African leaders (including representatives from the three Protectorates) met at Bloemfontein. They came in response to an appeal from Pixley Seme, who, while studying at Columbia University in the US, had been influenced by such moderate black American leaders as Booker T. Washington, with his stress on education, and Dr W. E. B. DuBois who underlined the need for strong organization. While still in the US, Seme had spoken of the 'Regeneration of Africa', declaring that 'I am an African and I set my pride in my race'. He claimed that 'the African people, although not a strictly homogeneous race, possess a common fundamental sentiment', and must take their future into their own hands (Meli 1988: 25). It was in this spirit of nascent African nationalism that he called for the establishment of a 'Native Union' in South Africa, to provide a representative and responsible outlet for African opinion, and to help counter exploitation. Africans, Seme wrote, must learn to co-operate and overcome old tribal feuds. 'We are,' he said, 'one people' (Karis and Carter 1972: 72).

In his opening address to the 1912 conference Seme repeated his call for unity. 'We have discovered,' he said, 'that in the land of our birth Africans are treated as hewers of wood and drawers of water.' The whites, he continued, had formed a Union without consulting Africans. The conference had been called in response to that: 'for the purpose of creating national unity and defending our rights and privileges'. Seme said he recognized the difficulty of gaining unity because this was the first time that so many 'different tongues and tribes ever attempted to cooperate under one umbrella in one great house' (Liebenberg et al. 1994: 5–7). Seme gained broad support, including that of the traditional rulers. Queen Regent Labolsibeni of Swaziland gave £3,000 to help launch the newspaper *Abantu Batho*. Philip Modise, the representative of the Basuto king, said that while in the past Africans 'were identified with different tribal names and dialects, just as the different trees in the woods were known by different names . . . they were now trees of one and the same forest.'

The delegates responded to Seme's call by forming the South African Native National Congress (NNC) – later to be renamed the African National Congress (ANC) – and electing Rev John Dube, a headmaster from Natal, as its first President. Dube, like Seme, had been educated in the US (as well as South Africa), where he had been influenced by the moderate black leader Booker T. Washington, who emphasized self-help and commercial activity. In his letter accepting the presidency Dube wrote that he would be guided by a 'hopeful reliance in the sense of common justice and love of freedom so innate in the British character' (Hill and Pirio 1987: 228). In his first address he called on members to move 'Upwards! Into the higher places of civilization and Christianity – not backwards into the slump of darkness, nor backwards into the abyss of the antiquated tribal system. Our salvation is not there, but in preparing ourselves for an honoured place amongst the nations' (Marks 1986: 52). Yet, the situation was never clear cut. The Congress members could not escape the tensions and ambiguities of being people of two cultures, influenced by traditional forms and loyalties as well as the new European order. Looking back in 1930 Dube wrote: 'The foundation of the African National Congress was laid at the great Conference where all the principal chiefs and nearly all the chiefs in the land were represented' (Walshe 1987: 33).

As Dube suggested, the Congress was a band of respectable, prudent men, drawn from a cross section of the African elite: traditional chiefs, clergymen, writers, school teachers and clerks. Chiefs were given their own chamber. The executive, led by Dube, was drawn mainly from the Cape, and from educated men, six of whom had been to college in Britain and two in the US. According to Meli: 'There is a strong element of elitism inherent in the utterances of the early African radicals.' They wanted equal rights for civilized men, although they were not always in agreement on what constituted civilized (Meli 1988: 24). Yet, from the beginning Dube and his fellow NNC members committed themselves to a racially inclusive, liberal nationalism, in contrast to the exclusive nationalism of most whites. They resolved to seek their aims by peaceful means and to encourage mutual understanding and unity across tribe and race. Their moderation was illustrated in July 1913 when Congress passed resolutions of condolences to the government on the death of J. W. Sauer (Minister Native Affairs); dissociated itself from the current industrial struggle on the Witwatersrand; and expressed a preference to achieve its ends 'through constitutional rather than violent means' (Plaatje 1982: 203). It was further illustrated by co-operation with liberal whites at home and continued attempts to gain redress by appeals to Britain. Despite all the evidence, or perhaps because few other options were available, the NNC clung to the hope that 'if South Africa were really British, then any suffering taking place in that country must be of concern to His Majesty the King and the British public' (Plaatje

1982: 203). Congress meetings passed resolutions of loyalty to the crown, and sang the national anthem.

Yet, for all its moderation, the formation of the NNC was a major step in African political development. The novelty as well as the moderation was evident in Dube's letter accepting the Presidency. He wrote of a renaissance and called for an awakening of African political life, based on prudence, restraint and respect for the rulers God had placed over them. His stated policy was 'reliance on the sense of common justice and love of freedom so innate in the British character' (Lodge 1983: 3). From the beginning Congress saw full citizen rights for Africans as an ideal to be achieved within a united non-racial state. However, developments had left it with no choice but to target issues which were of concern mainly to Africans in a white-dominated state: land, labour, wages, taxation, the franchise, Native marriages, Native beer, schools and churches. When the NNC finally agreed a constitution in 1919 its focus was on African concerns. It numbered among its aims to act as a representative of Native opinion; to inform Parliament and government on Native aspirations; to educate Africans on their rights, duties and obligations; to encourage mutual understanding among tribes and unite their political efforts; to eliminate tribal feuds; to propose laws beneficial to Africans; to oppose the colour bar; to seek constitutional redress of grievances; and to do 'everything directly or indirectly to maintain and uplift the standards of the race morally and spiritually, mentally and materially; socially and politically' (Karis and Carter 1972: 78).

With no direct power and committed to constitutional action the NNC's agenda was shaped by reaction to the government policies and proposals. That presented a constant dilemma. How should it respond to government offers which fell short of its hopes? Should it, for example, participate in the separate Native Councils? Some members stated that the NNC must stick firmly to principles and refuse to compromise, while others argued pragmatically that half a loaf was better than none. The pragmatists said that the councils would offer a channel to promote Congress's views. That was rejected by *Abantu Batho*, which argued that all representation should be in non-racial bodies, with 'equal rights for all civilized men'. It claimed that Africans should not only be able to vote, but to hold any office, whether it be in politics, the armed forces or the civil service (Walshe 1987: 55).

The 1913 Land Act and Segregation

The first major challenge for the NNC came with the passage of the Land Act in 1913. In introducing the legislation the government was attempting to secure white political support, and counter Hertzog's appeal to Afrikaners. However, the Act's main impact fell on Africans. It was based on the principle of territorial segregation by which specific areas were designated for African settlement – in reality the old Native Reserves – while elsewhere most of their rights were removed. The intention was to forbid the purchase or leasing of land by Africans outside the reserves. The long term implication of this was to remove the means by which many Africans had stayed outside the farm and mines labour system. But for a time the legislation was unevenly applied, and, in the case of the Cape it was declared illegal in 1917 because it infringed the franchise arrangements.

Initially only 7 per cent of the Union's total land area was allocated to Africans although promises were held out of more to come. The reserves varied in size from large blocks of land, like the Transkei, to small, scattered fragments, such as those in northern Natal. In the case of the Transkei the situation had been shaped by the Glen Gray Act of 1894, which Rhodes had introduced as Prime Minister of the Cape. The act had included a tax regime, which in part was aimed at producing migrant labour; a land tenure system to help create a class of food producing small holders; and a new form of local government through a council system. The implementation of the act was slow and uneven and had met some resistance, but a reserve like the Transkei had 'come to resemble a tropical colony of African peasants rather than – as in most parts of South Africa – a settler domination'. Within such areas the government relied upon the support of African allies, usually in the form of traditional rulers – chiefs and headmen (Beinart and Bundy 1987: 7/12).

The 1913 Act was not limited to land holding, it also changed arrangements for the payment of rents and labour tenancy, both of which gave white landowners greater leverage over their black tenants. As a result white agriculture expanded at the expense of peasant African farmers; and, at the same time the restrictions put

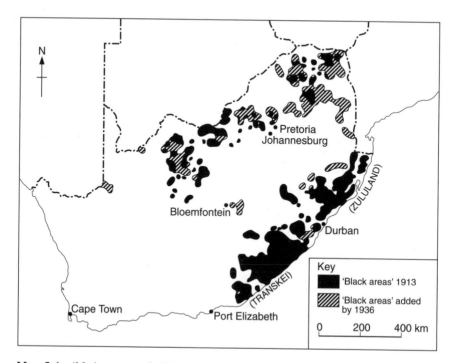

Map 5.1   'Native reserves', 1913 and 1936 (adapted from D. Denoon and B. Nieko, *Southern Africa since 1800*, second edition [London: Longman, 1984, 168])

on Africans helped to ensure a supply of cheap labour for white farms, mines and the urban areas. Outside the reserves rural Africans faced great hardship and uncertainty. Families which had lived for generations in what became 'white areas' were forced to move or pay in terms of rent or labour. Dube spoke of 'cruel and undeserved afflictions wrought by the harsh enactment on numberless aged, poor, and tender children of this, my and their own native land' (Marks 1986: 64).

Yet, while the suffering was clear enough, the concept of 'segregation' on which the Act was founded, and which became the chief vehicle of government policy towards Africans, was open to diverse interpretation, both by whites and blacks. As Nigel Worden has pointed out segregation was distinct from white supremacy in that its underlying principle was enforced separation not just subordination (Worden 1995: 72). However, for a time segregation was seen as a middle way between 'assimilation' (to which the Cape system pointed) and 'repression' (as reflected in the old Boer republic approach). Yet, the middle way meant different things to different people and its emphasis changed over time. The ambiguity rested on the meaning of the term 'segregation', the policy's long-term implications, and the gap between theory and practice. The uncertainty was compounded by the contrast between those who believed that segregation was a permanent solution to race relations, and those who saw it as a temporary expedient to allow different societies to develop at their own pace. From the government's viewpoint the ambiguity (whether intentional or not) had the advantage of providing an umbrella ideology which appealed to diverse interests and beliefs. Among whites the beliefs included – that segregation was a means of providing a cheap supply of labour; of avoiding social contact with blacks and overcoming the danger of being swamped by them; of ensuring that Africans did not degenerate in an urban setting; of countering the threat of miscegenation; of offering different people the opportunity to develop in their own way; and of preserving traditional African structures to counter the danger of class formation. As segregation became more established it replaced for some white liberals the old belief in assimilation with that of differentiation based on 'culture'.

The idea of territorial separation was not new. It had been advocated by the Native Affairs Commission in 1905. Subsequently scholars have debated the aims and implications of the policy. Howard Wolpe, for example, has stated that the core objective was to ensure cheap labour for the capitalist exploitation of the mines. The government, argued Wolpe, imposed a system of migrant labour and native reserves to free the mine owners from paying both wages on which a whole family could live, and from paying for social services. To ensure the operation of the migrant system the reserves had to be entrenched as they were in 1913 (Wolpe 1972: 60). However, William Beinart has suggested that Wolpe's views, while having substance, are too narrowly based. Beinart, who gave attention to the part played by Africans, wrote that the policy was not simply imposed from above by the state, but was influenced by the views of rural Africans. Migrancy, argued Beinart, had attractions for some Africans – including the migrants who wanted to retain a stake in the rural community, and for chiefs and headmen who wanted the young to return with their wages and to recognize their authority. 'Many African communities,' wrote Beinart, 'wanted to retain their hold over men who went out to work and tried to devise methods of ensuring their return. As long as land was available in communal land tenure systems this also remained an attractive option for the migrant men themselves. Migrancy could therefore be seen to have arisen as much out of the dynamics of African societies as the demands of the mines.' Such attempts by Africans to defend the rural areas, said Beinart, 'were not segregationist in the sense the whites understood the term. But these could be compatible with elements of segregation in certain respects', as a means of expressing identity, of controlling residual lands, and of expressing support for chiefs. 'The system,' he wrote, 'was at least initially, a compromise between capital and peasantry – it reflected the inability of the state to transform African society' (Beinart and Dubow 1995: 8–10 and 180).

With such diversity of views it is not surprising that the NNC equivocated when faced with the principle of segregation, as implicit in the Land Act of 1913. Some members favoured it because it protected what they had; and others assumed that there could be parallel developments which preserved African land rights in the reserves, while at the same time gaining political rights through the extension of the Cape system across the whole country. Some were not, there-fore, opposed to segregation in principle provided it offered both secure land and increased political rights. However, other NNC members were implacably opposed from the beginning. The Transvaal section, for example, flatly rejected the Act's segregationist assumptions, and pledged to counter 'such narrow and sectional race policy – conceived in evil and nourished on class and race hatred'. The overall result was that Congress spoke with different voices. Dube himself can be accused of that. Initially he completely opposed the Act, speaking of the 'selfishness and greed and godless persecution' (Walshe 1987: 46). Yet later he wrote to Botha saying: 'We make no protest against the principle of segregation so long as it can be fairly and practically carried out.' But, he added, the new Act was not fair to Africans and seemed designed to drive them into the labour market (Karis and Carter 1972: 85). Dube's position was not opposition based on prin-ciple but on the realization that the policy was impractical. That was crystallized at the NNC's 1914 conference. At that conference the government's Secretary for Native Affairs, Edward Dower, urged the NNC to abandon its proposal to send a delegation to Britain. Instead he advised it to concentrate on the positive aspects of government policy – including additions to the reserves, the extension of in-dividual tenure and the introduction of more Native Councils. In reply Dube repeated that he did not oppose the principle of land segregation, but pointed out that the areas allocated to Africans were far too small and it would require a major land redistribution in favour of Africans if it were to be done fairly. He did not believe that was possible while Africans had such inadequate political represen-tation. The way forward was therefore along the political road to full African participation in government.

Despite Dower's advice an NNC delegation, led by Dube, went to Britain to plead its case. As in the past it gained public attention and support from churches and liberal sympathizers. However, the British Government, which had already consulted Botha, was firm in its view that responsibility lay in Pretoria not London. In the event the delegation served only to underline the NNC's moderation (by repeating that it did not oppose the principle of Botha's proposals) and its weakness in the face of government opposition. Most of the delegates returned to South Africa empty handed, but Sol Plaatje, a strong opponent of the Act, remained in Britain conducting a solo campaign against it, and writing *Native Life in South Africa*. Plaatje's message was that the Act had reduced the rights of all Africans and driven many from land they had occupied for generations. He wrote of the arrest of progress, and 'exploitation of the cruelest kind' which would reduce Africans to serfdom. With reference to the British claim to have no power in the matter, Plaatje concluded that without such protection Africans were now 'under task-masters whose national traditions are to enslave the dark races' (Plaatje 1982: 72–6).

Shortly after the return of the delegation the First World War started. The NNC decided to postpone further political agitation, but the land/segregation question would not go away. When the government's Beaumont Commission toured the country to search for additional areas for the Native reserves, and to recommend how the existing fragmented pieces could be consolidated, Africans who gave evidence again revealed a variety of views about the principle of segregation. However, all were united in saying that if the policy was to be implemented substantially more land had to be allocated to Africans. That proved to be an insurmountable political obstacle. Following its investigations the commission reluctantly concluded that it was too late to define large, compact areas for the reserves. It might be possible to achieve small adjustments, but it simply was not practical politics to make major changes because of white opposition. Reviewing the commission's report at its 1916 conference the NNC spoke of disappointment, broken promises and a situation that would leave Africans in a subordinate position for all time. The conference concluded that as the policy was impractical and unjust it must be abandoned.

The government adopted a very different approach in response to the commission's report. In 1917 it introduced the Native Administration Bill, with the intention of setting Native administration apart from the rest of the government machine. The bill proposed to set up a rigid division between Native areas and the rest of the country, to legislate for Natives by proclamation and to establish separate Native courts and councils. Natives would only be permitted to reside outside the reserves in so far as they served white interests. In direct contradiction of the Cape tradition Botha said that the government wanted to avoid the mistaken approach of racial equality. Natives, he said, could gain political rights in their own areas but not elsewhere (Walshe 1987: 57). In the event that bill never became law, because it ran into white opposition over the continuing investigation of African claims, and because it infringed the Cape franchise arrangements. However, it was an indication of the government's thinking, which became more explicit in a lecture given by Smuts in London in May 1917. In that he had a double message: the need for white unity, and importance of the separate treatment of Africans. 'We have felt more and more,' he said, 'that if we are to solve our native question it is useless to try to govern black and white in the same system, to subject them to the same institutions of government and legislation. They are different not only in colour but in minds and in political capacity, and their political institutions should be different.' He explained that Natives would be free to go and work in white areas 'but as far as possible the administration of white and black areas will be separated' (Smuts 1942: 24–6).

In South Africa the continued uncertainty surrounding segregation and the Land Act resulted in the NNC reacting strongly against a government claim that it had accepted the principles behind the policy. It also resulted in a change of Congress leadership in 1917 when Dube was replaced as President by the more aggressive S. M. Makgatho from the Transvaal. The lesson that most, if not all, NNC followers absorbed was that social and economic issues were interlocked with political power and representation in parliament. Without political power their social and economic concerns would not be adequately addressed.

6

The Great War and its Aftermath

In August 1914 war broke out in Europe. The Union entered immediately, 'as a subordinate part of the British Empire, committed by the British declaration of war (Garson 1979). Inside South Africa the Native National Congress threw its weight behind the imperial cause, stopped political agitation and offered to fight for the crown. The offer was viewed with disquiet by some whites. *The East Rand Express* commented: 'The Empire must uphold the principle that a coloured man must not raise a hand against a white man if there is to be any law or order or respect.' On behalf of the government the Secretary of Defence explained that it was 'anxious to avoid the employment of its native citizens in warfare against whites' (Plaatje 1982: 304). The government accepted the offer to serve but not to carry arms. However, an exception was made in the East African campaign, where the Germans effectively used African troops. In response an armed Cape Coloured Corps was formed. The bulk of blacks who were recruited served in the Native Labour Contingent – 17,000 served in East Africa and 25,000 in France.

The Afrikaner Rebellion and South West Africa

The war placed immense strains on whites and especially Afrikaners – reopening wounds which had not had time to heal; forcing stark choices which would have been blurred by time; and facing them with the basic question 'Am I prepared to fight for and even die for the British Empire?' For those whites with the strongest commitments on both sides the response was immediate – most English speakers rallied to the flag, while hard-core Boer republicans saw an opportunity to regain their freedom. However, for many Afrikaners there was no such certainty. The conflicting responses were reflected in disputes over specific issues: whether, for example, military service should be compulsory, and/or whether South Africans should fight outside the Union. Hertzog reluctantly agreed that the Union was formally at war, but urged that action should be limited to defending its own borders. Botha's message to parliament was simple: 'The Empire is at war; consequently South Africa is at war with the common enemy.' He and Smuts accepted the imperial call to arms as 'the way of faith, duty and honour', but they too recognized the political dangers in the situation (Kruger 1969: 83).

Those dangers soon revealed themselves. The division between the government and the militant republicans was so deep that it led to rebellion and virtual civil war. The incident that sparked it off was the British request that the Union invade neighbouring German South West Africa. There seemed to be little danger of a German attack on the Union (although later it transpired that the German Foreign Office had floated the idea of promoting a rebellion among Afrikaners) but the British wanted to secure the coast line to protect the shipping lanes around Africa. When Botha put the British request to the cabinet it split. The opponents argued that the Union had done enough by offering to defend its own borders and place facilities at the disposal of the imperial forces. However, in the closest of votes – five to four, with Botha and Smuts in favour – it was decided to accede to the British request. Botha then summoned parliament to approve the decision. He told the MPs that it was both a duty and in their interests to mount the invasion. He mentioned the possibility that if South Africa refused Australian and Indian troops might be called

Louis Botha and J. C. Smuts in imperial uniforms during World War I (courtesy of *The Star*)

to undertake the task, thereby removing South Africa's opportunity to occupy the territory and by implication to absorb it into the Union. Despite some division inside the SAP and strong opposition from the NP, Botha, with UP and Labour support, gained a large parliamentary majority. Yet the dispute was far from settled. General C. F. Beyers, the Commandant General, refused to lead an expedition against South West Africa, and resigned his post. Other prominent Afrikaner military figures joined the chorus of disapproval: including past heroes, such as Generals Koos de la Rey and Christian de Wet; and they were joined by serving officers such as Lieutenant Colonel Manie Maritz (Commander of the district bordering South West Africa) and Major J. C. G. Kemp (who commanded the Potchefstroom District). Centres of resistance to the government emerged in the Free State, the North Western Cape and the Western Transvaal. In the OFS, although Hertzog and Steyn personally disapproved of the use of violence they were not prepared to condemn the rebellion outright. When Botha asked Steyn to repudiate Maritz, Steyn refused unless he was allowed to express his general disapproval of the South West Africa campaign. Meanwhile the rebels were active. In October 1914 Maritz contacted the Germans and laid plans to attack Cape Province, while de Wet and Beyers spread the rebellion internally.

Eventually about 12,000 rallied to the rebel cause (7,000 in the Free State; 3,000 Transvaal, and 1,300 the Cape). It was a substantial force, but the revolt was ill prepared and conducted. It lacked unity, centralized control and agreed objectives. Beyers, for example, simply wanted to make an 'armed protest'; Maritz to invade the Cape; de Wet to occupy Pretoria and declare a Republic. Most of all the rebels faced a determined government. When persuasion failed Botha proclaimed martial law, and pressed ahead with speed and determination. He personally took command of the Union forces, and deliberately used only Afrikaner troops to avoid a further division of Boer and Briton. As he was keen to settle the rebellion internally he kept in reserve a British offer to divert Australian and New Zealand forces to support him. Botha's strategy proved to be remarkably successful, and by February 1915 the rebellion had been crushed with comparatively light casualties: 190 rebels and 132 government troops were killed. On the whole the rebels were treated leniently, but Jopie Fourie, a serving army officer, became a martyr to the cause when he was shot after being court marshalled. Even in defeat the rebels were seen as heroes by many Afrikaners. In August 1915 6,000 women marched on the Union buildings in Pretoria to plead for the release of the rebel leaders, and sympathizers formed a mutual aid society to pay off their fines. In parliament Hertzog called for the immediate release of the prisoners and for a full amnesty for all who had taken part in the rising.

With the rebellion over Botha organized the invasion of South West Africa. Again he took personal command, and again he proved to be an outstanding strategist. By July 1915 he had achieved complete success, and lost only 113 men in gaining a victory which had long-term consequences for the Union. By driving the Germans from southern Africa he not only served the Empire, but gave South Africa control of a large, sparsely populated territory. In 1919 it became a League of Nations mandate under Union administration. Yet, Botha knew that his military successes were bought at a heavy political price. The rebellion and the South West Africa campaign polarized views, increased white divisions and hardened Afrikaner nationalism. The Nationalists branded Botha and Smuts as traitors and British henchmen, and their accusations intensified when Smuts took command of the imperial forces in East Africa, and was fêted in Britain, where he served in the war cabinet. Lord Buxton, the Governor General, predicted it would 'take years to bring the racial position [between Boer and Briton] back to that which existed or was thought to exist, say two years ago' (Garson 1979).

The 1915 Election

In October 1915 Botha called a general election. In terms of seats the SAP won 54; the UP 40; the NP 26; Labour 4; and Independents 6. This left the government in power, but underlined white divisions. In its election campaign the SAP had emphasized its commitment to the war effort, and to a united South Africa based on a single white nationalism. Although it failed to gain an overall majority of seats, its position was secure because it could rely on wholehearted Unionist support in prosecuting the war. The UP, with its English-speaking base and commitment to the Empire, gained seats through an electoral arrangement with the SAP, which avoided split votes, and further it benefited at the expense of Labour as patriotism overrode class divisions among British workers. Yet the UP was left in a frustrating position. Formally it was in opposition, but, because it was committed to the war, and to keeping the SAP in power, it acted more as a pressure group than a separate party. Botha resolutely refused to form a coalition with the UP, realizing that to do so it would dash his ambition to reunite Afrikaners by wooing them back from the NP. Even so, the jingoists in the UP so offended even moderate Afrikaners that Botha suffered from guilt by association.

Despite Botha's hopes the main message to emerge from the election was the scale and depth of the Afrikaner divide. This was masked by the relatively small number of seats won by the NP, but was clearer if measured in votes. The NP polled 78,000 against the SAP's 94,000. As the NP voters were drawn almost exclusively from Afrikaners, whereas the SAP had English-speaking as well as Afrikaner support, the figures signified a substantial shift of allegiance. Probably as many Afrikaners voted for the NP as for the SAP. The NP won all but one of the OFS seats, and it strengthened its position in the Cape, where Malan left the pulpit to lead the provincial party, and launch the newspaper *Die Burger*. S. B. Spies concluded that the NP 'probably had greater cohesion than any of the other parties in the war years. It was par excellence the party for the Afrikaners. Afrikaners who sympathised with the rebellion or republican independence or simply greater rights for Afrikaners . . . saw the National Party as the constitutional vehicle to achieve their aims' (Liebenberg and Spies 1993: 128). NP voices supporting republicanism became louder. In 1917 Tielman Roos, the NP's Transvaal leader, seized on US President Woodrow Wilson's appeal for national self-determination by using it as the basis for a claim for republican independence in South Africa. Despite Hertzog's ambivalence on the issue the NP adopted republicanism in its programme.

The Versailles Conference and Black Frustration

South Africa's contribution to the allied war effort enhanced its international position and its autonomy within the Empire. A government delegation, led by Botha and Smuts, enjoyed separate status at the 1919 Versailles Peace Conference. Like the representatives of Australia, Canada and New Zealand they signed the peace treaty not as part of the Empire but in their own right, and Smuts personally was prominent in the formation of the League of Nations. It was a sign of the increasing autonomy of the Dominions. Two other South African delegations arrived at Versailles. They came from opposite ends of the political spectrum – the Native National Congress and the NP. The NP delegation, led by Hertzog, failed to gain a hearing at the conference or an interview with Woodrow Wilson. They did, however, see Lloyd George, the British Prime Minister, who gave them short shrift. When Hertzog pleaded for the return of republican status to the old Boer republics, leaving the Cape and Natal to decide for themselves, Lloyd George dismissed the proposal, pointing out that the delegation represented only one party and not even the majority of white South Africans. The British Government, he said, would not reject a constitution which had been agreed by representatives of all the whites, and for good measure he added that the blacks were overwhelmingly opposed to a republic.

The NNC delegation was optimistic. Surely, they reasoned, their wartime loyalty and commitment to the Empire would bring its rewards. They recalled that Sir Douglas Haig, the British Commander, and King George V himself had congratulated the Native Contingent in France; and there had been encouraging statements from British politicians. Sir Richard Winfrey, Secretary for Agriculture, had written to Plaatje in 1917 saying that 'at the close of the War we shall do all in our power to help you regain that justice and freedom to which as loyal British subjects your people are entitled' (Walshe 1987: 62). Furthermore blacks also hoped to benefit from the liberal principles promoted by Woodrow Wilson. Addressing the NNC conference S. M. Makgatho, the new President, noted that Botha and Smuts had set off for Versailles saying that they would represent the views 'of the two great races' – Afrikaner and British. 'So where,' he asked 'do we come in?' What did Botha and Smuts know 'about the abomination of the Pass Laws or the atrocities of the Land Act, enacted by them?' (Karis and Carter 1972: 109). Makgotho contrasted that with Wilson, who had sought black US opinion and had taken a black adviser with him to Versailles.

It was therefore in anticipation of reward that the Congress delegation set out both for London and Versailles – the first time the NNC had appealed directly to an international body outside Britain. The delegation's ambitions were nothing less than to reverse the Union's constitutional and political structures. An open letter was sent to the King requesting justice and an end to discrimination based on colour. It asked him to change the constitution, to give natives an effective voice in the Union's affairs by enfranchising 'the natives throughout the Union so that they could protect their interests and check reactionary laws' (Karis and Carter 1972: 141). Even in their representations at Versailles they still placed reliance on the

British imperial ideal. 'We have come,' they said, 'not to ask for independence, but for an admission into British citizenship as British subjects so that we may also enjoy the free institutions which are the foundations and pillars of this magnificent Commonwealth' (Walshe 1987: 64).

However, within South Africa the Union government was drawing different lessons from the wartime experience of Africans. Far from contemplating rewards for blacks it saw dangers. Smuts admitted to his 1917 London audience that the military value of the Natives had been an 'eye opener', especially the fighting skills shown by those Africans who had been armed by colonial governments. Smuts was worried that if allowed to develop it could 'become a menace not only to Africa, but perhaps to Europe itself . . . It can well be foreseen that [Native] armies may yet be trained . . . [which] might prove a danger to civilisation itself' (Smuts 1942: 28). He therefore urged that one outcome of the war should be agreement by the imperial powers to follow the Union's example by preventing the military training of Africans. On the broader international front Botha and Smuts dismissed the NNC's Versailles claims. As leaders of the Union's constitutional government they claimed to speak by right for all South Africans. The NNC's answer to that was along traditional imperial lines. 'We have come not to ask for independence,' said the delegates, 'but for an admission into British citizenship . . . that we may enjoy the free institutions which are the foundation and pillars of this magnificent Commonwealth' (Walshe 1987: 64). Yet it was the government's voice and not that of the NNC that was heard by the ministers and officials in London and Paris. In Britain the NNC delegation again gained sympathy and public attention but nothing else. At Versailles it was ignored. It returned home with nothing to report but frustration.

The failure of the delegation was not a surprise. The war had not changed the British Government's view of the Union's constitutional position; indeed the white government's support for the war effort inclined London to be more generous than ever towards Pretoria: to believe that in terms of Britain's overall interests the 'hands off' approach had paid dividends. Equally the NNC delegation had no real chance of an effective hearing in the massive, complex and confused peace conference. In retrospect all that became clear, but in the euphoria of the moment, in the expectation of reward for its loyalty, the NNC had failed to appreciate that. When the full realization came it was a stunning blow. They had achieved nothing from their wartime loyalty, their appeals to the King and to London, and they had been ignored internationally. The NNC's peaceful, constitutional approach had led nowhere. What could be done? Congress had no clear answer. The men who led it had not changed overnight. They were still predominantly moderates, most of whom had no stomach for mass action or militant methods. But the hope of British intervention had gone. 'That cow,' said Professor D. D. T. Jabavu, 'has gone dry' (Karis and Carter 1972: 120).

For Africans the 1919 delegation was a watershed. It had been the first attempt to internationalize their claims outside the imperial setting; and it failed. The year 1919 was also a watershed in that it was Congress's last major attempt to gain direct British intervention in the Union's affairs. From time to time in the future approaches would be made to London, but they were more gestures than substance. When the 1919 delegation failed the moderate men who led the NNC had largely run out of effective options. For a time Congress (renamed the African National Congress [ANC] in 1923) lost its vigour and direction. It continued to see its tasks as those of furthering African views and interests – by advocating constitutional change to achieve a multi-racial state, by gaining educational and social facilities for Africans, and by opposing discrimination, such as the Land Act and the pass laws. However, not only had Congress failed to achieve its aims, it now faced changing economic and social conditions. A recession was driving blacks and whites into the urban areas, where, as they competed for jobs, the whites demanded racial privilege. The native reserves were patently unable to sustain a growing population. During the 1920s and 1930s it became clear that the balance between migrant labour and the reserves had changed. While initially the reserves had acted as a security and supplement for the migrant workers, now the wages of the migrants became the means of sustaining those who remained in the increasingly impoverished reserves. In response a more militant strain emerged in Congress leading to internal divisions. Some members, especially in the Transvaal, took an increasingly forceful line in support of black urban workers. After a stormy meeting in 1919 Plaatje complained about the aggressive demeanour of the Transvaal representatives, who initiated a campaign against carrying passes, in which more than 2,000 Africans handed in or threw away their passes, and more than 700 were arrested. They also gave support to strike action by municipal workers, and in 1920 to a major strike by black miners on the Rand.

Most Congress leaders, especially in the Cape where they were less conscious of industrial tensions, continued to favour petitions and delegations rather than strikes and boycotts, and they continued to seek 'differentiation of treatment . . . between those who were educated and civilised and those who had not yet reached that stage' (Lodge 1983: 5). In that spirit they gave evidence to government commissions and attended conferences under the terms of the 1920 Native Affairs Act. Characteristic of the moderation in their continued campaign to gain redress through constitutional channels was the evidence given to a commission by Rev Z. R. Mahabane, President of the Cape Province. Speaking personally Mahabane called for alteration in the South Africa Act, for more African representation in government, and the right of any British subject, irrespective of race, to sit in parliament. He recognized, however, that whites feared being swamped by African votes. To allay this fear he suggested that at this stage Africans should not ask for equality. Instead he proposed that Native constituencies (each returning two members) should be established – three in the Cape, two in the Transvaal and one each for the Free State and Natal. Mahabane went on to say: 'I am against social equality with the white man, because I know we are not equal, but as far as politics is concerned I see no danger in equal rights.' Finally he tried to reassure the white commissioners by stating that even if Africans were to outnumber the whites in parliament 'the native would never be able to outclass the white man intellectually' (Karis and Carter 1972: 117). Despite such subservience a more militant strain emerged not only in the ANC, but in two new organizations – the Industrial and Commercial Workers' Union (ICU) and the Communist Party of South Africa (CPSA) – which are discussed later.

White Politics: The Rise and Fall of the SAP Government

Inside South Africa the government soon faced difficulties. In August 1919 Botha died. Widely admired both as a man and a leader he had attracted great personal support. However, he did not bequeath white unity to his successor, Jan Smuts. Smuts, who had spent much of the war abroad, returned home only a few weeks before succeeding to the Premiership. The international scene had suited his expansive ideas, and convinced him that his broad holistic views had practical advantages in building unity and statehood at home. Hancock wrote: 'He calculated that South Africa no longer had anything to gain by challenging the British Empire, as Hertzog tried to do at the Paris Peace Conference, but that she had everything to gain in combination with the free nations who were transforming the Empire into a Commonwealth' (Hancock 1968: 5). Smuts believed that the greater the constitutional freedom enjoyed by the Union the easier it would be to build a strong white nation at home; while, at the same time, reinforcing the ties with Britain and the other dominions which were built upon consent. Smuts therefore saw common interest between a developing South Africa and a developing Commonwealth.

At home Smuts inherited a situation in which the NP was gaining ground, as the country moved into post-war economic depression. That was the setting for the February 1920 election. Hertzog went forth criticizing the government and its economic policies, proclaiming the importance of Afrikaans, preaching the need for sovereign independence and claiming the alternative to an NP victory was decline to the old status of crown colony. It was an appeal which won the hearts of many Afrikaners, stirring memories among the older generation and promoting fresh hopes among the young. Hertzog accused Smuts of being out of touch with the aspirations of his own people. On his part Smuts claimed that the Union had 'de facto' independence, and equality of status within the Empire. He emphasized the Union's sovereign status within the League of Nations and the Commonwealth; and affirmed three principal needs – to build on the British connection; to gain white conciliation at home; and to foster industrial development. The result of the election was political stalemate. The NP (in the rural areas) and Labour (in the towns) gained at the expense of the SAP and the Unionists. In terms of seats the NP became the largest single party: with 44 compared with the SAP 41; UP 25; Labour 21; and 3 Independents. However, Smuts remained in power with the support of the United Party and Independents.

Despite the disputes between the SAP and NP, the election stalemate revived hopes among some Afrikaners of 'hereniging' (Afrikaner unity). Efforts were made to bring the SAP and NP together, including personal discussions between Smuts and Hertzog and joint party conferences. The efforts failed because there was no meeting of minds, particularly on relations with Britain. Smuts opposed a precise definition of the relationship and preferred to let matters take their course. In 1920 he told parliament that the connection was more than a constitutional issue, because in a dangerous world South Africa must work with others to promote and protect her own interests, 'but never in a selfish way'. She must aim, he said, 'to co-

ordinate her interests with those of the British Empire and the world as a whole'
(Hancock 1968: 41). Smuts's wider vision alarmed the NP; Hertzog wanted a right
to secede from the Empire, and he wanted it in writing. Malan spoke of the dangers
of being dragged into conflicts which had nothing to do with South Africa. Thus
the efforts to bridge the gap between the SAP and NP served only to highlight
differences between them.

Following that failure Smuts called another election in February 1921, after only
eleven months. That resulted in a further reshaping of white politics. Smuts, having
failed to unite with the Afrikaner NP, led his party into a merger with the predominantly English speaking UP, to form a new South African Party (SAP).
Strengthened by the realignment and by improved economic circumstances,
the new SAP scored an impressive victory: winning 79 seats to the NP's 45 and
Labour's 9. Smuts gave three cabinet seats to Unionists, including the leader, Sir
Thomas Smartt. The result was a new white political map, in which Hertzog, who
had been in the original Union cabinet, was now leader of the opposition and
spokesman for Afrikaner nationalism; while Smartt, the old opposition leader,
whom Hertzog had accused of putting Empire before South Africa, now sat in
government.

Behind the election statistics broad trends in white politics can be discerned.
Two major political groups had emerged. One, led by Hertzog, was the party of
Afrikaner nationalism, and it was noticeable that support for the NP remained
firm so that it lost no seats in the election. The new SAP, led by Smuts, preached
conciliation based on the ideal of a single white nation, but it was compromised
by its failure to attract more Afrikaners, and had to place increasing reliance on
support from English speakers. It was a situation that Botha had always sought to
avoid. Although Smuts assured his Afrikaner followers that the Unionists were
much changed – that the merger marked a further step in conciliation, that it spelt
the end of the party of Rhodes and Jameson – not all his supporters saw it that
way. Some SAP Afrikaners bewailed the abandonment of 'heriniging'. Further,
the Unionists were commonly associated with capitalists, so that Smuts was
increasingly portrayed as their instrument against the white workers. Associated
with that was the claim that he was more sympathetic to black labour, which was
cheaper than white, and by extension that he was more liberal towards blacks generally. It was an accusation that would have bemused most blacks but was believed
by NP followers. The overall results of the 1921 realignment were therefore first
to widen the gap between Afrikaner Nationalists and those seeking conciliation,
and second to broaden the SAP but to leave it as a looser and more fractional
party.

In 1921, before setting out for the Imperial Conference in London, Smuts asked
parliament to accept two principles: that South Africa should stand as a self-reliant
state, independent in all essentials; and at the same time co-operate with other
members of the Empire and the League of Nations. At the conference Smuts
submitted a memorandum on the constitutional status of the dominions. It envisaged 'a Commonwealth', a body that would 'no longer be an Empire but a
society of free and equal sister states.' Smuts had already pointed the way along

this road at the 1917 Conference when he introduced a resolution calling for a readjustment of the Empire's constitutional arrangements, to emphasize dominion self-government and a voice for each in foreign policy-making. Sadly for Smuts, his 1921 proposal was opposed, notably by W. M. Hughes, the Australian Prime Minister, who wanted no change. Smuts's initiative therefore came to nothing, whereas had it succeeded he would have gained prestige at home and abroad for a development in imperial relations that followed some years later.

The Government Clashes with Blacks and Whites

The new government had little time to reflect on these broader issues before it faced a series of internal upheavals. The main clashes were with Africans and whites, but Pretoria also had difficulties with Indians when it proposed further restrictions on their rights. In 1921 a government commission recommended a scheme for voluntary repatriation to India, and segregation for those who remained, with strict limits on their trading rights and licences. This met with stern opposition from India as well as from Indians inside the country. At the 1921 Imperial Conference, India proposed that Indians living in the Union should be granted South African citizenship. Smuts firmly opposed the proposal.

The first of the tragic clashes with Africans also came in 1921. In Queenstown an African religious sect – the Israelites, led by Enoch Mgijima – had settled illegally on a farm, Bulhoek, and refused to move. In earlier years the sect had gathered at Passover and dispersed, but in 1920 they had stayed to build a tabernacle and huts, following a vision experienced by Mgijima. After protests from local blacks and whites about the sect's cattle infringing on grazing and allegations of theft, the authorities attempted to persuade the Israelites to move but failed. Then in May 1921 an ultimatum was issued backed by a powerful force of 800 police. The Israelites stood firm and launched a suicidal attack, in which 163 of them were killed and 129 wounded. In the following year excessive force was used again, this time against another small group of Africans, the Bondelzwarts of South West Africa. The Bondelzwarts had believed that when South Africa assumed control from the Germans they would regain their traditional land and leaders. Their hopes were dashed. Pretoria imposed new controls and measures, including a dog tax. As a result the Bondelzwarts defied the government – refusing to pay tax and hand over five suspects to the police. Eventually this led to clashes in which the government again employed ferocious tactics – using a force of 370 men and a military aircraft to bomb the tribesmen – 117 Bondelzwarts were killed, including women and children. The Labour Party labelled Smuts 'The Bloody Jeffreys of South Africa' (Muller 1969: 357).

The Bulhoek and Bondelzwarts clashes were exceptional in their tragic loss of life, and the prominence they received because of Pretoria's involvement. Yet, in other ways, they represented the tip of an iceberg of local rural disputes, which, by the 1920s, were found across many parts of the country. Something of a rural resistance culture developed. It was characterized by a blending of traditional tribal beliefs and Christianity, and African separatist movements which were not beholden to the white man's state. One example was the Wellington Movement in the Transkei, led by Wellington Buthelezi. Its main features were 'its radical separatism, its attempts to boycott the state's institutions, to withdraw into African churches [and] to seek actual or imagined Africanist solutions' (Beinart and Bundy 1987: 23). Because the rural movements were local, transient and without clear structures, they were usually dealt with by local officials and seldom gained the attention of the central state. Equally they were difficult to link into the national black movements. In the case of Bulhoek the NNC supported Mgijima and his followers, in so far as it saw them as victims of the 1913 Land Act, but it urged them to abandon the disputed land to avoid the impending violence. More usually, however, the national movements were not involved in the local confrontations.

Other problems with black and white workers arose from economic and industrial developments. Under the pressure of global economic recession South Africa had left the gold standard in 1920. As the recession deepened increasing numbers of Africans and whites (mainly unskilled Afrikaners) were drawn into the urban areas. Many Africans lived in such squalid conditions that the ANC complained they were being forced into serfdom. The competition for jobs led to increased racial tension, and helped the emergence of the Industrial and Commercial Union (ICU) which for a time harnessed black workers into a mass movement. The government's response was to introduce the Native Urban Areas Act of 1923, which was intended to tidy up the position of urban Africans. The original draft legislation was drawn up by the Native Affairs Department. Although it made no mention of political rights for Africans, it supported improved welfare and social services, and, most important of all, it proposed granting them property rights in towns. However, at the same time a Transvaal Local Government Commission, chaired by C. F. Stallard, was also investigating the position of urban blacks. The Stallard report adopted a very different stance. It laid down as a principle that: 'The native should only be allowed to enter urban areas, which are essentially the white man's creation, when he is willing to enter and minister to the needs of the White man, and should depart therefrom when he ceases so to minister' (Lipton 1985: 18). Although it also favoured improved services, it stated that Africans should be kept in separate locations, and carry 'passes' or reference books, so that the flow of labour into the urban areas could be controlled.

In parliament it was the Stallard approach that carried the day. After Hertzog had raised strong objections to Africans gaining property rights, the bill was referred to a select committee. The committee took Hertzog's line – denying Africans property rights, and retaining strict controls including the pass system. Smuts emerged from the process with little honour. While in the main parliamentary debate he had supported the original proposals, as a member of the select committee he failed to defend the principle of black property rights, or even to consult the Native Conference about the issues. It was another example of the way in which his 'liberal' ideas on race bent easily before white pressure. The outcome of the legislation was a boost for segregation and migrant labour. Added to which, further legislation placed African conditions of work under criminal rather than civil law so that breaches of contract or labour agitation became punishable as crimes.

*   *   *

The main challenge to the government at the time came not from blacks but from militant white labour. Although the white unions continued to be led by English speakers, many miners were now Afrikaners. The mine owners, themselves under economic pressure, were eager to reduce costs by cutting wages and employing more Africans. In 1922 they cut white wages. The unionized white miners, determined to defend their position, came out on strike. There had been earlier industrial confrontations, but not on the scale or with the associated violence of 1922. As the strike intensified order broke down along the Rand, with gangs of miners attacking buildings and people. The most militant union leaders urged the establishment of a workers' republic along Soviet lines. 'Backed by the newly formed Communist Party of South Africa, workers elected strike committees and formed strike commandos. The red flag flew over Johannesburg Town Hall' (Worden 1995: 52).

Smuts responded by proclaiming martial law, and sending in police and troops. Pitched battles were fought, in which 230 people were killed including 50 policemen. When the strike was finally broken four miners were hanged for murder and others were imprisoned. In November 1923 the Supreme Court declared as 'ultra vires' regulations protecting white miners. Subsequently their wages were cut, and the principle of job protection was dropped. The government (and the mine owners) had won the immediate battle but at a heavy price. Hertzog described Smuts as a 'man whose hands dripped with the blood of his own people' (Muller 1969: 357). The white miners were equally bitter. For them Smuts had become a brutal oppressor, a creature of the owners, an ally of 'Hoggenheimer'. A Labour cartoon showed Smuts in the sky 'showering peace and goodwill on Europe but bombs and frightfulness on South Africa' (Hancock 1968: 15).

In 1922 the government suffered a further set back, this time related to expansion of the Union. Smuts, who shared Rhodes's earlier vision of a greater South Africa stretching north across the highlands of East/Central Africa, was always eager to extend the Union's frontiers. As a step along that road he hoped to persuade Southern Rhodesia to enter the Union as its fifth Province (incidentally strengthening his own political base because Rhodesia's white population was predominantly British). Smuts personally toured Rhodesia to plead the case, and offered generous terms – enhanced representation at the centre, and a financial subsidy. The NP strongly opposed the proposal. They pointed out that if it went ahead the Union would acquire a substantial number of blacks and relatively few whites, and they branded the whites as imperialists, who would strengthen the British connection and cement Smuts in power. The NP's fears were resolved by the white Rhodesians themselves. They voted against joining the Union, because they feared Afrikaner domination and centralized control from Pretoria, and suspected that they would suffer economic discrimination. In 1923 Southern Rhodesia became a self-governing British colony.

The NP/Labour Pact

The SAP government's trials and tribulations, especially the Rand strike, served to strengthen the Labour Party and give it common cause with the NP. Despite their differences the NP and Labour were united in their antagonism towards the government, and their determination to defend white interests against the blacks. On that base they formed a pact to fight the next election. Hertzog and Creswell, the Labour leader, reached agreement on four major points: that the country was being ruined by the government and its capitalist allies; the pact parties would retain their separate identities but form an electoral alliance; the NP would concentrate on domestic measures required to promote the prosperity of the country and not press for secession from the Empire; and that in government the pact would introduce a programme of social and economic reform to further white interests.

The movement of poor Afrikaners to the towns and cities strengthened and reshaped Afrikaner nationalism and the National Party. Faced by the wealthier English speakers and in competition with Africans the urban Afrikaners' sense of grievance and solidarity was intensified. Their attitude hardened towards race issues, as did their criticism of the financial power of the English and Jews. The poor Afrikaners lost more of their independence in the cities; deepening their sense of grievance and hardening their concept of nationalism. The promotion of white urban labour interests not only drew Labour and the NP together, it led to the underlying theme of keeping blacks out of skilled work, and, as far as possible, out of the cities. The attitude evolved that town was not the place for blacks – that there 'a "good kaffir" got "spoiled"'. The report of the Native Affairs Commission in 1921 stated that: 'It should be understood that the town is a European area in which there is no place for the redundant Native' (Sparks 1990: 135). In line with this thinking the NP's commitment to Afrikaner upliftment covered urban as well as rural dwellers, and led to state intervention – a form of socialist nationalism.

In both Pact parties militant elements supported a republic, but from very different premises. The NP's republicanism was based on Afrikaner nationalism; whereas Labour militants wanted a workers' republic. When the SAP branded the Pact as an 'unholy alliance' of Bolsheviks and Christian National Republicans, the Pact parties countered by criticizing the government's financial and administrative record, its support for capitalism, its failure to protect white labour, its promotion of black interests and its subservience to Britain. The opposition leaders even reversed roles, when Creswell attacked Smuts's attitude to the Empire and Hertzog proclaimed the rights of white labour. 'The native can be used to advantage', he said, but not 'where the services of the white man can and ought to be used' (Hancock 1968: 159).

Surrounded by problems the government steadily lost ground. When, by early 1924, through by-election defeats, its majority had dropped from twenty-four to eight Smuts called a general election for June. He believed he could win by fighting a campaign which attacked NP republican ambitions in urban areas, and by raising fears of socialism in rural seats. However, the Pact fought an effective campaign. It claimed that a further period of SAP government would result in a country controlled by capitalists and dominated by black labour. Rallying to the cries of 'civilized labour' and the black menace, the Pact gained an emphatic victory. The NP won 65 seats and Labour 18, to the SAP's 53 and 1 Independent. Although the campaign had been fought on the old issues of relations with Britain and Afrikaner identity, victory was also built on racial concerns. In de Kiewiet's words: The Pact Government was 'a white man's front against the natives' (De Kiewiet 1957: 224).

7

The Pact Government
and Segregation, 1924–1929

As Prime Minister of the Pact government Hertzog formed a joint NP and Labour Party cabinet. Thus, as with Botha's and Smuts's administrations, it contained both Afrikaans and English speakers, and like them it was concerned to forward white interests. However, the Pact gave a different emphasis to these interests. The previous governments had attempted to bridge past divisions by building a common white nationalism within the British Empire; whereas the aim of the Pact was to offer its followers protection from what it perceived to be the overlapping threats of imperialism, capitalism and blacks. Oswald Pirow, a militant nationalist cabinet member, claimed that Hertzog's aim was to continue 'his war against Imperialism until he had reversed the Treaty of Vereeniging and removed all traces of inferiority as regards the Boers' (Pirow: 100). Labour was also concerned about imperialism, but in its case it feared the link with capitalism, and the capitalists' ambition to reduce costs through a freer labour market and by substituting black for white labour. The NP shared that concern because many white workers and most work seekers were Afrikaners, including the poorest and least skilled. Thus the Pact combined the interests of a nationalist party determined to promote the interests of Afrikaners, with those of a white labour aristocracy intent on defending its privileges. The buckle that joined them was not the search for a common nationalism but defence against the threats of imperialism, capitalism and blacks.

As government leader Hertzog was admired as a man of courtesy and strong principles, who acted with courage and determination. His followers lauded him for promoting the position of Afrikaners and the poor whites. 'It was Hertzog,' they claimed, 'who performed the indispensable and inestimable service of really placing the two [white] races on a footing of equality.' Under his leadership, they said, Afrikaners gained equality of language, institutions and culture, and through his 'civilized labour policy' he built 'a bridge over which English and Afrikaners could advance to meet each other on a basis of common fears and common hatreds.' Further, they claimed it was he who later secured full freedom and sovereignty for South Africa within the Commonwealth (Roberts and Trollip 1947: 183).

The Pact partners were convinced that white interests and status could only be defended effectively if the machinery of the state was in their hands and not those of the SAP. Their fear was not that blacks posed an immediate threat to the state, but that the inexorable growth in their numbers would steadily undermine white security and living standards. Such fears were prompted by the economic pressures which had drawn both whites and blacks to the towns. In 1900 less than 10 per cent of Afrikaners were urban dwellers; by 1926 the figure stood at 41 per cent (Adam and Giliomee 1979b: 150). In NP eyes, the chief danger lay in the vulnerable position of the 'poor whites'. The Carnegie Commission, appointed by Hertzog in 1924 to investigate the problem, found that between 200,000 and 300,000 whites were 'very poor'. These formed a vulnerable frontier between black and white societies and one that the government feared could be penetrated to allow a 'debasing stream of uncivilised blood to pour through' (De Kiewiet 1957: 221). The Pact government set out to transform the frontier into a barrier, by strengthening the position of whites and by solving once and for all the Native problem.

Yet, alongside the common interests that drew the Pact partners together there were also clear differences. Labour was an urban party led by English speakers and

J. B. M. Hertzog
(courtesy of the
South African
High
Commission)

had members who were socialists; whereas the NP was predominantly Afrikaner, it had strong rural as well as urban interests, and pursued a distinctive form of nationalism. To establish a working relationship the two parties not only stressed their common interests but trimmed their differences. In deference to Labour the NP played down republicanism, while on its part Labour restrained its socialist wing. Nevertheless, the paradox remained. The Labour Party was concerned with class interests – it sought to represent and protect a white labour aristocracy – whereas the NP was determined to avoid class divisions among Afrikaners. The NP's priority was nation not class, 'the volk' not the workers. It helped poor Afrikaners so that they would identify themselves with the nation rather than joining a class struggle. For NP supporters the Pact was a means of forwarding their nationalist aspirations, undermining conciliation and challenging the British link.

There were also tensions inside the parties. Some of the NP's most committed nationalists were uncomfortable associating with Labour and its British trade union style. They criticized Hertzog for leading them into that position, and for being too moderate in his approach both to Labour and to Britain. Within the Labour Party a division existed between those whose priority was the defence of a white labour aristocracy and a socialist wing that put more emphasis on class than race. That division led to conflict within the cabinet. For example, despite Hertzog's declared opposition, Walter Madeley (a Socialist Labour cabinet member) received a black delegation from the ICU. Hertzog, with the support of Creswell and the majority of the Labour Party, therefore removed Madeley from office. Both the common ground and the differences within the Pact can be traced in the four policy areas on which the Pact government concentrated its attention. They were: (a) the promotion of white labour; (b) the development of Afrikaner culture and identity; (c) clarification of the relationship with Britain; and (d) a comprehensive Native Policy.

The Promotion of White Interests and Afrikaner Culture

Self-preservation of one's own people was the first law of nature, stated the Minister of Mines in 1926 when he introduced the Mines and Works Amendment Act ('The Colour Bar Act'). All previous Union governments had advanced the interests of white labour, but, as the minister's statement indicates, the Pact gave it a higher priority and backed it by further legislation. To reduce white unemployment it created new jobs, replaced blacks with whites, and established a colour bar. Such steps were based on an innate and largely unquestioned assumption of white racial superiority. To most Europeans, wrote de Kiewiet, 'the inborn inferiority of the native remained a truth beyond serious contention' (De Kiewiet 1957: 226). In 1924 a Department of Labour was established with the prime functions of promoting employment for poor whites, and substituting white for black labour. In 1925 a Wages Board was created, with the specific task of ensuring that white wages did not fall below the level necessary to maintain a 'civilized' standard of living, which was a life 'tolerable from the European standpoint'. In contrast native wages were to satisfy 'uncivilized' standards – to meet 'the bare . . . necessities of life as understood among barbarous and undeveloped peoples' (Hancock 1968: 207). The result was a great gap between white and black incomes.

In its commitment to white labour the Pact was fortunate to enjoy a period of economic recovery, which enabled it to expand white employment. Departments of state, municipalities and nationalized industries were told that they must give preference to whites. Nowhere was that clearer than in the Railways and Harbours. In 1924 only 4,760 whites were employed in its work force; by 1929 that had grown to 16,248; and by the 1950s the figure climbed to over 100,000 (Adams and Giliomee 1979b: 151). Bolstered by the economic expansion and the government's efforts the position of poor whites steadily improved, but it was not until the economic boost of the Second World War that virtually full white employment was achieved. Even so, an element of discontent remained among poorer Afrikaners, who compared their lot not with Africans but with the more affluent English-speaking, whites.

The promotion of Afrikaner culture reflected NP rather than Labour Party priorities, but there was a link in that the provision of educational opportunities for poor Afrikaners and their children improved their employment prospects. The government took vigorous steps to further the cause. In 1925 Parliament unanimously agreed that Dutch should be taken to include Afrikaans, because the language had advanced sufficiently to serve for administrative and legal purposes. Following that, Afrikaans became increasingly prominent for official business. When the government set out to ensure that the civil service was bilingual, the opposition accused it of favouring its own supporters. Although the culture drive gained official support the grass-roots work was undertaken by the churches, schools, newspapers, families and Afrikaner voluntary groups. Language was a key issue. In 1919 Gustav Preller, a journalist and strong advocate of Afrikaans had written: 'Language unity is the natural outcome of national unity, the necessary precondition for a national culture' (Hofmeyr 1987: 105). And it was people like Preller to whom Hermann Giliomee referred when he pointed out the importance of 'language manipulators' in developing Afrikaans – professionals in education, the media and the church – whose position depended on the language. They took on the massive task of 'building a nation from words' (Giliomee 1987). In 1923 work had started on the translation of the bible into Afrikaans, which, when completed ten years later, 'promised to have the same influence on the language as had Luther's German and King James's English versions' (Kruger 1969: 141).

Among non-government Afrikaner bodies the most controversial was the Broederbond. Founded in 1918 it was dedicated to furthering Afrikaner values and power. It did so in a narrow, sectarian and secretive way. It was confined to men who were Protestant, financially sound, and who believed in the 'eternal existence of a separate Afrikaner nation with its own language and culture'. In daily affairs it gave 'preference to Afrikaners and other well disposed persons and firms in economic, public and professional life' It recruited those 'who are wholly devoted to the service of the Afrikaner nation', and 'cling to the Christian National viewpoint of the Afrikaner' (Moodie 1975: 102). Hertzog never joined – it was too extreme for him – and later he made a bitter attack on it. It was not therefore directly associated with the government, but many government and other Afrikaner leaders were members. For the Broeders politics was not a discrete activity; it permeated social and economic life. They spread their message through both established and new Afrikaner organizations; cultural groups, youth and women's clubs, and the church. Their commitment and ambition were captured in 1943 by Hendrik Verwoerd, a future Prime Minister, when he called on the Broederbond to 'gain control of everything it can lay its hands on in every walk of life in South Africa. Members must help each other to gain promotion in the civil service or any other field of activity in which they work with a view to working themselves into important administrative positions' (Thompson 1985: 46).

The Union's Constitutional Status

South Africa's constitutional status was also of greater concern to the NP than Labour. Within the international setting Hertzog was determined to establish – and demonstrate to the world – South Africa's sovereign and independent status within the Empire. His government set out to show this in a number of ways. For example, it reduced imperial preferences on British goods from £860,000 to £300,000 per annum; it sought to diversify trade links by sending Trade Commissioners to the US and Kenya; and a trade and shipping agreement was signed with Germany. In 1925 the government introduced a protectionist Customs Tariff Act which was welcomed by local industries and farmers and opposed by the mine owners and commerce. In more formal terms, Hertzog did not press for a republic or a break with the crown, but he was determined to remove the ambiguity which clung to South Africa's status.

Despite Smuts's protests to the contrary Hertzog believed that the Union was still seen to be subordinate to Britain. He did not accept, as Smuts argued, that South Africa's signature on the Versailles Treaty had fully demonstrated her equality. Hertzog committed himself to eliminate any uncertainty, to ensure that South Africa enjoyed sovereign independence within the Commonwealth. It was a time of intense international activity in which Britain became involved in conferences and treaties. In doing so other states often assumed that Britain and the dominions were one; that Britain acted on behalf of all. Hertzog rejected that and wanted his rejection stated unambiguously in a document. It was against this backdrop that he attended the 1926 Imperial Conference. There he submitted a draft declaration, which when amended became the Balfour Declaration. This stated that Britain and the dominions 'are autonomous communities within the British Empire, equal in status, in no way subordinate to one another in any aspect of their domestic or external affairs, though united by a common allegiance to the Crown, and freely associated as members of the British Commonwealth'. Hertzog was delighted with the outcome. He returned home in triumph, claiming that: 'No declaration could be devised by which the country's liberty in a most unlimited manner could be so clearly demonstrated . . . No one need bother in future about South Africa breaking away from the Empire. As a result of the work of the Imperial Conference, the old Empire no longer exists. All that remains is a free association'. In 1927 a Department of External Affairs was formed and diplomats exchanged with Holland, Italy and the United States.

Yet Hertzog's optimism was premature. Even the Balfour declaration was disputed within the NP. While Hertzog was fully satisfied with it other NP members were not. They clung to their republicanism, and would never be content until that was achieved. Others wanted the right of secession from the Commonwealth and neutrality in war spelt out specifically. Hertzog resisted that because he argued that those rights were now established and an attempt to specify them would only raise the sovereignty question again. In many respects Hertzog's position was now closer to Smuts's than his militant NP colleagues. Both men were agreed that the Union's interests were served by Commonwealth membership. However, they saw it in different contexts. Smuts's wider vision placed membership in an international setting; whereas Hertzog's prime concern was internal affairs. He accused Smuts of trying to build the Commonwealth into a super authority. That was untrue. At the 1923 conference Smuts had advanced similar proposals to those now contained in the Balfour Declaration. He too supported a community of equal states, but for him the greater the equality the greater the ties. For Smuts the Commonwealth was more than the sum of its parts, it was an international force for good. The difference between the two men was captured in their attitudes to neutrality. Hertzog stressed that independence included the right to neutrality. For Smuts that was the wrong emphasis. For it signalled that South Africa was ready to opt out of its international responsibilities.

The strong emotions that clung to relations with Britain surfaced again in the flag dispute of 1926/7. The debate was so fierce that it threatened to undermine the Union's political fabric. Previously the British flag (Union Jack) had been flown, but the government now proposed a distinctive South African flag. There was an immediate dispute about whether a new flag was needed at all, and following that what it should incorporate. The controversy extended into the government where Labour did not oppose a new flag, but wanted the Union Jack included, while some NP ministers favoured a 'clean flag' with no British symbols. D. F. Malan, who introduced the bill to parliament, was among the clean flag advocates. He stated that the question had nothing to do with the material welfare of the country. 'It has to do with the nation itself. It has to do with the very existence of the nation as a separate entity. It has to do with our national life and sentiment. It has to do with our national status . . . It has to do with the soul of the nation' (Stultz 1974: 28). Hertzog himself infuriated many English speakers by describing the Union Jack as 'merely a piece of cloth'. At the other extreme were those who wanted no change from the Union flag. The controversy was finally settled by a double compromise. First a new national flag was introduced, based on the original Dutch horizontal stripes of orange, white and blue, with a central shield incorporating the Free State flag, the Transvaal's 'Vierkleur' and the Union Jack. Second, it was further agreed that the Union Jack could be flown alongside the new flag.

Native Policy and Segregation

The protection of white interests was at the heart of the government's Native policy. Hertzog's ambition was to settle the 'Native Question' once and for all, and, like Smuts before him, he personally took the portfolio of Native Affairs. The principles on which he based his policy were: that white civilization must remain supreme for the sake of all blacks as well as whites; that Natives must be removed from the common voters' role; that Natives must have their own areas in which to develop; and that the Coloureds must be treated apart from the Natives. The policy was encapsulated in the label 'segregation' which was revitalized under the Pact government. As previously noted, segregation was not new in principle or practice. It was already embodied in the Mines and Works Act of 1911, the Native Land Act of 1913, the Native Administration Act of 1917, and the Natives (Urban Areas) Act of 1923 – but it remained open to different interpretations and policy outputs. The Pact government gave it a firmer framework, based on the assumption that it implied more than a separation of territory or functions but a division of people (Beinart and Dubow 1995: 3). De Kiewiet later commented: 'The language of public discussion and political debate freely used such terms as "native question" and "segregation", as if the native question concerned only natives and as if segregation meant a real separation between two distinct communities.' Whereas, in reality the life and activity of white and black were not separate, and did not operate in separate spheres (De Kiewiet 1957: 179–80).

The concept of segregation was accepted on both sides of the white parliament. There were differences of emphasis but not of substance. Smuts made that clear later when he lectured at Oxford in 1929. Smuts, unlike Hertzog, always argued that no final solution was possible, that some matters had to be left for the future. However, for the present he saw Africans as 'children of nature', and said it was clear that a race 'so different in its mentality and culture from those of Europe, requires a policy very unlike that which would suit Europeans'. If Africans were to advance they must not be forced into alien European institutions. The way forward, he said, was to build on traditional foundations. From time immemorial the Natives had been subjected to the stern, despotic authority of chiefs. If that broke down and tribal discipline disappeared, native society would disintegrate into chaos. The solution was to develop separate institutions for Africans in their own areas. Yet he added provisos. One concerned industrial work, where it was impossible to divide black and white. Industrial segregation, he stated, 'would be both impracticable and an offence against the modern conscience'. But he opposed a permanent black urban population. He regretted that Africans had been allowed to settle permanently outside native areas; because that raised 'a problem for the whole principle of segregation, as they claim to be civilized and European', and do not wish to return to native areas or 'forego their new place in the sun among whites'. For the future, said Smuts, men should be allowed to move to urban areas only to work, but should keep their roots and their families in the Native reserves. In terms of parliament Smuts concluded that Africans should be represented, but by a few white members. His preference was for separate racial electoral rolls, but he recognized that there would be a spirited defence of the Cape's common voters' roll (Smuts 1942: 52–82). Smuts's views on strengthening traditional foundations were similar to those of a close follower, Heaton Nicholls, who became a strong advocate of segregation in the late 1920s. Nicholls's message was that traditional African communities must be encouraged to counter the danger of communism. Segregation afforded the opportunity to do that; to nullify the threat of a militant urban proletariat. 'The policy of a Bantu nation,' he wrote in May 1929, 'as distinct from that of a black proletariat – and that stripped of all the verbiage, that is the real issue in Africa – obviously brings with it pride of race' (Marks 1986: 97).

There was therefore much common ground between the major white parties. However, Hertzog's approach was more forceful and strident. His ambition was to settle Native Policy once and for all, not to leave it for future generations. In practice his policy was erected on three main pillars. First was the protection of white labour and economic interests. Although he realized that complete separation was impossible, because the economy depended on black labour, he believed that protection was needed to underpin white supremacy. Second, he supported territorial division, based on the conviction that 'it is the best both for the Native and the European that so far as the occupation of land is concerned the Natives should be separated from the Europeans' (Karis and Carter 1972: 173). He recognized, however, that the existing Reserves needed expansion because they could not support the increasing African population. Third, he wanted to create institutions for Africans, but they would be subordinate to and separate from those of the white state. Hertzog did not rule out entirely the possibility that blacks could eventually stand as equals to whites, but the possibility was so remote and uncertain for him that it was of no practical significance. He stressed ethnic differences in 'nature, custom, development and civilization'. He concluded that: 'As against the European, the native stands as an eight year old against a man of mature experience – a child in religion, a child in moral convictions, without art, without science' (Moodie 1975: 261).

To achieve those ends Hertzog introduced four bills into parliament in 1926. Three of these were directed at Africans. One concerned the franchise and parliamentary representation, by which Hertzog sought to remove Africans in the Cape from the common voters' roll. Instead he offered Africans throughout the Union the right to elect indirectly (through chiefs, headmen and councils) seven white representatives to the House of Assembly and four to the Senate. Hertzog explained his proposal not in terms of African rights but as a measure 'to preserve white civilization through the unity of the white races'. He argued that leaving Africans on the common roll would divide whites into rival camps, with one group standing alone and the other having millions of Natives behind it. Christian principles, he said, stood high, but self-preservation stood higher 'because it was the only way in which humanity and Christianity itself could be defended' (Le May 1995: 175). A related bill made provision for African Councils, to be composed of indirectly elected members and government nominees. The third bill focused on the land. It proposed adding 7.25 million morgen to areas earmarked for Native Reserves in the 1913 Act – making a total of 17.25 million morgen in all, or 12.4 per cent of the Union's land area. However, Hertzog underlined that the Reserves 'would never become the independent states of which some Natives sometimes speak' (Walshe 1987: 110).

The fourth bill dealt specifically with the Coloureds, whom Hertzog wanted to exclude from some aspects of the segregation policy. In broad terms he accepted that whites and Coloureds shared economic, cultural and even political interests. In 1929 he stated that 'it would be foolish to drive the Coloured people into the arms of the enemies of the Europeans – and that will happen if we expel him, if we allow him eventually to come to rest in the arms of the native'. Hertzog therefore proposed extending the Coloured franchise across the country, but he did not favour social integration. 'The place of the educated Coloured,' he declared, 'is with his own people and not the white man' (Giliomee 1995: 215). However, Hertzog's Coloured policy ran into difficulties. In the first place there were problems in distinguishing the Coloureds as a distinct group from either whites or Africans. Hermann Giliomee noted that during the first three decades of the Union 'no clear cut division existed between whites and Coloureds whose lower classes lived interspersed', and Hertzog himself later admitted that no clear legal distinction had been laid down between Coloureds and Africans (Giliomee 1995: 203). An even greater problem for Hertzog was that most of his followers did not share his views of the Coloureds, and so were not prepared to support his policy. They did, however, share his much less sympathetic attitude towards Indians, whom they saw as an alien community. An attempt to segregate Indians for trading and residential purposes was applauded by the whites, but opposed not only by local Indians but the Indian Government. Negotiations between the two governments led to the 1927 Cape Town Agreement, by which Pretoria's immediate proposals were withdrawn, a more vigorous repatriation scheme was introduced, and an Indian Agent General was posted to the Union. The Agreement temporarily improved relations but did not offer a permanent solution for Indians resident in South Africa.

Despite Hertzog's efforts the four bills were not enacted. The proposed change in the Cape franchise ran foul of the constitution's entrenched clauses which required a two-thirds majority of both houses sitting together. Hertzog did not have the parliamentary strength to push it through. When he failed in that he withdrew all the bills. It was suggested to him that if he introduced the others separately he could gain part if not the whole of his scheme. That he would not countenance. For him each bill was part of an overall strategy. In essence the strategy, as far as Africans were concerned, was to offer them a deal based on the principle of segregation. In return for losing the Cape franchise they would gain more land, have their own councils and an indirect voice in parliament. Those constitutional arrangements would signal that Africans would not share the same sense of identity or nationhood as whites, nor would they enjoy the same rights as citizens of the state. Instead they would have their own lands, and tribal institutions.

Although frustrated on the four bills, the government pushed through the Native Administration Act in 1927. This was presented as an administrative rather than a political measure, but it was based on similar principles to Hertzog's bills. It reflected the government's opposition to 'the nineteenth century Cape ethos of assimilation and inclusion of educated Africans into a common civilization' (Rich 1996: 35). The act was designed to separate African affairs by reinforcing the policy of 'indirect rule' through chiefs and councils. Africans were to develop along separate 'tribal' lines, not as part of a South African nation. The act also strengthened the position of the Department of Native Affairs, so that within the state machinery Africans were also kept apart. 'Natives' were to be cared for by 'experts'. The legislation also extended the powers of the Governor General (designated 'Supreme Chief' but acting on the advice of the government) to take steps against those who promoted hostility between whites and Africans. Finally, it provided legal means to counter the increasing influence of organizations like the ICU.

African Reactions: the ANC

The late 1920s were difficult, uncertain times for black political activity. There was no unity of response either to Hertzog's segregation proposals, or to where the main focus of attention should be directed. Some Africans continued to see virtues in segregation, and sought to improve the terms rather than dispute the principle. They argued that it gave them the opportunity to preserve their traditional way of life, their culture and authority structure; while others said that racial division, and particularly territorial division, was a way of protecting the weaker (African) peoples. However, those who argued that way then added that it should be on a fair basis and Hertzog's territorial proposals were not fair. In rural areas – both in the reserves and white farms – it was a time of increasing black discontent. In white farming areas – such as Natal where wattle and sheep farming were expanding – the main pressure was on tenant labourers and squatter peasants. In the reserves, which were suffering from overcrowding and land degradation, Africans reacted against the government's attempts at agricultural improvements, which included stock culling, reclamation and rehabilitation. Added to that was government legislation which increased taxes in the Cape and Natal, and alarm at Hertzog's proposals. The resistance, which was often directed at Chiefs and headmen, was small scale, spasmodic, dispersed and difficult to organize; but it was no less real for that (Bundy 1987: 255).

The ANC took little advantage of the rural discontent. It suffered at the time from internal divisions between moderates and radicals; financial and administration problems; and provincial rivalries. As in the past, moderate leaders in the Cape retained some faith in the imperial connection. Inside the Union their aims were still to extend political and civil rights, to win better social and educational facilities and to gain incorporation into a non-racial society; and to do so by constitutional means. They failed to realize that it was leading nowhere, and even those who became disillusioned found it difficult to reorientate their thinking – to create a new mind set. In 1923 the ANC published a Bill of Rights. It was in the old vein, claiming the inalienable right of British subjects to liberty, justice and equality before the law, and calling for the implementation of Rhodes' formula of 'equal rights for all civilised men south of the Zambesi'.

Some ANC moderates attempted to co-ordinate their activities with liberals across racial lines, which led to the formation of Joint Councils and the Institute of Race Relations; and other attempts were made to merge black efforts, through such schemes as the Non European Conference. The moderates also tried to use the narrow channels offered by the government to advance their point of view. These included the annual Governor General's Native Conference, which Hertzog himself attended in 1925 to explain the principles behind his policy. He told the conference that in terms of land 'the native should be separated from the European', but he made clear that 'the Native Areas will never become independent or semi independent states'. Instead they would be under the government's leadership with delegated local powers (Karis and Carter 1972: 173–4). Although the conference members expressed their gratitude to the Prime Minister for coming, he failed to convince them. That became even clearer at the meeting in the following year. As ever the tone was mild but the message was clear. Selope Thema attacked the very foundation of Hertzog's policy, which, he said, was intended to divide people – splitting Africans into separate tribal groups, and keeping Africans and Europeans apart. It was, said Thema, hateful to be divided into tribes; and 'it was impossible to evolve a Nation within a Nation . . . a separate Bantu Nation and a separate European Nation . . . The only conclusion they could come to was that the Natives must be represented on equal terms with whites' (Karis and Carter 1972: 181). A motion from Thema – rejecting Hertzog's Representation of Natives Bill, defending the existing Cape franchise, and proposing the extension of voting rights to the northern provinces – was carried by an overwhelming majority. Hertzog had failed to persuade even the moderate African leaders.

Not all ANC members were moderates. James Thaele, who had been educated in the US, where he had come under the radical influence of Garvey (see below), argued that the only means by which Africans could achieve their ends was by political and trade union activity. 'We are fed up,' he wrote, 'with the white man's camouflage, his hypocrisy, his policy of pinpricks.' Thaele appealed to Africans 'to use all means to rouse the African race from their long sleep' (Lodge 1983: 6). Men like Thaele realized that they were not operating in a broad imperial setting, but within a white dominated state. To be effective would require a revision of organization and methods, and a new foundation for their claims. Josiah Gumede, who later became a member of the communist party, alongside his affiliation to the ANC, came to a similar conclusion. Gumede accepted that there were different approaches within the ANC, and tried to marry them together. In a letter, dated September 1927, he stated that he knew there were 'two wings of the Bantu movement for political and economic emancipation from the tyranny of European rule, the conservative and the radical'. However, he argued that in the same way that a bird needs two wings to fly so did the ANC to operate. It was possible, he claimed, to differ and yet work together for the benefit of the oppressed people (Karis and Carter 1972: 304).

In 1927, shortly after paying a visit to the Soviet Union, Gumede was elected ANC President. He introduced a new dimension into Congress by linking its struggle with the common values of oppressed people around the world as they faced the 'monstrous burden of Imperialism'. All races, he declared, suffer under the 'capitalist class which grinds the White and Black alike the world over' (Walshe 1987: 175). Gumede's election temporarily steered the ANC towards a more radical approach, but it did not last. His term as President was brought to an end in 1930. In his address to the annual conference in that year he pulled no punches. He urged members to adopt a militant policy to bring liberation. He spoke of the Union dragging blacks deeper into slavery, and claimed that elsewhere the oppressed were rising against imperialism, with an impending revolution in India against the British. 'Everywhere,' he declared, 'the oppressed people were being inspired by that ideal of emancipation, which found expression in the Russian revolution.' He dismissed appeals to Britain as futile, and insisted 'we have now to rely on our own strength, on the strength of the revolutionary mass of workers the whole world over with whom we must join forces. We have to demand our equal economic, social and political rights. That cannot be expressed more clearly than to demand a South African Native Republic, with equal rights for all, but free from all foreign domination' (Karis and Carter 1972: 309–10).

The conference was deeply split. Assembled against Gumede were the moderates, including the chiefs and many Christians, who made it clear that they did not want atheists, militants and communists operating through Congress. They carried the day. In Gumede's place they elected Pixely Seme, Congress's founding father, who had become a leading conservative member. However, Seme's election did not heal the ANC's wounds. He was as uncompromising as Gumede, but in the opposite direction. He described communism as 'humbug', and when he unveiled Congress's future direction there was no mention of mass action, but instead of self-help and unity between black and white (Walshe 1987: 181).

The Industrial and Commercial Union (ICU)

As the ANC quarreled new movements emerged to challenge the government. The largest of them was the Industrial and Commercial Union (ICU). It was formed by Clements Kadalie, who had emigrated from Nyasaland to South Africa, and first came to prominence when he led a dock strike in Cape Town in 1919. Under Kadalie's leadership, the ICU quickly spread across the Union. It was an 'all in' union drawing support from rural as well as urban blacks, to become the first effective 'mass' black movement. In a period of recession, increased competition between white and black labour, and forced removal of Africans from the land, the ICU attracted wide support. Its appeal in the rural areas was captured in the cry of Chief Msigana Mtembu from Zululand, who stated: 'We have become a poor people through lack of something to sustain us. The land which we owned in the past has been taken from us . . . we have no cattle to speak of' (Marks 1986: 94). The ICU projected its message by vigorous publicity, through its newspaper (*The Workers' Herald*) and powerful orators like Kadalie himself and A. W. G. Champion in Natal. Kadalie, who was critical of Smuts and his association with capitalism, initially supported Hertzog, but inevitably that did not last, and the ICU attacked his Native bills.

The ICU concerned itself with the immediate day-to-day concerns of its followers – such as wages, social benefits, passes, and night curfews; and land and rents for its rural followers. However, it also advanced broader political aims as the only way to achieve its ends. Kadalie condemned racism, capitalism and religion, and called for a redistribution of land. Champion saw the ICU filling a role similar to that of a British trade union, by the 'gradual introduction of political and industrial democracy by and through the emancipation, economically and politically of African workers' (Walshe 1987: 194). These ICU aims were explicitly stated in its *Economic and Political Programme* in which Hertzog's bills were attacked and support given for the Cape franchise. In his introduction to the programme Kadalie quoted Marx in saying that in the last analysis every economic question is a political one, so that failure by the ICU to concern itself with politics would leave 'the political machines to the unchallenged control of our class enemies' (Karis and Carter 1972: 331). He urged his followers to agitate for change. In 1927 Kadalie personally appealed to the British Trade Union Conference at Blackpool, drawing attention, among other things, to the discrimination of the Native Administration Act of that year. If that were not revoked, he said, if Africans were denied all legitimate expressions of grievances and aspirations they would come to hate the white man as an oppressor. Kadalie argued that although narrow African nationalism could be a fatal path to follow, if the Union's policy continued unamended that was the path Africans would take.

The ICU's impact was remarkable. For a time it brushed aside difficulties as it spread across the country – combining the strength of a mass trade union with the drive of a political party. It shared with the ANC a commitment to a united South Africa offering equality of opportunity and African participation in a single society. However, there was no co-operation between the two organizations. Both missed an opportunity – the ANC to gain a powerful union ally; the ICU to work with an established political party. In general the ICU's tone and methods were more radical than the ANC's. Kadalie labelled ANC moderates as 'good boys', but the ICU's relations with communists were even stormier. Although few in numbers, communists had infiltrated the ICU and become influential in its organization. Kadalie, despite quoting Marx and referring to a class struggle, was fiercely opposed to them. He accused them of trying to dominate the ICU and use it for their own ends. As a result communists were ousted from the National Executive in 1926, by which time they occupied five of the eleven places. Later they were expelled from the organization as a whole.

Initially the ICU fed on its own success. Its membership, which was already 39,000 in 1926, had risen to an estimated 100,000 by the end of 1927. But almost as quickly it went into decline: rocked by internal squabbles, organizational overstretch, financial scandals, and frustration among the rank and file. W. G. Ballinger, who came out from Britain in 1928 to work for the ICU, found it ill organized, casual in its financial dealings and lacking control. In the internal struggles Champion broke away to form the Natal ICU, and established an alliance with the local traditional chiefs. These internal weaknesses were magnified by implacable white opposition (including the storming of the Durban office in 1929) and by the government's antagonism, which wrongly saw it as a bolshevik movement. Pretoria's response culminated in the 1930 Riotous Assembly (Amendment) Act, which was directed against the ICU, and led to restriction orders being placed on its leaders. By the early 1930s the ICU had fragmented into a number of small, ineffective bodies. It had moved across the South African sky like a bright comet, but from its trail lessons could be drawn: the importance of identifying people's day-to-day concerns in rural and urban settings, the co-ordination of political and workers' demands, and the effectiveness of mass action. In the long term the ICU was less important for promoting new ideas than for demonstrating the potential power of a mass black movement.

Garveyism: 'Africa for the Africans'

While the ICU was an important but temporary movement there were other long-term influences at work in black politics during the 1920s. Among these was the impact of external ideas, including a movement led by Marcus Garvey urging African self-reliance. Garvey, a flamboyant Afro-American, had formed the Universal Negro Improvement Association (UNIA) in the US. He spread his ideas abroad through a newspaper (*The Negro World*), the formation of groups, and the word of his disciples. With his cry of 'Africa for the Africans', and the vision of a black republic spread across the continent, his approach linked back to the Ethiopian movements and forward to Black Consciousness. Garvey quickly gained followers in South Africa. In the 1920s they included millennium groups who preached the coming of a fleet bringing black Americans to liberate the continent. With pardonable exaggeration Nathan Ntengo wrote: 'Even the deaf, dumb and half dead have caught the vision of Mr Garvey that Africa must be freed from the hands of the exploiters' (Hill and Pirio 1987: 227). Even if not among the 'half dead', Garvey's influence certainly spread into the ANC and the ICU. In the ANC James Theale radicalized the Western Cape branch – endorsing the call for 'Africa for the Africans'. In August 1922, he declared that 'the salvation of our race [and] the Negro races throughout the world does not depend on the white man; but solely depends upon the Negroes themselves'. The ANC's newspaper *Abantu Batho* commended Garvey's warning that 'the only avenue through and by which the Negro will win the respect of the world is by self-exertion and contribution in the founding of a Black Government by black men for black men' (Hill and Pirio 1987: 232/237).

Garvey's ideas overlapped with those of the communist party once Moscow declared in favour of a Native Republic (see below). The various strands – Garveyism, communism and Congress – were linked together through individual members; such as Gumede, who was described in a police report as 'one of the most dangerous agitators in the country, who not only works for the communist party but also corresponds with Marcus Garvey' (Hill and Pirio 1987: 237). Inevitably the government became concerned with the spread of Garveyism, which challenged not only white control in South Africa but imperial control across the continent. In 1923, when reports were received that Garvey was planning a visit to Africa, Pretoria immediately declared him a prohibited immigrant. However, it was not only the white government that saw him as a threat. The first warning Pretoria received about Garvey came in 1920 from another Afro-American, Samuel Augustus Duncan, who had broken away from UNIA. Duncan stated that Garvey was 'engaged in the most destructive and pernicious propaganda to create disturbances between whites and coloured people in the British possession' (Hill and Pirio 1987: 223). In 1930 Bishop G. B. Young of Texas, told a Methodist Conference to stop complaining and instead use the opportunities that existed for that was 'how the American Negro has made it and you will have to come along the same road' (Walshe 1987: 164). Duncan and Young reflected a more moderate stream of Afro-American advice, which advocated racial co-operation and harmony. Similar external black advice came from James Aggrey from the Gold Coast. Aggrey, who arrived in South Africa in March 1921 with the Phelp-Stokes Education Commission, spoke strongly against Garvey. While he urged Africans to help themselves, it was within a Christian context of racial co-operation, and encouraged the formation of Joint Councils between whites and Africans. He told an audience at Lovedale College: 'Do not have anything to do with Marcus Garvey.' Instead he urged them to have faith in the spirit of union and British justice, so that 'before long South Africa will be the best place on earth for white and black; so that Great Britain may lead the whole world' (Hill and Pirio 1987: 229).

The Communist Party of South Africa (CPSA)

As its clashes with the ICU indicated another newcomer to the scene was the Communist Party of South Africa (CPSA). Founded in July 1921 as a white workers' party, by the merging of a number of Marxist groups, it was from the beginning a faithful subordinate of the Moscow based Communist International (Comintern). It was a further example of an external ideology penetrating, and shaping, South African politics. However, inevitably the communists faced dilemmas in matching their global vision with the local situation. For instance, South Africa's working class was far from a united body. It was composed of whites, who enjoyed certain privileges – but were themselves divided between European immigrants and Afrikaners drawn off the land – and blacks, most of whom were migrant workers. The CPSA actively supported the 1922 white miners' strike – calling on white workers to unite. That turned out badly, for not only did the strike fail, but it set worker against worker on racial lines. As far as the CPSA was concerned that was remedied in 1924 when it opened its doors to all races; after which it fought against racial discrimination.

Unlike the ICU, the CPSA was never a mass party. It aimed at commitment not size, and gained its black members through diligent organization, night classes, and targetted trade union activity. By 1928 it had an estimated 1,750 members of whom 1,600 were Africans, but the whites retained a powerful influence disproportionate to their numbers. The members were dedicated and tough. They spread their influence both directly through party activity, and by penetrating other movements. Like other political organizations the CPSA suffered from internal disputes and squabbles. These were exacerbated by the resistance it encountered within established black movements to an alien doctrine, and by the intervention of Moscow.

The Soviet leaders saw South Africa as part of its global stage, as an opportunity to attack British imperialism and capitalism through support for a colonial nationalist movement. In South Africa's case that was linked to three important decisions. First, in 1927 a directive from Moscow stated that the party must fight to establish an 'independent native republic'. Second, in 1928 the Comintern labelled South Africa as a colonial situation of a special kind, in which the colonialists were based inside the country. Third, Moscow decided that the Union would have to pass through the earlier stage of establishing the native republic, before moving to a socialist state. The 1928 decision called for a 'Native Republic as a stage towards a workers' and peasants' Government with full protection and equal rights for national minorities'. This would involve 'the return of the land to the landless', liberation from British imperialism, and the formation of a workers and peasants' government (Walshe 1987: 177). The CPSA's task was 'to influence the embryonic and crystallising national movements among the natives' (Bundy 1987: 261). It saw nationalism not as an end in itself but as a stage towards a socialist society. The existing capitalist/imperialist state was to be overthrown by a revolutionary movement which would establish a transitional state based on black nationalism. In time that would give way to a workers' state which would be part of the global socialist movement.

In pressing its aims the CPSA was told to pay particular attention to the ANC – aiming 'to transform it into a fighting nationalist, revolutionary organisation against the white bourgeoisie and British imperialists' (Ellis and Sechaba 1992: 18). It therefore infiltrated members into the ANC and recruited from inside Congress. Josiah Gumede, a founder member of the ANC, and a member of the 1918–19 delegation to London and Versailles, exemplifies this. He returned to South Africa in 1919 a disillusioned man. However, the gloom lifted in 1927, when Gumede visited the Soviet Union for the first time. On his return he told a Cape Town ANC audience that African people had a choice – either to accept imperialism, which had inflicted terrible suffering on them, or to unite 'with the only country in the world where freedom existed, and that country is Workers' Russia'. James Thaele, who chaired the meeting, and was himself a communist, urged members to realize that the communists 'were the real friends of the oppressed people' (Walshe 1987: 175). That call was heeded when Gumede was elected ANC President, although, as noted above, he faced strong opposition and his period in office was relatively short.

In contrast with Gumede's claim that freedom existed in the Soviet Union, Moscow's attempts to impose discipline and ideological uniformity on the CPSA led to considerable internal tensions and strains. Fierce internal disputes became common. Some members, for example, continued to challenge the step-by-step approach of seeking a native republic before moving to socialism. In 1929 Douglas Wolton, following a visit to Moscow, drew up a list of 'right-wing opportunists and deviationists', including such prominent figures as S. P. Bunting, and J. A. LaGuma, who were then expelled from the party. The full extent of Moscow's iron discipline was illustrated by the fate of three intransigent CPSA members – Lazar Back and the brothers Maurice and Paul Richter. They went to the Soviet Union in the mid-1930s to seek support for their position in a domestic SACP quarrel. In Moscow they were first detained, then arrested, and in 1938 the Richters were executed, while Back died in a concentration camp in 1941 (Ellis and Sechaba 1992: 20).

Yet, despite their small numbers, despite the factions and quarrels, and despite Moscow's ruthlessness, communism with its seductive message and its discipline persisted to exercise a considerable influence in South Africa's politics.

8

From Pact to Fusion: Economic Depression and Black Opposition, 1929–1939

When Hertzog called an election in 1929 the Pact Government went to the polls with confidence. It had presided over a period of increasing white prosperity and achieved many of its original objectives. It appealed to the electorate on the grounds of economic success, industrial peace, balanced budgets, the achievement of international equality of status, and the promotion of the Afrikaans language. But above all, its main theme at the election was 'the Black Peril'. Repeating its determination to resolve the Native question once and for all, the government campaigned on the black threat to white supremacy. It claimed that white civilization was endangered by Smuts and the SAP, because they stood for equality between black and white. They did not. Smuts and his party also believed in white supremacy, but their message was less simplistic and emotional than the NP's. In 1924 Smuts had explained: 'My whole political effort and public life . . . has been to establish and tender firm and secure white civilisation', but if 'we want to enrich our position merely as a white oligarchy by getting round us a ring fence of hate from all the other communities in South Africa, we shall have a very hard and difficult row to hoe in future. That is not the way to establish a white South Africa' (Hancock 1968: 209). Then shortly before the 1929 election Smuts spoke of creating in the future a British confederation of states – a 'great African Dominion stretching unbroken throughout Africa'. The NP seized on this. They ignored the fact that Smuts had said he was committed to white control of the proposed confederation, and instead denounced him as an 'apostle of a black Kaffir state . . . extending from the Cape to Egypt'. To vote Smuts, they said, was to vote black (Hancock 1968: 218).

The election was a triumph for the NP. It won 78 seats against 62 for the SAP, 8 Labour, and 1 Independent. The Pact continued but Labour was much weaker. More than ever it was the junior partner. It had suffered losses because many Afrikaner workers had heeded the NP's message that it was the party that could serve both their economic and nationalist needs. With the NP in the ascendant the government looked secure. However, dark economic clouds lay on the horizon. Like the rest of the world South Africa was struck by the Great Depression which began in 1929. The impact was not as severe as in some other parts of the world, and was uneven between different industries, but it was severe enough, and caused great misery for many people of all races. The government tried to erect protective barriers but could not deflect the storm. Between 1928/1929 and 1931/1932 the national income dropped by 19 per cent. The gold mines survived well, but diamonds suffered badly, as did agriculture, especially farmers who relied on the export trade. Unemployment increased sharply among all races. By September 1933 roughly 22 per cent of white and Coloured men (188,000 in all) were unemployed, and they included many who were driven from the land. The Carnegie Commission, which reported in 1932, found that 30 per cent of white families were 'so poor they cannot adequately feed or house their children' (O'Meara 1983: 37). However, the commission rejected the views of Afrikaner militants that the problem could be placed on the doorstep of British imperialism and capitalism. There were no statistics for African unemployment, but it was substantial. The 'civilized labour' policy, which sought to cushion white unemployment by replacing black labour by white, was designed to force Africans back to the reserves. But the reserves were overcrowded and impoverished, so that, despite the government's efforts, many blacks made their way to the edges of towns and cities, forming unemployed squatter communities, which heightened white fears of 'the black peril' (Liebenberg and Spies 1993: 245). The economic crisis formed the stage for the political developments of the time.

When Britain, in response to the depression, left the gold standard in September 1931 a fierce debate ensued about whether the Union should follow suit. The debate concerned economic policy, but it had a parallel agenda – the Union's status in relation to Britain. Pretoria decided not to follow Britain, partly because of the economic advice it received and partly to demonstrate its independence. However, the SAP, the business sector and Teleman Roos (a former NP member who re-emerged to lead the campaign) urged the government to follow London, as money started to stream out of the country. By the end of 1932 the stream had become a flood. Under enormous pressure, and with the prospect of ruin ahead, the government recanted and left the gold standard. An improvement in the economic situation followed almost immediately. However, the crisis had been so profound that it left the government stunned and vulnerable.

In the wake of the crisis Smuts proposed the formation of a broadly based coalition government. Although he and Hertzog had been political opponents for more than twenty years, and had differed recently on the gold standard question, paradoxically the aftermath of the crisis underlined their common ground rather than their differences. In the context of the crisis their past disputes appeared to be of emphasis rather than direction, of means rather than ends. Both believed in white supremacy; both supported the development of a white nation drawn from the two cultures; and both had shown themselves leading practitioners of political partnership – Smuts with the UP and Hertzog with Labour. Even in relations with Britain there was common ground. In the past Hertzog had feared British domination, but for him the Balfour Declaration had disposed of that. Yet, while Hertzog was sympathetic to Smuts's approach, others in the NP were not. Since Hertzog's acceptance of the Balfour Declaration many republicans in the party had lost faith in him.

Malan opposed a coalition with Smuts because he believed it would dilute national-ist principles. However, despite that opposition and despite hesitation among some SAP members, Hertzog decided to accept Smuts's proposal. In public he said that 'the nation' favoured a coalition, and economic conditions demanded it; but he confided to NP members his fears that if they rejected the offer the NP would be defeated at the next election. 'We will,' he said, 'suffer defeat and it will be the end of Afrikanerdom' (Muller 1969: 368). The agreement went ahead. A government was formed with Hertzog as Prime Minister, Smuts his deputy, and a cabinet composed of six members from each party. Points of agreed principles were published – including the Union's independent status; equal language rights for English and Afrikaans; a civilized labour policy; and a Native policy based on sepa-rate political development. In February 1933 the new government was formed, and an election called for May.

Fusion: The Formation of the United Party

In the election the governing coalition parties gained an overwhelming majority, with 144 seats against 6 for the opposition (including 2 Labour and 2 Natal Home Rulers). With such strength in numbers, and the administration working effectively, Hertzog and Smuts discussed the prospect of fusion between the two parties. Hertzog's perception of the political scene had changed. Now he believed that the SAP and their English-speaking supporters were prepared to accept 'South Africa first', as well as equality between the language groups. Nor did he still fear imperial or English cultural domination. To underline that point he referred to an amend-ment in the SAP programme, which stressed that even though a member of the British Empire, the Union had no obligation to other countries which would derogate from its independent status. Nothing remained to divide the parties, said Hertzog, except fear that they would deceive each other. That he dismissed. He saw no reason why English and Afrikaans speakers could not 'work together in all respects' (Moodie 1975: 119).

Yet differences had to be surmounted before fusion was possible. Smuts, for example, reacted angrily at Hertzog's early efforts to reassure the hard-line NP members clustered around D. F. Malan. Even when that was settled disagreements of principle remained about the divisibility of the crown, the right to neutrality in war and the right of secession from the Commonwealth; and there were differences of emphasis over Native policy. In the end pragmatism triumphed. Both were committed to white supremacy, both were concerned to stabilize the economy, and they agreed to disagree on the constitutional issues because they assumed that such issues were unlikely to arise. The two parties therefore gave unanimous support to the Status Bill which formalized the Union's sovereignty, recognized her free association to the Commonwealth, and confirmed the Union's Parliament and government as the sole legislative and executive authorities. However, ambiguity persisted. For Smuts the Status Act not only legalized existing practice, but tied the Union more closely to the Empire – in which 'the freedom of the parts is making for the salvation of the whole'. For Hertzog the Act was a new, positive step to underlining the Union's independence and removing the old constitutional disputes (O'Meara 1983: 47).

Given that background it was not surprising that despite Hertzog's and Smuts's best efforts opposition to fusion developed in both the parties. The constitutional issues on which they agreed to disagree had been, and would continue to be, central to the dispute between the party of white conciliation, and the party of Afrikaner nationalism. Within the SAP suspicion of Hertzog persisted. Some from the party's English-speaking wing saw fusion as a plot to weaken the British link, and the more determined of them rallied behind Colonel Charles Stallard to break away and form the Dominion Party. A greater split arose in the NP. The Nationalist critics of fusion, led by Malan, refused to push aside such prickly issues as the right to neutrality and secession. They oppposed fusion on principle. For them nationalism and unity had to be based on an exclusive Afrikaner unity. Nor did they accept that the Statute of Westminster offered full independence. Their aim was an independent republic. They were affronted by the symbols of imperialism – flag, anthem, and the sovereign's head on coins and stamps – which they saw as continuing signs of humiliation. How, they asked, could English speakers be true South Africans when they paid allegiance elsewhere?

Despite the divisions Hertzog and Smuts reached agreement. In June 1934 Hertzog published their 'Programme of Principles', which he had drafted personally. It was a mixture of precise points and vague ideas, covering constitutional, economic and social issues. The guiding purpose of the new party, it said, was to develop 'a predominant sense of South African national unity, based on the equality of the Afrikaans-speaking and English-speaking sections of the community', while recognizing their distinctive cultural inheritance and bilingualism (Hancock 1968: 256). The programme underlined the Union's sovereign independence within the Commonwealth, and aimed at white unity, based on 'South Africa first', and 'the spiritual and cultural possession of the people' (Kruger 1969: 173). It offered freedom to advocate any form of government for South Africa, and undertook to resolve the Native question by accepting the primacy of white civilization without depriving Natives of their right to develop on separate lines. Following the acceptance of the programme fusion came about in December 1934 with the formation of the United South African National Party, usually shortened to the 'United Party' (UP). Later, under pressure from his NP critics, Hertzog confirmed that, despite accepting fusion, he would never co-operate with people 'who are not prepared to acknowledge and accept complete equality and complete justice between the English and Afrikaans sections of our People as laid down in the Programme of Principles of the United Party' (Moodie 1975: 189).

The 'Purified' National Party

Hertzog could only have met Malan's demands by abandoning his efforts to work with Smuts. He refused and the NP split. In three of the provinces a large majority of the party followed Hertzog. The Cape was different. There, under Malan's leadership, the Nationalists voted overwhelmingly against fusion. In the Transvaal only one MP followed Malan – J. G. Strijdom, a future Prime Minister, who declared that the National Party must be maintained on 'a purified foundation'. After that party members often referred to themselves as 'Purified' [Gesuiwerde] Nationalists. Like its predecessor the new NP was a federal party with clear differences between the provinces. The new party had economic as well as political and ideological interests to satisfy. Initially its main electoral base was in the Cape, where it drew support from fruit, wine and wool farmers, who complained that they did not benefit from imperial preferences. It also had backing from the infant Afrikaner financial institutions, including SANLAM, a finance and insurance group which had grown on the basis of agricultural savings, and which owned Nasionale Pers and its Cape newspaper *Die Burger*. Added to that the new NP gained support from poor farmers and the unemployed not only in the Cape but to the north, and from a rising class of petty bourgeoisie and professionals – teachers, clergymen, civil servants and small businessmen – who were 'anti imperialist, anti semitic, and anti black'. These supporters were attracted by economic as well as nationalist motives, as they waged a struggle to establish themselves in the English-speaking cities, and to ensure their own economic rewards. As Merle Lipton commented: 'economic issues – pork barrel politics – were always a prime concern of the Afrikaner national- ist movement, to the chagrin of some of its more idealistic exponents' (Lipton 1985: 269).

In parliament the new NP sat in opposition. Freed from Hertzog's compromises, sharpened by the internal controversy, and composed of committed nationalists the NP gave full rein to its 'purified' ideas. For it the soul of Afrikanerdom was at stake. 'Only in the nation as the most total, most inclusive human community can man realise himself,' declared Dr Nic Diederichs. The nation was 'the fulfilment of the individual', and Afrikaners were a 'nation', not a 'section'. 'If there is a "section" in this country,' he declared, 'then we may in all honesty say that our English fellow citizens . . . are no nation in the true sense of the word but a section of a nation overseas' (Moodie 1975: 157–9). Malan shared similar convictions: 'We hold this nationhood as our due,' he declared, 'for it was given to us by the Architect of the Universe. Afrikanerdom is not the work of man but the creation of God' (Moodie 1975: 1).

In furthering its ideas the NP was determined to avoid class divisions among Afrikaners. The aim was to build a united, exclusive nation. The leaders knew that if they could hold the volk together demography among whites was on their side. The 1936 census revealed that for every 100 English speakers over the age of 21 there were already 115 Afrikaners. More significantly, for the future – for every 100 English speakers aged between 7 and 21 there were 185 Afrikaners, and for every 100 English speakers under 7 there were 212 Afrikaners (Stultz 1974: 93). Malan spoke of a second Great Trek, this time to the towns. In the past, he said, Afrikaner destiny had been worked out on the veld; now it was in towns and it must not be allowed to divide the nation (Moodie 1975: 201). Diederichs claimed that the worker was the 'most reliable Afrikaner. He must be drawn into the nation to be a genuine man. There must be no division or schism between class and class'. The danger, he said, came from forces seeking to unite the Afrikaner worker with the proletariat of other lands: 'the headquarters of this movement is in Moscow'

(Moodie 1975: 168). Geoff Cronje warned: 'We must not allow the city Afrikaner to become a different kind of Afrikaner from his fellow on the farm.' The NP's declared aim was not to overthrow capitalism but to gain a rightful share of its spoils; to 'mobilise the People to conquer this system and transform it so it fits our ethnic nature' (Moodie 1975: 203–4). To these ends the NP therefore encouraged the development of Afrikaner businesses, banks and insurance companies.

Hertzog attacked the extremism of the purified NP and the increasing influence of the Broederbond. His fears were fuelled when Van Rooy, the Bond chairman, urged the Broeders to pursue political as well as cultural aims, including 'a completely independent, truly Afrikaans government for South Africa'. The main object, he said, is 'that Afrikanerdom shall reach its ultimate destiny of domination in South Africa' (Adam and Giliomee 1979: 112). In pursuing these aims the Broeders succeeded in cutting out its dead wood, and recruiting an increasing number of the Afrikaner elite: teachers, lawyers, clergy, civil servants and university staff. By the late 1920s academics from the University of Potchefstroom were playing a leading role, infusing a rigorous brand of conservative Calvinism. 'A picture emerges of an immense informal network of influence in all regions and in all sections of the Afrikaner community . . . organized into a militant, highly disciplined body' (O'Meara 1983: 64). But Hertzog would have none of it. He accused the Broeders of aiming not only at cultural development but political power: nothing less, said Hertzog, than control of the state. He reproached them for causing white disunity, for 'awakening irreconcilable aversion and hatred between the races' (Afrikaans and English speakers), and using language, religion and history 'to fight, slander and crush one another' (Le May 1995: 179). The NP and the Broederbond were, he said, two sides of the same coin. He named Malan as a Broeder, an identity to which Malan admitted with pride.

Despite the committed opposition of the NP the fusion government prospered. The mid to late 1930s was a period of economic growth, with a steady rise in the price of gold, agricultural price stability and the development of secondary industry. The government took advantage of the situation to build up the country's infrastructure (tarred roads, airways, improved harbours), to establish new services (including the South African Broadcasting Corporation), and to improve the lot of poor whites. The result was increased urbanization, leading to more day-to-day contact between the races, more pragmatism, but also more prejudice and the undermining of white hopes of greater segregation. The reward for the government's economic success and its reconciliation of Afrikaans and English speakers came in a renewed mandate at the 1938 election. In the campaign the NP concentrated on racial issues, claiming that it alone would keep South Africa secure for whites. It promised legislation to prevent mixed marriages and to enforce urban residential segregation. Although the NP gained seven extra seats it was far behind the UP in terms of votes: 448,000 for the UP to the NP's 240,000. In numbers of seats the party positions after the election were (with previous seats in brackets); UP 111 (117); NP 27 (20); Dominion 8 (5); Labour 3 (4); Independent 1 (4).

The NP had certainly not lost ground. The election had confirmed it as the vehicle of a revived Afrikaner nationalism. Hertzog himself had underestimated the strength and attraction of this appeal to an exclusive identity. He retained his

conviction that Afrikaner speakers alone could not constitute the nation. In defiance of his views the NP was given an enormous boost by the Great Trek
centenary celebration of 1938. The government helped to fund the festivities but
the NP highjacked them. Henning Klopper, a leading Broederbond member, who
helped initiate the celebrations, set the tone by declaring that the future belonged
to the Afrikaners if they could unite. He saw past disasters, suffering and adversity
as 'some of the best means in God's hand to form a people' (Le May 1995: 182).
The culmination came on 16 December – The Day of the Covenant – with
ceremonies at Blood River, and an even larger one at the laying of the foundation
stone for the Voortrekker monument outside Pretoria. More than 100,000 people
(perhaps ten per cent of the Afrikaner population) were present, but Hertzog did
not attend as he was not invited to speak, and Smuts was there only in a private
capacity. Surrounded by symbols of Afrikaner nationalism, a wave of patriotic
emotion and enthusiasm welled up which persisted after the ceremonies, and helped
the NP's cause. Malan wrote: 'Genuine religion, unadulterated freedom, and the
pure preservation of one's white race and civilization are essential requirements for
our own People's existence. Without this the South African people can have no
soul and also no future' (Thompson 1985: 40).

Hertzog's Native Bills

Although the UP government was committed to white control there were internal
differences of emphasis in its policy towards Africans. Smuts had an evolutionist
approach. Unlike Hertzog, he still believed that it was impossible to lay down a
permanent solution. As a result, he was taunted by critics as either having no
policy or of wanting a 'Kaffir state'. The truth was that Native Affairs were not high
enough on Smuts's agenda to resist Hertzog when the Prime Minister revived his
1927 proposals. Previously these proposals had run into the sand, because a change
in the Cape franchise required a two-thirds majority of both Houses of Parliament
sitting together. Hertzog had been unable to achieve that, but substantial inroads
had already been made into the effectiveness of the Cape African vote by increasing
the size of the European electorate. In 1930 the Women's Enfranchisement Bill
gave the vote to white but not black women. In the following year the Franchise
Laws Amendment Act removed 'civilization tests' for white men but not for blacks.
The result was that by 1935 African voters had been reduced to 2.5 per cent of the
Cape electorate. However, Hertzog was not content. He clung to the principles in
his earlier bills, and now with the combined strength of the United Party behind
him he could act.

A parliamentary committee reported in favour of concentrating on two bills
rather than the four which Hertzog had favoured in 1927. Hertzog accepted this
and in 1936 laid the two bills before parliament – one concerned with political
representation, the other with land. The Native Representative Act removed
Africans from the Cape voters' roll. Instead they would elect three white representatives to the House of Assembly, and Africans from all four provinces would
indirectly elect four whites to the Senate, and to a Native Representative Council.

The second piece of legislation, the Native Trust and Land Act, enlarged the Reserves from the existing 10.4 million to 17.6 million morgen, as previously proposed in 1927. It also imposed further limits on Africans outside the Reserves. In introducing the bills Hertzog was opposed by a handful of liberal UP members, including a cabinet member, Jan Hofmeyr. Hofmeyr criticized the concept of communal representation, because, he said, it 'implies a divergence of interests between Europeans and non Europeans', whereas, he said, their interests were common. He warned against sowing the seeds of future conflict (Paton 1964: 227).

Hofmeyr's stand challenged the very principle of segregation. In contrast, the NP criticized Hertzog's proposals because they did not push segregation far enough. Malan led the attack. He opposed not only any form of African representation in parliament, but the establishment of a Native Representative Council and the transfer of land to the Reserves. Despite that Hertzog gained the necessary majorities for both pieces of legislation. Significantly, however, he had failed to rally support for his original scheme for the Coloureds. In an atmosphere of increasing white prejudice – with demands that Coloureds be placed on a separate roll – Hertzog's proposals were too liberal for most of the UP as well as the NP. The fate of the proposals for Coloureds reflected a period of deteriorating race relations. One reason for this was the changing socio-economic scene. In 1932 the Native Economic Commission reported an alarming situation in the Reserves; with overstocking, erosion and an inability to feed the growing population, driving more people to the towns. Africans, like Afrikaners, were becoming an increasingly urban people. By 1936 1.7m Africans were living in the urban areas, which was double that of 1911 (Kruger 1969: 182). Yet, while whites wanted blacks to provide labour in the urban areas, they still resented and tried to resist the social consequences that followed. The result was that increasing formal restrictions were placed on urban blacks, and, as a consequence, increasing conflict arose between blacks and the authorities.

Black Opposition to Segregation

Among whites an element of controversy persisted over Hertzog's Native Bills. Considerable ambiguity still clung to 'segregation', but overall it was accepted as the basis of policy towards blacks. Segregation also continued to pose problems for blacks. As in the past there remained a diversity of views. In their frustration, and the uncertainty of what they could do, black leaders took divergent and sometimes conflicting stands. The role of the mainstream churches was one point of dispute. The Synod of the Church of South Africa rejected segregation, stating that the country was 'irretrievably both White and Black, and the two elements in her body politic are necessary to each other and are mutually interdependent'. However, despite that and the continuing commitment to Christianity among many black leaders, communists and radicals criticized the church. Kadalie claimed that it had been thoroughly reactionary and had always sided with the rich against the poor (Walshe 1987: 161–2). Similar differences were found between those blacks who favoured co-operation across race lines, and those who believed that only by standing alone could blacks succeed. James Thaele regularly attacked European paternalism and called for Africans to stand alone. He criticized the 'white' churches and called for the establishment of a united church bringing together the separatist black churches. Alongside that, chronic tension continued about the influence of communists.

Many of these differences were buried, at least for the time being, in opposition to Hertzog's Native policy. There were, however, organizational problems. The ICU had collapsed, the SACP was riven by internal disputes – its membership falling to between 200–300 – while the ANC, under Seme's cautious conservative leadership, was almost moribund. In their place a new broad-based body was formed – the All Africa Convention (AAC) – which brought together leaders from the four provinces and a variety of organizations – including the ANC and what remained of the ICU. At the AAC's first meeting, in December 1935, 400 delegates assembled at Bloemfontein, under the chairmanship of Professor D. D. T. Jabavu. The meeting condemned Hertzog's proposals, saying that they were not designed to promote harmony and peace; instead their logical outcome 'will be the creation of two nations in South Africa, whose interests and aspirations must inevitably clash and lead to conflict'. Segregation was dismissed as unjust and impracticable. The only way it could be implemented fairly was through the creation of two separate states, which was not desirable and in any case was not proposed by the government. It was wrong, stated the meeting, to place the destiny of the underprivileged in the hands of a dominant group however well intentioned that group. Pretoria's proposals denied blacks participation in government, which was not only unjust but would inflame passions and cause discontent. The government's assertion of a permanent trusteeship role relegated Africans to the status of a child race. In place of segregation, the AAC called for a common citizenship in a single state. The way forward, it stated, was the 'creation of a South African nation, in which, while the various groups may develop on their own lines socially and culturally, they will be bound together by the pursuit of common political objectives'. The interests of all South Africans were 'inextricably interwoven', and the attempt to deal with people separately was bound to defeat itself (Karis and Carter 1973: 31–4).

The AAC sent a delegation to Pretoria to press its case. It was received politely, but Hertzog was unmoved. He explained to parliament that the 'first duty of the white man is to himself. Whatever the rights of the Natives may be, they have no right to call upon us to do anything which might jeopardise our supremacy'. Arrangements for African representation must not conflict with the white man's authority (Walshe 1987: 121–3). This rejection placed the AAC's moderate leaders in a quandary. When Jabavu reported to the AAC's 1936 conference, he spoke of the collapse of European morality, which, he said, had been further demonstrated by Hertzog's assertion of dominant self-interest. Jabavu declared that most white members of parliament had descended to the level of the jungle. The result was that while Africans had asked for legitimate rights they had imposed on them legislation 'embodying our own political inferiority and segregation'.

Jabavu was facing the eternal dilemma of the liberal confronted by intransigence. What should they do? Should they boycott the new arrangements as unacceptable, or should they participate while continuing to protest, or should they preach open defiance and resistance? Jabavu confessed that they were confronted by a greater problem than ever before. He repeated the demands of the last meeting, but offered no clear means of achieving them. However, his tone was more militant than in the past. If segregation and the colour bar remained, he told the delegates, 'we want a separate State of our own where we shall rule ourselves freed from the present hypocritical position'. He spoke of blacks using their economic strength to boycott white businesses; of a policy of 'bottled revenge', designed to shake whites out of their complacency, and he even discussed open resistance to the government – of trying to win 'our rights by using the fear of bloody revolution'. However, he counselled against that, because it would end in disaster. The African movements of the day, he stated, had neither the organization nor the mass support to take matters further (Karis and Carter 1973: 18–19). Jabavu had identified the major problem facing black leaders. They were united in opposition to the government's policies but what tactics could they and should they employ?

In responding to that question a new militancy could be detected even among those who previously had adopted a moderate approach. It was captured in a pamphlet – *The Crisis* – in which Selby Msimang (the General Secretary of the AAC) expressed indignation at the exclusion of Africans. We have been treated, he wrote, as rebels in our own country. He concluded that Africans could no longer loyally serve a government 'which has openly disowned us and told us in brutal language that we can never, never be free'. The government must be resisted even if it meant going to prison. There were two alternatives. First to accept segregation – that European and African interests were different. If that were the case then Africans must demand 'a complete segregation on a fifty-fifty basis to enable us to establish our own state and government', and it must be a territorially consolidated state, not one of islands dotted all over the country. That, he said, would not be the choice of Africans, but, if whites were committed to segregation, they could not have it both ways and therefore should establish two states. Alternatively Africans should take their fate in their own hands. The method required 'no machine guns, no bombs, no aeroplanes', but will, determination and constant agitation. It would be necessary to educate Africans to make them aware of their subordinate position, and inculcate self-reliance. Paradoxically, argued Msimang, Hertzog's policy may have behind it the hand of fate by bringing Africans together to exercise their strength. 'May we live to see,' he concluded, 'the history of the overthrow of the Russian Empire by the governed repeated in our own Fatherland' (Karis and Carter 1973: 57/61).

With militancy in the air, protest meetings were held, strong resolutions passed, new methods discussed and proposals made for action; but there was neither a body organized to take militant action, nor leaders thirsting for a fight. That was the situation in the ANC. Pixley Seme, as President, went out of his way to emphasize co-operation between black and white, and within the African community he worked closely with the chiefs. Under Seme, who gave little time to political activities because of his busy lawyer's practice in Johannesburg, the ANC went into decline, and split into competing factions. In 1933 the Bloemfontein Congress was only attended by 69 delegates, of whom 37 came from the local area (Walshe 1987: 254). Membership figures are unreliable, because accurate records were not kept, and some members failed to pay dues, but even so the picture was bleak. Dr Silas Molema estimated that the ANC's total paid-up membership was only 253: and Govan Mbeki sadly recorded that in Natal 'Congress is dying' (Meli 1988: 88). 'Is it worth continuing?' was a question Rev James Calata asked as he toured branches across the country in 1936. His hesitant reply was 'Yes', but it was a discouraging scene.

Congress was kept alive by the efforts of local leaders, and conscientious, if moderate men like Calata, who was President of the Cape Province, and Rev Z. R. Mahabane, who succeeded Seme in 1937, to become national President for the second time (He had previously served between 1924 and 1927.) In the late 1930s, under their leadership, the ANC began a slow revival. It was done by appealing to established values – Christian beliefs, respect for chiefs and common citizenship – and by using the few legal channels open to Africans. Like other bodies the ANC had to decide whether or not to participate in the government's new structure. Again there was division. Mahabane favoured participation, and even described the Native Representative Council as the 'official mouthpiece of the African people'. Similar divisions were found in the AAC, where the majority of leaders shared the moderate views of Mahabane. When the AAC met in December 1937 four members of the Native Representative Council (NRC) were among its leading figures. A policy statement, written by Professor Jabavu and Msimang, explicitly recognized members who had been elected to government bodies as 'the accepted mouthpiece of Africans in their various representative State Chambers'. Other members of the NRC were encouraged to attend AAC meetings to discover African views on a variety of issues and to gain a mandate. The ANC adopted a similar approach, and also gave its support to the Native representatives in parliament, nominating Dr D. Molteno and Margaret Ballinger. When Molteno was returned Congress members chaired him through the streets of Cape Town, and Mahabane wrote to Ballinger to express confidence in her as 'our representative' (Walshe 1987: 256). Moderation reigned.

Part III

World War II and Apartheid

9

World War II and its
Aftermath, 1939–1948

Britain's declaration of war against Germany in September 1939 split the Fusion Government apart. Five cabinet members supported Hertzog in opting for neutrality; six backed Smuts's call to fight. When Hertzog introduced a neutrality motion into the House of Assembly, Smuts countered with an amendment proposing participation in the war. In a dramatic confrontation Smuts triumphed by 80 votes to 67. Hertzog immediately asked the Governor General to dissolve parliament and call an election. He refused. Instead, he invited Smuts to form a government. Smuts then led the Union into the war, and was backed by the majority of the UP, plus the Labour and Dominion parties. However, Hertzog took 38 UP MPs into opposition. Fusion had floundered on the rocks of war.

The war exposed the very questions that Hertzog and Smuts had pushed aside when they had fused their parties: neutrality and loyalty to the crown. Now they could not be ignored. For Hertzog the struggle was between distant European powers and of no concern to South Africa; for Smuts it impinged directly on the Union, because she could not cut herself off from international affairs. For him it was in South Africa's own interests to support Britain and further she had an obligation to do so through the crown. Keith Hancock contrasted the two approaches by the use of the word 'We'. For Hertzog it simply meant 'We South Africans'. For Smuts 'We' meant '"We South Africans", "We members of the Commonwealth," "We free men," "We humans"' (Hancock 1968: 313). Hertzog believed that if South Africa entered the war it was because a section of whites cared more for Britain than South Africa. To allow such a view to prevail would undermine the principle of sovereignty and the two-stream unity for which he had struggled all his political life. For Smuts the Union could not afford to be isolated in a dangerous world, in which there was no limit to Hitler's, and later Japan's, ambitions. Safety lay in fighting with Britain and the Commonwealth. He could see no alternative, but he recognized the price to be paid at home. 'Smuts risked the policy of "conciliation" and the future of domestic politics of the Union in order that South Africa might contribute to the defeat of Hitler' (Stultz 1974: 66).

War again reopened old wounds, leading to bitter personal divisions among whites. Serving soldiers and militant Afrikaner nationalists had fist fights in the streets. Most English speakers and a good number of Afrikaners supported Smuts, but many Afrikaners opposed him. Some Nationalists not only believed that Hitler would win, but were sympathetic to him and his national socialist creed. But it was hatred of Britain rather than support for Germany that was their main motivation. Their feelings were later captured by Annie Swardt. 'The thought,' she said, 'of South African, and especially Afrikaner soldiers fighting England's war against Germany was totally abhorrent to me. At that time the dominant forces in my own life were my hatred of England, my love of South Africa and my desire for a republic' (D'Oliveira 1977: 51). South Africa's best hope, such people argued, was to cut its ties with Britain. A student journal at Potchefstroom University stated that not only was it unjust for South Africa to 'wage war against a friendly nation [Germany], but we have . . . to support our only foreign enemy! For no nation other than England has ever threatened our existence' (Moodie 1975: 192).

In the tense war atmosphere, and with opposition to Smuts's government to bind them, Malan and Hertzog set out to rebuild their political relationship Hertzog spoke of 'co-operation between the . . . two parts of national minded Afrikanerdom' (Muller 1969: 376). However, standing in their way were issues related to nationalism and republicanism. Despite his sense of betrayal at the decision to go to war Hertzog continued to advocate the two streams approach, convinced that only mutual respect and tolerance could build a sound white nation. With regard to a republic it was not a pressing issue for him. He wanted individual party members to be free to express different views; he was opposed to any move until it was backed by a substantial majority of whites; and he rejected any suggestion to bypass parliament. Finally he did not want to break with the Commonwealth. Two months after the declaration of war he said he would not 'be placed in the category of those who desired to break all constitutional ties with Britain' (Roberts and Trollip 1947: 22). With varying degrees of intensity most NP members disagreed with him. Many argued that if the English speakers were not prepared to assimilate to an Afrikaner way of life they must accept an inferior civic status; and many favoured a full commitment to republicanism. To achieve that they were prepared, and some even eager, to break with Britain.

Despite such differences Malan and Hertzog reached sufficient agreement to reunite, including postponement of the republican issue. They took the view that in such a critical situation and, despite their differences, they should combine on the bigger issues. At the NP's Cape Congress in December 1939 Malan's proposal that Hertzog should become leader of the reunited National Party was accepted. Yet tension persisted. Many of Malan's supporters believed that Hertzog lacked true nationalist conviction. Men like Strijdom and Verwoerd thought it impossible to work with him when there was such a gulf of principle, and some openly acted against the spirit of the Malan/Hertzog agreement. N. J. van der Merwe and C. R. Swart arranged a national gathering to consider ways of establishing a republic; while Strijdom and Swart undermined Hertzog's position with slogans like 'Stick to Principles not Leaders', and warned against slavish acceptance of the leaders' views (Muller 1969: 378).

The discontent intensified as German armies swept across Europe. In the belief that Britain would lose the war and the Commonwealth collapse, a new sense of urgency arose in the NP to take advantage of Britain's weakness and to avoid association with a defeated power. In July 1940 Hertzog and Malan protested against continued participation in the war, and called for demonstrations in favour of peace. Militant NP members wanted more – they wanted to abandon the constitutional procedures advocated by Hertzog, commit the NP to support an independent republic and leave the war. A campaign was launched to undermine Herzog's position. Although Malan was not personally involved in it he was increasingly sympathetic to the militants. Matters came to a head at the Free State Congress in November 1940. Hertzog, who was the party leader in the Free State, proposed that under any new constitution there should be equality between English and Afrikaans speakers. He was heavily defeated. He therefore resigned and soon afterwards withdrew from parliament, convinced that after all his years of leadership there was no place left for his brand of Afrikaner nationalism. Hertzog died shortly afterwards, in November 1942. Of the MPs who had followed him against Smuts in 1939, 10 joined a new party, the Afrikaner Party, based on Hertzog's principles, 2 returned to Smuts and the remainder stayed with the NP.

Despite Hertzog's disappearance Afrikaner nationalism was deeply divided. As well as internal NP divisions, there were now Hertzog's disciples in the Afrikaner Party and 'right wing' movements had sprung up – including the New Order and the Ossewa Brandwag (OB). Malan's greatest threat was the OB. Its origins were in the 1938 Trek celebrations. After the wagons had passed through Bloemfontein a group of enthusiasts, led by Dominee C. R. Kotze, formed the OB to perpetuate the trek spirit. From the beginning it had a military stamp, based on the Voortrekker commando system, but it claimed to be a cultural movement operating in parallel with the NP. Its first Commandant General, Colonel J. C. C. Laas, stated that its objectives included: 'The perpetuation of the spirit of the ox wagon . . . giving expression to the traditions and principles of the Dutch Afrikaner; protecting and promoting the religious cultural and material interests of the Afrikaner; [and] fostering patriotism and national pride.' These ends would be achieved by festivals, erecting memorials, military exercises, folk dances, music and drama, and by fostering Afrikaner history and literature (Roberts and Trollip 1947: 73 and 231).

Laas was succeeded in December 1939 by Dr J. F. J. (Hans) van Rensburg, an efficient organizer, and an admirer of Hitler and national socialism. Driven forward by its emotional appeal, the OB at its peak in 1942, claimed a membership of 250,000. Its most extreme element, the 'Stormjaers', launched a campaign of sabotage, to which the government responded by arresting its leading figures. At one stage 4,000 of them were in internment camps, including John Vorster (a future Prime Minister). Vorster later repeated the claim: 'We were not so much pro German, but anti English and pro Afrikaner. We wanted to be free of the English and we wanted our republic' (D'Oliveira 1977: 60). The OB not only hindered the government's war effort by forcing it to keep troops at home to guard strategic points, it was also a threat to Malan. Although it claimed to be a cultural movement, Malan recognized its political ambitions, and was not prepared to accept a parallel movement which recruited separately and claimed to represent Afrikaner nationalism. When the OB issued a draft republican constitution with a strong national socialist flavour, Malan dismissed it as foreign ideology with support for an authoritarian state. 'We cannot,' he said, 'ignore the fact that the kernel of national socialism is a dictatorship or, at least, the dominance of an enforced one party system.' In contrast, claimed Malan, the history of Afrikaners had been away from dictatorship. 'That is why our forefathers were Protestants, Huguenots and Voortrekkers. That is why we could become an Afrikaner nation. It is in our blood' (D'Oliveira 1977: 56). Malan therefore called on NP members to break with the OB, and his call was heeded by the great majority of the party. For the government Harry Lawrence, the Minister of the Interior, cheerfully concluded: 'Instead of the government having to ban the OB, Dr Malan has done it for us' (Roberts and Trollip 1947: 119).

Malan's struggle with the OB did not lessen his or his party's opposition to the war. Their continued condemnation of the government's war effort reached a crescendo in 1942, before the fighting turned in favour of the allies. A party congress in September 1942 discussed breaking away from Britain, and forming a republic. It asked: 'Whether South Africans were defending their own country by fighting in the Middle East?' and 'What was the Union doing fighting on the same side as communists of the Soviet Union?' It also attacked the use of blacks in the forces, even as non-combatants. At the same time, Malan outlined the party's programme. In it South Africa was to become a republic, dissociated from the crown and Empire and from any other foreign power. It would follow a path between dictatorship on the one hand and British traditions on the other. The republic would be built on the principles of Christian Nationality and offer equal cultural rights to both white language groups, while rejecting false British liberal doctrines. European civilization would be safeguarded by a policy of guardianship towards blacks, and restrictions on capitalism (Hancock 1968: 372).

In spite of such opposition at home the Union forces fought successfully. They led the defeat of Italians in Ethiopia; they fought in North Africa and Madagascar; and, after Smuts had gained parliamentary approval for service outside the continent, they joined the Italian campaign. In all about 200,000 South Africans, drawn from all sections of society, and including many Afrikaners, served in the forces. Of these 6,840 were killed, 1,841 went missing, 14,363 were wounded and 14,589 were taken prisoner (Mansergh 1963: 296). Yet within this common effort the race issue persisted. African and Coloured troops were used mainly in non-combat roles. Yet in March 1942, when the Japanese were sweeping all before them, Smuts said he would arm African and Coloureds if the country were directly threatened by Japanese. The NP said that such a desperate response showed the weakness of the Empire and the inaccuracy of Allied propaganda. Later, in May 1944, Smuts signalled to Pretoria while on a visit to London suggesting that it was time to arm Coloured soldiers. Hofmeyr, acting in Smuts's absence, called a cabinet which unanimously opposed the proposal because the political price was too high for any military gain it might bring.

The 1943 Election and the Allied Victory

Smuts called an election for July 1943. Inevitably the central issue was the war, which by then was going well for the Allies. To gain wider approval the NP modified its message. It put less emphasis on republicanism, offered full equality to English-speaking whites, propounded a policy of trusteeship for blacks, pointed to the danger of communism spreading among the blacks because of the alliance with the USSR and attacked price rises and wartime inconveniences. In the event the UP won easily gaining 105 seats (plus the support of the 2 Independents and the 3 Native representatives), while the opposition was reduced from 63 to 43 (Hancock 1968: 383). However, the NP won all the opposition seats, as Malan put to flight his Afrikaner rivals. Following the election the NP turned away from foreign affairs to concentrate on building up its support among Afrikaners at home. Yet again an election had served to underline the persistent division in the white community. Taking account of uncontested seats the government was estimated to have gained 640,000 votes (64 per cent) and the NP 362,000 (32 per cent), but only 32 per cent of Afrikaners supported the government, while the NP attracted the majority of them. (Roberts and Trollip 1947: 159).

The division was again reflected in conflict over education. In 1943 a conference of Afrikaner school inspectors declared: 'A nation is made through its youth being taught and influenced at school in the tradition, customs, habits and ultimate destiny of its volk' (Thompson 1985: 50). In April 1944 a passionate parliamentary debate followed a government regulation, which specified home tongue education in the early years, the introduction of the second language as the student advanced, combined with an element of parental choice. Teacher training was to be bilingual. This was similar to the position Hertzog had always favoured, but it still met resistance from both extremes: English speakers who rejected bilingualism, and Afrikaners who opposed parental choice. A predikant asserted: 'God has willed that there shall be separate nations each with its own language, and . . . mother tongue education is accordingly the will of God. The parent should accordingly have no choice in the case' (Thompson 1985: 49).

The allied victory in 1945 was a time of triumph for Smuts and the UP. The government moved into the post-war period anticipating the fruits of success. The war had caused little physical hardship at home, and had even brought an economic boom. During the war South African industry had faced a major challenge. Demand increased especially in the manufacturing sector, both in the country itself – which was cut off from overseas sources – and in terms of the war effort. At the same time many skilled men were drawn into the forces leaving gaps which had to be filled by those with less experience and lower qualifications. Industry responded well, not only meeting internal demands but making a substantial contribution to the war through ship repairs, and the manufacture of munitions and vehicles. Between 1939 and 1945 the value of gross output more than doubled, from R281m. to R608m. The increased activity had direct social consequences. It finally resolved the poor white problem, and, at the same time, drew large numbers of blacks into industrial employment and into the urban areas. In these conditions a blind eye was turned to many of the restrictions which had earlier been applied to black labour. While in the war years white employment in manufacturing industry rose by 20 per cent (93,000 to 112,000), black employment increased by 74 per cent (281,000 to 608,000).

Yet soon the government was facing new domestic problems – reabsorbing the returning troops, a shortage of urban housing for whites and blacks, demands for improved social and administration services, and increasingly issues concerned with race relations. In handling these matters the government revealed its shortcomings. The cabinet, which was dominated by Smuts, contained too many mediocrities. It also faced new international pressures as a post-war consensus emerged against racism and colonialism. Despite Smuts's prestige and experience he could not divert mounting criticism of the Union. That criticism played its part in reinforcing divisions within the white society and between white and black. More than ever domestic and foreign policy became locked together, and increasingly it was race that dominated the scene.

Race Relations

The problem of race relations dogged Smuts's every step in his two major roles; global statesman and Union politician. He was under conflicting pressures from the two settings. Reflecting on the international scene he appreciated the dilemma but he had no remedy. He said: 'Colour queers my poor pitch everywhere. But South Africans cannot understand. Colour bars are to them part of the divine order of things. But I sometimes wonder what our position in the years to come will be when the whole world will be against us' (Hancock 1968: 473). In the ferment of war and under post-war pressure he mused and reflected, and expressed liberal ideas, but he was not prepared to commit himself. His usual position was that the matter was best left to future generations. This lack of precision alienated him from both ends of white opinion. In May 1941 he had told the Senate that the presence among them of representatives of Native opinion marked an enormous progress in public opinion. 'Do not mind being called agitators,' he told these white representatives, 'but get on with the job' (Hancock 1968: 476). Yet, although they did agitate they achieved few results. One of them, Margaret Ballinger, complained that 'none of our non-European communities in this country can look forward to anything that we can call real citizenship' (Hancock 1968: 478). At the same time the international pressure, which put Smuts in such a quandary, had a reverse affect on many whites. They saw it as a threat to their survival and were determined to resist.

The central question boiled down to whether the government was prepared to abandon the concept of a white-dominated state, and move, even if slowly, to a society in which race would be subordinated to a common citizenship with equal political rights for all. Smuts realized that the white electorate would never stomach such a change. 'What will it profit the country,' he asked, 'if justice is done to the underdog and the whole caboodle then, including the underdog, is handed over to the Wreckers?' (Hancock 1968: 488). Yet there was more to it than that. Smuts's own government was deeply divided on race issues, and in 1945 the Labour and Dominion Party members resigned partly because of these differences. The UP itself contained a range of attitudes from hard-line racists to the renowned liberals like Hofmeyr. Nor did Smuts ever abandon his own belief in the superiority of European civilization, although he realized that the policies which flowed from this position were neither equitable to blacks nor acceptable to the international community. During the war, with blacks increasingly drawn into the urban economy, he had said that segregation was dead, but he avoided spelling out the alternatives, because he believed, 'it is demanding too much of human nature to ask black and white to be just and fair to each other.' The result was, as Smuts confessed, that on racial issues 'I am suspected of being a hypocrite because I can be quoted on both sides' (Hancock 1968: 450). Yet, when forced to the wall, he believed in continued white control. 'In the last resort,' he confessed, 'I take the side of the European and what he stands for in this continent' (Poel 1973: 101). He did not close future options, but for him fundamental change would have to come from generations as yet unborn. Such indecision left a fertile field for his opponents. 'On the colour problem,' said Malan, 'he never sounded a clear note.'

Racial tension increased during the war and in the immediate post-war years. That was the case with Asians. Until 1943 there had been no formal restriction on their ownership of land, but as their numbers increased and their settlements spread white resentment increased. The government responded by restricting them through the 'Pegging Act'. Then in March 1946, under further white pressure, the Asiatic Land Tenure and the Indian Representation Act were introduced, which further limited settlement but contained changes in the franchise whereby Asians would for the first time be able to choose white representatives at national and provincial level. This satisfied nobody. It antagonized some whites, including UP supporters; it was rejected by the South African Indian Congress; and the Indian government raised the issue at the United Nations and cut trading links with the Union.

The situation was no better with Africans. The government offered improved services, but no more. In February 1947 Smuts claimed that the government had a good case, 'but the Natives want "rights" not improvements. There we bump up against the claim for equality which is most difficult to satisfy' (Hancock 1968: 481). Hofmeyr warned that even African moderates and chiefs were increasingly critical of colour discrimination, and could be swept into the extremist camp. In its attempts to square the circle the government refused to extend the indirect parliamentary representation, but tried to enhance the prestige of the Native Representative Council (NRC). That failed. The NRC was a purely advisory body which was given a low priority in the welter of government business. Time after time, the requests of that moderate body were frustrated – when it invited Ministers to attend its meetings; when it sought to extend its numbers and functions; when it called for increased Parliamentary representation; and when it asked for the abolition of the pass laws. It was, as members concluded, no more than 'a toy telephone'. The frustration reached a climax in 1946. The NRC met during a major strike among black miners. Instead of being informed and consulted it was ignored, and was addressed by civil servants not ministers. The Council responded by passing a resolution to adjourn until all discriminatory legislation had been abolished.

The government's reaction to the problems of urban blacks and black labour was to appoint the Fagan Commission to investigate the situation. When the commission reported in 1948 its major premise was that while a degree of control could be exercised it was impossible to prevent blacks – not only men but women and children – from moving to the urban areas. They had to be accepted as a permanent part of the urban population because economic development had entwined the races together. Equally, argued the Commission, total territorial separation was a self-deceiving dream, and dependence on migratory labour was largely obsolete. However, because of differences between the races, residential separation and distinctive administrative structures were desirable. Within that context a degree of responsibility should be delegated to Africans themselves in their own areas. The commission's message was that South Africa was a dynamic society in which it was essential to retain flexibility for growth and development, while at the same time offering greater stability for black labour. The UP government accepted Fagan's report. 'You might as well try to sweep the ocean back with a broom', said Smuts, in commenting on attempts to keep Africans from the urban areas. Another government minister agreed with the views of businessmen that industry could not function efficiently with migrant labour – that a permanent black, urban workforce was needed (Lipton 1985: 21).

Shortly after the publication of the Fagan report the NP produced its own investigation – a report from a group chaired by Paul Sauer. Based on very different assumptions from Fagan's it pointed to an alternative road for the future. As far as possible, said Sauer, the races should live and develop apart and blacks should only come to the towns as labour, on a temporary basis without gaining rights. 'The process of detribalisation should be arrested', stated Sauer. 'The entire migration of Natives into and from the cities should be controlled by the state . . . Natives from the country areas shall be admitted to the urban areas or towns only as temporary employees, obliged to return to their homes after the expiry of their employment.' Surplus labour in the urban areas 'should be returned to their original habitat' (O'Meara 1996: 35). It was a return to the old segregationist ideas, to the Stallard principles of the early 1920s. As then, the NP did not want to halt industrialization and economic growth, but rather to control its social implications by imposing strict segregation based on a racial hierarchy. And so, when they came to power, they took out their brooms and tried to sweep back the ocean.

10

African Nationalism
Transformed, 1939–1948

African political activity was transformed between 1939 and 1948. In the late 1930s
it was weak and uncertain. By 1948 an African nationalist movement existed which
had distinctive aims, and the organization and strength to pursue those aims vigorously against the white-controlled state. The decade saw African nationalism move
from low-key protest to a movement which increasingly challenged the government. The transformation came about from a combination of new circumstances,
a new generation of African leaders, the impetus of fresh ideas from inside and
outside the Union, and the failure of the white government to respond to black
demands. The ANC, which took on a new lease of life, was central to this.
However, there remained many hurdles to overcome. These included the persistent
opposition of the white state, and the old internal problems of divisions, organization, finance and communications. At the time the ANC had no full-time
employees but relied on the commitment of those who gave their voluntary
time and effort.

The Influence of War

The main change in external circumstance and ideas came as a result of the
war. The early reaction of African leaders was less enthusiastic and clear cut than
in 1914. The ANC made clear its opposition to fascism, but said that support for
the government was conditional on gaining better conditions for Africans. The
conference of December 1939 advised Africans not to participate in the war until
the government had granted full citizenship and democratic rights. At the same
time communist members and the CPSA dismissed the war as a capitalist struggle
which should not be supported. Despite that many Africans ignored such advice
by volunteering their services, and, as the war developed, both the ANC and
CPSA became more sympathetic to the Allied cause (in the CPSA's case after the
USSR was attacked). Experience within the forces had an impact as men from
different races served alongside each other, although not with equality. In 1940 a
Native Military Corps was formed, and Denys Reitz, the Minister of Native

Affairs, defended the arming of Africans in the North African campaign (Walshe 1987: 269).

In the darkest days of the war, when the Union itself seemed vulnerable, the government called on all South Africans, irrespective of race, to rally together in defence of the state. Despite past disappointments, such calls revived the hopes of moderate African leaders that change could be achieved by co-operation and working within the system. The drive for co-operation was further enhanced by changing economic circumstances. As noted above, with whites away in the services and a growing economy, more blacks were drawn into urban employment. In February 1942 Smuts called for a united war effort, urging all his fellow countrymen to stand 'together in the hour of danger'. He said he recognized the permanence of urban Africans, and admitted that the whites had neglected their social welfare duties towards Africans. Although he repeated his belief in white trusteeship, he attacked the NP for ignoring Africans as part of the social order. The Native, said Smuts, was 'carrying the country on his back' and was an integral part of the common economic order. 'Segregation,' he declared, 'has fallen on evil days' (Walshe 1987: 269).

At the same time external ideas and principles generated by the war fueled the Union's internal debate. In 1941 the two major western leaders, Winston Churchill and Franklin Roosevelt, drafted the Atlantic Charter, proclaiming justice, freedom and rights for all. African leaders seized on it. A committee, established by Dr Alfred Xuma, the ANC President, was formed to examine the Charter. That committee reached two main conclusions: first, that all peoples had the right to choose the form of government under which they live; and second that the need for economic and social development applied as much to the blacks of South Africa as the people of Europe. However, when these findings were brought to Smuts's attention he dismissed them. In contrast with his liberal sentiments of February 1941, he stated that the Charter did not apply to African problems and conditions. Instead he repeated his faith in white trusteeship – a reaction which encapsulated the government's more usual response to African demands. That was further confirmed at the 1943 election, when, to counter the NP's racial appeals to the white voters, the UP reasserted its old Native policies and rejected calls for reform to meet black aspirations. It became clear to African leaders that Smuts's 'trusteeship' offered little more than Hertzog's 'segregation', and was another factor in radicalizing African opinion.

The African National Congress (ANC)

In the late 1930s it was unclear which of several black and non-racial movements would survive and which among them would become the most powerful. In the event it was the long established ANC. In 1940, with the election of Dr A. B. Xuma as President, the ANC came under the control of a new generation of leaders. Xuma was a physician who had spent several years abroad and returned home with an American wife who played a leading part in the ANC's women's wing. Xuma was an intelligent, efficient and charming man. He made a major contribution to the revival of the ANC, so that when he lost office in 1949 he had reshaped a small ramshackle organization, whose main activity was the annual conference, into an effective political movement. Among his lasting contributions was a major improvement in the ANC's organization and its financial position. Even so the limited scale of the enterprise can be measured by the fact that when Xuma took over the ANC had less than £1 in its coffers; when he left it had about £4,000. Yet, for all his virtues he could be aloof and proud; he was more at home in an elite organization than a mass movement.

Xuma and the ANC executive had to decide how closely to work with other organizations. A number of options were open – to work across the races, to combine with other African and black organizations, or to retain a distinctive identity. Xuma opted for the latter. He did not turn his back on co-operation. For example, as ANC leader he became chairman of a national Anti Pass Campaign, which operated between 1944 and 1946, and brought together several organizations; and in 1947 Xuma signed the 'Doctors' Pact' with Drs Dadoo and Naicker of the Indian Congress to work together against the government's discriminatory policies. However, his main preoccupation was to strengthen the ANC as *the* African organization, and to ensure that it took the lead in any co-operation. That became clear in his dealings with the All African Convention (AAC). The AAC's aim to become a co-ordinating body for all African organizations (and even some non-African) came to nothing, in part because Xuma and his executive were not prepared to absorb the ANC into a broader, more diffuse body. If the ANC was to participate it was as the leader. Xuma stressed that Congress must have a sense of purpose, and give a positive lead. 'One must lead public opinion,' he wrote, 'to see the need for reforms by stating the case to its final and logical conclusions' (Walshe 1987: 264).

To help achieve that goal the ANC published two major documents in 1943. The first was a crisper, clearer constitution, which stressed the need for African participation in all aspects of the state, and terminated the House of Chiefs. It also opened up the possibility of membership across the races, in that it would permit any person to become a member 'who is willing to subscribe to the aims of the Congress and to abide by its constitution'; whereas the 1919 constitution had restricted membership to 'the aboriginal races of Africa' (Karis and Carter 1973: 101). The second document was *African Claims*. In his introduction, Xuma said that the Atlantic Charter must be applied everywhere including the British Empire, but, he continued, African leaders were not foolish enough to believe that they would be granted rights merely by asking. A long, difficult road lay ahead. In following that road *African Claims* asked for nothing less than full equality within the state. It was a call for the establishment of a new order based on a common citizenship and individual rights irrespective of race. The challenge, said the document, was for Africans to organize themselves so that they could move along that road together, 'under the mass liberation movement, the African National Congress'. Africans should not be seen merely as pawns. Alien governments, however well-intentioned, are not accountable to the indigenous population, and Africans now called 'for full citizenship rights and direct participation in the councils of state'. A just and permanent peace was only possible if the claims of citizenship were accepted for all. 'In South Africa,' stated the document, 'Africans have no freedom of movement, no freedom of choice of employment, no rights of residence'. It called for the abolition of discriminatory legislation – the Land Acts, the Pass Laws, the Native Urban Acts – and for the introduction of a Bill of Rights to end racial discrimination, and extend equal rights to all adults, including the vote and membership of parliament (Karis and Carter 1973: 209–15).

Xuma created a new sense of purpose and drive in the ANC but he was not able to resolve all its internal tensions. In restoring its position as the leading African movement, in seeing it 'as a great umbrella under which all Africans could find shelter', it became an even broader and thereby diverse movement (Mandela 1994: 90). The inevitable price to pay was internal division. The movement was united in its opposition to the government's racist policies and in its determination to gain equal rights for all, but such broad objectives left ample room for differences of emphasis, means and priorities. Should Africans co-operate with other racial groups or simply rely upon themselves? Should the ANC use the tactics of a mass movement or concentrate on a political elite? Should it use or ignore the constitutional channels still open to it? In response to such questions three broad overlapping ANC streams emerged: first, the main stream; second the Nationalists (as represented by the Congress Youth League); and third, the communists. In 1946 the National Executive was increased from 11 to 22, which enabled all three streams be represented in the central organization.

The main stream, which was led by Xuma, was more militant than the old Congress, but had clear traces from the past – the Christian element, the links with liberals from other races, the elitist air, its reliance on deputations and written submissions, its doubts about mass action, and its readiness to use the confined outlets offered by the government. In 1946 the government's Native Representative Council included among its members several ANC leaders – Xuma, Z. K. Matthews, Selope Thema and A. W. G. Champion. Yet, even in the main-core attitudes had hardened. That can be seen in the case of Xuma himself. At the time of the 1948 election he complained of a 'despotic racial oligarchy'; he dismissed trusteeship as a euphemism for exploitation, and although he was willing to work with people from other races (and accepted support from the Indian Congress to attend the United Nations) he kept white liberals at a distance. Even so Xuma came under pressure from younger ANC members who were dissatisfied with the old compromises. Their challenge added urgency and edge to the whole movement.

The Congress Youth League (CYL)

The choice for the young ANC militants was either to leave Congress to form their own radical organization, or to stay inside and revitalize it from within. Both approaches were tried. In 1943 Paul Mosaka broke away to form the African Democratic Party, which had similar objectives to those of the ANC, but favoured more radical, dynamic methods based on a mass movement. It failed to establish itself and soon disappeared. More important in the long term was the formation inside the ANC of the Congress Youth League (CYL). Socially the CYL leaders were similar to other Congress leaders, in that they were mainly middle-class professionals with strong educational backgrounds. It was led by a group of out-standing young men, including Anton Lembede, A. P. Mda, Jordan Ngubane, Nelson Mandela, Oliver Tambo, Walter Sisulu and Robert Sobukwe. The inten-tion, said Ngubane, 'was to establish a pressure group inside the ANC'. They even compared themselves to the Broederbond within the NP (Karis and Carter 1973: 102).

The CYL members saw themselves as a new driving nationalist force within Congress; introducing novel ideas, tactics and commitment, and questioning old assumptions. They scorned collaboration with any government institutions. Initially they had Xuma's support, but they soon adopted a more militant stance than he favoured. For them, although Xuma with his range of contacts and his efficiency 'exuded a sense of security and confidence', he was too moderate. 'Everything,' wrote Mandela 'was done in the English manner, the idea being that despite our disagreements we were all gentlemen' (Mandela 1994: 92). Further Xuma believed that it would be rash and premature to launch mass campaigns because of the limits of the ANC's organizational capacity and its discipline. In contrast the CYL's 1944 manifesto spoke of 'struggle' and 'fighting', and its leaders were prepared to confront the government through mass action. Mda spoke of using 'our atomic weapon; the withdrawal of labour' (Karis and Carter 1973: 103). However, the CYL only had limited contact with the trade unions, and their main concern was not to promote a class struggle but 'the encouragement of an assertive "African Nationalism" bolstered by economic strength and cultural self consciousness' (Walshe 1987: 355). They were socialists, but for the most part in the spirit of the British Labour Party; and they were suspicious of communist influence, stressing the need for vigilance against that and other non-African ideologies. In December 1947 CYL members, including Mandela, introduced a motion demanding the expulsion of communists from the ANC but it was defeated.

The CYL's aim was to build an African national identity. Its 1944 manifesto stated that although Africans had been defeated in battle, they refused to accept further oppression. Most whites, stated the manifesto, assumed that their destiny was to dominate blacks, but that only roused in Africans 'feelings of hatred of everything that bars his way to full and free citizenship'. Trusteeship was a disguise for white domination: 'An eyewash for the civilised world and an empty platitude to soothe Africans into believing that all oppression is a pleasant experience under Christian democratic rule.' Looking to the future Africanism must be promoted by self-reliance. It was pointless to dwell on past faults. The need was to be positive and advance, and support the ANC in the conviction that 'the cause of Africa will triumph', that Africans will 'occupy their rightful and honourable place among the nations of the world'. The CYL 'must be the brains trust and power station of the spirit of African nationalism'. Its creed was to be based on the 'divine destiny of nations'. It was prepared to borrow from foreign ideologies but not as wholesale imports. African national liberation must be achieved by Africans themselves, working together in a unity – from the Mediterranean to the Indian and Atlantic Oceans – and speaking with one voice (Karis and Carter: 1973 300–6).

Anton Lembede, a charismatic figure and brilliant public speaker, was the outstanding leader in the CYL's early days. He preached African nationalism, rejecting the deference paid to European ideas, and emphasizing the need for African self reliance and dignity. 'The history of modern times,' he wrote in May 1946, 'is the history of nationalism. Nationalism has been tested in the people's struggles and the fires of battle and found to be the only antidote against foreign rules and modern imperialism.' Plainly the 'nationalism' to which Lembede referred was anti-colonial nationalism which in the immediate post-war years spread across the Middle East, Asia and North Africa. He called on the CYL to involve itself in this historic process, based on a number of cardinal principles: that Africa is a blackman's country; that Africans are one; that leadership must be drawn from Africans themselves; that co-operation with other black races may be desirable on specific issues but 'non European unity is a fantastic dream which has no foundation in reality'; that the divine destiny of African people is national freedom; and following freedom would come socialism. The CYL's motto, wrote Lembede, was 'Freedom in our life time' (Karis and Carter 1973: 318). Lembede did not live to pursue his dreams. He died in July 1947 aged 33, and was succeeded as CYL leader by A. P. Mda. Mda lacked Lembede's dynamic personality, but he was clear minded and well organized. In Mandela's opinion Mda was ideally suited to build on the foundation established by Lembede. Mda, said Mandela, was more broad minded, mature and tolerant of a wider range of views, including communists, than Lembede. His approach to nationalism was more moderate and less tinged by Lembede's racism. Mda 'hated white oppression and white domination, not white people' (Mandela 1994: 101).

In 1948 the CYL issued a further document, the *Basic Policy*, which reflected Mda's wider views. It reiterated the commitment to African nationalism, the 'creed of the oppressed African people', but accepted that the 'different racial groups have come to stay'. It recognized the rights of minorities, but the African 'has a primary inherent and inalienable right to Africa' which is his continent and Motherland. 'Africans as a whole have a divine destiny which is to make Africa free among the peoples and nations of the earth.' To achieve that they 'must build a powerful National liberation movement,' led by Africans. The *Basic Policy* was many sided – political, economic, educational and cultural – with calls for the removal of racial discrimination, the granting of citizenship rights, democratic representation in parliament, and 'the division of land among farmers and peasants of all nationalities in proportion to their numbers'. It ended by calling for a united effort by Africans in 'their Herculean efforts to emancipate themselves and to advance their cause and position economically, culturally, educationally, socially, commercially and physically' (Karis and Carter 1973: 107 and 324).

The Communist Party of South Africa (CPSA)

Differences arose in the Youth League about co-operation with other races and organizations. Some, like Lembede, were strong Africanists, but others were prepared to co-operate with 'radicals' as distinct from 'liberals' of other races. The difference was most marked over the relationship with communists, the third main element in the ANC. The CPSA was about 2,000 strong at the time, with Africans forming the majority, but whites, Indians and Coloureds having prominent roles. During the 1930s it had been torn by internal disputes. While these did not disappear they became less marked as the party rallied behind Moses Kotane (who became General Secretary in 1939) and gave its support to Moscow's wartime policy. As the challenge to the government intensified so communists came to play an increasingly important part in the struggle. They were effective because of their commitment and discipline, their penetration of other organizations including trade unions and Congress, and their careful placing of members in key positions. The CPSA was on common ground with Congress in opposing the government's discriminatory policies and in working towards a non-racial society. White communists with their determined stand against the government also gained African support as Native Representatives in Parliament.

The communists were able to work through and with the ANC because of two major ideological assumptions decreed from Moscow. The first, which was shared by many militant non-communists, was that the South African state was built on colonialism of a special type, whereby the white colonialists were not drawn from a separate metropolitan power, but were settled in the colony itself. The second assumption was that the first step towards a socialist state was to establish an independent native republic. By making this assumption the CPSA was able to support the nationalist cause rather than commit itself immediately to a class struggle, although that would follow. In seeking a native republic the CPSA was instructed to work within the ANC to transform it into a 'fighting nationalist revolutionary organisation against the white bourgeoisie and the British imperialists' (Ellis and Sechaba 1992: 18). But the relationship was often tense. Some ANC and YCL members belonged to the CPSA, but the majority rejected Marxism, and many were openly critical of a movement which was based on an alien ideology, took its orders from Moscow, had non-Africans among its leaders and saw its cooperation with the ANC only as a stepping-stone towards a communist society. However as the struggle intensified the common ground between the ANC and the CPSA became more important than the differences.

A New African Nationalism

The momentum the ANC had gained during the war intensified with the peace. An increasingly important international element came into play to reinforce and expand the ideas already generated during the war. In the past blacks had looked in vain to the British government for support. Now they turned to the United Nations and from small beginnings it provided them with an increasingly important platform. The lobbying started in the UN's early days as two South African issues arose: the status of South West Africa and the Indian government's complains at the treatment of Indians in the Union. Despite Pretoria's protests South Africa's critics argued that neither of the two cases could be confined to the Union's domestic jurisdiction because South West Africa was a mandated territory which should now fall under UN trusteeship, and the treatment of Indians was a source of friction between two member states and a potential threat to world peace. It was clear, however, that behind those specific issues was a broader question. They were hooks on which to hang an attack on South Africa's racial policies. Xuma, with help from the Indians, visited the UN in 1946 where he presented a petition to the Secretary General, which complained of blacks being driven into a blind alley, and having the same status as those who lived in colonies. From the beginning these complaints gained considerable international sympathy.

Smuts was distraught as attacks rained down on the Union government. For him the UN became unrecognizable as the organization he had helped to create, or the one he believed was needed. Instead of concentrating on broad global order and security, as he thought it should, it became in Smuts's words 'a cockpit of emotion, passion and ignorance' (Walker 1968: 762). In 1947 he spoke of a 'solid wall of prejudice' against the Union's racial policies and 'floods of emotion fanned by mischievous propaganda'. When asked in parliament what would be the situation if the UN applied sanctions against South Africa he did not dismiss it as an absurd idea. That, he said, 'would constitute a war measure . . . We are in a delicate and even dangerous situation' (HA 21/1/1947). Smuts's early responses characterized the reactions of successive South African governments over the next forty years. The details of the responses altered but not the substance. Smuts, like those who followed, protested that the attacks were against policies that lay within the Union's domestic jurisdiction and were therefore outside the competence of the UN. At the international level his voice was largely ignored.

By 1948 African nationalists had developed a set of claims and demands which differed substantially from those of the past. No longer were Africans seeking partial representation and rights; no longer were they claiming a limited sectional voice; no longer were they asking to be judged by tests based on white civilization (such as the Cape franchise) in which implicitly or explicitly it was assumed that they would be in a political minority. Now their claims were for an end to segregation and trusteeship, the abolition of racial discrimination in all its forms, political and constitutional equality and a common citizenship which recognized that South Africa belonged to all its people. The practical implications of these claims were that government of the state would become representative of and responsible to the majority – a majority that was black and predominantly African. The state would therefore be built on the foundation of a common South African identity, and not on a racial oligarchy. No longer would South Africa be 'a white man's country.'

Nobody, including those who made the claims, anticipated that such a change could be achieved overnight or without a prolonged struggle. The methods to be used would be more militant than those in the past. That was demonstrated by the 1946 African miners' strike on the Rand. The African Mine Workers' Union had been formed in the early 1940s. In 1946 the union, led by J. B. Marks – a member of the ANC and the CPSA – called out its members in a claim for ten shillings a day, family housing and two weeks' holiday per year; 70,000 miners answered the call. The government reacted ruthlessly: arresting leaders, surrounding the miners' compounds with police, and raiding the union offices. The police also broke up a march of miners, killing twelve of them. By chance the Native Representative

Council was meeting at the same time. When the government ignored the Council, even those moderate men were incensed and abandoned their meeting. In the end the government crushed the strike and the union. Fifty-two leaders, including Marks and Kotane, were arrested and prosecuted for incitement and then sedition. It was a foretaste of things to come.

11

The National Party
Government, 1948–1961

Smuts called an election in May 1948. To fight it, both the major parties formed alliances with smaller parties – the UP with Labour, and the NP with the Afrikaner Party (AP). As the AP, led by N. C. Havenga, was part of Hertzog's heritage, its alliance with the NP renewed hopes of Afrikaner unity, and moderated the NP's image. Paradoxically, however, the Afrikaner Party was the route by which some OB members, like John Vorster, eased themselves back into mainstream policies, when Malan refused their immediate readmission to the NP. The alliance of 1948 therefore appeared to heal the rift of 1941 among Afrikaner nationalists.

The UP's election manifesto was safe and dull. It called for national unity, the maintenance of the Union's existing economic and constitutional position, and continued white immigration. It went on to confirm the Commonwealth connection, to emphasize Smuts's leadership, to speak of trusteeship in race relations and the need for development over time. In relation to urban Africans the UP relied heavily on the Fagan report. Smuts derided the NP's call for separation. 'The idea,' he said, 'that the Natives must all be removed and confined in their own kraals is in my opinion the greatest nonsense I have ever heard' (Heard 1974: 33). The NP's message was sharper. It toned down its anti-British and republican stance to concentrate its attacks on the government – its incompetence, Smuts's obsession with global affairs and his vagueness on colour issues. It criticized the UP's liberalism and weakness in the face of the twin dangers of communism and 'the black sea of South Africa's non European population' (Heard 1974: 33). Malan asked: 'Will the European race in the future be able to, but also want to retain its rule, its purity, its civilization, or will it float along until it vanishes without honour in the black sea of South Africa's non European population?' The UP's liberalism was, argued Malan, a slippery slope to communism. 'A vote for Jan Smuts is a vote for Joe Stalin', proclaimed an NP headline (Hancock 1968: 500 and 502). As an alternative to the slippery slope the NP offered 'apartheid' (or 'separate development'). 'We can act in only one of two directions', stated the NP election manifesto. 'Either we must follow the course of equality, which must eventually mean national suicide for the white race, or we must take the course of apartheid through which the character and future of every race will be protected' (Le May 1995: 202). In practical terms, said Malan, apartheid meant outlawing marriages between blacks and whites, abolishing African representation in parliament, recognizing the reserves as the true home of the natives, exercising control over their entry into towns, maximizing segregation, and the protection of the white workers. Coloureds, he said would have a position between whites and Natives, but should lose their vote on the common roll; while Indians were a 'foreign element', who should be repatriated back to India (Stultz 1974: 136–7).

Although the NP had gained ground at recent by-elections the government was confident that it would win the election. In the event the NP/Afrikaner alliance triumphed – gained 79 seats (70 NP and 9 AP) against 65 for the UP and 6 Labour. Even Smuts lost his seat – at Standerton in the Transvaal. A variety of explanations (either singly or in combination) were advanced for the NP's victory. First, that it rested on the vagaries of the electoral system, whereby, although the UP gained many more votes, the NP gained the seats because of unbalanced constituencies and the uneven distribution of voters, with UP supporters clustered in urban areas (the percentage of votes cast was UP 48.7; NP 35.7; Labour 4.9;

Dr D. F. Malan
(courtesy of the
South African
High Commission)

and AP 1.6). Second, that the NP was better organized and motivated so that it maximized its resources, whereas the UP gave too little attention to party organization. Third, that Smuts had spent too much time on international affairs and was out of touch with developments at home. Fourth, was the effectiveness of the NP's emotional appeal for Afrikaner unity. Fifth, that the government had been incompetent in handling post-war problems. Sixth, that recent economic changes (and government incompetence) had told against the interests of traditional UP supporters, such as the farmers of the Western Cape and the Transvaal. In Dan O'Meara's judgement the election was not won by the nationalists as lost by the government (O'Meara 1996: 37). Seventh, Newell Stultz suggests that the die had been cast in 1939 when Smuts split the party of conciliation to prosecute the war, and so opened the door to a future NP victory (Stultz 1974: 65). Finally, that in 'apartheid', the NP had a positive message which appeared to offer whites certainty in race relations. In Hermann Giliomee's words the NP combined for Afrikaner nationalists the double attraction of 'putting the Kaffir in his place', and 'getting "our" country back' (Adam and Giliomee 1979a: 115). Whatever the explanation, and it was probably a combination of many or all those above, what was clear was that for the first time Afrikaner nationalists had sole control of the government.

The 1948 election result came as a surprise even to the NP. But for them it was a wonderful surprise. 'At last,' they rejoiced, 'we have got our country back' (O'Meara 1996: 43). The victory heralded a major change in white South Africa's political leadership; in the composition of the power elite; and in the government's orientation. Subsequent election victories in 1953 and 1958 cemented the established NP's grip on power to make it the established party of government, while the UP steadily lost ground. The NP government set itself three main tasks – first to build up the power of the state; second to ensure that the state was controlled by Afrikaner nationalists and promoted Afrikaner interests; and third to implement apartheid. In doing so it also set out to cement the social and economic interests of Afrikaners, through job reservations and welfare provision for white workers, subsidies for farmers, socially engineered upward mobility for the middle class, and support for the expansion of Afrikaner capital enterprises by overt and covert state support. The combination of political, social and economic patronage and rewards goes far to explain the strong sense of unity which developed among Afrikaners in the 1950s and 1960s, and their increasing support for the NP (Hyslop 1996). In undertaking these tasks the government was led in its early years by three prime ministers: D. F. Malan (1948–54), a quiet, pious and determined man; Jan Strijdom (1954–8), 'The Lion of the North,' aggressive and forthright; and Hendrik Verwoerd (1958–66), a dominant, doctrinaire, powerful leader. Each step in the chain of succession was seen by the government's opponents as a further hardening of attitudes – from Malan, the father of modern Afrikaner nationalism; to Strijdom the advocate of 'baaskap'; to Verwoerd, the architect of apartheid.

Like all major parties the NP had its internal differences: based on personalities, provinces, class, ideology and competition for power. These often led to bitter quarrels, personal feuds and 'baronial politics' (O'Meara 1996: 51). Yet despite that the NP usually succeeded in presenting a monolithic face to its opponents. This was partly explained by its strong organization, based on a provincial structure and reaching down to active local branches; but equally important the NP saw itself as, and was seen by its supporters as, the Afrikaner nation in politics. The party was linked to a network of Afrikaner institutions, and a high proportion of NP voters were also party members. As a result differences were contained within 'the volk'. Overriding their disputes NP members had a transcending loyalty to their cause, and when there were doubts the leaders could always beat the tribal drum. For the NP 1948 was more than a simple change of government: it was a people inheriting their God given right; the right of the Afrikaner nation to control South Africa. 'In the past we felt like strangers in our own country', said Malan, 'but today South Africa belongs to us once more' (Geldenhuys 1977: 43). They saw other groups as less than 'true' South Africans – the blacks because South Africa was a white man's country; the English speakers and anglicized Afrikaners because their loyalties lay elsewhere.

Having gained power the NP leaders were determined to retain it. They granted, for example, six parliamentary seats to the whites of South West Africa, who in 1950 dutifully returned six NP members. The NP's determination was built on its belief that not only the future of the state but the future of the Afrikaner as a people was at stake – their language, religion and culture. It was convinced that to remedy the past subordination of Afrikaners by an anglicized elite it had to build a state controlled by Afrikaner Nationalists, and ensure that the levers of government and state patronage were used to enhance Afrikaner status, pride and rewards. As a result no English speaker served in the cabinet, most senior civil service jobs went to Afrikaners, and Afrikaners were appointed to top military posts. The culture of civil service neutrality was abandoned, and between 1948 and 1960 the number of Afrikaners in public service doubled. At the same time immigration policy was tightened up to reduce the inflow from Britain. Previously, the UP had encouraged a vigorous flow of white immigrants, especially from Britain, arguing that this was to satisfy the need for skilled workers and to strengthen the white community. However, in NP eyes it was seen as a means of 'ploughing under' the Afrikaner. Not only did the NP government reduce the number of British immigrants, it diluted their political influence by extending the period of residence from two to five years before they could vote.

The Decline of the United Party

Within the white parliamentary system the UP initially assumed that it would soon regain power. Instead it steadily lost ground. When Smuts, who had dominated the party, died in 1950, there was no major figure to replace him. Hofmyer had died young, late in 1948, and the rest of the leadership was mediocre. Afrikaners continued to drift away, leaving the UP an increasingly English-speaking party, although with a body of Afrikaner supporters and an Afrikaner leader – J. G. Strauss until 1955 and then Sir de Villiers Graaf. However, the UP continued to attract support – from inertia, from established social and political divisions within white society, and from deep antagonism to the NP which was exacerbated by the government's Afrikanerization programme. Backed by non-parliamentary groups, like the Torch Commandoes, and with the backcloth of the African Defiance Campaign, the UP made a great effort at the 1953 election – attacking the government's apartheid policies, its assaults on the constitution and its authoritarian methods. The NP countered by accusing the UP of being soft on the race issue and of having support from communists. In the event the NP won most seats, increasing its overall majority from 5 in 1948 to 25 in 1953 (including those from South West Africa); but the UP still polled many more votes – gaining 54 per cent compared with the NP's 44 per cent. The government claimed that the result reflected the will of the people. In Kenneth Heard's judgement, however, the result was a reversal of majority opinion: 'it reflected not "the will of the people" but the combined effects of demographic factors and the electoral system's built-in capacity for distortion' (Heard 1974: 69).

A similar pattern emerged in the 1958 election, although by then the UP was less hopeful of success, and the NP was confident enough to discuss the prospect of establishing a republic. 'The day of the republic,' said Strijdom, 'is approaching much faster than the United Party realizes' (Heard 1974: 74). Again in 1958 the NP increased its majority of seats and again the UP polled more votes although the gap had narrowed (50 per cent against 48.5 per cent). Also by the late 1950s the UP was clearly divided between liberal and conservative wings, and eventually it split in 1959 when eleven of the more liberal members broke away to form the Progressive Party (PP or 'Progs'). In its attempts to hold the party together in the frustrating experience of opposition UP policies were often vague compromises, little more than modifications of the government's position, and based on the government's agenda. The UP's position in relation to the government's racial policies was described as 'Me too, only not so loud' (Heard 1974: 75).

Although the UP was a declining force the atmosphere in parliament was often acerbic. In part that was because the government was frequently looking over its shoulder, seeking to redress what it saw as past sins by English-speaking capitalists, the British and their UP allies. In NP eyes there was much unfinished business. It believed that the poorer economic status of many Afrikaners could be attributed to English-speaking domination, and it saw control of the state as a means of righting past economic wrongs. Verwoerd had already told an NP congress in 1939 that state power was the best weapon for Afrikaners to assume their 'legitimate share of commerce and industry' (O'Meara 1996: 76). Under the NP government, therefore, a series of steps were taken to further Afrikaner economic interests – more protection for white workers, support for Afrikaner business enterprises, the extension of the public sector and granting of contracts to Afrikaner companies. During the 1950s, state employment increased rapidly from 481,000 to 798,000, with Afrikaner males as the main beneficiaries.

The symbols of the old imperial link also came under attack. The government enacted that the Union Jack would no longer be flown at official ceremonies; 'God save the King' was abandoned as 'Die Stem' became the sole national anthem and appeals to the British Privy Council were suspended. The old imperial link was also involved in the fierce political battle over the Cape Coloured franchise. The government was determined to remove the Coloureds from the common voters' roll because their presence offended against its rigid views on race, and because most Coloureds supported the UP. In April 1951 the Separate Representation of Voters Bill was introduced to remove Coloureds from the common roll and give them separate representation through four white MPs. However, because of entrenched clauses, which included the old Cape franchise, to change the franchise required a two-thirds majority of both houses sitting together. The NP argued that the entrenched clauses had no validity; that change only required a simple parliamentary majority because the Status Act and the Statute of Westminster (1931) had made the Union's parliament supreme. It was no longer bound by an act passed by the British parliament, with its entrenched clauses. The bill duly gained a majority, but less than two-thirds. The opposition therefore referred the matter to the courts. A long dispute ensued, not only between the NP and the UP, but between the government and the courts.

The matter was settled in 1955 by the new leader Strijdom. Strijdom, who represented a harsher Transvaal strain within the party, was more authoritarian and less concerned with constitutionalism than Malan. He decided to override the constitution by expanding the size of the Senate and the Appelate Division of the courts, and packing them with hard-line NP supporters. Therefore the enlarged Senate (89 compared with the previous 48) ensured the required two-thirds majority to pass the bill. The government rejoiced. Jan de Klerk, the Minister of Labour, declared: 'We are taking this step because we are Calvinists who believe that God is sovereign and hands over the sovereignty to the legal rulers of the land. We therefore have the right to determine what must be done and nobody, not even the highest court, has received that power from the Creator of Heaven and earth' (Liebenberg and Spies 1993: 342).

On the franchise the NP government had finally succeeded. However, on another aspect of the old relationship it did not – the future of the three British Protectorates (Basutoland, Bechuanaland and Swaziland), which rested on the Union's borders. The government wanted to absorb them into the Union because they were seen as a dangerous model for African development, and even more as a slight on South Africa's independence. In 1950 Malan publicly told a visiting British minister that apart from 'the question of grievous mistrust' – whether South Africa could be trusted 'with the protection or promotion of native interests' – the failure to transfer the territories 'affects our status'. Unlike any other Commonwealth member the Union has to harbour territories 'entirely dependent on her economically and largely also for defence, but belonging to and governed by another country'. He asked if anybody could blame South Africa if she felt she had been 'relegated to a position of inferiority; a semi-independent or third class country' (Mansergh 1952: 928). The British ignored the request because South Africa's racial policies had already become a matter of international concern. That concern was encapsulated in the word 'apartheid'.

Apartheid

Apartheid was both a creed and a set of policies. The policies were in many ways a continuation of those developed under segregation, but now they were applied with a thoroughness not previously envisaged, and were underpinned by a burning conviction of right. It represented a major step of degree, even of kind, in policy towards blacks. Apartheid appealed to faith and fear: faith that a resolution could be found to the problems of race relations while retaining white supremacy; fear that without authoritarian measures the whites would be swamped. It was backed by biblical references to the division of peoples, and, as with many other NP policies, the belief that God's hand was behind it. It was God, proclaimed the Dutch Reformed Church, who had shaped the nations, and ordained the existence of races and nations as separate units. It was therefore 'imperative that these creations be recognized for the sake of the natural development through which they could fulfil themselves'. God 'gave each nation a feeling of nationhood and a national soul' (Le May 1995: 201). M. D. C. de Wet Nel, who became Minister of Native Affairs in 1958, spoke of God giving a 'divine task and calling to every people', each of whom 'has the inherent right to live and develop.' He claimed that: 'To our people [apartheid] is not a mere abstraction which hangs in the air. It is a divine task which has to be implemented' (O'Meara 1996: 73). Allied to the religious claims a body of doctrine was developed by academics, theologians and politicians to underpin apartheid. Prominent in this field was the South African Bureau for Racial Affairs (SABRA) which was established soon after the NP came to power to investigate the 'colour question' based on 'the scientific study of racial affairs'.

Alongside the doctrine, and the 'divine task', was naked self interest: the determination to retain white and in particular Afrikaner dominance. The aim of apartheid was first and foremost to safeguard the racial identity and dominance of whites, by development along separate racial lines. The claim that all races had rights was balanced by the fear that whites could be overwhelmed by the black majority. The apartheid solution therefore was to retain the power of the state and the economy in white hands, and in other respects to follow separate roads. Malan wrote: 'The difference in colour is merely the physical manifestation of the contrast between the irreconcilable ways of life, between heathenism and Christianity, and finally between overwhelming numerical odds on the one hand and insignificant numbers on the other . . . Small wonder that the instinct of self preservation is so inherent in white South Africans. He has retained his identity all these years. He is not willing to surrender it now' (Le May 1995: 209). Characteristically Strijdom was even blunter: 'Our policy,' he said 'is that to protect the white man these discriminatory laws . . . are necessary to place the power to govern in the country in the hands of the white man so that he can retain or maintain his supremacy or "baaskap"' (HA 7 May 1957).

Apartheid was not a single, cohesive policy. Some intellectuals advocated total separation with the exclusion of Africans from white towns and rural areas. Most supporters, however, favoured 'practical apartheid', whereby labour would be strictly controlled. (Worden 1995: 93). Nor was the application of apartheid set in concrete; rather it evolved as circumstances and ideas developed. Although in its election campaign the NP had advertised the concept with vigour, apartheid was initially as much a slogan as a clear set of policies. Malan himself admitted that the races were so interdependent economically that they could not be completely separated into territorial spheres. In 1950 he stated that complete territorial segregation though ideal 'was impracticable [because] our whole economic structure is to a large extent based on native labour' (Lipton 1985: 30). However, he rejected claims that apartheid was a policy of oppression. 'On the contrary,' he said, 'like the wire fence between two farms it indicates a separation without eliminating necessarily legitimate contacts in both directions . . . [but] serves as an effective protection against violations of one another's rights' (Le May 1995: 207). The wire fence, however, was chiefly designed to keep Africans out of the white areas, other than those required for labour. The government pursued policies which were designed to ensure that white farmers were provided with cheap labour, and restrict the flow of blacks to the urban areas. The latter was achieved by 'Influx Control', which was designed to limit the number of Africans entering urban areas, to ensure that their stay was temporary; to control the allocation of labour; to exercise social control by means of segregation, and to offer white security.

The introduction of apartheid called for the use of state power on a scale previously not envisaged – creating new administrative and political structures, moving and resettling large numbers of people, controlling daily lives, and drawing firm legal distinctions between individuals based on their race. It required a comprehensive and detailed policy of social engineering. Initially the full rigour may not have been there, but apartheid legislation was quickly introduced – such as the Prohibition of Mixed Marriages Act in 1949, which ended marriage across racial lines. Then in 1950, with the appointment of Dr Hendrik Verwoerd as Minister of Native Affairs, a sense of pragmatism was replaced by a sustained, ideological approach. Creed and policy were married together as Verwoerd, with Dr W. W. M. Eiselen, his permanent secretary (who had previously been a university lecturer in ethnography and Bantu Languages) built up a department whose influence penetrated throughout the government. From that base, apartheid came to infiltrate itself into the lives of all South Africans. In broad terms it could be divided into 'petty apartheid', which was concerned with people's daily lives – the buses and trains in which they could travel, the doors they could use to enter public buildings, the seats they could sit on in parks, and so on – and 'grand apartheid' which was designed to divide South Africans, and the geographical area of the state, on racial lines. A stream of legislation emerged: the Population Registration Act (1950) which labelled every individual by race; the Group Areas Act (1950) which delimited living areas; the Bantu Authorities Act (1951) which reinforced traditional African tribal structures; the Separate Amenities Act (1953) which divided the use of public amenities; and the Bantu Education Act (1953) which defined African education.

The Group Areas and Education Acts provide clear examples of apartheid thinking. The Group Areas Act was designed to make residential separation compulsory. To achieve its ends it cut across established property rights, and led to the forced removal of many Africans, Indians and Coloureds from their homes. For example, in Cape Town Coloureds were removed from District Six, near the city centre; and in Johannesburg 'black spots' such as Sophiatown, Martindale and Newclare were eliminated. These removals went ahead despite massive protests at home and abroad, and condemnation from people like Father Trevor Huddleston who described them as legalized theft carried out by policemen with guns. Yet, the government saw it as part of a greater cause. T. E. Donges, the Minister of the Interior, claimed: 'It is the price we have to pay in order to achieve certainty . . . It is a sacrifice we will have to make in order to bring about conditions most favourable for inter-racial harmony' (Liebenberg and Spies 1993: 323). In defending the Bantu Education Act, Verwoerd explained that the act avoided giving the wrong type of education to Africans. He stated that mission schools, which had previously been the main African education providers, had failed because they had ignored the reality of the situation. They had created false hopes that Africans could occupy positions in European society. 'The Bantu must be guided,' he said, 'to serve his own community in all respects. There is no place for him in the European community above the level of certain forms of labour' (Karis and Carter 1977: 29). They cannot improve, he said, if the result 'is the creation of a frustrated people, who, as a result of the education they receive, have expectations in life, which circumstances of life in South Africa do not allow to be fulfilled' (Carter 1962: 103).

In line with such thinking Verwoerd supported the migratory labour system. In 1952 he refused a request from the mining companies to house a higher proportion of African families on their new Orange Free State gold mines. 'Migratory labour,' responded Verwoerd, 'is the best system, and not only did the government support it, there is also good reason to believe the Bantu people prefer [it]' (Lipton 1985: 26). Yet, although the government wanted separation between the races, it rejected the UP's assertion that this would lead to a politically and economically fragmented South Africa. Verwoerd initially denied that apartheid implied the creation of separate Bantu states. He told the Senate in 1951 that the opposition was wrong in claiming that he was forming 'an independent Native State . . . a sort of Bantustan with its own leaders . . . that is not the policy. The Senator wants to know whether the series of self governing areas will be sovereign. The answer is obvious. How could small scattered states arise? We cannot mean that we intend by that to cut large slices out of South Africa and turn them into independent states' (Wolpe 1972: 82). He stressed that although Africans could develop 'local self government' in their own areas, 'all the areas will be within the geographical and economic unit of the Union of South Africa . . . also in respect of any international relations concerning the defence of the country. It speaks for itself that South Africa is the trustee and ruler of the whole' (Liebenberg and Spies 1993: 346). Verwoerd was equally, if not as openly, dismissive of a Commission report – the Tomlinson Commission – on the development of African areas which had been set up before his appointment to Native Affairs. The commission concluded that apartheid could only succeed in reducing the flow of Africans to urban areas and in promoting racial harmony if the government were prepared to invest heavily in the development of the reserves (£104 million in ten years). It further recommended that industries should be established inside the reserves backed by white capital. Verwoerd rejected these assumptions. He opposed the introduction of white capital because it could lead to integration, and he argued that Africans were not psychologically adapted to develop industries. Instead Verwoerd offered development along traditional tribal lines.

By the end of the 1950s therefore 'the long existing racial segregation of South African society had been radically extended' (O'Meara 1996: 71). The UP persistently criticized the government's racial policies but it did not offer a clear-cut alternative. It could see that apartheid was impractical as well as unjust, but it was too wedded to continued white dominance to offer blacks more than a continuation of past 'trusteeship' and 'segregation' policies. They were more flexible and less rigorous than apartheid but they were far from satisfying black aspirations. By the start of the 1960s there were only two shows on the road: apartheid and African Nationalism.

12

African Opposition: Communists, Congress and the Pan Africanist Congress

Inevitably many of the ideas and activities of African nationalism came as a reaction to the policies of the new NP government. As in the past, the political agenda was largely determined by those who held power. Even under the UP black leaders realized that the chance of gaining their ends through existing constitutional channels were slim, but many had clung to the hope that peaceful agitation would open up new opportunities. Now the NP introduced a sterner ideology with a determination to see it through, whatever the opposition. The Transvaal ANC spoke of the 'dark and desperate phase into which the African people of South Africa are entering' (Walshe 1987: 290). On racial issues the new government, unlike the UP, was not inhibited by an internal liberal wing, or concern with international opinion. It almost gloried in defiance. Black political leaders operated under increasingly severe laws and suffered from persistent harassment by the government.

The government tried to demonize its opponents by grouping them together as 'communists' or 'fellow travellers'. As soon as it came into office it set up a committee to investigate communism in the Union. The outcome was the Suppression of Communism Act of 1950, which declared unlawful the Communist Party or any other organization which was promoting communist activity. A wide definition was given to 'communism', so that it included any doctrine or act 'which aims at bringing about any political, industrial, social or economic change within the Union by the promotion of disturbances or disorders, by unlawful acts or omissions or by the threat of such acts or omissions' (Carter 1962: 65). This 'statutory communism', as it became known, was designed to emasculate opponents outside parliament. In anticipation of the Act the CPSA disbanded itself in 1950.

In the period that followed the disbanding of the CPSA the communists were in some disorder, as they debated their future in terms of organization, strategy and ideology. Initially the situation was easier for black communists, most of whom found a home in Congress, where many (but certainly not all) members welcomed them as fellow opponents of racism and apartheid. For white communists there was a period of indecision and stock taking, during which some formed the Congress of Democrats; until finally in 1954 the party was reborn in a new secret form as the South African Communist Party (SACP). During the interim years a lively internal debate had developed, and inevitably it was concerned with the relationship between the class struggle and nationalism, and that between imperialism and capitalism. In the debate, there was broad agreement that South Africa was a unique case in which permanent settlers controlled the system of exploitation – based on discrimination, migrant labour and a racially divided working class. It was further agreed that the black working class had grown in size but not class consciousness. From these premises one section of the old party – which turned out to be a minority – argued that the nationalist movement was the home of the bourgeoisie and not the working class. It was irrelevant, they claimed, that the bulk of the middle class was white and that of the working class was black. The working class should therefore develop its own organizations. However, a majority of members sought a more pragmatic, middle-ground approach by taking their stand on the Union's position as that of 'colonialism of a special kind'. According to this approach, South Africa exhibited 'the characteristics of both an imperialist state, and a colony within a single indivisible political and economic entity . . . The Non European population, while reduced to the status of a colonial people, have no territory of their own, no independent existence, but is almost wholly integrated in the political and economic institutions of the ruling class'. Although for communists the nationalist struggle was seen as a transitional phase, this broad interpretation offered an ideological mid-point between the class and nationalist positions, and it offered a means by which the ANC and the SACP could work together. It was the foundation on which an alliance was built, and formed the ideological glue which held together an SACP/ANC alliance for the next four decades' (Everatt 1991).

Increased Militancy and the Defiance Campaign

As reflected in the ANC/SACP alliance the new government's actions radicalized black opposition, and drew it together. Differences still remained in the ANC over tactics and collaboration with other racial groups and communists, but for many the common struggle overrode other differences. After riots in Durban in 1949, when Africans attacked Asians, and in which 142 were killed and over a thousand injured, the Indian and African Congresses agreed to avoid a recurrence by working together, under the guiding principle of equal rights for all South Africans. In 1951 the leaders of the two Congresses gave flesh to the bones by agreeing to launch a joint mass defiance campaign directed against the pass laws, the Suppression of Communism Act, the Group Areas Act, and the Separate Representation of Voters Act (designed to remove the Coloureds from the common roll). At the same time the ANC became more militant. In the face of apartheid even a moderate like James Calata said that African nationalism must assert itself against unrestrained white nationalism. 'Africa is our homeland,' he said, 'and while we do not deny any human being of any race, colour or creed, the right to become African or South African, nevertheless we maintain that we are the real South Africans' (Walshe 1987: 358). The ANC Youth League proposed a 'Programme of Action', based on non-violent but radical activities – including strikes, civil disobedience, non co-operation and boycott of all racially divided institutions. The National Executive endorsed this approach in December 1949. Congress also authorized symbolic actions, such as a clenched right hand salute, and singing the anthems 'Nkosi Sikelel'i Afrika' and 'Mayibuye Afrika'. However, the more aggressive tactics did not signal a major departure for the ANC's aims as set out in 'African Claims'. Nor did Congress abandon the principle of non-racialism. Instead it was 'inspired by the desire to achieve national freedom', and throw off white domination and apartheid (Walshe 1987: 291).

One of the early casualties of the period was Xuma. He was voted out of office in 1949. Faced by demands for greater militancy and mass action he suggested instead a steady development of the ANC's membership and organizational strength before launching into such new activities. In response to the CYL's claim that mass action would lead to mass membership, Xuma argued that it would only lead to confusion before a stronger framework was in place. In the congress which followed Xuma lost the Presidency, to be replaced by another physician, Dr James Moroka. Moroka exercised a looser grip on the party. He came to office without much ex-perience of political leadership, and as he lived in the Free State he was remote from the main centres of activity and decision making. That gave an opportunity for others, including the CYL, to dictate the pace and move the ANC from petitions and deputations to mass action, strikes and boycotts.

The change in approach led to the 1952 Defiance Campaign. It was the largest African political protest yet staged. It received support from the South African Indian Congress and gained widespread national and international attention. In December 1951 the ANC's annual Conference told the government that unless it repealed six named racist laws, demonstrations would start on 6 April, 1952 (the 300th anniversary of the arrival of the Dutch to settle the Cape) as a 'prelude to the implementation of a plan for the defiance of unjust laws' (Karis and Carter 1973: 413). When the government dismissed the demand, the ANC issued a pamphlet *300 Years of Sorrow, Sin and Shame*, and followed with the Defiance Campaign. It marked a new stage in the struggle both in terms of the size of the protest and the severity of the government's response. The campaign started with small groups of volunteers going into urban areas without passes, and entering stations and post offices through the 'Europeans Only' doors. On arrest they refused to pay fines and went to prison. The government responded severely with arrests and banning orders – seeing civil disobedience not as a protest but a crime. The campaign reached a peak in September 1952, with 2,058 arrests. The organizers stressed that the campaign must be non-violent. That held good in the early months, but during October and November, as discipline fell apart, rioting occurred, leading to about 40 deaths including six whites. The ANC leaders condemned the violence. Ironically, therefore, both the CYL and Xuma had proved to be right. The mass action had mobilized many more supporters, and the ANC membership rose dramatically from about 20,000 to 200,000; but in the end its organizational capacity was inadequate to control such a major campaign.

The campaign confirmed a number of lessons for the ANC. First, that the government was not prepared to respond to requests and petitions; that there was no constitutional route to liberation. Second, that militant action could gain mass support, but good organization was needed to control it and make it effective. Third, that the government would use its full powers to counter black political activity; that liberation could not be achieved without substantial suffering. Following the campaign the ANC was under continual pressure from the government. Earlier it had sought to avoid direct clashes; now the message was confrontation. According to Mandela the ANC emerged from the Defiance Campaign as a truly mass organization with experienced activists who had braved the authorities and removed the stigma of imprisonment. 'From the Defiance Campaign onwards,' he wrote 'going to prison became a badge of honour among Africans' (Mandela 1994: 129).

Given the conditions under which it operated the ANC's achievements were considerable, but it still had clear limitations. Its impact varied sharply from area to area. In the Defiance Campaign itself almost three-quarters of the support came from the towns of the Eastern Cape and Port Elizabeth in particular. It also remained a predominantly urban movement – led by an educated middle class and followed by urban workers. Rather than major efforts (like the Defiance Campaign) many African protests, both in urban and rural settings, were linked to local – bread and butter – issues. Soweto, for instance, at this time was little involved in national campaigns, but was the setting for a determined bus boycott from 1954 to 1959. Local protests were also the feature of African rural activity.

Albert Luthuli receiving the Nobel Peace Prize (courtesy of *The Star*)

The Native Affairs Department's reports between 1948 and 1952 spoke of 'considerable organized resistance', and 'serious retardation of government policy due to 'malicious agitators'. Colin Bundy records substantial rural discontent – including Zoutspanberg and Sekhukhuniland (1941–4); Witzieshoek reserve (1950–1), Marico reserve (1958); the Natal reserves (1958–9); and Pondoland (1960). These were local in origin and concerned with the government's agricultural policy in the reserves. If the ANC was involved at all it followed in the wake. Bundy concluded that national organizations, like the ANC – 'physically located in urban centres, ideologically concerned with the vanguard role of the Proletariat or with wringing political concessions for modernisers – were structurally ill-equipped to respond to the inchoate and murmurous patterns of peasant resistance. They failed to follow or to lead them' (Bundy 1987: 274, 276, 281). Tom Lodge reached a similar conclusion. He stated that the two most successful resistance movements of the time – judged by duration, scale and their success in frustrating state control – were the rural peasant resistance and the women's campaign against passes. In both cases they were initiated by local and spontaneous reactions (Lodge 1987: 317).

The Defiance Campaign led to a further change in ANC leadership. Moroke was arrested in July 1952 along with other ANC leaders, including Mandela and Sisulu. However, in court Moroke insisted upon conducting a separate defence because he claimed not to have been consulted about the campaign and he refused to be associated with communists who were among the accused. Moroke pleaded for leniency. Inevitably he was then ousted from the Presidency, to be replaced by Chief Albert Luthuli from KwaZulu. Luthuli, who unusually had a rural background, was a man of dignity, determination, faith in the cause and quiet, personal charm. 'A man of patience and fortitude', wrote Mandela (Mandela 1994: 133). The government had already told Luthuli that he must choose between the ANC and his chieftainship. He chose the ANC. He remained a man of moderation, retaining his Christian faith and opposition to violence. 'I am in Congress precisely because I am a Christian', he said (Sparks 1990: 279). In his 1955 Presidential message (read for him as he was under a banning order) he reaffirmed that the ANC, having accepted the multiracial nature of the country, supported an inclusive African Nationalism, resting on the principle of freedom for all and embracing all people 'regardless of their racial and geographical origin'. The ANC, said Luthuli, also opposed tribalism, and aimed to lead Africans from tribalism to the brotherhood of man (Karis and Carter 1977: 214). Luthuli was suspicious of left-wing elements in the ANC but supported moderate socialism in the style of the British Labour Party. In 1960 he was awarded the Nobel Peace Prize. Yet, like others, he came to realize that his moderate approach had gained little. 'Who,' he asked, 'can deny that thirty years of my life have been spent knocking in vain, patiently, moderately and honestly at a closed and barred door?' (Karis and Carter 1977: 435)

In September 1953, Nelson Mandela, as President of the Transvaal ANC, captured the mood of the day in a speech in which he called on Congress to adopt an aggressive but non-violent approach. The speech was read for him as he too was under a

Oliver Tambo and Nelson Mandela in the early 1990s (courtesy of *The Star*)

banning order. These orders, which were designed to remove leaders from the struggle by restricting their movements and activities, were issued simply on the minister's instructions. 'Banning,' wrote Mandela, 'not only confines one physically, it imprisons one's spirit. It induces a kind of psychological claustrophobia that makes one yearn for not only freedom of movement but spiritual escape' (Mandela 1994: 134). Despite the banning, in his 1953 speech he called on his listeners to continue the struggle against the government's harassment; to be flexible in response to changing circumstances; and to identify with the broader international liberation movement. The Defiance Campaign, he stated, had generated a new spirit in the people. It had 'inspired and aroused our people from a conquered and servile community of yesmen to a militant and uncompromising band of comrades in arms'. The government's immediate response, Mandela continued, had been to ban those who had championed the cause of freedom of the oppressed, and had 'uncompromisingly resisted the efforts of imperialistic America and her satellites to drag the world into the rule of violence and brutal force'. In the longer term the government's intentions were reflected in the Bantu Education Act which aimed 'to teach our children that Africans are inferior to Europeans', and to sustain white supremacy by beating down the blacks.

Resistance must continue, argued Mandela, but it had to reflect the new situation. The Defiance Campaign had run its course. We have 'to recuperate our strength and muster our forces for another and more powerful offensive against the enemy'. In the light of these circumstances it was necessary, he stated, to reinvigorate the ANC: 'to resist to the death the stinking policies of the gangsters that rule our country'. He recommended his 'M' plan, based on the creation of small local cells, which would improve commitment and internal communication, strengthen local branches, respond to the will of the people, and make it difficult for the government to penetrate the organization. He further recommended action based on day-by-day activities: such as union meetings in buses and trains, ANC groups visiting homes, and parents teaching their children that 'Africans are not one iota inferior to Europeans'. On a broader front he urged his listeners to see themselves as part of an international movement which was sweeping imperialism from Asia, and now challenging it in Africa. He finished by quoting the Indian leader, Jawaharlal Nehru: 'There is,' said Nehru, 'no easy walk to freedom anywhere, and many of us will have to pass through the valley of the shadow [of death] again and again before we reach the mountain tops of our desires' (Karis and Carter 1977: 106–15).

The Congress of the People and The Freedom Charter

In August 1953 Professor Z. K. Matthews, addressing the ANC's Cape province, called for a Congress of the People – to bring together representatives of all South Africans to reach agreement about the future of the country. The idea fired the imagination. A National Action Council was formed – consisting of the ANC, the South African Indian Congress, the South African Coloured People's Organization and the Congress of Democrats (a small white group). A wide range of organizations was invited to participate in the Congress including the governing National Party. None of the white parliamentary parties responded, but elsewhere the Congress generated great enthusiasm. Many organizations gave their support – churches, women's groups, trade unions and political parties – and public consultations were held throughout the country. 'Nothing,' said Luthuli 'in the history of the liberatory struggle in South Africa quite caught the popular imagination as this did' (Karis and Carter 1977: 59). Mandela wrote that the dream was to make it a landmark in the history of the freedom struggle, 'to create a clarion call for change. Our hope was that one day it would be looked on with the same reverence as the founding convention of the ANC in 1912.'

More than 3,000 delegates assembled for the Congress at Kliptown, near Johannesburg in June 1955. They ranged from liberal-minded churchmen to hard-line communists. While the great majority were Africans, there were also 320 Indians, 230 Coloureds and 112 whites. On arrival they were presented with a document, drafted by a committee of the National Action Council. That document became the Freedom Charter and was accepted at the meeting by acclamation before the police broke up the Congress on the second day. The Charter does not concern itself with methods. It concentrated on broad aims and ideals, which were to be the lode star of the ANC and anti-apartheid organizations in the years ahead.

The Charter is committed to a multiracial society and an inclusive nationalism built on civic not ethnic identity. 'South Africa,' it declares, 'belongs to all who live in it, black and white.' It claims that the basis of authority is the will of the people, which can only be achieved in a democratic state, without distinction of race, sex, or belief, and in which individuals enjoy equal political and legal rights. 'Every man and woman shall have the right to vote and stand for all bodies that make law.' However, the Charter also speaks of equal rights for national groups and races. 'All national groups,' it states, 'shall be protected by law against insults to their race and national pride. All people shall have equal rights to use their own language and to develop their own folk culture and customs' (Karis and Carter 1977: 205). Further aims concerned the economy, work, housing and education. The state, as seen in the Charter, should play an active role in the economy, so that: 'The national wealth of our country, the heritage of all South Africans, shall be restored to the people', through nationalization of the mines, banks and monopoly industries. Land, without being nationalized, was to be redistributed more evenly 'amongst those who work it.'

From the beginning the Charter attracted controversy – about its drafting, its interpretation, and its implications for the future. For the ANC the controversy intensified as it moved towards its annual conference in 1955, where the Charter was due to be presented. In the event it was decided to postpone deliberation for a special conference in March/April 1956. With regard to the drafting, the group (a small committee of the National Action Council) that had presented it to the Congress claimed that they had distilled the ideas and hopes of the thousands of groups and individuals who had made submissions. It was, claimed the group, a 'bottom up' exercise. Critics dismissed that. They said that the group had ignored the consultation process, so that even Luthuli and Matthews did not see the draft before it was presented. It was, said the critics, a 'top down' exercise by a small group which contained a disproportionate number of communists and whites. Even after the Charter had been accepted by the Congress there was uncertainty about whether it was a draft open to amendment or a finished document to be accepted whole. Luthuli initially saw it as a draft and favoured amendments, but eventually accepted it as a whole to prevent internal divisions.

There was equal controversy in interpreting the Charter, and its implications for the future. The debates turned around three main issues: race, the role of communists, and revolution. For the 'Africanists' inside the ANC one of the sticking points was the statement that 'South Africa belongs to all', thereby abandoning what for them was the inalienable rights of Africans to ownership, with other sections as 'guests' of the African nation. Further, they argued, that to regard blacks and whites as 'brothers' was to distort a situation in which Africans were treated as 'slaves'. Instead they claimed they would regard people as individuals and it was on that basis that future citizens would be accepted. Potlako Leballo attacked foreign ideologies and called for a return to 'Africa for the Africans'. On the eve of the 1955 annual conference a leading Africanist, Peter Molotsi, wrote that the aims of the Charter could not be achieved unless there was a return to the ideology underlying the 1949 Programme of Action. 'There can be no question,' he wrote, 'as to the correctness and dynamism of African Nationalism as an outlook for giving the African people the self confidence and subjective liberation, without which no national oppression can be effectively challenged' (Karis and Carter 1977: 69). At the conference itself sections of a letter from Xuma were read out in which he supported the Africanists approach. He accused the present leadership of abandoning the nation-building plans of the 1940s, and working with other racial groups, which unlike Africans, did not have to make sacrifices themselves (Karis and Carter 1977: 242/3).

Directly linked to the Africanists' concern about the influence of other groups was the position of communists within both the ANC and the trade unions. This concern was not confined to the Africanists. Luthuli himself expressed fears. On the eve of the 1955 conference he wrote that he would consider resigning the Presidency if there was too much over centralization or if the ANC were to 'tie ourselves so fast to the Congress of the People'. Also the Liberal Party had only sent observers, not delegates to the Congress, because it was suspicious of the role being played by communists. Joseph Ngubane of the Liberals said that the ultimate aim was 'to condition the African people for the purposes of accepting communism via the back door' (Karis and Carter 1977: 64). When communists responded that there was no mention of class struggle, or vanguard party in the Charter, their critics replied that this was only because the Kremlin had decreed that the move to communism must be taken step by step, and the first step was to support national liberation.

Without doubt communists played an active role in preparing the Charter and without doubt they saw it only as a step to their final objective, but for many non-communists that was acceptable in the struggle against the evil of apartheid. Despite his doubts about communism, Luthuli was confident that the ANC was not under communist control, and he was not prepared to split the party on this matter. E. P. Moretsele, a prominent non-communist ANC member, explained that communists were in the ANC, but that was not grounds for a split. 'Most of them,' he said, 'are hardworking, sincere members who abide loyally by the Constitution and aims of the national Congress. As long as they continue to do so they are welcome.' Nelson Mandela adopted the same position. However, this was an issue which persisted and later helped to split the ANC. It also convinced the government that the ANC was a communist organization, or at least a communist front.

In Pretoria's eyes the Charter was a revolutionary document, whose aims could only be realized by violence. On 27 September 1955, the police made their largest raid yet searching properties and arresting up to 500 people, followed by restrictions and banning orders. Subsequently the government made the Charter a central document in the Treason Trial which started in 1956. The ANC rejected the claim that it was 'revolutionary' in that it was not an attempt to overthrow the state by violent means. However, Mandela realized that it was in some senses 'revolutionary' precisely 'because the changes it envisages cannot be won without breaking up the economic and political set-up of present South Africa' (Karis and Carter 1977: 64).

In summary the Freedom Charter contained a mixture of aims based on liberalism, egalitarianism and socialism, leaving it open to a variety of interpretations. One ANC leader called it a 'hodge-podge' (Karis and Carter 1977: 60). Probably that was inevitable, for it was an attempt to satisfy diverse interests in a broad statement of ideals. At the time most whites dismissed the Charter as at best an unreliable wish list, and at worst a call to bloody revolution. For the ANC, consciously or un-consciously, the ambiguity had advantages. The Charter helped to hold members together beneath 'a great umbrella under which all Africans could find shelter' (Mandela 1994: 90). In the years ahead the ANC consistently advocated the Charter, but interpreted and reinterpreted it according to the times and circum-stances. Despite its ambiguity; 'it captured,' wrote Mandela, 'the hopes and dreams of the people and acted as a blueprint for the liberation struggle and the future of the nation' (Mandela 1994: 162).

Responding to the spirit of the Charter and the calls of leaders like Luthuli and Mandela the ANC continued its activities against the government's racial policies. It opposed the forced removal of Africans, and the introduction of the Bantu Education Act. Women members led a campaign in 1956 against the introduction of passes for women, which culminated in a mass demonstration at the Union Buildings in Pretoria. Women were also prominent in local protests 'not so much [as] a feminist attempt to overthrow the existing social order as opposition to state interference in the established rights and status of women' (Worden 1995: 101). The ANC joined with other black organizations in criticism of the Tomlinson Committee, with its proposals to intensify the separation of the races. An 'All In' conference rejected the concept of separate national homelands, because it would undermine co-operation between the races and remove African rights in the Union as a whole. The ANC leaders hoped that their efforts would be like an incoming tide, with wave after wave steadily making their way up the shore. If that was the hope the government was equally determined to turn back the tide. In an attempt to do so it arrested 156 people in December 1956, charging them with treason.

Those who stood before the court at the Treason Trial were a mixture of races and of political beliefs – Africans, whites, Indians and Coloureds; moderates like Luthuli, and hard-line communists like Joe Slovo, stood side by side. After an initial period in prison the accused were released on bail but their personal lives and that of their organizations were greatly disrupted by regular court appearances. Eventually the charges against all the accused were dismissed or withdrawn, but in stages. It was not until March 1961, after more than four years, that the last of the accused were found not guilty and released. The trial had its impact on the government's oppo-nents in contradictory ways. For a time the movements were thrown back on their heels as the energies of the leaders were consumed in defending themselves. During 1957 and 1958 the level of activity against the government fell, but even then it did not stop. For example on 26 June 1957 the ANC arranged a 'stay at home', and in December it adopted a new constitution – the 'Tambo Constitution'. Meanwhile, among those standing trial, a new unity was being forged. The common experience brought most of them closer together in their opposition to the government and made future co-operation easier. By 1960 agitation against the government was more intense than ever.

Africanists and the Pan Africanist Congress (PAC)

Ironically, despite the broad sense of unity engendered by the Treason Trial, the ANC found itself fighting an internal battle in the late 1950s. The challenge came from a group who initially were called 'Nationalists' but later were known as 'Africanists'. Like the Youth League before them, they were militant young men in a hurry, frustrated by what they thought was lack of drive in the ANC's leadership, and what they claimed was the failure of the leaders to represent the true aspirations of the mass of the African people. The internal division was exacerbated by the ANC's acceptance of the Freedom Charter: the 'Kliptown Charter' as the Africanists disparagingly called it. Reflecting views that had been advanced by Marcus Garvey in the 1920s, they objected to the Charter's claim that South Africa belonged to all who lived in it; its undertaking to protect the rights of all national

Robert Sobukwe
(courtesy of *The Star*)

and racial groups; and to the prominent role played in drafting it by whites, particularly the Congress of Democrats.

The Africanists claimed that they were returning to the ANC's true principles – those of 1912 as revived in the 1940s by Anton Lembede of the Youth League. They saw themselves as the rightful custodians of African nationalism, whose objectives would be achieved, said Nana Mahomo, by 'involving the common heritage of the black man – his colour, his culture, his language . . . creating out of the myth and the reality of race a feeling of common destiny for all black men who have suffered and shared oppression' (Liebenburg 1994: 104). The Africanists were strongest in the Transvaal and particularly the ANC's Orlando branch, which was led by Potlako Leballo. Their initial hope was to reshape the party from inside, like the Youth League before them. However, perhaps because of different circumstances and/or a lack of patience, they broke away. The break came at the ANC's Transvaal's provincial conference in November 1958. In his presidential address Luthuli not only attacked the government, for injecting 'the virus of prejudice and sectionalism' and pandering to racism, but he went on to criticize those Africans who were emulating the government, 'in claiming exclusive control of South Africa . . . We have seen developing – even though it is at an embryonic stage – a dangerously narrow African nationalism' (Karis and Carter 1977: 310). The Africanists were incensed. They tried to shout down Luthuli's supporters, and although they were in a minority they attempted to take over the conference. They were thwarted by the vigorous efforts of Oliver Tambo, who ensured that majority views prevailed. The Africanists therefore withdrew and in the weeks that followed were joined by sympathizers in the Cape and Natal.

In April 1959 the Africanists met at the Orlando Communal Hall. Surrounded by posters proclaiming 'Africa for the Africans', 'Imperialists Quit Africa'; and 'Forward to the United States of Africa', they formed the Pan Africanist Congress (PAC). Robert Sobukwe, an academic from the University of the Witwatersrand, was elected President, and Leballo became National Secretary. Young men and intellectuals were prominent. Of the fifteen members elected to the national executive, eight were teachers or former teachers, three were university students, three were small businessmen, and one a trade unionist (Karis and Carter 1977: 315). The delegates adopted a constitution, a manifesto and an oath of allegiance. For organizational purposes they divided the country into six rather than four regions, but otherwise their structure was similar to the ANC's – with local branches and regional executives, answerable to a national executive and an annual conference. However, because it did not inherit an administrative structure, the PAC was plagued by organization problems from the start, and never fully resolved them. Its members tended to rely on emotion and rhetoric rather than routine organization, to believe that they had only to point the way and all would be achieved. Sobukwe declared 'all we are required to do is show the light and the masses will find the way' (Liebenburg 1994: 105). The PAC also tended to concentrate on grand causes rather than immediate bread and butter issues, so that even in Orlando they had only limited popular support.

Despite its weaker organization the PAC offered a clear alternative to the ANC. Both movements claimed to have the same broad goal – a non-racial South Africa

– yet they differed in a number of ways: over the routes to that goal, their interpretation of 'non-racialism', and the form of the state. The ANC angered Sobukwe and Leballo, by treating all who opposed the government as potential allies, whatever their motives or beliefs. Such alliances, argued the PAC, were based on the false premise that co-operation could exist between the oppressed and the oppressor, whereas it was only possible between equals. That left the ANC vulnerable to white communists and their 'foreign ideologies' based on class interests and class divisions. Africans, the PAC argued, had to create their own structures. Further it accused the ANC of acting as a party which was seeking a place in parliament, thereby implying that the present structure was legitimate and only needed amendment. The ANC failed to see that South Africa was not an island, that the struggle was both national and continental. The 'national' aspect, they stated, involved the return of the land to the Africans, its rightful owners. There could be no compromise on that: no bargain between the conquerors and the conquered, between the dispossessor and the dispossessed. The African nation had been suppressed. 'We claim Africa for the Africans; the ANC claims it for all', wrote Sobukwe. The 'democratic' struggle was essentially a recognition of numbers, the acceptance of the majority. 'The Africans,' concluded Leballo, 'are in the fortunate position of being not only the rightful owners of the land but also the majority of the population'. The Africanists were not simply seeking a place in the present structure – the whole structure had to go (Karis and Carter 1977: 500–10).

At the PAC's inaugural conference Sobukwe spoke of a new scramble for Africa by the Soviet Union and the United States, which could only be countered by Africans working together across the continent. He quoted Dr Kwame Nkrumah of Ghana and Dr Azikiwe of Nigeria in their determination to resist outside powers and put Africa's interests first. He endorsed Nkrumah's vision of throwing off white domination to build a United States of Africa. It is, said Sobukwe, 'the sacred duty of every African state to strive ceaselessly and energetically for the creation of a United States of Afrika stretching from the Cape to Cairo, Morocco to Madagascar'. All attempts to balkanize Africa should be resisted. He dismissed the claim that the Union was an exceptional case because of its social mix. It was an African country like any other which had been colonized by an alien minority. Its problems could only be solved in a continental setting, and that is why the Africanists rejected not only apartheid but multi racialism, which was simply 'racialism multiplied'. For Sobukwe and the PAC the aim was 'government of Africans, by Africans, for Africans' with an 'African' defined as one who gives loyalty to Africa and is prepared to accept African majority rule. 'We guarantee no minority rights, because we think in terms of individuals, not groups', he said (Karis and Carter 1977: 513).

Sobukwe went on to argue that the myth of racism had been propounded by white imperialists to justify their exploitation of the indigenous masses. In South Africa the whites claimed to be guardians and yet treated Africans as savage and backward. Although Indians were also 'a foreign minority group', they too were oppressed. However, the merchant class, from which most Indian political leaders were drawn, had become tainted with the virus of cultural and national arrogance. Democracy could therefore only be achieved by the efforts of Africans themselves. For the future 'the illiterate and semi literate masses constitute the key . . . of any struggle for true democracy in South Africa' (Karis and Carter 1977: 515). To be effective an African consciousness had to be revived in exclusive organizations under the banner of African nationalism. He spoke of 'the humiliation and degradation of the indigenous African people', the theft of their land, and their treatment as inferiors. Recognizing the importance of self-respect and self-reliance he announced a 'status programme', to free the African mind, for once that was free the body would follow. 'We are blazing a new trail,' Sobukwe declared, 'We invite you to be creators of history. Join us in the march to freedom.' With these commitments in mind the PAC leader believed that the decks were now cleared for a decisive conflict. The final outcome was not in dispute. The PAC would be the 'advance guard' of the African masses, leading them to freedom as a single African nation, in a state based on 'an African socialist democratic order', rejecting the exploitation of the many by the few, seeking an equitable distribution of wealth and income, but avoiding the totalitarianism of the communist state.

When Sobukwe was questioned on the Africanists' attitude to whites, he argued that history showed that a privileged group never voluntarily relinquished its position. He recognized that 'there are whites who are intellectually converted, but because of their position materially, they cannot fully identify themselves with the cause. They want safeguards and checkpoints'. He explained that the African masses 'do not fight an abstraction. They do not hate oppression or capitalism. They concretise these and hate the oppressor [which] in South Africa is the white man. But they hate these groups because they *associate them with their oppression!* Remove the association and you remove the hatred . . . We do not hate the European because he is white! We hate him because he is an oppressor' (Karis and Carter 1977: 510). Sobukwe claimed to have no anti-white feelings. However, only when Africans had gained equality of status would racism disappear. 'Our contention,' he said, 'is that the Africans are the only people who, because of their material position, can be interested in the complete overhaul of society.' Europeans cannot identify with it because they benefit materially from the system. Whenever Europeans co-operate with Africans they demand 'checks and counter checks . . . they stultify and retard the movement of Africans . . . consciously or unconsciously promoting sectional interests' (Pogrund 1990: 105). That was true of white communists, but Africanists' suspicion of whites was not confined to communists; it extended to white liberals and missionaries like Trevor Huddleston and Ambrose Reeve. The PAC's manifesto spoke of African leaders who had been so seduced by the whites that they had come to 'regard as equals the foreign master and the indigenous slave, the white exploiter and the African exploited' (Pogrund 1990: 92).

In summary Robert Sobukwe identified three basic PAC commitments. First, that the movement must directly involve the great mass of Africans. Second, that an exclusive African nationalism must be established to provide equality for Africans and to weld the masses together through a 'loyalty higher than that of the tribe and giving formal expression to their desire to be a nation.' Third, that the struggle in South Africa was part of a continental struggle, with the ultimate goal of creating a United States of Africa. The PAC manifesto spoke of South Africans working to find 'expression for this nation in the merger of free independent African states: a United States of Africa'.

Although the PAC claimed that its ultimate aim was a non-racial society, there was an element of ambiguity in the message. Its call for a government of 'Africans' had similarities to Hertzog's earlier call to 'Afrikaners'. Both claimed to be building self-confidence for a particular group so that it could gain equality of status. Yet to many it seemed implausible to propose change on exclusive lines to achieve an inclusive society. Sobukwe personally stressed that ethnic origin was not the issue; that once oppression was removed everybody would be treated as individual citizens. However, not all his followers were as clear minded. Opposition to whites had a strong emotional appeal to Africans who had suffered oppression and discrimination for generations. Therefore, among Africanists two interpretations of nationalism coexisted. One was an inclusive approach, in which once oppression was removed all people, irrespective of race, would be embraced as members of an African nation and a state founded on democratic majority rule. The other was exclusive, and based on race. In that approach non-Africans were seen as at best 'guests', and at worst 'aliens' in an African dominated state, and in pursuit of that state it might be necessary to drive the white exploiters into the sea.

Part IV

The Wind of Change

13

The New Republic, Sharpeville and the Granite Response

On Strijdom's death in August 1958 Dr Hendrik Verwoerd became Prime Minister. The 'Verwoerd years' was a time of profound changes in the quest for national identity and the structure of the state, as the government set out to develop grand apartheid and defend itself against its many opponents. Verwoerd, a man of burning conviction, great determination, and formidable powers of work, had already made his stamp on government as Minister of Native Affairs. He was inspired by the belief that he had been divinely chosen to lead the Afrikaner people under God's guidance. 'We', he said, 'as believing rulers of a religious country, will seek strength and guidance in the future, as in the past, from Him who controls the destiny of nations' (Hepple 1967: 134). In white politics his political inheritance was much more secure than Malan's had been ten years earlier. The NP now had a grip on government; the bulk of Afrikaners were massed behind it; the white opposition was weak; the economy flourished and the framework of apartheid was in place. African nationalism was active but did not appear to be a threat to the state. The government and the white society were enjoying a period of confidence. That did not last. In the early 1960s confidence was replaced by crisis. The roots of the crisis were in the past, but they gained a new intensity from African nationalists and international critics. Challenge mounted on challenge to produce a cumulative sense of peril.

The Republic

The year 1960 opened dramatically when Verwoerd announced that the white electorate would be asked to decide by referendum whether South Africa should become a Republic. 'This,' Verwoerd told Parliament, 'has indeed been the basis of our struggle all these years: nationalism against imperialism. This has been the struggle since 1910; a republic as opposed to the monarchical connection . . . We stand unequivocally and clearly for the establishment of the republic' (Moodie 1975: 283). Yet, not all his NP colleagues shared Verwoerd's determination. He went ahead despite doubters who pointed out that the NP had never gained a majority

H. F. Verwoerd
(courtesy of the
South African
High
Commission)

of votes at an election. With the UP strongly opposed to a republic these doubters feared defeat. In the referendum campaign Verwoerd appealed for white unity, without which he claimed it would be impossible to solve racial problems. He confirmed that the two official languages (Afrikaans and English) would be retained, and appealed to English speakers to vote for a republic in the cause of white unity. In the event Verwoerd's confidence was rewarded. A remarkable 90.73 per cent of the electorate voted, giving a majority of 850,458 to 775,878 for the Republic. Verwoerd was triumphant. The ideal which Afrikaner nationalists had harboured since Union had been made flesh. In thanksgiving at the Voortrekker Monument, having paid homage to Kruger, Hertzog, Malan and Strijdom, he attributed victory to the hand of God. 'It is,' he said, 'the day of answered prayer; it is the coming of the republican dawn; it is the sun breaking through the morning mist . . . Through so many years we longed and prayed for this moment and now it is here' (Moodie 1975: 285).

In itself the republican referendum would have made 1960 a year of intense political activity, but in the months between Verwoerd's announcement and the referendum itself the country was in turmoil, shaken by a series of internal events whose impact was intensified by the international reaction. The unquestioning assumption of white domination of the state was severely shaken, and from this came changes in government policy, black nationalism and Pretoria's international relations. Although the NP government was determined to hold onto power, it could not prevent the impact of events elsewhere in Africa spilling over the borders, promoting hopes among blacks and anxiety among whites. The UN declared 1960 the 'Year of Africa', as sixteen African colonies gained their independence. Many whites believed that their worst fears about black rule were confirmed when white refugees fled through South Africa from the chaos of the Congo. In this political climate Verwoerd's vigorous defence of the white position drew increased support for his republican campaign.

In South Africa itself the first major event to follow the announcement of the referendum was the visit of the British Prime Minister, Harold Macmillan. When Macmillan arrived in February the government ignored his request to meet ANC leaders, but it could not ignore what followed. In private Macmillan told Verwoerd that Britain could no longer continue to support South Africa's claims that her racial policies were outside the competence of the UN. Apartheid, explained Macmillan, created tension between states which could not be contained within the Union's borders. He followed up these private conversations with his 'Wind of Change' speech to a joint sitting of the South African Parliament. The speech came like a hammer blow. To the surprise and chagrin of his hosts Macmillan challenged their concept of nation and state. In doing so he exposed the fears of many whites: about the strength of African nationalism, about decolonization and about international action. He unearthed the fears, stripped away the illusions of unquestioning western support, and was bitterly condemned for doing so.

It was the tone as well as the content of Macmillan's speech that angered many whites. They sensed a smugness in the British position of claiming to have backed both a winner and a just cause. Macmillan's message was that anti-colonial nationalism which had swept across Asia was now sweeping across Africa. With his eye on the cold war, Macmillan said that western interests were best served by coming to terms with it. The great issue of the second half of the twentieth century, he said, is whether the uncommitted peoples of Africa 'will swing to the East or the West. The struggle is joined and it is a struggle for the minds of men'. He claimed, however, that British policy was not based on opportunism but on a conviction of right — a claim the NP dismissed as characteristic British cant. Britain, said Macmillan, was determined 'to create a society which respects the rights of individuals — a society in which men are allowed to grow to their full stature'. He recognized the baffling problems that faced South Africa, but said there were aspects of Pretoria's policy which it was impossible for Britain to support, 'without being false to our own deep convictions about the political destinies of free men'. Macmillan set these developments in a sweep of history, stretching back to the Romans and reaching forward to generations as yet unborn. He hinted at inevitability, for while the growth of an 'African national consciousness' took many forms, it could not be stopped: 'It is happening everywhere. The wind of change is blowing through the continent' (Mansergh 1963: 347–51).

Verwoerd replied immediately. He was at a disadvantage because Macmillan had not observed the normal courtesy of providing a copy of his speech beforehand. However, for many whites, Verwoerd's impromptu response was one of his finest hours. He thanked Macmillan for his frankness, and said that Britain and South Africa would remain friends because they were both committed to western values and to peace. However, they had clear differences in Africa. Verwoerd claimed that South Africa was in tune with developments in the continent, whereas he warned Britain that its aims would be defeated by its policy changes. The attempt to do justice to all should imply being just to whites as well as blacks. It was the whites 'who brought civilization here, who made the development of Black nationalism possible'. The whites, continued Verwoerd, had made South Africa their mother-land, but 'we also see ourselves as part of the Western world, a true White state in Africa, with the possibility of granting a full future to the Black man in our midst'. This made South Africa 'indispensable to the White World . . . We are the link. We are White, but we are in Africa. We link with both, and that lays on us a special duty' (Botha 1967: 55–6).

Later Verwoerd said that simply because the whites were outnumbered, they must not allow their rights to be swallowed up, or be satisfied 'to compete with the Black masses on an equal basis, which in the long term can only mean a Black government'. He foresaw communism and black dictatorships emerging in the new African states, which the black masses would find more onerous than white leader-ship. The objective, concluded Verwoerd, should not be human or political intermingling, but co-existence. He accepted that black states were coming into existence, but their development should 'take place from the bottom upwards, and gradually', at the speed at which they are capable of advancing. Meanwhile 'we will see that we remain in power in this White South Africa' (IRR 1959/60: 281).

An insight into Verwoerd's character came in his private conversations with Macmillan. The British Prime Minister outlined a consensus view of politics, in which the government's task was to respond to changing views and circumstances, to find the main stream of opinion. Verwoerd rejected that. His experience was rooted in different soil: in which Afrikaners had struggled to preserve their identity against powerful enemies; in which there was no consensus to reflect; in which success had come from intransigence – from a dogmatic conviction of right and a refusal to compromise. Verwoerd said he preferred to set his own course, rather than 'be carried along willy nilly by the stream'. His aim was to influence the course of history, and satisfy 'the desires of that section of the nation whose support I enjoy' (HA 5 February 1960). For him, wrote Macmillan later, apartheid 'was more than a political philosophy, it was a religion; a religion based on the Old Testament rather than the New. He had all the force of argument of some of the great Calvinist leaders . . . that he alone could be right' (Horne 1989: 194).

Sharpeville

The dust had not settled from Macmillan's visit before the tragedy of Sharpeville hit South Africa. Late in 1959 both the ANC and the PAC announced that they would launch campaigns against the pass laws. The PAC, eager to gain the initiative, moved first launching its campaign on 21 March, calling on Africans to defy the pass laws and offer themselves for arrest. The PAC assumed/hoped that their call would steadily build up into a massive response, and, as the prisons were filled and industry ground to a halt, the government would be forced into concessions. It was a step, said the PAC, along a road leading to political independence by 1963. Sobukwe and other PAC leaders insisted that the campaign must be peaceful to avoid a violent government reaction, and they informed the police of their plans (Lodge 1983: 203). In the event the African response was at best patchy, but at Sharpeville, south of Johannesburg, a crowd of about 5,000 gathered around the police station offering themselves for arrest. The incidents that triggered off the violence are disputed, but after a long stand off the police fired into the crowd killing 67 and wounding 186. Many were shot in the back as they fled. On the same day at Langa, outside Cape Town, three Africans were killed and 50 wounded. Because of the scale of the tragedy Sharpeville would have stood out whenever it had happened; but it was not the first time that the police had killed demonstrators. Others are forgotten but Sharpeville remains: it remains because it was seen as part of the struggle which was bringing Africans into power elsewhere in the continent, and which, predicted Robert Sobukwe, would bring 'freedom and independence' to South Africa. Those who fell at Sharpeville were seen as martyrs in a righteous cause, and victims of a brutal regime.

In the wake of Sharpeville the rival ANC and PAC organized marches, days of mourning and boycotts. In Cape Town there was a major strike. These demonstrations were a living witness of black demands and revealed to many whites for the first time the potential of mass black action. Yet, although the activities captured black enthusiasm they ran into problems. Some arose within the organizations themselves – from poor communications, inadequate funds, inexperienced leadership and continued rivalry – but the greatest obstacles arose from the government's response, which reflected both its concern and determination. It took time and experience for the government to bring to bear its full power, but following Sharpeville, Pretoria declared a state of emergency, outlawed the major African political parties, and arrested African leaders.

As Pretoria fought to regain control it became clear that Sharpeville had changed the political context – reshaping African nationalism and the government's response to it. There were Africans who continued to support non-violent methods, either from principle or from fear of the government's security machine. Albert Luthuli himself, who remained committed to non-violence, was awarded the Nobel Prize for Peace in 1960. For many ANC members the final attempt at peaceful pressure came in March 1961 from the 'All In African Conference'. This was presented as an umbrella organization but was Congress dominated. A highlight of the meeting was the public appearance of Nelson Mandela, who had temporarily been unbanned. He called for a national convention of all races to prepare a new constitution, and for a campaign of non co-operation if the government did not respond. Following the meeting Mandela wrote in vain to the UP seeking its support for the convention. The alternatives, he said were 'talk it out; or shoot it out' (Karis and Carter 1977: 635).

Launching the Armed Struggle

The government was in no mood to 'talk it out'. African nationalists therefore turned to revolutionary methods. Protest turned to violent resistance; defiance to a liberation struggle. Armed sections emerged – 'Umkhonto we Sizwe' (Spear of the Nation) from the ANC, and 'Poqo' (Meaning 'only' or 'pure') from the PAC. (Later the PAC's armed wing was renamed 'The Azanian Peoples' Liberation Army' or 'APLA'.) In the months and years that followed the government and the underground movements became locked in a fierce struggle – of raids, sabotage, torture, assassinations, imprisonment without trial, killings, informers, emergency laws, dramatic arrests and escapes. Many government opponents fled the country some to return later as freedom fighters. The early escape and re-entry routes were through the British High Commission Territories. Inevitably this created tension between Pretoria and London: Pretoria complaining that the British were supporting enemies of the state; London complained that South Africa was raiding across the borders. In October 1962 the ANC held its first conference in exile, at Lobatsi in Botswana, where it still emphasized political action, but for the first time acknowledged its links with its armed wing Umkhonto we Sizwe (MK). The PAC established themselves at Maseru in Basutoland. Yet neither London nor Pretoria saw it in their interests to pursue the dispute too far. Pretoria tightened its policing of the borders, and gained valuable information from those who were arrested. For their part the British were not prepared to turn the refugees back, but they tried to hurry them on, restricted the activities of those who remained and banned the establishment of guerilla camps.

In the immediate aftermath of Sharpeville there was great optimism among African nationalists. This was fed by the surge of decolonization elsewhere in Africa, by the conviction that their cause was just and therefore must succeed, and by the strong international reaction to Sharpeville. So confident were PAC leaders that they repeated that freedom would be achieved by 1963. Although less specific the ANC was preaching a similarly upbeat message. In December 1961 Oliver Tambo, after reaffirming to an international audience that the ANC's aim was a non-racial South Africa embracing all her people, claimed that the whole African continent was bursting into freedom. 'This,' he said, 'is Africa's age – the dawn of her fulfilment. Yes, the moment when she must grapple with destiny to reach the summit saying – ours was a fight for noble values and worthy ends, and not for lands and the enslavement of men . . . To us all free and not free, the call of the hour is to redeem the name and honour of Mother Africa' (Reddy 1987: 33–6).

The decision to turn to arms ran against previous ANC beliefs and history, and was not taken lightly. In June 1961 Mandela proposed to the national executive that violent tactics be employed. He later explained that it was 'only when all else had failed, when all channels of peaceful progress had been barred to us, that the decision was made to embark on violent forms of political struggle . . . the Government had left us with no choice' (Mandela 1978: 160). To persuade colleagues he argued that 'it was wrong and immoral to subject our people to armed attacks by the state without offering them some kind of alternative'. The African people, he said, would take to violence with or without the ANC and therefore it was better to have it under control (Mandela 1994: 259–60). Although Mandela carried most of his colleagues with him, the national executive decided that Congress itself (as distinct from Umkhonto) would remain non-violent but would not stop members adopting different tactics.

Umkhonto – or 'MK' as it became known – was therefore initially formed outside the ANC, and unlike the ANC, it opened its ranks to whites, Indians and Coloureds. The 'National High Command, which was mixed race, identified four options: sabotage, guerilla war, terrorism or open revolution. It decided initially to confine itself to sabotage (although a few units failed to comply and used terrorist measures) while at the same time developing a guerilla army in exile. When the MK launched its first sabotage attacks in December 1961 against power stations and government buildings, it issued a pamphlet, which reflected both the old hopes of reaching agreement, and the new recognition of the need to fight. 'We hope,' it said, 'we will bring the Government and its supporters to their senses before it is too late [and] before matters reach the desperate stage of civil war.' But it went on to state: 'The time comes in the life of any nation when there remain only two choices: to submit or fight.' While previously peaceful methods had been employed now was the time to fight. The government had increasingly employed violence, leaving the liberation movement no choice but to respond in kind. The pamphlet did not name the ANC, but claimed that MK was fully backed by the 'national liberation movement . . . [was] under the overall political guidance of that move-ment', and had support from people of all races (Lodge 1983: 234 and Ellis and Sechaba 1992: 33).

Joe Slovo, a member of the high command, argued that by confining itself to sabotage MK fulfilled three aims: it placed the moral responsibility for a slide into war onto Pretoria; it helped to identify which of the activists were suited to aggres-sive action; and it was a form of propaganda which encouraged others to act. Incidents became common. Between September 1961 and June 1963 at least 193 cases of MK sabotage came before the courts, extending from such minor acts as putting burning matches into letter boxes to blowing up power lines. They were seen as forerunners to the overthrow of the white state. The ambitious scale of the high command's thinking was revealed in plans for 'Operation Mayibuye'. It was to start with landings of freedom fighters by sea and air. Their tasks were to estab-lish bases, recruit new members and mobilize the black masses. Risings were planned in four areas (Port Elizabeth, Port Shepstone, Northern Transvaal and the North West Cape). It was assumed that the campaign would be backed by substan-tial international support from African and socialist states. Although the nationalists realized that the government would resist they optimistically believed 'that the state structure will collapse sooner than we at the moment envisage' (Karis and Carter 1977: 684).

Meanwhile in terms of propaganda, Mandela, as MK leader, was gaining a national and international reputation for his articulate defence of the struggle, and, as he eluded the government's efforts to arrest him, he became known as 'the Black Pimpernel'. In January 1962 he secretly slipped out of the country to attend a conference in East Africa, after which he visited Algeria (where he undertook guerilla training and arranged training for MK recruits) and finally to Europe. 'Wherever I went,' he wrote, 'I found sympathy for our cause and promises of support.' However, he was arrested in August 1962 shortly after his return to South Africa. Although there was insufficient evidence at that time to link him with MK, he was imprisoned for three years for inciting workers to stay away from their posts, and for leaving the country without a visa. In contrasting ways the trial was a triumph both for the government, which had caught its man; and for Mandela who used the court as a platform to promote the ANC's message.

Despite Mandela's growing fame the MK campaign had only a limited impact. Inside the country it gained sparse press coverage and the damage it inflicted was often superficial. Greater attention at that time was paid to the more aggressive Poqo. Poqo (or the Azanian Peoples' Liberation Army – APLA, – as it later became known) was formed by militant members of the PAC, and the restraining hand of Robert Sobukwe was removed when he was imprisoned along with 18 other PAC leaders for inciting people to disobey the pass laws. Like MK, Poqo's impact was patchy, much depending on local leadership, but it flourished in the Western Cape, Vereeniging and Krugersdorp, and, unlike MK, it operated in rural areas. Poqo's appeal was cruder, simpler and more violent than the MK. It was the first African movement in South Africa to adopt a strategy which explicitly involved killing people. A Poqo pamphlet of December 1961 stated: 'Africa will be free on January 1st. The white people shall suffer, the black people will rule. Freedom comes after bloodshed. Poqo has started' (Lodge 1983: 243).

Poqo's violent course was shaped with a number of aims in mind: to defend itself by murdering informers and police; to terrorize the white population by random killings; and to lay the found for a general rising (Lodge 1983: 246). Its approach included attacks on chiefs in rural areas (with a number of unsuccessful attempts to assassinate Kaiser Mantanzima in the Transkei) and in February 1963 five whites were murdered at a road camp near Bashee River, including a woman and two young girls. A small scale Poqo rising took place at Paarl in November 1962, where it had established control of the African township by terror tactics. When the police challenged that by their own aggressive actions, the local Poqo leaders led a crowd of about 250 men armed with axes and pangas to attack the police station where some Poqo members were held. When the marchers were repulsed they rioted through the town burning, looting and killing, before order was restored (IRR 1963: 16). Like MK with its Operation Mayibuye, Poqo laid plans for a general rising. Potlake Leballo, who in Sobukwe's absence became national leader, set 8 April 1963 as the date. As a prelude to the rising every branch was to undertake a recruitment drive with a target of 1,000 members each. Then on the appointed day the members would lead a mass rising with simulta-neous attacks on strategic places, such as police stations, accompanied by the indiscriminate slaughter of whites, who Leballo described as 'the forces of dark-ness'. The slaughter of whites would last for four hours after which those who survived would be allowed to stay if they supported the new government (Lodge 1983: 247).

★   ★   ★

The African nationalists had seriously overestimated their own strength and under-estimated the determination and power of the government. At first the government did have difficulty in coming to terms with the new threat. Early in 1961 Verwoerd admitted: 'We regard the present situation as very serious', but added that the government was well equipped 'to halt the reign of terror' (HA 23 March 1961). Following Sharpeville, Pretoria moved quickly – prohibiting public meetings, banning the ANC and PAC as unlawful organizations, declaring a state of emer-gency and rounding up political opponents. It did not end there. The government steadily increased its security grip in the months and years ahead through fierce laws (such as the Sabotage Act of 1962 and the '90 Day Act' of 1963); through police action; and through better intelligence gained from informers and from the use of torture. The police scored major successes against both the PAC and the ANC. One MK member stated: 'Having talked of fascism for a decade and more, the movements were nevertheless caught by surprise when the police behaved like fascists' (Lodge 1983: 239).

Both MK and Poqo suffered from internal weaknesses. They were penetrated by informers, and Poqo in particular was plagued by factionalism and weak leadership. Leballo, from his base in Basutoland, rashly called a press conference late in March 1963 (shortly before the proposed rising) at which he claimed that the PAC had 150,000 members. He announced that a general rising was imminent leading to independence, and that killing whites would be part of the revolution. Following that the Basutoland police raided the PAC offices and seized documents, which may have fallen into Pretoria's hands. In any case PAC couriers were arrested in South Africa carrying messages to members. Arrests followed. By mid-1964 John Vorster, then Minister of Justice, claimed that Poqo had been smashed with the arrest of 3,264 of its members. Subsequently he announced that 202 had been convicted of murder, 395 for sabotage and 1,000 for other offences. The ANC also suffered a devastating blow. In July 1963, the police scored their greatest triumph when they raided a house in Rivonia, owned by Arthur Goldreich, where they arrested most of MK's high command, including Walter Sisulu, Govan Mbeki, Ahmed Kathrada, Leonard Bernstein, Arthur Goldreich, and Bob Hepple. The police seized docu-ments outlining the MK's plans which were later used in court against the Rivonia plotters and others who were not present, including Mandela. Although some of the plotters escaped from prison, including Goldreich, it was a major blow to the ANC/MK.

The black movements were battered and in disarray. In their post-mortems they came to realize that they had been far too optimistic and amateurish. They had acted on faith without adequate resources and preparation. They lacked bases, organ-ization and discipline, and had failed to mobilize mass support. The masses, said Joe Matthews, had no knowledge of what was happening. 'We were going to war without the people with us. The vanguard was isolated and this allowed the police to infiltrate easily.' Yet, although African nationalism was badly wounded it was not dead. Again Mandela used the court to assert his beliefs. When he and other MK leaders were tried in 1964, ANC supporters gathered at the court with their banners, singing liberation songs. As he entered the court Mandela raised a clenched fist and declared 'Amandla' (power); to which his followers replied 'Ngawethu' (to the people). From the dock he declared: 'During my lifetime I have dedicated myself to the struggle of African people. I have fought against White domination, and I have fought against Black domination. I have cherished the ideal of a democratic and free society in which all persons live together in harmony and with equal opportunities. It is an ideal which I hope to live for and to achieve. But if needs be, it is an ideal for which I am prepared to die' (Karis and Carter 1977: 679). It was magnificent but was it a meaningless gesture? At the time it seemed that it was, as he and his fellow prisoners were found guilty and sentenced to life imprisonment.

By the mid-1960s African nationalism was in disarray. The leaders were in prison or exile; the organizations banned. The optimism of the early 1960s gave way to gloom. Previously African nationalist parties may have knocked at the government's door in vain; but at least they had been there to knock. Now they appeared to have been swept aside. At the same time the economy soon recovered and with it white affluence and confidence. Yet there was a paradox. The balance of South African politics had changed. While in the past the African nationalists had been obliged to react to the government's agenda now it was the government that was reacting to African political activity – both actual and potential. Pretoria's mind was occupied by the threat to the white system that came from African nationalists and their allies inside and outside South Africa. Government policy was increasingly shaped with this in mind, as witnessed at home by the security legislation, the increased expenditure on the police and armed forces and the extension of the Bantustan policy; and abroad by a foreign policy which was characterized by the search for status and security in a world that became increasingly opposed to apartheid and increasingly sympathetic to African claims.

In Africa decolonization gained pace. In April 1960 Eric Louw, the Foreign Minister, accurately predicted that white rule would soon be confined to the Portuguese territories (Angola and Mozambique), Rhodesia and South Africa itself. Pretoria strongly criticized the colonial withdrawal. It accused the European powers of appeasement, of betraying the white man and his civilization, and of exposing the continent to communist penetration by handing over power to immature regimes. Verwoerd claimed that 'multi-racialism' was a euphemism for promoting black interests at the expense of whites, and while the British claimed to find apartheid abhorrent, he found their treatment of white men in Kenya and Tanganyika abhorrent. And worse followed as troubles developed in the neighbouring white-controlled territories. In Rhodesia the local whites illegally declared independence from Britain, and in Angola and Mozambique African liberation movements challenged Portuguese control. These troubles were compounded by increasing international antagonism to the white rulers of southern Africa, led by the new black African states.

Verwoerd and the Granite Response

The government's response to the crisis of the early 1960s was dominated by the stern, authoritarian figure of Verwoerd. His conviction of right came fully into its own following Sharpeville. Appeals to jettison or at least modify apartheid came from all directions – from the UP, from business interests, from members of the Dutch Reformed Churches, from international organizations, from western states and even from cabinet colleagues. Verwoerd dismissed them all. For him there was no sense in retreat, nor was he prepared simply to rely upon security measures to counter the challenge of African nationalism. Instead he saw an opportunity to implement his policies with greater determination. He drove onwards not backwards. However, for a time his own fate hung in the balance. In April 1960 a white man, David Pratt, attempted to assassinate Verwoerd, shooting him twice in the head. Remarkably Verwoerd survived and made a complete recovery. His extraordinary escape and personal courage enhanced his reputation. While still in hospital he sent a message telling his wavering cabinet colleagues to stand firm. In a public speech read out for him, his message was not to retreat, but to apply apartheid more thoroughly. He said that although recent events had given cause for reflection there was no reason to abandon existing policies. Indeed he saw an excellent opportunity to push forward more energetically.

Verwoerd was convinced that the explanation for Sharpeville and black radicalism lay not in the government's policies but in misunderstandings at home and abroad, which were fostered by the subversive doctrines of liberalism and communism and exploited by revolutionaries. It was the misinterpretation and the consequences of misinterpretation that must be changed not the policy. He told the NP that as national survival was at stake it must stand by its racial policies 'like walls of granite', and granite is the image that clings to Verwoerd – hard, solid and unbending. The crisis simply reinforced his personal resolution, as he explained to his wife: 'If I cannot save the country I would rather resign. I will never be an accomplice to the destruction of our people by abandoning our policy' (Kenny 1980: 186). If few whites could match Verwoerd's determination, most came to share his conviction that seeking compromise with black movements and international opinion would only lead to the destruction of the white nation of South Africa.

Verwoerd's determination was further tested by relations with the Commonwealth. Following the declaration of a Republic, South Africa had to reapply for membership. Like many Afrikaner nationalists Verwoerd had little enthusiasm for the organization, but to gather support during the referendum campaign he had urged voters to back 'a democratic republic within the Commonwealth' (Hepple 1967: 7). When he set off for the 1961 London conference he said that he favoured retaining membership, provided the Republic's sovereignty was not infringed and there was no interference in her domestic affairs. At the conference, however, he agreed to discuss the government's racial policies; but while some Commonwealth leaders were prepared to separate that issue from continued membership, others were not. Under a barrage of criticism Verwoerd withdrew the application because he believed the critics were intent on undermining South Africa's sovereignty. His mission had failed in the sense of having to abandon membership, but on his return Verwoerd was met by ecstatic supporters waving banners, proclaiming 'Believe in God; Believe in your People; Believe in Yourself'. Far from mourning a defeat they rejoiced at what they saw as the death of the imperial factor. Verwoerd told his followers: 'We do not come back as a people who had had a defeat. It's a happy day for South Africa. What happened was no less than a miracle. So many nations have had to get their complete freedom by armed struggle . . . But here we have reached something that we never expected (Hepple 1967: 9).

Verwoerd was speaking then to committed NP followers still fighting past battles. 'Freedom' for them was freedom from the old imperial enemy; but even the UP quickly accepted the loss of Commonwealth membership. In the referendum the UP had fought for continued membership and against a republic, but once the decision was taken it accepted the situation. The UP came to realize that its image of the Commonwealth — crown and flag, like-minded political leaders, and being 'British' — had gone, that membership could only be gained by abandoning white dominance. That was too high a price. Only a few months after the withdrawal Sir de Villiers Graaff, the UP leader, said that the cost of re-admission might be too high, and the party conference agreed to reapply only 'if it were in South Africa's interests'. After that there was no more talk of returning to the Commonwealth.

Redefining Nation and State

Verwoerd's distinctive response to the increasing pressure was to redefine 'state' and 'nation' within an apartheid framework. Previously the NP had been committed to Afrikaner control of a republic. Ironically it was when that aim was achieved that its limitations became clear. Afrikaner dominance had been achieved within the white political system, but now the system itself was in danger. The whole white edifice was under threat. To defend it the government shifted its ground from preaching an exclusive Afrikaner nationalism to an inclusive white nationalism; from calling for Afrikaner solidarity to a call for all whites to rally together in defence of the state. Verwoerd claimed that the change was possible because the establishment of a republic had removed the old external influences and white divisions. That was at best only a part of the story. He also recognized the need to defend the white state against black nationalism and the international anti-apartheid movement. In doing so he claimed that strife between English and Afrikaners was a thing of the past. Now whites must look to the future. 'In that future,' he said, 'we see the revolution of Africa and the growing problems for South Africa. For the sake of the future we must stand together as whites' (Moodie 1975: 277–8).

In October 1961 Verwoerd called an election, claiming that the country was at the start of a new era. He campaigned on the themes of security, white unity and apartheid. The election, said a cabinet minister, was a 'mobilization order for the struggle that lies ahead. We will die, each and every one of us, rather than give up our nationhood' (Karis and Carter 1977: 656). Verwoerd himself declared: 'I see the National Party today not as a Afrikaans, or English, or Afrikaans–English party, whatever it has been in the past. I see it as the party that stands for the preservation of the white man, of the white government in South Africa' (IRR 1961: 14). Persuaded by that rallying cry, most whites backed the government. The NP not only increased its number of seats, but for the first time at an election gained a majority of votes. Meanwhile the white parliamentary opposition was in disarray, as a group of 'liberals' split from the UP to form the Progressive Party (PP). Yet, despite the call for white unity, the NP remained predominantly Afrikaner in its culture, style, leadership and government patronage. Verwoerd broke new ground by appointing two English speakers to the cabinet, but in reality the English voters were invited to support an Afrikaner government which was committed to the defence of the white state. The minority of English speakers who voted for the NP did so not because they expected to gain a full share in government, but because they believed its tough approach offered them security and social privilege. *Die Burger* joked that the English joined the Progressives, voted for the UP, but thanked God for the Nationalists.

A further indication of the government's new approach came in immigration policy. As late as January 1959 Verwoerd was still arguing for tight controls, repeating the accusations that the UP was trying to swamp Afrikanerdom by bringing in 'foreign' whites. That changed as those old fears were subordinated to new needs to strengthen the white community. The NP's suspicion of the British, Mediterranean Europeans, Roman Catholics and Jews did not disappear, but it was subordinate to the greater fears of black revolution. Again Verwoerd tried to put a gloss on it by claiming that the achievement of a republic had entrenched Afrikaner values and so allowed a new approach to immigration. However, in 1965 he dropped the veil when, in defending the changed policy, he said: 'Our motto is to maintain white supremacy for all time to come over our own people and our own country, by force if necessary' (HA 5 February 1965). With that commitment in mind a record number of white immigrants entered South Africa.

Bantu Nations and Bantustans

Verwoerd's new vision was of a multi-national not a multi-racial state. Alongside the concept of a white nation based on race, the government promoted the idea of distinctive African ('Bantu') nations, and separate Coloured and Indian 'national groups'. The government rejected any attempt to bring the diverse peoples together into a single nation based on loyalty to a united South African state. When the government referred to 'South Africans' it meant whites. It dismissed African nationalism as a sham based on a false interpretation of African identity and loyalty and rejected the ANC's call for one nation based on one state. Instead, it argued, Africans belonged to distinctive nations. The way forward, therefore, was to promote separation between the nations. Verwoerd proposed 'to realign the white and bantu nations . . . on their separate and natural evolutionary courses by means of a dynamic programme of reconciliation' (Moodie 1975: 264).

Apartheid had many faces. To its critics, inside and outside South Africa, it was crude racism. To its advocates it was built on the cultural and ethnic differences which distinguish nations, and which Afrikaners had pursued over their long troubled history. In 1959 M. D. C. de Wes Nel, the Minister for Bantu Affairs, said that God had given a divine task to each separate people: that peoples (like individuals) had inherent rights to live and grow, and 'that the personal and national ideals of every individual and every ethnic group can best be developed within its own national group. It was a mistake to try to place diverse people into the same mould' (Moodie 1975: 265). Dr Eiselen, the Secretary of Native Affairs Department, stated that the first duty of black leaders is 'not to become black Europeans but to raise their people to a higher Bantu culture', and Verwoerd dismissed African intellectuals as 'black Englishmen' (Sparks 1990: 194–5). Based on such convictions the government's policy was to divide up the geographical area of the South African state between these nations. The great bulk of the land, roughly 87 per cent and including all the main urban areas, was reserved for the white nation; while the Bantu nations, whose members constituted a large majority of the population, were to share the remaining 13 per cent. The old African reserves became 'homelands' or 'Bantustans', where each Bantu nation would develop separately. It was through these Bantustans that Africans would gain their political rights, even if they lived outside the territorial area but were associated by tribal origins. Africans would require special permission to live in the white state, which would only be granted to those required for work, and they would enjoy no permanent rights there.

The multi-national state concept was attractive to the government leaders because in their eyes not only did it retain white dominance over the bulk of South

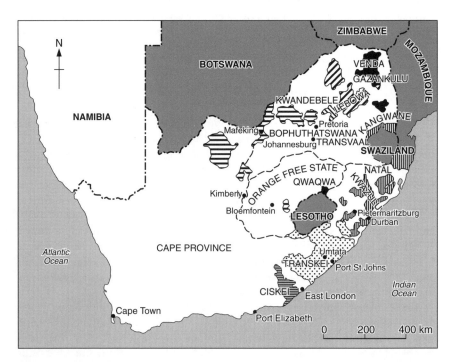

Map 13.1   The Bantustans (Homelands) (adapted from J. Omen-Cooper, *History of Southern Africa* [London: James Currey, 1987, 214])

Table 13.1   Government's national groups (1960), in millions

Xhosa	3.4
Whites	3.1
Zulu	3.0
Coloured	1.5
Northern Sotho	1.1
Southern Sotho	1.1
Tswana	0.9
Asians	0.5
Tsonga	0.4
Swazi	0.3

Africa it also countered claims for majority rule. They argued that no one nation formed a majority within the existing state. Instead there were national minorities, each with its own identity and destiny. De Wet Nel declared: 'The Zulu is proud to be a Zulu and the Xhosa proud to be a Xhosa, and the Venda is proud to be a Venda.' The lesson of history, he concluded, is that ethnic groups, whites as well as Bantu, gained their fulfilment and happiness from separate development, 'the only basis on which peace, happiness and mutual confidence can be built.' He idealized nationalism as a force which brings out 'the best things in the human spirit', leading to 'beautiful deeds of idealism and sacrifice and inspiration.' 'Should the Bantu not have it?' he asked. South Africa, he claimed offered a lesson to the rest of the world. 'The calling of this small white nation is to give the world the basis and pattern on which the different races can live in peace and safety in the future, each within its own national circle' (Moodie 1975: 266 and 290).

The implications of different interpretations of state and nation can be seen through population figures. In 1960 the total population of South Africa was about 16 million. According to the ANC there were therefore 16 million 'South Africans'. An alternative, was to divide the population into racial groups, as the PAC was inclined to do. In which case there were 10.8m. Africans; 3.1m. whites; 1.5m. Coloureds; and 0.5m Indians. The government's multi-national approach is reflected in table 13.1.

The Bantustan policy was not fixed. It evolved as circumstances changed and as government thinking developed. That was well illustrated in 1959. Early in the year Dr Eiselen, the Secretary of Bantu Administration, reaffirmed the established position that Africans would remain subordinate in a white-controlled unitary state. He wrote that the degree of autonomy granted to the Bantu would 'fall short of the actual surrender of sovereignty by the European trustees . . . The maintenance of White political supremacy over the country as a whole is a "sine qua non" for racial peace and economic prosperity' (*Optima*, March 1960). Shortly afterwards, Verwoerd introduced the Bantu Self Government Act which opened up the opportunity for Bantustans to gain a degree of internal self-government. That would match with Eiselen's position. However, in explaining the new legislation, Verwoerd, conscious of increasing international pressure, went much further. He said that the speed and extent of political progress would depend on the wishes of the people and the performance of the separate nations; and 'if it is within the power of the Bantu and if the territories in which he now lives can develop to full independence, it will develop that way' (Kenny 1980: 206). It was a remarkable shift from the government's previous position.

In advocating this shift of policy Verwoerd was conscious that economic ties continued to draw the races together, and even he realized that that would continue, that industry would still act as a 'magnet which draws the Bantu into "European South Africa"'. However, his hope was to limit that as far as possible. He wanted to reconcile economic development with the social and political apartheid. In addressing parliament he suggested three steps to achieve that goal. First, he said that industries in white areas should be mechanized as far as possible and staffed mainly by whites. Second, that more industry should be developed on the borders of the Bantustans so that labour could commute each day to work, thereby avoiding any question of residence in white areas. Finally (and this was new), he envisaged a smaller white state. 'The danger of economic disruption is much greater when there is a mixed fatherland', he stated. 'I would prefer to have a smaller white state in South Africa which will control its own army; its own navy; its own policy . . . in the event of an emergency . . . than a bigger state which has already been surrendered to Bantu domination.' Such political independence, he claimed, would be fully compatible with economic interdependence (Lipton 1985: 31).

Although presented in ideological terms Verwoerd's change of policy came as much from pragmatism as conviction. He later confessed that the prospect of independence for the Bantustans 'is not what we would have liked to see. In the light of pressures being exerted on South Africa there is, however, no doubt that eventually this will have to be done, thereby buying for the white man his freedom and the right to retain domination in his own country' (HA 10 April 1961). He spelt out the same message to whites during the 1961 election campaign. They must realize, he said, that in the end they could only rule over their own territory and over their own people: that they would have to learn to maintain friendly relations with neighbouring black states. In 1962, explaining to the cabinet his plans for the Transkei, Verwoerd's pragmatism and conviction were equally balanced when he said the plans would confirm to the world the government's just intentions and at the same time give western members of the UN the means of countering action against South Africa.

The implications of the shift in policy were profound. The existing South Africa was to be carved up into a series of separate states – a large white state and a series of Bantu states. The Bantu states, based on separate national identities, would become 'foreign', and the Africans living in them or associated with them would be 'foreigners'. Connie Mulder, a cabinet minister, declared: 'If our policy is taken to its full conclusion, there will not be one black man with South African citizenship. There will no longer be a moral obligation to accommodate these people politically' (Sparks 1990: 183). To its supporters the government conveyed this as a message of hope. It was, insisted Verwoerd, a practical and just outcome. Pretoria would offer the same opportunities to Africans as the imperial powers offered to their colonies. South African diplomats later recalled a meeting at which Verwoerd outlined his plans. He presented the policy as one that they could present to the world – as fair and practical, offering security to the whites, justice to Africans, and satisfying the demands of the international community. Those who attended the meeting emerged elated, convinced that Pretoria had a policy that was fair to all and could be defended at home and abroad.

Yet, although the government gave increasing prominence to its Bantustan policy, considerable uncertainty remained. Verwoerd was said to have regretted conceding the principle of independence, and there was scepticism in the NP about the ability of Africans to manage their own affairs, and concern about the dangers of letting them try. For every government statement which recognized the possibility of the Bantustans advancing to independence there was another saying that it might never happen. Verwoerd himself was often ambiguous as he tried to persuade the party faithful that the policy, although sounding new, was a development from the past. White fears and doubts persisted. They were given voice in parliament by UP members who asked: Would the Bantustans form part of a federal structure? If they were offered independence would they not become hotbeds of opposition to the Republic? Would they not provide bases for guerilla fighters? Verwoerd said he recognized the dangers, but argued that it was easier to confront an external foe than internal revolutionaries. They might, he said, become Cubas or Zanzibars on the borders, and that may be dangerous – not only inconvenient but dangerous – 'but if three million whites have to live together in one state with four times as many of those who are liable to create a Cuba surely it is much more dangerous' (HA 23 April 1964).

Uncertainty surrounded the lot of Coloureds and Indians in the new scheme of things. It was easier to state the questions than offer answers. On what grounds could the Coloureds and Indians be said to be 'nations'? Where were their homelands in which they could develop separately? Dr A. L. Geyer, a diplomat, admitted that while 'in the case of Africans I know the answers . . . When I think of the Coloureds my thoughts arrive at a dead end and I prefer not to go any further' (Van der Merwe 1971: 10). For the NP the Coloureds – most of whom spoke Afrikaans and many of whom had Afrikaner blood – were a vulnerable aspect of the policy. Suggestions were aired inside the party about incorporating them into the white political system. Verwoerd would have none of it. He dismissed these 'dramatic ideas' as a dangerous springboard for integration and biological assimilation. Yet even Verwoerd was uncertain about the Coloureds. He took the unusual step of summoning the NP's Central Council to gain its support on this issue, and at another time mused about the possibility of political separation with economic interdependence and a 'state within a state' for Coloureds. Yet they were only musings and official policy remained that the Coloureds and Indians were 'separate racial groups aspiring to be nations'. Referring to the Coloureds Verwoerd drew a distinction, which critics would see as raw racism, but which he presented as the difference between 'citizenship' and 'the components of a homogeneous nation'. While, he said, there was no doubt 'that the Coloureds are citizens of this country: there is just as little doubt that they are not part of the homogeneous entity that we can describe here as "the nation"'. He asserted that while the establishment of the Republic had removed the past distinction between English and Afrikaner so that they now formed a single nation, that did not imply further unification with the Bantu or Coloureds or Indians (IRR 1961: 135, 141). Indians were, however, afforded greater recognition than in the past. Previously there had been much talk of their repatriation as an alien group, but in 1961 the Minister of the Interior declared that they are a permanent part of the population. 'We must realize,' he said, 'that they are South African citizens and as such are entitled to the necessary attention and consideration' (Steward 1977: 172–3).

By the time of Verwoerd's death in 1966 the political map of South Africa had been redrawn. It was now a Republic, in which the NP government appealed to a white, rather than an Afrikaner nationalism. The concept of apartheid had been reshaped into a multi-national mould which could lead to a physical division of the country into a set of 'nation states'. However, within that mould 'nation' was defined in different ways. The white nation was distinguished by race, embracing all whites. The old white divisions and prejudices were subordinated to the preservation of control of their state. The Coloureds and Indians were also defined by race, despite the absence of homelands and the ambiguity of the Coloureds' position. In contrast Africans (the Bantu) were grouped not by race, but by tribal association, however fragile that was in many cases. Finally, although the government claimed equality between the national groups, Pretoria decreed that the preponderance of territory, riches and power lay with the white nation. The Bantu nations were confined to small, underdeveloped and fatally fragmented territories.

Sharpeville and the development of the early 1960s had signalled a major change in South African politics. Political developments were increasingly shaped by white attempts to defend their power and privilege against black demands. On the surface the white government gained a firm grip as it stamped on African political parties, but African numbers continued to grow, more blacks were drawn into the urban areas, the Bantustan policy failed to gain acceptance, international pressure increased, troubles continued on the borders, and claims for a more just society persisted. The government was trying to hold down the lid of a boiling pot. For a time it succeeded.

14

Vorster and the Development
of the Bantustans

On 6 September 1966 Verwoerd was assassinated as he was taking his seat in the House of Assembly. His assailant, a white parliamentary messenger, was later certified as insane. Shortly before his death Verwoerd had called an election. Security was still the dominant issue, for although black nationalism at home was moribund there were disturbing events elsewhere in Africa, not least in Rhodesia where the white minority's Unilateral Declaration of Independence (UDI) in November 1965 had brought international sanctions to South Africa's doorstep. At the election the government's message was that safety depended on a strong, determined government that would defend white rights while dealing justly with blacks through the apartheid policy. The UP countered by pointing to the dangers of the Bantustans – the Cubas on the borders, as they described them – but the government carried the day winning more seats than ever. When the House reassembled the NP had 120 seats, the UP 39, and the Progressive Party (PP) 1. (The single PP member was Mrs Helen Suzman, who for years to come fought a vigorous, isolated battle in parliament promoting liberal values.)

Recoiling at the death of the dominant Verwoerd, the NP chose John Vorster to replace him. Once again the party had turned to a man with a tough image. In Vorster's case this rested both on his wartime record as a general of the 'Ossewabrandwag' (for which he had been interned), and more recently as Minister of Justice, when he had ruthlessly fought African nationalism. Vorster made clear his view that: 'The security of the state is the supreme law . . . I regard the security of the state as priority number one.' Like most whites he believed that communism was the chief threat, underpinning the government's radical opponents. 'The communists,' he said, 'have been organising for years to take over South Africa . . . South Africa has always formed part of their world plan' (Geyser 1977: 2).

Despite the shock of Verwoerd's death, Vorster's transition into the premiership was smooth. At home he inherited a strong position. As well as the NP's parliamentary position, the white population was enjoying a period of confidence and of economic growth. In 1968 Vorster himself declared: 'It seems only yesterday that supporters, as well as opponents . . . wondered what the future of the Republic would be. Now, after seven years, South Africans have the answers to most – if not all – of their questions. Doubts have gone and fears have vanished' (*Southern Africa* 1968: 371).

Division in the National Party

Despite the confidence, divisions emerged among whites. The old Afrikaner/ English gulf had never been completely bridged, but more significant for the future a rift appeared within Afrikaner nationalism. Even in Verwoerd's time a few dissatisfied 'right-wingers' had complained that the NP was betraying its inheritance by wooing English speakers, and giving too much rope to Africans. Now, a clearer split emerged under Vorster. In part this arose from criticism of his leadership. The right wing of the party had supported him, believing that he would be one of their own. He certainly was no 'liberal', as he had shown as Minister of Justice, but he was less dominant than Verwoerd. He was fully committed to retaining white control and imposing apartheid, but, unlike Verwoerd, he was not an ideologue. He was pragmatic and relaxed in style. In cabinet he acted as a chairman collecting the sense of the meeting rather than dominating proceedings. Vorster argued that he was keeping firmly to the principles of his predecessors but implementing them in changing circumstances. For example, to reduce international criticism he was ready to accept diplomatic links with black states and to tolerate a small element of racial mixing in sport. Outside the inbred setting of the NP such steps seemed of little significance, but inside they created divisions, and sharpened a developing ideological split, between those who were categorized as 'verligtes' (enlightened) and those as 'verkramptes' (hard-line).

The rift also revealed and reflected growing class divisions among Afrikaners. Economic growth, the social and economic rewards of political power and urbanization had transformed Afrikaner society. New interests co-existed with traditional values. In 1970, 80 per cent of Afrikaners were urbanized, and those in white-collar occupations – as distinguished from agriculture and blue-collar jobs – had increased from 29 per cent in 1946 to 65 per cent by 1977. In Merle Lipton's judgement: 'The origins of the verligte/verkrampte split lay in the diverging interests of these classes.' By 1970 Afrikaners were no longer a society of farmers and workers. They dominated the civil service, they had moved into commerce and finance, and generally the gap between English speakers and Afrikaners had been greatly diminished. 'While,' wrote Lipton, 'the "verligtes" were Afrikaners who had made it and no longer needed protection against blacks, English or foreigners, "verkramptes", still wanted the retention of "Afrikaner first" policies. They tended to be less well off and less educated, although they also gained support from those with vested interests in nationalism (teachers and clergy) and in continued Afrikaner hegemony (the political and bureaucratic establishment)' (Lipton 1985: 306). Yet, Hermann Giliomee rightly pointed out that the division was less about economic issues than about status and identity. 'At the very core of the struggle,' wrote Giliomee, 'was a battle among Afrikaners about the true purpose of the state and the goals of Afrikaner nationalism, in which "verligtes" saw themselves as whites as well as

Afrikaners, while "verkramptes" identified themselves primarily as Afrikaners' (Giliomee 1992: 346).

Not all NP members were committed to either side of the dispute and within the groups were shades of opinion – derived from gut feelings, economic interests, theological principles, personal loyalties and ideological commitment. Both sides were firmly committed to apartheid and to white dominance; but while 'verkrampters' believed that continued white rule depended on rigid opposition to change and that concessions endangered the whole edifice of apartheid, 'verligtes' were convinced that future security depended on a degree of flexibility and change to protect the core of white authority. Also, lurking behind the dispute was the conviction among 'verkramptes' that the party should remain the political arm of exclusive Afrikaner nationalism.

The 'verkrampte' were led by Dr Albert Hertzog (son of J. B. M. Hertzog). Vorster dismissed him from the cabinet in 1968 because of Hertzog's opposition to government policies. Following that, in April 1969, Hertzog launched an impassioned parliamentary attack against the political merging of Afrikaners and English speakers in the new white nationalism. The central issue, declared Hertzog, is that the whites, 'the civilized people . . . dare to rule as a minority'. Among the whites are two peoples both with great but distinctive strengths. First, the Afrikaners, who 'are permeated by that great complex of principles called Calvinism; that code of moral, ethical and religious principles. They form part of our being'. From this tradition Afrikaners recognize the diversity of creation; they gain a love of freedom for their own people; and stand firm against any who unlawfully challenge their authority. It is because of this, said Hertzog, that 'the Calvinist Afrikaner, the nationalist, makes such an ideal fighter and such a good soldier for white civilization'. The second are the English, who do not share that tradition. Instead, he said, they espouse 'liberalism' which is so deeply engrained that they 'find it difficult to take action against those communistic and leftist movements when these movements make attacks upon them.' Indeed, without the Calvinists the English would have collapsed before the challenge. It is the Calvinist, proclaimed Hertzog, who is the soldier and champion of his own and the English speakers civilization. For the future, as in the past, it is the Calvinists on whom reliance must be placed for the preservation of civilization (HA 14 April 1969).

The government reacted fiercely to Hertzog's attack. Verkrampte support was strongest in the Transvaal, and it was there at the 1969 Provincial Congress, that the NP leadership sorted out the 'verkrampte' goats from the 'verligte' sheep by asking for individually recorded votes on specific government policies. The sticking point was sports policy. Hertzog stood firm against a tour by a New Zealand rugby team which included Maoris. 'It will,' he complained, 'lead to social integration, since they will dance with Afrikaner girls at social functions' (Liebenberg and Spies 1993: 435). In the formal break that followed the most committed 'verkramptes' left the NP to form the Herstigte Nasionale Party (HNP) under Hertzog's leadership.

Vorster, who realized that many who remained in the NP retained 'verkrampte' beliefs, picked a cautious route between the two wings. He did not want to be condemned as the leader who broke the unity of the Afrikaner volk and abandoned traditional values. When, for example, the HNP renewed the attack on white immigration, Vorster argued that the immigrants were needed for the economy and to strengthen the white nation. However, he added: 'There will be no immigration scheme which will prejudice the survival of the Afrikaners or materially change the composition of the people' (Geyser 1977: 99). More generally Vorster's approach to white nationalism had echoes of J. B. M. Hertzog's two streams policy. Vorster stated that the future of Afrikaners and English speakers was linked together by a commitment to South Africa. He promised: 'We can work together with the retention of our identities, each with his own language, his own customs, but a common love and loyalty binding us to one fatherland, South Africa' (Geyser 1977: 101).

When Vorster called an election in April 1970 the campaign was fought with the intensity of an Afrikaner civil war. One of Vorster's avowed aims was to crush the HNP and reassert the NP as the undisputed voice of Afrikanerdom. The government said it was calling the election to 'ensure a permanent home for Whites; and to have a united English and Afrikaans-speaking White nation'. Eager to avoid further defections to 'the right', Vorster reiterated that apartheid would be vigorously pursued. In response the HNP called not only for rigid implementation of apartheid, but for Afrikaner pre-eminence, and for economic development to be limited by the availability of white labour. The HNP accused the government of betraying its trust, and in more specific terms it continued to oppose mixed sport in any form, the exchange of diplomats with black states, and increased immigration. In the event the HNP was heavily defeated. It gained no seats and only 7.3 per cent of votes cast. Vorster triumphantly declared that the HNP had been destroyed.

In the Afrikaner turmoil the UP saw a glimmer of hope for itself. Taking advantage of the divisions and accusing the government of inefficiency and arrogance, it regained some electoral ground for the first time since 1948. It won back eight seats at the expense of the NP – all in constituencies which it had held until 1961. The overall result was NP 111 seats, UP 47, and PP 1. However, for the UP it was a false dawn. Soon internal splits appeared between its old guard and its Young Turks who were eager for reform. The UP was no threat to the government, but the NP was able to use its divisions to advantage, by emphasizing the need for white unity in the face of threats from African nationalists and communists. When in 1973 Japie Basson (UP) criticized the Immorality and Mixed Marriages Act, Vorster retorted that the people (whites) demanded: 'Absolute assurance . . . that we will continue to preserve the white identity'. P. W. Botha, the Minister of Defence, declared: 'We are being threatened by the global and overall strategy under the leadership of aggressive communism'. He claimed that it was directed not against apartheid as such or to promote individual rights, but 'against stability, security and progress'. As the onslaught was total – including economic and cultural threats and propaganda – the response must also be total. In that spirit he advocated better relations among all whites (with greater respect for the Afrikaans languages), 'separate developments' to foster good relations between black and white, and the need to counter the hostile news media.

Apartheid and the Development of the Bantustans

Vorster was as committed as Verwoerd to the principles of apartheid. If we want peace, he declared in 1969, 'the development must not be towards each other, but away from each others'. In 1971 he said he had told the Bantu leaders: 'Look we are different to you and we have our land you have your land. You will have no say over my land and my children.' Then he confirmed: 'I am not prepared to integrate with them on any basis whatsoever. And that is also the view of the Black leaders. Indeed anybody with self respect will take such a view whether White or Black' (Geyser 1977: 146). To abandon apartheid would, he claimed, bring chaos and the downfall of all population groups. It was based on moral, Christian foundations. 'We instituted the policy of separate development,' said Vorster, 'not because we considered ourselves better than others . . . but because we said we differed from others. We prize our otherness and are not prepared to relinquish it' (Geyser 1977: 96). However, he explained to a private NP meeting that he did not see apartheid as an end in itself. 'The cardinal principle of the NP,' he stated, 'is the retention, maintenance and immortalisation of Afrikaner identity within a white sovereign state. Apartheid and separate development is merely a means to achieve and perpetuate this' (Giliomee 1992: 347).

Having inherited the Bantustan policy, based on the concept of multi-nationalism, Vorster's government steadily developed it. It was an attempt to preserve white dominance through massive social engineering. The cost for the government was high, in terms of subsidies and forming new administrations, but the greatest price was paid by Africans, not least those forced from 'white areas' to be resettled, often onto desolate land. Even so the government remained adamant that African rights must be confined to the homelands. M. C. Botha, the Minister of Bantu Administration, stated that the Bantu were in white areas not 'because it is their natural and traditional area . . . [but] because of the work they want to do for the sake of personal earnings and to supplement the white lack of man power'. If there is no work there will be no place for them. 'The white area is the homeland of the whites; here the whites rule and here the whites have exclusive and sole control' (HA 4 February 1974).

The Bantustan policy continued to generate uncertainty and criticism at home and abroad. Many whites, including NP members, remained sceptical. The government, immersed in its own doubts, moved in crab-like fashion, as it sought to brush off its critics and reassure its followers; trying on the one hand to persuade Africans that the Bantustans offered them great opportunities, and on the other to reassure whites that they had nothing to fear. In April 1968 Vorster confirmed that Bantustans could not gain independence without full parliamentary approval. In 1969 M. C. Botha set out five 'determining factors' which a Bantustan would have to meet before gaining independence. These factors were so demanding that few existing states could match them. When P. W. Botha was questioned about the dangers of Bantustans harbouring guerillas and controlling the coastline, he snapped back that the dangers could be countered by gaining the goodwill of the Bantu peoples. But then, on a harsher note, he said that the Bantustans were so dependent on the Republic they had no choice but to seek friendship. Finally, he repeated Verwoerd's point that it was better to have enemies outside than inside the state (HA 27 May 1968). A parliamentary committee reported in favour of placing defensive 'white corridors' between Venda and the border with Rhodesia, and along the KwaZulu coast between Richards Bay and St Lucia. In 1971 Vorster confirmed that they could have their own Defence Departments, but later he claimed that they 'are the luckiest people in the world as it was not necessary for them to spend a penny on defence . . . because they know they have nothing to fear from South Africa' (IDAAF 1971: 444). In 1974, when P. W. Botha confirmed that he had been negotiating with the Bantustans about their establishing armed forces, he warned against recklessness in arming Africans because South Africa's history was full of tragedies.

Since 1963 the Transkei had managed many of its internal affairs, while Pretoria retained control of security, foreign affairs, immigration, customs and banking. In 1971 the Bantu Homelands Act gave similar powers to the Ciskei, Venda and Lebowa. In 1973 the Bantu Laws Amendment Act speeded up land consolidation and the subsequent movement of people, so that by the time Vorster resigned as Premier in September 1978 two Bantustans – Transkei and Bophuthatswana – had gained 'independence'; and six others – Ciskei, Gazankulu, KwaZulu, Lebowa, QwaQwa and Venda – had 'full self governing status'. On several occasions Vorster claimed that the Afrikaners had never intended to subordinate the Bantu nations; the responsibility, he said, lay with the British. He told an Afrikaner audience that it was not the policy of their ancestors 'to annex these people and to make them citizens of the state. If it had not been British policy to bring these people within the British sphere of influence and make them British subjects, they would, as far as we are concerned, still have been independent' (Geyser 1977: 74).

Vorster's claim about the British role was part of the presentation of policy which Pretoria had developed by the late 1970s. The government Yearbook of 1978 claimed that South Africa had never been a single, integrated socio-political system. It was British imperialism which had forced the independent nations together under a single political authority. 'This artificial unity', it was claimed, 'brought into political juxtaposition disparate and incompatible ethnic and racial groups', whereas the key to South Africa 'lies in the unique diversity of culture, ethnic origins, faiths, languages and levels of socio and political development'. Although the population could be divided into four broad racial groups, the society could not be reduced to a simple black–white polarization. Rather it was a complex multi-ethnic, multi-national mixture, in which the black population 'comprises several principal ethnic groups regarded as separate embryonic nations'.

Within this complex society, stated the Yearbook, the white nation was the product of three centuries of history so that the whites rightly defined themselves as 'a permanent African nation', living in a part of the continent which has become their only fatherland'. Neither the white nor black nations had a prior claim to all South Africa. Each had a claim to that part which history had given it as a homeland. The government's aim was self-determination for all, thereby eliminating the domination of one group and allowing the development of self-governing nations. The Yearbook concluded that government policy was not built on an assumption of superiority but on the fact of diversity. From that six premises could be drawn. First, whites could only maintain their national identity as long as they controlled 'that part of South Africa which history gives them as their homeland.' Second, if majority rule were introduced the whites would be an impotent minority. Third, sovereignty must be given to each of the nations that the British had compelled to live together. Fourth, permanent white control of all the people was neither practical nor morally defensible. Fifth, the policy was in line with the rise of global national consciousness. Sixth, separate territorial bases would be provided for the white and black nations (SA Yearbook 1978: 204–9).

The Bantustan Leaders

The African leaders who were prepared to work within the Bantustan system had to accept, to a greater or lesser degree, the government's structure of separate national groups and the restrictions on African political rights inherent in the policy. From time to time they made attempts to co-ordinate their efforts. In November 1973 a 'summit meeting' of six leaders was held, (two others refused to attend because they opposed the principle of federation, which was on the agenda). At that meeting an elated Chief Kaiser Matanzima of the Transkei stated: 'My dream has come true', and he compared the meeting with a 'UN of Black South Africa'. Chief Buthelezi of KwaZulu declared that the architects of apartheid would not have believed that their policy would be the foundation of black unity. At that and subsequent meetings the leaders voiced their opposition to the pass laws and influx control; they gave support to a South African federation with the black homelands as provinces; and above all they insisted that land problems must be resolved, both by giving more land to the Bantustans and consolidating the fragmented pieces into which each Bantustan was divided.

However, when the leaders met Vorster in 1974 and 1975 he stood fast against their claims. He told parliament that a federation would mean abandoning white sovereignty. 'I am not,' he said 'prepared in respect of the whites to abdicate any part of their sovereignty to other people or nations' (HA 4 February 1974). Nor would Pretoria move far on the land issue. It was willing to undertake limited consolidation but not to grant more land. M. C. Botha bluntly told the leaders that if they wanted to link additional land to independence 'they will have only themselves to blame if their independence is retarded or comes to grief in the process'. He asserted that all land was in the gift of the whites. 'We,' he declared, 'as the givers must determine what land should be given and it is not for those who receive to point out what land they should have' (IDAAF 1972: 548). Following that a parliamentary committee opposed any increase in the total area, but supported greater consolidation. It recommended, for example, that Bophuthatswana be reduced from nineteen separate pieces to six; and, most spectacular of all, that KwaZulu be reduced from the existing one hundred and eighty pieces to ten. Even then the results were disappointing. Vorster stated that the government tried to achieve as much consolidation as possible, but for practical reasons (which was a euphemism for white opposition) it was not possible to go further.

The attempts by the Bantustan leaders to co-ordinate their efforts soon fell apart. Pretoria divided them, by playing to their separate interests and handling them on a bilateral basis. Promises of solidarity came to nothing as each leader pursued his own agenda with the central government. In the end each took what he could get. Matanzima, for example, originally called for the creation of a greater Xhosaland, to incorporate not only the Transkei but the Ciskei, East Griqualand, and the white area between the Fish and Kei Rivers, including East London. When both the government and the Ciskei leaders dismissed the claim Mantanzima dropped it. His small consolation was that a 'white spot' – the tiny coastal resort of Port St Johns – was absorbed into the Transkei. The fuss that surrounded that transfer underlined the constraints under which Pretoria worked as it sought to balance the demands of the white electorate and the Bantustan leaders. The local whites as Port St Johns resisted the transfer on two grounds: first that the white community opposed it, although that community was tiny; and second because of the security implications, although the small port was silted up and had not been used since the First World War.

Some Bantustan leaders came to accept the situation and tried to gain as much as possible by negotiation. Chief Matanzima of the Transkei was the most prominent among them. He claimed to be a realist, who recognized that the whites had power and would not willingly surrender it. It was better, so he argued, to gain what they could rather than crying for the moon. He said there was no middle road; the choice was either to accept Pretoria's policy or gain nothing. With the whites controlling the state the alternative to Bantustans would be to wait 'for the day (it might be a thousand years) when the Bantu will have a vote in the Parliament of South Africa' (Hill 1964: 66). A second reason was Matanzima's claim that with increased land allocations, the Bantustans would satisfy the traditional aspirations of the African peoples. Like the government, Matanzima did not envisage a single nationalism embracing all South Africans, or even all Africans, but a patchwork of separate nations. For him an individual's identity and rights were derived from his/her origins. 'I am a disciple of nationalism,' said Matanzima. 'I believe in Xhosa nationalism because I was born to it . . . My heritage commands me in the name of nationhood to sacrifice the best of my abilities to the advancement of my own nation in its own country according to the terms of its own culture.' He pointed out that the Transkei had existed long before apartheid, and now it offered freedom to the Xhosa people who are 'doing no more than regaining sovereignty over their traditional territory'. He compared the position of the Transkei and the Xhosa people with that of Israel and the Jews. It was a homeland for all Xhosa whether or not they lived there (Leatt 1986: 125–7). Chief Lennox Sebe of the Ciskei, spoke in the same vein when he said that he would die a happy man if one day he could stand before his great ancestors who had fought the British, and say: 'Father, there is your nation' (Leatt 1986: 126).

A third reason for the leaders' acceptance of the government's policy was that the Bantustans offered them personal rewards, prestige and power. Leadership in the Bantustans became centralized, and confined to a small group which exercised patronage and nepotism. The structure of authority and rewards restored the claims of traditional chiefs whose authority rested on client-patron relationships, family ties, the control of land distribution and traditional subservience. In the Transkei, at Matanzima's insistence, and despite Pretoria's hesitation, only a minority of the legislature was elected, while the majority was composed of traditional chiefs and nominated members.

The government pushed ahead with the Bantustan policy. By the early 1980s four Bantustans (Transkei, Bophuthatswana, Venda and Ciskei) were 'independent' in terms of South African legislation. The others had 'self-governing' status. Yet for all the claims of fairness and practicality, the rationalizations, the pomp and cere-mony of 'Independence Days', the establishment of new government structures, the Bantustan policy was running into the sand. In the first instance it was not fair. The distribution of resources and power across South Africa continued to be predominantly in white hands. In the search for separation large numbers of Africans, and many Coloureds and Asians were forced to move. The Africans were often dumped in inhospitable areas with few resources for development. Second, despite the movement of people, it failed to separate the races. The 1970 census figures revealed that. Pretoria put a gloss on them by pointing out that while in 1960, 36.5 per cent of the African population lived in homelands, by 1970 that had risen to 46.5 per cent. The gloss masked the fact that the African numbers had grown so quickly in the period that the total number living in white areas had risen from seven to almost eight million; and that took no account of the numerous 'illegal' blacks living in white areas, or the redrawing of some homeland boundaries so that, without moving, 300,000 Africans who had previously lived in white areas were now in Bantustans. The grand apartheid design simply was not working. The 'white' urban areas continued to draw Africans to them, because the homelands remained poor, overcrowded and further burdened by the forced dumping of the weak, the old and the economically inactive. Third, the reactions of the inter-national community, far from applauding Pretoria's efforts, ranged from cool to bitter hostility. The international consensus was that the Bantustan policy had changed nothing of substance. Whites still dominated blacks and the full apparatus of apartheid was still in place with its degradation of people based on race. Far from equating the Bantustans with the independent former colonies, they were dismissed as puppets. Finally, the whites discovered that the policy did not offer them secu-rity, as the 1976 Soweto rising revealed. Instead of finding a clear path ahead the government had marched into a 'cul-de-sac'.

Vorster Opposes Integration and Power Sharing

Like his predecessors, Vorster was unsure about the future for the Coloureds and Indians. As with all Afrikaner leaders he showed more concern for the Coloureds than the Indians, but even for them he had no clear vision. He said that he recog-nized the dilemma whereby the white nation and 'the nascent Coloured nation' lived side by side within the borders of the same state, and he admitted that it was not practical for either the Coloureds or the Indians to have their own homelands. Nor was it reasonable, he said, for the whites to exercise guardianship over the

Coloureds indefinitely. A 'modus vivendi' had to be found, but he firmly excluded the idea of Coloured representation in the white parliament. One of Vorster's first tasks as Prime Minister was to deal with an initiative towards the Coloureds which Verwoerd had started but not completed. Verwoerd's aim had been to separate completely white and Coloured political activity, and in 1964 he had introduced the Coloured Persons Representative Council Act. However, the act had not been implemented by the time Vorster came to power. Before going ahead Vorster appointed a white commission under S. L. Muller to investigate the situation. That commission recommended that the existing system of indirect Coloured representation in the white parliament should be abolished; that Coloured politics should be allowed to develop without interference from other groups; and that the Coloured Representative Council should be enlarged and its powers extended, but it should remain subordinate to the white parliament.

Whatever the details of the arrangements – whether for Coloureds or Indians or Africans – Vorster's broad approach was always away from integration or power sharing. He never tired of stating that whites must not share with blacks. 'I am not,' he stated, 'prepared to integrate with them on any basis whatsoever' (Geyser 1977: 146). He argued that trying to share power would lead to destruction. In 1973 he declared: 'He who plays with divided power over his people, who is prepared to give any other person a say over his own people, he is an enemy of his people . . . It will lead to the downfall of his people' (Geyser 1977: 193). Vorster was convinced that it was the whites, and Afrikaners in particular, who had previously guided black advancement. 'It is we,' he said, 'who led them to that stage [self-determination] and that is right and moral according to our policy', but it would be 'futile, dangerous and deceitful to play around with the concept of power sharing . . . which could only engender frustration and create the greatest possible chaos in South Africa' (Geyser 1977: 270).

15

Black Resistance:
Inside and Outside the Republic

The banning of the ANC and PAC left a vacuum in black political activity inside South Africa. In part that was filled by two very different movements – Inkatha and Black Consciousness. Outside the Republic exiled members of the ANC and PAC built external organizations directed against Pretoria and its apartheid policies.

Buthelezi and Inkatha

Like other Bantustan leaders, Chief Gatsha Buthelezi of KwaZulu was a pragmatist, in the sense of working within the system and deciding that the government's power was too great to challenge by armed resistance. Yet he stood out from the other Bantustan leaders – because of his strong personality, his ambition to be a national not just a sectional leader, the strength of Zulu support he generated, his refusal to kowtow to Pretoria, and above all because his stated intention was to work within the structure to undermine it. He called for dialogue across the races to avoid violent confrontation. At Lutuli's memorial service he called for 'freedom in our lifetime' and repeated his appeal for the release of Mandela and other black nationalists. He said that while these nationalist leaders might appear to whites to be 'subversive elements' to blacks they were heroes (Karis and Carter 1977: 688). Far from accepting the government's optimistic view of developments in 1973 Buthelezi said that after twenty-five years of NP rule, 'I do not feel less of a "Kaffir" than I did in 1948'.

To support his position and promote his views Buthelezi built up a powerful organization – 'Inkatha YakwaZulu'. Inkatha had first been established in the 1920s as a cultural/political movement by the Zulu aristocracy. Their aims were to gain recognition of the Zulu monarchy, to collect funds for the royal family and for general welfare, and to reinforce a sense of Zulu identity. Buthelezi revived the movement in 1975, but the focus was moved away from the royal family to broader aspirations. As Prime Minister of KwaZulu and President of the movement, Buthelezi was its dominant figure, while the Zulu monarch was restricted to a symbolic role. Buthelezi gave Inkatha a wide but ambiguous brief, describing it as

Chief Buthelezi
(courtesy of *The Star*)

a 'national cultural liberation movement'. It was, he said, 'a black nationalist grouping or a cultural grouping within the South African nation', which aimed to move to self-mobilization and away from reacting to government policy (Leatt 1986: 132). From a combination of dynamic leadership, pride, obedience, fear and patronage Inkatha quickly emerged as a large, disciplined organization. By 1980 it claimed to have 300,000 members, making it the largest political movement in the country.

From its earliest days Inkatha had two faces. One was that of a South African party, open to all people, ready to work with other nationalist movements, which were seeking to eradicate 'all forms of colonialism, radicalism, neocolonialism and discrimination' (Leatt 1986: 130). In this mode Buthelezi saw himself not only as the leader of Inkatha, but the inheritor of the ANC tradition. The movement even adopted the ANC colours. Buthelezi declared: 'We owe it to the founding fathers of the ANC now banned, and their successors, some deceased, some exiled and some incarcerated, to uphold the tradition of the titanic struggle for liberation' (Leatt 1986: 132). He claimed to have support from the imprisoned Mandela and Sisulu, and from ANC leaders abroad. There was contact at the time between Inkatha and the ANC, and they shared a strong opposition to apartheid, but there were also clear differences. If Buthelezi represented an ANC tradition it was that of the past, with its stress on non-violence and strong organization. Buthelezi, himself, recognized that and associated his movement with the founding fathers. 'They,' he wrote later, 'were the true South Africans who dreamt of a multi racial democracy and who mounted non violent tactics and strategies which would make the achievement of a multi party, multi racial democracy resting on a one man one vote system of government a reality' (Buthelezi 1990: 8).

The other face of Inkatha was that of a Zulu party, built on tribal traditions and loyalties. Within this second image it sought to dominate the KwaZulu homeland, by restricting the legislature to its own members, and opposing other political parties operating in KwaZulu. Even Pretoria baulked at that and pronounced that other parties must be allowed. However, in practice Inkatha was a predominantly, but not exclusively, Zulu movement. In KwaZulu as in other Bantustans, power was concentrated, and a career in the KwaZulu government was closely tied to Inkatha membership. Inkatha defended that in terms of 'African democracy', which it claimed was more suitable than western style multi-party democracy. Disagreements could be aired freely inside the party but not in public.

Buthelezi, in working to undermine the apartheid system, emphasized that the means must be non-violent. He saw the struggle being 'fought in our daily lives. We will fight,' he said, 'on the political front. We will fight it on the social front. We will fight it on the economic front' (Leatt 1986: 131). He rejected political rights based on ethnicity, called for a sharing of power, and rejected white dominance over other groups. The political rights of national groups and minorities should, he said, be recognized, but the final protection lay in individual rights and equality before the law. In this spirit Buthelezi mounted his challenge to the government and apartheid. Yet he discovered that instead of gaining recognition from other nationalists he came under increasing criticism from the ANC in exile and from militant youths inside the country. Buthelezi's severest critics dismissed him as a covert government collaborator, but even those who realized that this was untrue attacked him. They did so, partly because they saw him as a fallen angel, but more because they believed that his form of opposition to the government would divert the African masses away from support for what they saw as the true struggle. In contrast with the ANC, Inkatha was opposed to the armed struggle and international economic sanctions, and favoured the capitalist market economy. Buthelezi recognized the diplomatic achievements of the ANC in exile, but dismissed the armed struggle as irrelevant. It was naive to believe that sabotage would intimidate whites or rally blacks; better, he said, to concentrate on internal action, based on such factors as worker and consumer power.

The critics directed their attacks both at the Inkatha movement and Buthelezi personally. Some branded Inkatha as a Zulu 'Broederbond' and attacked Buthelezi personally as 'a sell out' and an interloper between the oppressor and oppressed. Buthelezi dismissed the criticism as the inbred frustrations of an exiled movement and the callowness of youth. He accused his critics of causing discord among Africans, and said he would not stand by and see the ANC commit political suicide by establishing itself on the lunatic fringe of society. When he addressed the European Parliament in 1980 he said that the armed struggle would not bring liberation, nor could the exiled ANC claim to be a government in waiting or to represent all Africans. As the struggle would be won inside the country by political means he called for international recognition of Inkatha. Yet ambiguity persistently surrounded Inkatha as a movement and Buthelezi as a leader. Was Inkatha a Zulu or a South African organization? Was it a liberation movement which could undermine apartheid, or by working within the system did it help to sustain it? Was Buthelezi personally an ally or an opponent of the ANC? Was Inkatha a liberation movement or a vehicle for Buthelezi's personal ambitions, or was it both? By opposing international sanctions and the armed struggle was Buthelezi a puppet of the government, whatever his intentions?

Black Consciousness (BC)

Black Consciousness (BC) emerged in the late 1960s and early 1970s. It was not a centralized movement and ironically was in part nurtured by apartheid, in that it gained much of its support in the universities established exclusively for African students. In 1969 these students organized themselves into the South African Students Organization (SASO), under the leadership of Steve Biko – a young charismatic man. That was followed later by the Black People's Convention (BPC), which had a wider social base. SASO and BPC were not secret organizations, and therefore although they challenged the government, they recognized that they had to operate within the limits of the law. Therefore they stressed their commitment to peaceful persuasion, claiming that, by dialogue and bargaining not by violence, they were seeking a free society based on universal suffrage.

Early responses to Black Consciousness were mixed. Initially it was even welcomed by advocates of apartheid. *Die Burger* saw it as a product of disillusionment with liberal doctrines, which showed that 'non-whites do not want to be objects of white politics any longer, but desire to determine their future for themselves as people in their own right' (Gerhart 1978: 269). In that light some people (including Africans as well as whites, Coloureds and Indians) saw it as a new form of racism, dividing not uniting people. The accusation persisted, as the great bulk of BC members were African, but Biko dismissed it, arguing that blacks must first develop their own identity and institutions, and their own psychological and cultural strength before they could co-operate with whites on the basis of mutual respect. Currently, he said, the oppressive machinery of state alienated blacks from themselves. The result is that 'powerlessness breeds a race of beggars who smile at the enemy and swear at him in the sanctity of their toilets'. He accused whites of perpetuating a super-race image by the use of force, on the assumption that what they cannot gain by respect they gain by fear. The fear had become systematized: blacks fear whites, whites fear blacks and the white government is built on fear. 'It

Steve Biko
(courtesy of Rex
Features
London)

is fear that erodes the soul of Black people', said Biko. It 'is a dangerous type of fear, for it only goes skin deep. It hides underneath it an immeasurable rage that often threatens to erupt' (Arnold 1979: 274–6).

Although BC publicly rejected violence, the statements of some of its more radical leaders were ambiguous. Speaking at a BPC meeting Harry Singh said the whites had plundered, raped and massacred from their arrival, and had no right to live in South Africa because they had taken the country by force. There was, he claimed, no experience in the world to surpass the brutality carried out on the blacks of South Africa. He concluded: 'We have now reached a point where we can also say an eye for an eye and a tooth for a tooth' (Arnold 1979: 226). Violent or not the government branded BC as a revolutionary movement. Even if there was doubt about its methods, it was, in Pretoria's eyes, revolutionary in its aims. It stood the government's policy on its head by seeking a unitary state dominated by blacks, not a multi-national state dominated by whites. 'This country belongs to Black people and to them alone', declared a SASO resolution. Whites 'who live in this country [should do so] on terms laid down by Blacks . . . This should not be construed as anti-Whitism. It only means that inasmuch as Black people live in Europe on terms laid down by Europeans, Whites shall be subjected to the same conditions here'. Within the new society blacks must close ranks to control the state (Arnold 1979: 40).

In terms of ideas, black consciousness fell within the broad 'Africanist' stream. When Biko was asked in court to explain the concept of black consciousness he said it was concerned with the condition of the black man in South Africa. The blacks were, said Biko, subjected to two forces. First they were oppressed by the state – its institutions and laws. Second, and more insidious, blacks had become alienated from themselves, because they associated what was good with whites and what was inferior with blacks. Black Consciousness opposed both those forces (Biko 1978: 100). On another occasion Biko said that being black did not depend on pigmentation but on mental attitude. 'Black people – real black people – are those who can manage to hold their heads high in defiance rather than willingly surrender their souls to the white man.' The aim of BC was to infuse a new pride; to counter the image of blacks as appendages to white society. 'Black people are out to completely transform the system and to make of it what they wish,' wrote Biko. The barrier to progress was white racism. The only way to counter it was by black unity. Biko recognized that Africans, Coloureds and Indians often despised each other, but argued that the explanation for this lay in white racism, oppression and exploitation. If South Africa were ever to see black and white living in harmony, said Biko, it could only be when the opposites (black and white) come together to form a synthesis (Biko 1978: 48/53).

Biko directed his ire not only at the government, but at white 'leftists' and 'liberals'. He rejected the communists' class analysis of society, arguing that colour not class was the greatest single determining factor in South Africa. There could, he said, be no rapport between white and black workers because white workers gained their privileges from racism. As a result those who are nearest the blacks economically are the most eager to underline the gap between them. 'Hence,' he argued, 'the greatest anti-black feeling is to be found amongst the very poor whites whom the Class Theory calls upon to be with black workers in the struggle for emancipation' (Biko 1978: 50). Biko was no less critical of white liberals: that 'bunch of do-gooders who argue that they are not responsible for white racism . . . who say that they have black souls wrapped in white skins', but in fact stifle and suppress blacks, 'with whites doing all the talking and blacks the listening.' White liberals, said Biko, always claimed to know what was good for blacks. He rejected their false belief in integration, which was based on the premise of bringing blacks into the white circle, and propagated by the 'come around for tea at home' set. He favoured integration only if it meant 'free participation by all members of a society, catering for the full expression of the self in a freely changing society . . . as determined by the will of the people'. The culture of the majority, he said, must determine the broad direction of a society. So that 'an Africa in which the majority of the people are African must inevitably exhibit African values and be truly African in style' (Biko 1978: 22–4).

Biko called for a black reawakening to their own values and dignity. Apartheid existed because of whites overpowering psychological dominance over black minds. 'We must realise', wrote Biko, 'that our situation is not a mistake on the part of whites, but a deliberate act', and no amount of moral lecturing could correct the situation. 'The most potent weapon in the hands of the oppressor is the mind of the oppressed.' To counter white power, argued Biko, blacks must use their group power (Arnold 1979: xix). He rejected Bantustans as the product of white thinking. Instead he wanted 'a total accommodation of our interests in the total country, not in some portion of it' (Arnold 1979: 59). The Bantustan solution was, he wrote, 'given to us by the same people who have created the problem. In a land rightfully ours we find people coming to tell us where to stay and what powers we shall have'. Economically the Bantustans gave blacks a raw deal, and politically they were 'the greatest fraud ever invented by white politicians'. The policy was designed with a number of malign intentions in mind: to create a false sense of hope among the blacks; to direct the struggle in a false direction by envisaging 'false freedoms'; to deceive the outside world; and to intensify inter tribal competition (Biko 1978: 81–2).

Although Biko accepted that men like Matanzima and Buthelezi believed that they could uplift Africans by their actions, and had shown courage and determination, he entirely rejected their position. They were, he said, 'subconsciously siding and abetting in the total subjugation of the black people of this country' by promoting tribalism. They were confusing the black people, and confusing themselves that they could exercise influence on the government. 'These tribal cocoons called "homelands" are nothing else but sophisticated concentration camps where black people are allowed to "suffer peacefully."' Matanzima and Buthelezi, wrote Biko, 'can shout their lungs out trying to speak to Pretoria through the phony telephone. No one is listening in Pretoria because the telephone is a toy'. Biko said that it pained him to see Buthelezi, 'a man who could easily have been my leader, being so misused by the cruel and exploitative white world'. Buthelezi, said Biko, was allowed to criticize the system in public because he was no threat to the state and it exonerated the government from the accusation of creating a police state. 'The combination of Buthelezi and the white press make up the finest ambassadors that South Africa ever had' (Biko 1978: 81–6).

The first BPC national congress was held in December 1972 – attended by two hundred Africans, Indian and Coloured delegates. They condemned apartheid, rejected the Bantustan policy, and opposed foreign investment, because it supported a white economic system which exploited black workers. As BC activities increased the government responded by forbidding its meetings and serving banning orders on its officials. Despite this BC protests continued, and clashes and confrontation persisted as the government tightened the screw. For example, BC rallies to celebrate the defeat of Portuguese colonialism in Mozambique and Angola went ahead despite a ban on them by Jimmy Kruger, the Minister of Justice. However, the government gave the movement no respite as it banned, detained and imprisoned the leaders, charging them with 'endangering the maintenance of law and order in the Republic', and conspiring to 'transform the state by unconstitutional, revolutionary and/or violent means'. Pretoria's brutality and disregard to human rights was appallingly exemplified in its treatment of Steve Biko. After earlier banning orders, Biko was detained without trial in 1976 for 101 days under Section 6 of the Terrorism Act. The act extended the definition of 'terrorism' to include activities which are intended to bring about social or economic change, or 'cause, encourage or further feelings of hostility between the White and other inhabitants of the Republic' (Arnold 1979: xxii). Biko was arrested again on 18 August 1977 under the same legislation. By 12 September he was dead, having been treated with extreme cruelty by his captors. In the official investigation which followed, nobody was found responsible for his death. The news of Biko's death and the callous response of the South African government shocked not only black South Africans but the whole international community. The *New York Times* stated that 'the death of Steve Biko has shaken South Africa more than any single event since the police opened fire at Sharpeville in 1960' (Arnold 1979: xxiii). An estimated 15,000 people attended the funeral, including the diplomatic representatives of thirteen western states. With Biko's death BC as a movement was suppressed, but before that the ideas of black consciousness had found root and flourished among black youth.

The ANC and PAC in Exile

Although Sharpeville had altered the balance of South African politics, that was not clear to the ANC and PAC, especially after the setbacks of 1963. The ANC's journal *Sechaba* later admitted that the arrests at Rivonia had 'smashed the very heart of the organisation' (Johns 1973: 152). The African parties were in a sorry state – their internal organizations smashed, their members dispersed, their leaders in prison or in exile. Some small-scale, intermittent activity continued inside the country but it was no immediate threat to the government. Yet Pretoria did not relax its grip, and continued to ban or bring to trial any ANC and PAC members it caught or suspected. Those who had escaped abroad faced the formidable task of rebuilding the parties in exile. The talk was no longer of a quick victory but of a long difficult struggle. Their first task was simply to survive, both as individuals and as organizations. To do so they had to rely on others – for refuge, for places to work and to train, and for support and resources – and in doing so they built up obligations, were influenced by the ideas and values of their hosts and sometimes were drawn into their internal affairs.

Urged on by some of their backers to combine their efforts the exiled ANC and PAC leaders made early attempts to work together, but there was no real enthusiasm on either side and the efforts soon broke down. The two parties remained fierce rivals, harbouring the divisions, the personal antagonisms and different ideologies which had led to their split inside South Africa, and adding to them in exile. Among other things a gulf remained over racial attitudes. Tennyson Makiwane, speaking on behalf of the ANC in November 1960 said: 'If the United Front were an anti white organisation, the ANC would not be part of it. The ANC stands for non racialism whether it is inside or outside SA' (Thomas 1996: 47). Although they were not prepared to work together the ANC and the PAC faced similar tasks and problems in exile. They fell under four headings: first, to build an organization that could survive; second, to retain links with supporters in South Africa; third, to gain a diplomatic status so that international support could be enlisted and Pretoria isolated; and fourth, to train and equip guerilla forces for an armed liberation struggle. Their shared problems included their dependence on others; shortage of resources; the need to establish new methods of working and training; the alien context in which they had to operate; personal tensions and rivalries; and the crises of morale and confidence that come to all exiles. Yet both the PAC and the ANC survived the ordeal. However, the ANC was the more successful.

The PAC, which had had little opportunity to put down roots even inside the country before it was banned in 1960, had made no prior arrangements to operate abroad. At first it assumed that the government would be toppled quickly, and so established itself on the borders in Lesotho where it had an unhappy time – penetrated by informers and riven by internal divisions. It was not until 1964 that the PAC followed the ANC in opening offices in London, Cairo, Accra and Dar es Salaam. It received support from China, and under Maoist influence it took a close interest in the peasantry, and it continued to emphasize that the struggle must be led by Africans. Tom Lodge identified three characteristics which told against the PAC. First, its ideological stand was negative (based on antipathy to external influences in the ANC) and was difficult to sustain when it became dependent itself on external support. 'In place of any analysis and discussion,' wrote Lodge, 'there was substituted a sterile and externally derived dogmatism'. Second, the PAC persisted in its indifference to effective organization and its reliance on spontaneity. As a result its activities in exile were often characterized by bureaucratic confusion and bitter squabbles. Third, because the PAC leaders came from a less privileged background than the ANC they were more susceptible to the temptations and pretensions of politics in exile. Lodge could well have added two more factors – namely erratic leadership (especially from Leballo) and the inadequacy of the PAC's alliances (Lodge 1983: 313).

Yet, despite the PAC's tribulations, the ANC never achieved its ambition to be accepted as the sole legitimate representative of South Africa's oppressed people. The PAC continued to be recognized. Indeed, for some African states the PAC's 'Africanism' and rejection of multi-racialism was clearer and more attractive than the ANC's position. The ANC was even accused of not being revolutionary enough. Also circumstances, both local and international, played their part. For example, the PAC was especially favoured in Tanzania after Leballo had helped to uncover a plot against President Julius Nyerere in 1970. In international terms the division in the communist camp led to a shift in support. At first China helped to train and equip both ANC and PAC guerilla fighters, but after the communist split China backed the PAC while the USSR supported the ANC. In the long term that told against the PAC, for China lost interest in Africa and became consumed in its own internal struggles. Subsequently the PAC was viewed with suspicion by the

Soviet bloc, so that, for instance, it was refused admission as a member of the 1966 pro USSR Havana Conference.

Even before Sharpeville the ANC had started to build an international presence. After the 1958 All-Africa Peoples' Conference call to boycott South African goods, Tennyson Makiwane was sent to London in 1959 to support the campaign. Next year, shortly before Sharpeville, Makiwane was joined by Oliver Tambo. In 1963 a third major figure arrived: Moses Kotane, the General Secretary of the SACP, who became Treasurer of the exiled movement and an important link with Moscow. When Tambo arrived in London he had little idea of the crucial role he was to play in the ANC's future. After Rivonia, with Luthuli under house arrest and Mandela and others in prison, Tambo, as leader of the exiled movement, came by default to be leader of all. He and his fellow exiles had to create new structures and operate in an unknown and alien environment. A Congress alliance was established between the broad-based ANC itself; the MK with its guerilla army; and the SACP. All three were bound together by their opposition to apartheid and the white state, but each enjoyed a considerable degree of autonomy.

Tambo's position was formalized step by step. Luthuli remained President until his death in 1967, after which Tambo was appointed acting President and finally confirmed in office in 1977. His style was mild, yet he had a strong will and became the hub that held the ANC together. His strengths lay in his ability to reconcile, to listen to others, to seek internal agreement without abandoning his main aims. His achievements were to build an organization in exile, to hold it together so that it did not disintegrate into factions, and finally to avoid major corruption. Even so, there were clear limits to his authority. He had no control over the SACP or directly over MK. Nor was he able to avoid internal clashes, or crises of morale and confidence, or gaps appearing between the leadership and the rank and file.

International Diplomacy

The exiled movements set themselves three main tasks – to stimulate mass action in South Africa, to gain diplomatic support, and to build guerilla armies. At first the most difficult was to promote direct action inside South Africa, because the movements had lost their domestic base. The exiles retained intermittent contacts with internal supporters and from time to time infiltrated trained members across the border, but the links were sparse and difficult to maintain. Nor did the government drop its guard. In 1971 Brigadier P. J. Venter, Chief of the Security Police, warned that the ANC and PAC were 'moving trained terrorists' into the country, and organizing 'a subtle and large scale brain washing of youth' (IDAAF 1971: 449). Frustrated in their efforts to promote activity inside South Africa the exiles turned their main activities to international diplomacy and preparing for the armed struggle.

In terms of international diplomacy the PAC and ANC made quick progress in gaining recognition. The 1960s was the decade of Africa, as new states emerged from the old colonies. These states, as well as recognizing the exiles paved the way for them at international institutions – including the UN, and the Organisation of African Unity (OAU) which was formed in 1963. By working together the African states and the exiles succeeded in making apartheid a prominent item on the international agenda, and rallying opposition against Pretoria. The appearance of PAC and ANC leaders before international organizations was important in affording them legitimacy, and from the beginning they sought to exploit their status. For example, Tambo, fearing that the Rivonia trialists might face execution, petitioned the UN Special Political Committee on their behalf the day before the trial started, in the hope that international attention would reduce the chances of death sentences. Yet, in some ways international organizations were a disappointment. The exiles naively expected too much from them. They anticipated that there was always substance behind the rhetoric. However, they soon discovered that the fiery language of the UN's General Assembly was not matched by action in the Security Council where the three permanent western members (US, UK and France) refused to support the armed struggle and opposed comprehensive economic sanctions. Similarly the exiles found that OAU members failed to live up to their word. In 1967, for example, the OAU promised to provide $80,000. In fact it produced less than $4,000.

The exiles also had to take account of the vagaries of international politics. The major East/West powers tended to interpret their relations in cold war terms; the African states to see them as an element of the struggle against colonialism. The emphasis of the exiles' diplomatic effort therefore varied according to the setting. In Africa, there were obvious advantages in co-operating with sympathetic governments, and being based near to South Africa itself. As a result the exiles came to site more of their activities on the continent. Over time they established major offices at Dar es Salaam in Tanzania and Lusaka in Zambia; broadcasting centres in Cairo and Addis Ababa; and guerilla camps in such countries as Zambia, Algeria, Tanzania, Uganda and Angola. Without doubt the African states were of great importance in the struggle against Pretoria. However, each government had its own agenda which took precedence over those of the dependent exiles, and the exiles sometimes brought troubles on their own heads by poor discipline in their camps or involving themselves in local politics. Further, Pretoria's own diplomatic efforts in Africa under Vorster made some headway and a group of states emerged which for a time adopted a more 'moderate' approach to South Africa. That was reflected in the 1969 Lusaka Manifesto which was accepted by thirteen African states. It differed from the liberation movements' policy by placing the emphasis on peaceful change rather than armed struggle; by accepting the Pretoria regime as the government of a sovereign state; and by separating the liberation struggle in South Africa from those in Rhodesia and Namibia, and giving the latter two priority in terms of timing.

The exiles' attempts to gain support in the West had mixed fortunes. Western government criticized apartheid, and slowly imposed limited forms of sanctions against Pretoria, but only the Scandinavians gave substantial financial aid, and that largely for humanitarian work. There was virtually no official support for the armed struggle. However, the West was important in that Pretoria looked there for its own international support. The exiles set out to undermine that, to gain what support they could from non-government bodies and to use the West's powerful media to forward their own cause. Instead, therefore, of emphasizing the armed struggle in the West the exiles concentrated on propaganda against apartheid, isolating Pretoria by means of boycotts and sanctions, and gaining what financial backing they could find. In that they gained support from anti-apartheid groups, churches and some political parties, and sections of the media. These alliances spread the anti-apartheid message and put pressure on western governments, banks and trading companies to cut links, so that steadily a climate of opinion was built up against Pretoria and its apartheid policies.

The most effective support for the exiles, especially for the ANC, came from communist states. Not only did the USSR give diplomatic support, it was prepared to underpin the armed struggle, based on the Soviet assumption that the West could be attacked through African and Asian nationalist movements. The support was offered from the beginning. In December 1962 the SACP sent a memo to Moscow seeking help. In the following month Arthur Goldreich, an SACP member, visited the USSR and Eastern Europe, where he obtained promises of substantial aid in terms of finance (rumoured to be $2.8m.), equipment and training. The promises were largely fulfilled. For example East Germany, a leading ANC backer, provided military training, paid for the ANC journal *Sechaba* and gave scholarships for African students. By the 1980s the exiled ANC had a budget of *c.*$100m. Half of this came from the communist bloc, much of it for MK activities, and most of the rest from the UN and Scandinavian countries.

The role of the SACP in relation to the ANC was always a matter of potential controversy. It remained a small multi-racial party which was influential because of its discipline, commitment and certainty of purpose. The communists never doubted that history was on their side. They saw the present struggle in South Africa as part of a three-stage progression: first, the overthrow of the white colonial state; second, the creation of a socialist state; and third, the achievement of a communist, classless society. The first phase coincided with Moscow's current interpretation of the cold war, in which it was better to avoid direct conflict with the West because of the danger of nuclear war. Instead capitalism would be attacked by supporting nationalist and socialist movements in Africa and Asia. The SACP's influence inside the ANC increased as international communist support increased. Its role became more prominent after the Sino/Soviet split which forced the ANC to choose between its communist backers. *Sechaba* later admitted that the Sino-Soviet split had thrown the liberation movement into disarray. 'One of the greatest tragedies of our time,' it stated, 'has been the discord in the socialist camp which has weakened the main shield of the people against imperialism' (Thomas 1996: 167). Because of the SACP link the inevitable choice for the ANC was the Soviet Union, which was accepted as leader of the world's revolutionary movement. The Soviet line was largely followed whether in condemning the Chinese invasion of Vietnam, or supporting the invasion of Czechoslovakia in 1968. On one issue at least, however, the ANC challenged Moscow's position. With his eye on broad East/West relations Krushchev, the Soviet leader, re-formulated the theory of the inevitability of war, arguing that socialist ends could be achieved by a policy of peaceful co-existence. At the World Congress of Peace

Forces in 1973 the ANC openly stated that liberation movements found it difficult 'to support the theory of peaceful coexistence among states of different social systems whilst at the same time they are fighting life and death struggles for independence' (Thomas 1996: 171).

Usually, however, the ANC/SACP alliance toed Moscow's line. That bred intolerance. Scott Thomas wrote: 'Whoever spoke against the Kremlin and its policies was branded as a deviant, Maoist and revisionist; or alternatively an imperialist and branded a fifth columnist against the liberation of South Africa (Thomas 1996: 162). The result was tension and discord, which finally led to an ANC split in October 1975. Eight members were expelled, including Tennyson Makiwane. Like Africanists in the past they complained about the undue influence of communists and whites in the movement. They accused SACP members of opposing 'the political philosophy embodied in the concept of African nationalism' and having their 'roots firmly fixed in the historically conditioned modes of thought that characterise white superior attitudes to blacks' (Lodge 1983: 303). The split did not lead to a major division and the rebels were written out of ANC history. Makiwane later returned to South Africa where he worked for the Transkei government, until he was assassinated in 1980, probably by ANC agents.

The Armed Struggle

In ANC eyes diplomacy and the armed struggle were twins. Although some MK members came to believe that Pretoria could be defeated militarily, and Tambo tried to keep up spirits by making extravagant claims about the effectiveness of the guerilla fighters, the usual message was that violence was not an end in itself. It was part of a strategy that combined mass action, diplomacy, economic pressure and armed struggle. 'Violence,' stated Tambo in 1966, 'is an extension of, not a substitute for, the forms of political action employed in the past. Its uses will be confined to the objectives of freedom for the oppressed people' (Johns and Davies 1991: 137). Although that message was based on principle, it was also a recognition of military limitations. The conventional wisdom for guerilla forces was that they needed to operate from reliable external bases on the borders of the target state, and they needed areas inside the country where they could disappear either by losing themselves in the people or in difficult terrain. Those conditions did not apply in South Africa.

South Africa was not only a powerful state but until the mid-1970s it was surrounded by a buffer of white-controlled territories – namely Rhodesia and the Portuguese colonies of Angola and Mozambique – which were fighting their own wars against liberation forces. To an extent, therefore, South Africa was able to fight its war by proxy outside its own borders. In the government's eyes all the guerilla fighters were terrorists and directly or indirectly enemies of South Africa. Voster declared: 'I know of no terrorism in southern Africa which, in the final analysis, is not directed against South Africa . . . The ultimate aim of all the terrorists is to take South Africa away from us' (HA 15 September 1966). To counter that a new Terrorism Act was passed in 1967, military expenditure was greatly increased, and informal alliances formed with the neighbouring white regimes. In 1966, P. W.

Botha said that 'the terrorists are underestimating our determination and our military power; such attempts can only lead to the death of these people' (HA 29 September 1966).

Because both MK and the Azanian Peoples Liberation Army (APLA) – the renamed armed wing of the PAC – had major difficulties in reaching South Africa to prosecute the war they ran into morale and discipline problems in the camps. The romance of becoming a guerilla fighter quickly wore thin when faced by life in a remote camp often with little prospect of real action. The guerillas had diverse experiences. Some were well trained, others were not; some lived in reasonably well-ordered camps, others did not; some were moved from camp to camp and country to country, others were not; some were subjected to brutal discipline, others were not. Yet whatever the conditions all suffered from the boredom and morale sapping experience of endless waiting. MK tried to overcome the problems of distance from its targets and inactivity by forming an alliance with the forces of the Zimbabwe African Peoples Union (ZAPU). Tambo declared that they marched 'as comrades in arms on a common route, each bound to its destination . . . to fight the common enemy to the finish' (Martin and Johnson 1981: 10). The MK's aims were to help overthrow the Rhodesian regime and to use Rhodesia as a conduit to penetrate South Africa.

Between the mid-1960s and the mid-1970s the Rhodesian war fell into three phases. The first culminated in 1967/8 with the combined ANC/ZAPU forces invading the Wankie area of Rhodesia from Zambia. The guerillas fought bravely but in military terms the Wankie campaign was a disaster. Most were either killed or captured. It taught them the hard lesson that guerillas were doomed if they attempted to fight set-piece battles against a better-equipped enemy fighting on its own territory, and with no easy retreat across a border or into the local community. The ANC retrieved what it could of the campaign by making it part of MK mythology, lauding the courage of their troops and identifying those who were killed as martyrs. In the second phase of the Rhodesian war, between 1968 and 1972, there was little direct action. The ANC/ZAPU alliance fell into disuse, and ZAPU was riven by internal divisions. When guerilla activity started again late in 1972 it was mainly led by Robert Mugabe's Zimbabwe African National Union (ZANU) operating from Mozambique. ZANU had loose links with APLA, which played a small part in the campaign. However, for the South African exiles there was no disguising the lesson that, given the existing conditions, guerilla attacks alone were not going to overthrow the Pretoria government.

However, a critical turning point came in 1974, when, following a military coup in Portugal, the face of southern Africa was changed as the Portuguese withdrew from their colonies. The retreat from Mozambique so exposed Rhodesia's mountainous eastern border to infiltration that in Pretoria's judgement the country was no longer defensible. The war dragged on, but eventually in 1980 the independent Zimbabwe emerged from the colonial Rhodesia. On the other side of the continent Angola became ensnared in a cold war conflict which drew in South Africa partly to support the anti-communist forces inside Angola and partly to defend Namibia's northern borders from the South West African Peoples Organisation (SWAPO).

The ANC's Morogoro Conference: 1969

In April 1969 the ANC held a conference at Morogoro in Tanzania. It was a far cry from the old conferences inside South Africa. Only 70 delegates attended, of whom 11 were not Africans. The Morogoro meeting captured much of the essence of life in exile – the problems, the hopes, the tensions, the strength of external influences. Although there was some optimistic rhetoric, with Tambo urging the delegates to 'cast their eyes southwards, to prepare to go home', it was in reality a bleak time for the movement – with uncertainty about its future, immediate morale and discipline problems, discontent in the MK camps, criticism that the leadership was out of touch with the rank and file, and complaints about poor organization and lack of communication. The conference was summoned to deal with these issues. At the start the National Executive resigned en masse, although most were re-elected. Later Joe Slovo admitted that: 'There were moments at the Morogoro Conference when the very future of our whole movement seemed in jeopardy' (Thomas 1996: 52). Yet, in the event, Morogoro not only helped to iron out immediate problems, but it clarified the ANC's current thinking, and it pointed out a future course. Tambo emphasized that the aim was to create a truly revolutionary movement. To that end it was decided to reorganize the external mission. In future it would concentrate more effort on the armed struggle and less on diplomacy, and it would foster its relations with communists and Afro-Asian states, the opponents of imperialism and supporters of the struggle, and give less attention to the 'incorrigible' West. A further major decision was to open up membership to all races for the first time. Although the National Executive Council was still confined to Africans, the MK's controlling Revolutionary Council was mixed race. Joe Slovo, Yusuf Dadoo of the Indian Congress, and Reginald September of the Coloured Peoples Congress, were appointed to it (Ellis and Sechaba 1992: 55).

Another product of the conference was a commentary on the Freedom Charter – the 'Revolutionary Programme'. Among other things it discussed individual and group rights, and in particular the relationship between Africans and other peoples. It declared that the ANC had been formed to unite Africans as a nation and to forge an instrument for their liberation. From the outset it had recognized 'the rights of Africans as the indigenous owners of the country, entitled to determine its direction and destiny', while at the same time accepting that other groups belonged to South Africa. It repeated the commitment that 'South Africa belongs to all who live in it'.

Looking to the future the Programme envisaged establishing a democratic state. To achieve that power had to be seized by the revolutionary forces led by the ANC. The new state would recognize that 'the people who have made South Africa are components of its multi-national population' but will in the future be 'one people inhabiting their common home'. The state would not be divided or dominated by one group, but based on the will of all. Parliament was to be transformed into an Assembly of the People. While at present 'the Afrikaner national group is lording it over the rest of the population', a democratic government would 'ensure that all national groups have equal rights . . . to achieve their destiny in a united South

Africa'. Recognizing that the struggle would be hard, it finished with a call to 'all
South African patriots whatever their race [to] take their place in the revolution
under the banner of the ANC' (*ANC Speaks*: 16–25).

The final communique from Morogoro set the Programme in an international
context and linked it to the armed struggle. It stated that although the national
character of the movement must be dominant, the struggle was taking place in the
context of an international 'transition to the Socialist system, and the breakdown
of the colonial system as a result of national liberation and socialist revolutions'. The
international balance of forces had changed in favour of the powerful socialist states
and those seeking liberation. South Africa was 'part of the zone in which national
liberation is the chief content of the struggle', with its own distinctive 'colonialism
of a special type'. The main content of the struggle was 'the national liberation of
the largest and most oppressed group – the African people', which involves 'a deepening of national confidence, national pride and national assertiveness'. However,
it was not enough to have a political/constitutional revolution – it must extend to
economic emancipation, so that the wealth of the land is returned to the people as
a whole. 'To allow the existing economic forces to retain their interests intact is
to feed the root of racial supremacy and does not represent even the shadow of
liberation.' To achieve these ends, stated the communique, the ANC recognized
that the military and political sides of the struggle were tied together, and that the
political had primacy. 'When we talk of revolutionary armed struggle we are talking
of political struggle by means which include the use of military force.'

Finally the communique outlined the strategy for the people's war. The revolution, it stated, could only succeed with the active support of masses. 'The enemy is
as aware as we are that the side that wins the allegiance of the people, wins the
struggle.' Power must reside not in an army but the masses 'at the head of which
stands its organised political leadership' [the ANC]. The campaign would be based
on the townships and urban working class, where as an alternative to jungles and
mountains, the fighters would be absorbed. The large well-developed black
working class, with its unions and institutions, was part of the liberation front. If
the confrontation was on racial lines that was of the enemy's making not the ANC's.
The ANC was opposed to racism, and it was still possible that part of white working
class would support the struggle. 'There is room in South Africa for all who live in
it but only on the basis of absolute democracy.' We are', declared the communique,
'revolutionaries but not narrow nationalists, and all committed revolutionaries are
our brothers to whatever group they belong'.

The Morogoro conference helped to overcome immediate problems but it did not
end the ANC's troubles. There were some activities inside South Africa, such as
pamphlet bombs which were set off in Johannesburg, Durban and Port Elizabeth,
and an ANC news sheet *Amandla-Matha* began to circulate. However, the guerilla
war made little progress, and the split developed which led in October 1975 to the
expulsion of a 'Gang of Eight'. Yet, despite the continued problems in the African
movements, including the old issue of the role of white communists, their position
improved in the mid-1970s. The international situation, especially in southern
Africa, where Angola and Mozambique came under black socialist governments

tied to the communist bloc, became more favourable. MK took advantage by moving its operations closer to South Africa's borders. In 1974 Chris Hani, an outstanding young MK leader, established a base in Lesotho, while Joe Slovo, the Chief of Staff of MK, moved to Maputo soon after Mozambique's independence. By the mid-1970s Pretoria faced serious security problems on its borders.

Part V

Renewed Black Challenge

16

Soweto and its Aftermath

Following the crisis of the early 1960s the South African Government recovered to enjoy a period of confidence: the economy grew steadily; white incomes increased; the NP retained its electoral support; and black nationalism was stifled at home. All that changed in the mid-1970s. International political and economic developments turned against Pretoria, to be followed by a major rising at home.

On the international front Pretoria came under mounting criticism at the UN, both for its apartheid policies and its continued administration of South West Africa/Namibia. In 1974 the General Assembly voted to suspend the Republic. That action was beyond its powers and was not confirmed by the Security Council, but it was an indication of the intense global hostility. Pretoria clung on to UN membership because it gave it the opportunity to respond directly to attacks; it valued the specialized institutions (like the International Monetary Fund); it confirmed South Africa's status as a sovereign state; and it thwarted any attempt to fill the empty seat with a black government in exile. Membership was retained but Pretoria no longer sat in the General Assembly and refused to pay its full UN dues.

The economic picture also became bleaker as conflict in the Middle East led to an oil crisis which shook the world economy. In South Africa itself the growth rate slowed down, inflation and unemployment increased and the economy went into recession. This lead to labour troubles among both whites and blacks. As the economy had expanded during the 1960s and early 1970s many of the old job barriers had been breached, but the recession led to a white backlash. Stoppages and threats of strikes arose among white workers in the railways, construction industries and even the mines. In the face of this pressure Pretoria reaffirmed its commitment to white labour. However, it soon faced much greater troubles among black workers.

Starting in Durban and spreading to the Eastern Cape and the Rand, African workers, dissatisfied with their lot, began to show their industrial muscle. In the first three months of 1973 there were 160 strikes, and in the period between January and September more than 70,000 workers were involved in industrial action. The employers had difficulty in dealing with the situation as many of the strikes were lightning affairs involving groups of workers without any formal organization. The Minister of Labour spoke of 'agitators', and told parliament that the strikes followed a pattern, which made clear that the claims for improved wages and union rights were 'only a smoke screen behind which there are other motives' (IRR 1973: 288). In contrast a report from the Institute of Race Relations suggested that among the factors which caused the strikes were rising costs, the increasing awareness of relative deprivation, and the pressure of limited opportunities due to job reservation.

Although the major labour troubles were in the industrial areas the greatest single tragedy came at a gold mine at Carletonville on 11 September 1973. The disturbances began in the vast mine compound which housed 8,470 men. According to a report by the Minister of Police the disturbance started when black workers threatened the mine manager and security guards and went on the rampage destroying mine property. When a small party of police arrived (22 of them) they were met by a barrage of stones. The police retaliated – at first with tear gas and battons, but when they found themselves surrounded by a mob who continued to attack, they defended themselves by opening fire. Eleven workers were shot dead by the police, while another was hacked to death by the rioters themselves (IRR 1973: 243).

The labour troubles of 1973 were forerunners of a revival of militant African political activity.

The Regional Scene

In southern Africa Portuguese rule collapsed after a coup in Lisbon in April 1974. Following that event black socialist governments came to power in Angola (threatening Pretoria's control of South West Africa); and in Mozambique (which undermined Rhodesia's security and threatened South Africa's north east border). Thus the defensive barrier of white-controlled territories which had stretched around South Africa was replaced by black states sympathetic to the liberation movements. For Pretoria the introduction of a communist government in Mozambique also had grave economic implications. Lorenco Marques was a major port for the Transvaal; many Mozambique workers were employed in the mines; Pretoria had invested heavily in the Cabora Bassa dam on the Zambezi; and South African business had substantial interests in the country. At first Vorster responded cautiously but positively to President Samora Machel's new Frelimo Government. He was not concerned, he said, with the type of government, but only that it is stable and friendly. Whoever, Vorster said, 'takes over in Mozambique has a tough task ahead . . . They have my sympathy and I wish them well' (Meredith 1980: 151). Yet, behind the sympathy was the message that a tough response would follow interference in South Africa's affairs, or help for her opponents. At this stage, however, Vorster rejected military action in Mozambique, even when a white-led coup was proposed, which Ian Smith, the Rhodesian leader, was keen to support (Smith 1997: 161).

Vorster's policy towards Mozambique formed part of a broader 'détente' initiative. It differed from the earlier attempts at 'dialogue' in that it concentrated on stabilizing the southern African region. In October 1974 Vorster declared that 'Southern Africa is at the crossroads and should choose between peace and escalating violence'. For Vorster the key to peace was a settlement of the Rhodesian dispute. He believed that if he could achieve that it would remove a major source of regional tension, bring credit to South Africa among both western states and black neighbours, and demonstrate Pretoria's regional influence. In any case, with the change of government in Mozambique, Vorster concluded that Rhodesia's eastern border was indefensible.

Vorster's views were challenged by Smith, who believed that the military effort could be sustained, and he could reach his own internal settlement. 'Uppermost in our minds,' wrote Smith, 'was the South Africans' eagerness to throw us to the wolves in their desperate panic to try to buy time and gain credit for solving the Rhodesian problem' (Smith 1997: 207). In contrast Vorster's proposals were welcomed by President Kaunda of Zambia. If Pretoria, said Kaunda, was ready to take the path of peace the rest of Africa would follow. Kaunda and Vorster tried to realize their aims by bringing the Rhodesian regime and its African opponents together in a peace conference at Victoria Falls. Smith dismissed it as 'a bizarre attempt to appease' but he was obliged to attend because his land-locked country was dependent on South Africa. The conference failed because there was no meeting of minds between white and black Rhodesians. Despite that Vorster kept up the pressure on Smith – by delaying supplies and withdrawing troops and equipment – and brought into play Henry Kissinger, the US Secretary of State, in a new initiative. That too failed, as did subsequent South African efforts. Years of escalating violence followed.

It was not only white Rhodesians who questioned détente. Sceptics were also found in Pretoria. They included P. W. Botha, the Minister of Defence, who gave more credence to military action than diplomacy. He found an outlet for his approach in Angola, which became a tangled web of competing African movements and superpowers, and provided a base for SWAPO attacks into South West Africa. Pretoria's early military intervention was to counter these incursions and defend its own border installations. However, as an Angolan civil war developed between the communist MPLA and UNITA (which initially had US backing) so a debate arose in Pretoria about military intervention. The Department of Foreign Affairs opposed it, Vorster himself was not enthusiastic, but in the end Botha's will prevailed. South African troops invaded Angola in October 1975. They enjoyed initial success as they advanced north towards Luanda. Then the MPLA government, close to collapse, called for outside help, and received it in the form of Soviet arms and Cuban troops. Faced by this greater force, and with political vacillation in Pretoria, the South African troops were obliged to withdraw to their own border in March 1976.

Then came Soweto.

The Soweto Rising

On 16 June 1976 secondary-school pupils in Soweto, the vast black township on the edge of Johannesburg, marched in protest against the government's insistence that in future increased use should be made of Afrikaans as a medium of instruction. By the time the students reached Orlando West High School their numbers had grown to about 14,000. There they met and clashed with the police. At first there were stones from the students and tear gas and warning shots from the police, but then the police fired into the crowd, killing at least one youth, Hector Petersen. Rioting followed, sweeping across Soweto, with several deaths including two innocent whites. The rioting persisted and spread like a bush fire. African youths took to the streets in many parts of the Republic and in some places they were joined by Coloureds and Indians. The young militants put pressure on adults to support them with strikes and civil disobedience. There was much loss of life and damage to property. Five days after the first outbreak Jimmy Kruger, the Minister of Justice, announced that on the Witwatersrand alone there had been 130 deaths and 1,100 people injured; and 33 Bantu administrative buildings, 27 beer halls and 90 schools had been burnt down. By the end of the rising the number of people killed and injured was higher still. The government's conservative estimate was 575 people killed and 2,389 wounded by the end of 1977 (IRR 1976: 51–87).

The Soweto rising was not planned and came as a surprise, to the government and the exiled African movements. Initially the students had no formal organization – they relied more on passion than discipline – but in August they formed the Soweto Students Representative Council (SSRC) and other councils followed around the country. However, organization was never a strong point with the students. Although the immediate cause of the rising was the introduction of Afrikaans as a teaching medium there was common agreement that deeper reasons lay behind it, but there was disagreement about what these were. For most Africans it was an outburst against the injustice and oppression of apartheid. Shortly before the rising Bishop Desmond Tutu had written to Vorster warning of the potential danger. 'I have a growing nightmarish fear,' wrote Tutu, 'that unless something drastic is done very soon, then bloodshed and violence are going to happen in South Africa, almost inevitably . . . A people made desperate by despair and injustice and oppression will use desperate means' (Liebenberg and Spies 1993: 462). Tutu was ignored because the government did not take the threat seriously. A couple of weeks before the rising a senior administrator described Soweto as 'very happy' (Brewer 1986: 67).

Even in retrospect the government rejected Tutu's analysis. Instead it pointed the finger at agitators. Vorster refused to believe that the youths had acted spontaneously; claiming that the rising was a deliberate attempt by 'certain organizations and people' to 'bring about polarization between Whites and Blacks'. He said that the continuation of such troubles must be expected: 'After all the communists have adopted this course and dare not deviate from it now' (HA 18 June 1976). Later, an official enquiry was conducted by Mr Justice Cillie. He recognized that there had been poor police intelligence and a breakdown of communication between the people and the urban administration, and he noted complaints about housing, low wages, influx control and transport. Yet he concluded that in themselves these matters had not caused the rising. Rather they had laid the ground for agitators who had intimidated people into action. His report concluded that 'it cannot be said that the riots were an expression of the Black man's wish or that, by rioting, he was raising his voice against oppression and for a more democratic dispensation in the Republic of South Africa' (Lodge 1983: 332).

Although general frustration lay behind the Soweto rising the language question had a special resonance. Many black teachers were not fluent in Afrikaans and it was not widely used among Soweto students, but it was more than a technical dispute. It was a confrontation of principle. For men like Dr Andreis Treurnicht, the Deputy Minister of Bantu Education, who was responsible for the policy, the use of Afrikaans demonstrated Afrikanerdom's pre-eminence in the state. He was determined to forward the cause by ensuring that Afrikaans, not English, was the second language for Africans. Therefore on one side of the language dispute stood Afrikaner nationalism. On the other stood black consciousness. When, shortly before his death, Steve Biko was asked if he could point to support for his movement, he replied: 'Yes – In one word: Soweto!' He added: 'The boldness, dedication and sense of purpose and clarity of analysis of the situation – all these are a direct result of black consciousness ideas among the young' (Motlhabi 1984: 146). Black consciousness, with its message of personal pride and independence had become the youths' intellectual and emotional polar star. For them, unlike Afrikaner nationalists, English was not linked to past defeat and humiliation, but was a global language which could help free them from the confines of the apartheid state. Pretoria's aims conflicted with their determination to demonstrate their identity by resisting the imposition of a language and culture associated with apartheid.

While, in the early 1960s, Sharpeville had caught national and international attention its direct impact in South Africa had been localized. In contrast Soweto spread across the country and persisted. It was a rising on an unprecedented scale, drawing in hundreds of thousands of people. Soweto, commented a black consciousness journal, 'amazed not only the outsiders but also the insiders because it was so big . . . The people walked the way of unity. And tall. We were reborn. We were new people' (Brewer 1986: 2). It was also interpreted in a different way. At Sharpeville, argues Dan O'Meara, those who died were seen as apartheid's victims; at Soweto they were seen as heroes in the struggle against apartheid (O'Meara 1996: 180). The 'heroes' were militant youths, who represented a new radical element in African society. They knew little of the old movements (ANC and PAC) and dismissed their elders as too submissive and lacking fire in their bellies. Leonard Mosala, a veteran ANC supporter, stated: 'They won't take anything we say, because they think we have neglected them' (IRR 1976: 57).

More clearly than before the government was forced to respond to an agenda set by its opponents. It had constantly to try to divert troubles, to counter internal and external pressures. It fully recognized the challenge to its authority. While at the time of Sharpeville Verwoerd had called on whites to stand like granite, now Pik Botha, the Foreign Minister, urged them to 'stand like a rock against the waves of the ocean' (HA 2 February 1978). Pretoria acted swiftly, and without mercy. The notorious Minister of Justice, Jimmy Kruger, commenting on the use of live ammunition by the police, said that blacks must be made 'tame to the gun' (O'Meara 1996: 193). Thousands of youths were arrested and brought before the courts or detained without trial; many others fled the country. The State President described 1976 as 'a watershed year, characterized on the one hand by far-reaching developments on the international scene and on the other by the emergence within the Republic of elements who believe that the attainment of meaningful political rights for all our people is only possible by totally destroying, if need be through violence and bloodshed, the existing political, economic and social order' (HA 21 January 1977).

By 1978 the rising was over, but the situation had shifted against the government. Soweto had shattered the Verwoerdian vision/illusion of apartheid as a moral cause and a practical policy; it ignited a major and sustained black challenge; it forced Pretoria into reforms which caused deep fissures among whites; it undermined détente; it changed the political mood by weakening white confidence and giving hope to African nationalists; it hit the economy – with R1,739 million of private investment fleeing the country in 1977/8; it ushered in a period of sustained and brutal conflict; and it eventually led to a new constitution based on a reinterpretation by the government of the concepts of 'nation' and 'state'.

The Revival of African Politics

Soweto gave Africans inside the country a sense of confidence that they could challenge Pretoria's power. It also recharged the efforts of the exiled parties, and it gave hope to the imprisoned leaders. Mandela later commented: 'My comrades and I were enormously cheered; the spirit of mass protest that had seemed dormant in the 1960s was erupting in the 1970s.' When some of the youths were brought to Robben Island, Mandela noted that they 'were a different breed of prisoner than we had seen before. They were brave, hostile and aggressive; they would not take orders . . . Their instinct was to confront rather than cooperate. The authorities did not know how to handle them' (Mandela 1994: 471).

The revival was more complex and dispersed than in the past. The work place and the school room became political battlegrounds, and action was promoted by diverse groups – student bodies, black consciousness members, trade unions, churches, civic and community groups. Initially their efforts were limited because they were unco-ordinated, but that also created difficulties for the government in countering the hydra-headed challenge. For a time there was no peace for Pretoria as a new militancy demonstrated itself in day-to-day confrontations – such as refusals to pay increases in bus fares and rents, or to accept the authority of the urban councils, or to kowtow to the police. The number of days lost by strike action by black workers steadily increased, so that while in 1976, 22,000 man days were lost, by 1980 it was 150,000, and rose above 200,000 in the following two years (Brewer 1986: 187). Funerals for those who had fallen in the struggle became stages for symbolic demonstrations of resistance, none more so than Steve Biko's funeral in September 1977.

Civic groups varied according to local circumstances. Some were formed by parents to moderate the behaviour of their children; but all challenged the authority of local councils. The most prominent group – formed in Soweto and known as 'The Group of Ten' – was led by Dr Nthato Motlana, a covert ANC member. It was initially a small elite body which claimed that the task of the leaders was 'to guide and lead the broad mass of labourers and to move ahead of their thinking and not simply reflect it' (Lodge 1983: 354). The Group gained considerable media attention as it organized protest meetings, opposed official policies, and challenged the government in court. The authorities harassed it with bans and imprisonment of the leaders, but despite that it survived and was reformed in September 1979 as the larger, more democratic Soweto Civil Association, with thirty-three branches.

Although black consciousness was outlawed, and most of its leaders detained, a new movement – the Azanian Peoples' Organization (Azapo) – was formed in May 1978, with the motto 'One People, One Azania'. It was more flexible than earlier BC groups, and set out 'to correct the errors of the past' by 'taking black consciousness to the broad masses', and co-operating with labour unions and civic groups. Azapo's aims were to form a national black consciousness body, to work for a common education system and a single parliament in a unitary state, 'to encourage black theology, and to direct itself to all black workers' (IRR 1978: 33).

The Reactivated ANC

The ANC played no part in initiating the Soweto rising, and even when the rising was in full swing it remained largely on the sidelines. The militant youths neither associated themselves with the old liberation movements nor attempted to co-ordinate their activities with them. While the ANC leaders had predicted that mass action would play a leading part in the struggle, when the youth of Soweto rose they either could not or would not take full advantage of it. Yet the ANC gained advantage. Some activists had been infiltrated across the borders before the rising, and that paid dividends, when, within days, an ANC pamphlet was in circulation calling on the youths not only to sustain their action but broaden it against the whole apartheid structure. A few ANC sabotage units went into action, and although their activity was on a small scale they too announced the party's presence. A further factor was the re-emergence of an older generation of ANC activists in the civic associations.

However, the main importance of Soweto for the ANC lay in its longer-term implications, by changing the political climate inside and outside the country and by giving the movement an infusion of new blood. The new blood came from the youth who fled the country – estimated at 4,000 – most of whom were successfully absorbed by the ANC. They provided new life, drive and determination. Many received military and political training at camps such as Nova Katenga in southern Angola, which became well known as 'The University of the South' – so well known that it was attacked by the South African Airforce in May 1979. The exiled ANC succeeded in recruiting the youths because it had a reasonably efficient organization, while its rivals did not. Black Consciousness had made little effort to build an external mission, and the old PAC weaknesses of poor organization and faction fighting persisted. Between 1975 and 1978 APLA did infiltrate a handful of fighters across the border and PAC cells were active in East London and Johannesburg, but it was all on a small scale.

In retrospect the ANC leaders realized that they had failed to take full advantage of Soweto. As a result the ANC/SACP alliance undertook a strategy review in 1978.

A small group was set up which had a balance of Congress and communist members and of the armed and political wings. Oliver Tambo chaired the meetings; the other members were Thabo Mbeki (ANC), Joe Gqabi (SACP/MK), Moses Mabhida (SACP/Trade Union); Joe Modise (ANC/MK) and Joe Slovo (SACP/MK). Previously the external alliance had placed its main reliance on the armed struggle – based on experience elsewhere (Cuba, Algeria, China and Vietnam), the writings of revolutionaries (like Che Guevara), and its determination to retaliate in kind to the state's violence. Now, however, with little progress in the armed struggle and the example of Soweto before it, the group recommended putting greater emphasis on developing and/or co-operating with internal political movements. It was still assumed that the armed section would provide the cutting edge, but a combined effort would be employed to achieve the overthrow of the white regime. Looking to the future this eventually led to ANC links with the United Democratic Front (UDF), formed in 1983, and the Congress of South African Trade Unions (COSATU) in 1985; but initially Inkatha was sounded out as a possibility (Barrett 1991).

Although mainly a Zulu movement Buthelezi claimed that Inkatha was the inheritor of the ANC's true tradition. Certainly he could boast of large numbers. By August 1978 Inkatha already claimed to have 150,000 paid-up members, with many more waiting to join. Buthelezi said that Inkatha was a grass-roots organization, dedicated to the total liberation of blacks by non-violent means. To achieve that unity was essential, and so it was ready to forge alliances. There were, said Buthelezi, only two alternatives: either the escalation of violence or negotiation. Inkatha was committed to negotiation. Yet he warned Pretoria that violence lay ahead if it did not change its policies. He appealed to Vorster to abandon apartheid and call a national convention (IRR 1978: 28).

In 1979 Tambo invited Buthelezi to London to discuss common concerns. In the event nothing came of it. Inkatha was wedded to policies that were inimical to the ANC: it opposed international sanctions; it favoured a free-enterprise economy; it criticized rent strikes, school boycotts and the burning of official buildings; and, although it opposed apartheid, it worked within an apartheid framework. Added to those policy differences was the problem of Buthelezi's mercurial character. The attempt to co-operate with Inkatha was, therefore, probably doomed from the beginning. Yet Hermann Giliomee saw it as a 'parting of the ways' among African nationalists. It dashed hopes that the government would be challenged by a mass movement that embraced Inkatha's non-violent strategy with the ANC's militant approach. The vision, wrote Giliomee, of 'a united front of the ANC and Inkatha was gone. They were no longer partners in the liberation struggle, but contenders for the support of the black masses' (Giliomee 1982: xviii). The ANC, having abandoned the Inkatha route, sought to work through trade unions, civic associations and black consciousness groups. Soon Buthelezi was being dismissed as a 'betrayer' of the cause (Brewer 1986: 256).

Despite the limitations revealed by Soweto the ANC came to symbolize the new resistance. The scale and range of its activity was circumscribed by its exile, by the government's opposition, and by the relatively small number of activists it succeeded in smuggling back into the country. For most Africans the movement at this stage was more one of symbols and slogans than a physical presence with a clear policy, but it was increasingly recognized as the flagship of African opposition. Its colours were displayed at political rallies and funerals; a 'Free Mandela' campaign was launched; copies of the Freedom Charter were circulated; from exile the leaders declared 1979 as the 'Year of the Spear' and 1980 the 'Year of the Charter'. In its revival the ANC re-emphasized its commitment to support across the races. Mandela even sent a message out of prison specifically supporting the involvement of whites in the struggle.

At the same time the ANC gained a higher international profile. Governments and international organizations, eager to demonstrate their opposition to apartheid following the Soweto rising and the murder of Biko, embraced the liberation movement they knew best. In October 1976 Tambo was invited to address the UN General Assembly – the first black South African to do so. He told its members that the shooting of innocent people at Soweto was not an aberration, but the 'concrete expression of the policy of the apartheid state'. South Africa was a colonial situation in which blacks had yet to be liberated. Vorster's regime, declared Tambo, was backed by international capitalism and could exist only 'because of the economic, military and political support it receives from the West'. He called for additional sanctions, including a mandatory arms ban, and concluded that while imperialism associates 'its own survival on the survival of the white minority regime, the confrontation between the ANC and the forces of imperialism led by the United States, cannot but grow sharper' (ANC Speaks: 198–211). A year later, in October 1977, following Steve Biko's death, the western powers agreed to support a UN mandatory arms ban against South Africa.

In exile the ANC was still not free of internal disputes. The problem of communist members again reared its head in the breakaway of Makiwane and his colleagues, and the formation of 'Okhela', a white group which aimed at countering communist influence. But the ANC's tensions were only irritants compared with the PAC's conflicts. In 1978 a bitter PAC leadership contest followed Sobukwe's death, in which Leballo overcame a challenge from Templeton Ntantala, the APLA leader. Leballo's triumph was, however, short-lived for in May 1979 he was replaced by a triumvirate. Still there was no peace. One of the new leaders, David Sibeko, who had been a Leballo supporter, was assassinated in Dar es Salaam by men from an APLA camp, who were then arrested by the Tanzanian authorities. Although Leballo continued to lead a small faction until his death in 1985 he had little power. That passed first to Vusi Make, and in 1981 to John Pokela. Under Pokela's leadership and that of Johnson Mlambo, who gained the leadership on Pokela's death in 1985, the PAC gradually overcame its internal problems and became an active if relatively small movement.

The Armed Struggles and the Government's Total Strategy

Tambo identified four pillars of the liberation struggle: a united mass movement; the international drive to isolate South Africa; the vanguard activities of the underground movement; and the MK's armed struggle. As with other ANC roles the post-Soweto period saw progress in the armed struggle. That was facilitated not only by developments inside the Republic, but by those in southern Africa following the emergence of black governments in Angola and Mozambique, and later, in 1980, by the transformation of Rhodesia into Zimbabwe.

In the aftermath of Soweto the struggle inside and outside the Republic intensified. Following a visit to Vietnam by MK leaders, Slovo drew up a three-year plan which set the war in a broad political setting. One of Slovo's aims was to make the ANC and MK into household names by means of 'armed propaganda', so that the population could eventually be mobilized for a people's war and a general rising. During 1977 and 1978, therefore, the MK concentrated on opening up communication and supply lines, infiltrating members across the border, forming cells and demonstrating that the movement was alive and active by small-scale attacks. The extension of ANC activities was revealed by government reports and court cases. The evidence was fragmentary but indicated the increasing tempo of the struggle. A selection of examples from 1978 demonstrate this. In February a bomb exploded at the Daveyton police station; in separate incidents several black policemen were assassinated; in April the police reported gun battles in the eastern Transvaal and northern Natal in which two policemen were seriously wounded in an ambush; in August the police and Bophutatswana forces clashed with guerillas; a number of witnesses at ANC trials were killed; and in December the Soweto Community Centre and a section of railway line in the Eastern Province were bombed (IRR 1978: 122–4). And so it continued. In August 1979, for instance, the police reported that over the past year 26 different arms caches had been uncovered – including 61 rifles, 3 machine guns, 14 hand guns, 29 machine pistols, 32 automatic pistols and two rocket grenade launchers; and in that same period attacks had been made on three more police stations – Moroka, Orlando and Booysens (Brewer 1986: 131). The first MK fighter of the new wave to be captured and executed was Solomon Mahlangu, who was given hero status by the ANC and had a training school in Tanzania named after him.

The MK's attacks were carried out in the teeth of strong government countermeasures. Those who were arrested and detained often suffered torture (including beatings, electric shocks, mid-air suspensions, partial suffocation and solitary confinement). Between March 1976 and July 1978 forty-four political prisoners died while in police hands. A series of major trials also took place. For example, in April 1980 nine young MK members, who had left the country at the time of Soweto, were tried for activities they had undertaken between November 1979 and February 1980. They were charged with assaulting the Soekmekaar police station with hand-grenades and rifles; to have planned an attack on oil storage tanks near Pretoria; and to have raided a Volkskas bank at Silverton when two people were killed. The accused were all found guilty of high treason as well as other offences. Three were sentenced to death (Ncimbithi Lubisi, Petrus Mashigo and Naphati Manana) and the rest to terms of imprisonment.

Alongside the specific incidents broader developments were taking place. Soweto and its aftermath had shattered the Verwoerdian apartheid vision. As a result the government steadily abandoned the high moral ground and replaced it by pragmatic policies designed to defend the white state. Faced by diverse problems Vorster spoke of dangers 'too ghastly to contemplate'. The change did not come easily and Vorster clung to some past illusions, but policies were now based more on responses to threats than a master plan. However, Pretoria tried to give coherence to its perception of danger by claiming that it faced 'a total onslaught'. In September 1977 General Magnus Malan, the Chief of Defence Staff, declared that South Africa was involved in 'a total war'. It is, he said, not confined to soldiers, everyone is involved and has a role to play. The aggressors' aim is 'total, not only in terms of ideology, but also as regards the political, social, economic and technological areas'. The enemy, said Malan, would use many techniques (coercive, persuasive and incentive) and attack on many fronts (political, diplomatic, religious, psychological, cultural and sports, as well as military). The enemy's aim was to overthrow the existing constitutional order and replace it by a communist black government (Grundy 1986: 11 and Geldenhuys 1981: 3).

Pretoria claimed that although the onslaught was directed against the whole western world, many western states failed to appreciate the dangers and therefore South Africa had to stand alone. Vorster spoke of moving closer to Israel's position where 50 per cent of the budget was spent on arms. The Republic, so the argument ran, was a special target for Moscow because of its strategic position, its mineral wealth, its strong economy and infrastructure, and because it stood as the barrier to Soviet domination of the whole African continent. As a conventional military attack was too difficult and expensive for the communists to mount they were using indirect tactics, such as economic boycotts and psychological warfare. In these circumstances it was logical to expect that they would promote revolutionary activities among the black population. The vehicles they employed for this were the ANC, PAC and SACP, supported by communist states, the OAU, the UN and western anti-apartheid groups. To counter the onslaught Pretoria committed itself to a 'total national strategy'. The 1977 White Paper on Defence stated that this was a 'comprehensive plan to utilise all the means available to the state . . . A total National Strategy is therefore not confined to a particular sphere, but is applicable at all levels and to all functions of the state structure' (SA Govt 1977: 5).

While in one sense, therefore, the message behind the total onslaught and total strategy was of danger for the whites, in another sense it offered consolation and bolstered their position. The total onslaught provided an explanation for the problems they faced; while the total strategy offered a means of countering the dangers by all working together. Army generals openly stated that the dangers were 80 per cent political and only 20 per cent military. As a result Pretoria tried to rally whites together, by adopting policies which combined direct security measures with reforms designed to remove the causes of conflict and to counter external criticism. There were, therefore, two parallel government streams running – first direct security measures and second reform policies. Which of the two was more prominent rested on circumstances and individual decision makers.

However, security was given priority. In secret, a decision was taken to build atomic weapons. They were intended to act as a deterrent to communist forces attacking the country, based on the assumption that in a crisis the West would come to Pretoria's aid to avoid the outbreak of an atomic war. The policy, initiated in Vorster's time was continued under P. W. Botha. In all six bombs were built (probably with help from Israel). They were designed to be delivered by aircraft, and were of the type and size used by the Americans against Hiroshima in 1945. These weapons, and the capacity to manufacture them, were eventually destroyed after F. W. de Klerk came to power in 1989.

Vorster's Electoral Victories and Reform

Vorster called two elections in the mid-1970s. The first, in April 1974, was timed to demonstrate the strength of support for the government by taking advantage of the UP's internal troubles, and by stressing white unity in the face of external criticism. His calculations were well founded. The NP more than regained the lost ground of 1970, winning 123 seats against the UP's 41, while the 'liberal' Progressive Party increased its representation from 1 to 7 seats. The clear message was that the government was secure within the white political system.

The next election was called in November 1977, after the Soweto rising, Vorster decided on it not from any threat from the opposition in parliament, but to demonstrate, at home and abroad, that the government had strong white support and to ensure discipline in the NP for the reforms he was introducing. Over the previous three years the UP had disintegrated – its leader, Sir de Villiers Graaff, had retired, and its members had split between the 'conservative' New Republican Party (NRP) and the 'liberal' Progressive Federal Party (PFP). On the right flank of white politics the HNP fielded candidates but made no progress. In the election campaign the NP played the loyalty card. Connie Mulder declared that the election was 'a golden opportunity to show the world it must not meddle in South Africa's affairs'. Vorster rightly calculated that security would be the main issue and the electorate would rally behind the government. The NP emerged with 135 seats, and 65.8 per cent of the votes cast. The 'dominant feature of the election', wrote Matthew Midlane, 'was that of white unity within the garrison state' (Midlane 1979: 371–87).

Another feature was that the PFP gained 17 seats from 17 per cent of the vote to become the largest opposition party. Led by Dr F. van Zyl Slabbert, it was the first official opposition in parliament to propose the removal of racial discrimination. Previously liberals, like Helen Suzman, had been lonely figures in the House of Assembly, snapping away at the government; but now the PFP moved into a more positive stance, proposing that a broad-based national convention should be called to hammer out a new constitutional dispensation. Further it laid out the approach it favoured, based a federal constitution, in which all races would participate, leading to power sharing between the ethnic groups, and the protection of minorities. Yet, while the PFP had made progress, and its ideas were a stimulus for the future, it suffered from obvious limitations. In its attempts to cross racial lines, it was not allowed by law to recruit black members, but in any case most black movements refused to co-operate. The party itself, which had been formed from the old Progressives and a few liberal UP members, was an alliance of capitalists, professionals and a liberal intelligentsia, and was predominantly English speaking. It had clear 'right' and 'left' wings, so that divisions arose – sometimes on class lines – over such issues as state aid for the economy, segregated schools and national security. However, above all it had no chance of office. It had improved its position but still stood on the wings of politics, far removed from real power. Its importance was not its immediate impact, but rather that it 'helped to keep alive ideas, institutions and multi racial contacts' that in the long term served 'as a bridge to a less racist and more democratic society' (Lipton 1985: 332).

For the moment, however, Vorster had achieved his aims of closing white ranks against internal and external threats, and demonstrating solidarity in the NP. Secure on its electoral base the government responded to the black challenge by a combination of repression (as noted above) and reform. In Vorster's time the reforms were mainly concerned with changes in the administration of black urban areas, and the removal of aspects of petty apartheid. In urban areas the powers of local councils were increased, an elected element was introduced, 99-year property leases were offered, and Connie Mulder, the Minister responsible, announced a five-year development plan. In terms of petty apartheid Vorster said that he intended to remove 'hurtful discrimination'. A cabinet committee proposed that discriminatory laws should not be maintained if they had fallen into disuse, or no longer removed friction between the races. Senator Horwood, the Finance Minister, told a Brussels audience that the aim was to eliminate discrimination based on colour. Such discrimination, he said, 'is an historical fact but sustained efforts are being made to move away from this situation' (IRR 1978: 362).

However, Voster's main contribution to reform was not in immediate steps, but the investigations he set in train for the future. They included a commission chaired by Professor Nic Wiehahn to look at industrial relations and trades unions; another under Dr P. J. Rieckert to examine the mobility of black labour; a cabinet committee chaired by P. W. Botha to investigate 'possible and desirable adjustments to the existing constitutional order'; and a commission under Professor Erika Theron to examine the position of the Coloureds. Even these tentative steps ran into opposition inside the NP, and there was outrage when Hendrick Schoeman, the Minister of Agriculture, suggested that the Immorality and Mixed Marriages Acts were unnecessary.

Yet Vorster's reforms, whether implemented or envisaged, were firmly contained within an apartheid framework. There was no moving from that. The sense of righteousness associated with Verwoerd may have disappeared, but the commitment to separation was as strong as ever. There are 'no black South Africans', declared Mulder when he announced plans for the urban areas. Township Africans would, he said, gain their political and citizenship rights in the homelands. Commenting on the 99-year leases he explained that the intention was not to cut urban Africans away from their homelands, but rather to make them less wary of acknowledging those ties by assuring them of their rights (IRR 1978: 320). Vorster himself always asserted that the state must be founded on grand apartheid. In November 1976 he stated that the recent troubles had convinced him that 'there is no way to handle race relations but the way of separate development'. Verwoerd's greatest legacy, said Vorster, 'was his vision of separate homelands which could be developed to full independence'. Without that, he said, South Africa would become another Rhodesia (O'Meara 1996: 195).

And so Vorster pushed on with grand apartheid. In 1976 the Transkei was granted 'independence', and Bophutatswana followed in the next year, but international recognition did not follow. Vorster accused the West of practising double standards by accepting independence elsewhere on the continent but not in South Africa. However, despite Vorster's efforts, problems arose with the Bantustans. At Bophutatswana's independence celebrations, Lucas Mangope, the Chief Minister, complained about the fragmentation of the homeland into seven pieces. He spoke of the Tswana's 'well founded bitterness on the question of consolidation', and 'of being granted independence but not sovereignty' (IRR 1977: 322). That was not the end of complaints. In April 1978 the Transkei was so incensed at Pretoria's refusal to transfer Griqualand East to the homeland that it broke off diplomatic relations with Pretoria. In real terms that counted for nothing but it demonstrated the frustration of the Bantustan leaders.

As with détente on the borders, Vorster's efforts at domestic reform ran into difficulties, and not only with the Bantustans. In the black urban areas there was a poor response to elections for the new councils. As a result they lacked legitimacy. Then, in August 1977, when proposals from Botha's constitutional committee were presented to the NP caucus, the 'verkramptes' immediately rejected them as leading 'to a multi racial dispensation whereby a "non white" could be declared President and the white parliament lose its powers' (O'Meara 1996: 199). Despite that Vorster and Botha pushed the proposals through, but the gulf persisted between those who wanted a rigid implementation of apartheid and the more flexible 'verligte' approach. If Vorster had any appetite for further reform – and there must be doubt that he had – it was quickly buried beneath his determination to avoid another party split and his personal weariness. His sense of drive had disappeared – due to policy failure, tiredness and his limitations as a leader. He acted as a man ready to retire. His indecision and his failure to mould the cabinet into an effective unit allowed powerful ministers to pursue almost independent policies. The two strongest were P. W. Botha, the Minister of Defence, and Connie Mulder, Minister of Information. Their scope for personal initiatives was such that in Botha's case the cabinet was only fully briefed on the Angolan invasion five months after it had started; and it knew little of covert operations in Mulder's department until they were exposed by newspapers and independent investigators.

17

Reform, Security and
White Divisions under P. W. Botha

In September 1978 Vorster resigned as NP leader and Premier, to take up the figure-head role of State President. Three candidates contested the NP leadership – Connie Mulder, P. W. Botha, and 'Pik' Botha. Mulder, a conservative, who was close to Vorster and leader of the Transvaal party, had long been considered the 'crown prince'. However, during the campaign news filtered out of a scandal in his Information Department. With Vorster's compliance, Mulder, aided by Dr Eschel Rhoodie (the departmental Secretary), and Van den Bergh (Vorster's security adviser), had launched a covert campaign which cut across the work of other departments, including Foreign Affairs. Expansive, sometimes bizarre schemes were launched, involving misuse of funds. These activities were in part a reflection of internal competition inside the government among factions which were linked to provincial power bases. The Cape Nationalists, led by P. W. Botha, 'had close connections with Cape capital and its press and the army'; while the Transvaalers, led by Connie Mulder, who were more 'verkrampte', were close to the security services, and to Transvaal capitalists (such as Marius Jooste and Louis Leyt) 'with whom Mulder's circle was involved in the business deals out of which the Muldergate scandal arose' (Lipton 1985: 316). Although news of 'Muldergate' started to circulate the voting was close, and P. W. Botha only defeated Mulder in a second ballot by 98 votes to 74. Botha then immediately set up an enquiry which exposed the full extent of the scandal. Its report of corruption, incompetence and internal division rocked white South Africa, undermining the Afrikaners' self-image of puritan righteousness and volk unity. Connie Mulder was forced to resign and was soon followed by an embittered Vorster who stood down as State President.

Botha, the new Prime Minister, had spent his working life in the National Party: first as a party official and from 1953 as an MP. He was appointed to the cabinet in 1961, and in 1966 became leader of the Cape Province and Minister of Defence. He was a tough, determined politician who did not suffer fools or opponents gladly, as epitomized by his nickname 'the great crocodile'. His personality and association with the military did not suggest that he would be a reformer, but reformer he became, and on a much greater scale than Vorster. Yet he never abandoned his tough security approach. He was, wrote Hermann Giliomee 'a man of maddening

B. J. Vorster and P. W. Botha (courtesy of *The Star*)

contradictions. In one sense reformer, but in others as determined as his predecessors to perpetuate policies that militate against a settlement' (Giliomee 1982: ix). Botha's dual approach was reflected in what became the two most influential branches of government – a security wing led by General Magnus Malan; and a constitutional reforming wing led by Chris Heunis, Minister for Constitutional Development. Although they represented different approaches and used different methods the two wings were united in the sense that their principal aim was defence of the white state.

Botha: Reform and Efficiency

Initially circumstances favoured reform. By the time Botha came to office the security forces had regained internal order; the economy was recovering; and on the international front conservative western leaders came to power who were prepared to pursue a policy of 'constructive engagement' rather than sanctions against Pretoria – Margaret Thatcher in Britain, Ronald Reagan in the US, and Helmut Kohl in Germany. Inside the country Botha promised a 'clean, honest administration'. He also promised greater efficiency, by improving the machinery of government and ensuring that it was effectively staffed and managed. In that he was profoundly influenced by his experience in Defence – in the way business was handled, in the appointments he made, and in his attitudes to security and foreign policy. Botha's was the age of the 'securocrats'. They were drawn from across the services, but the army replaced the police as the main source of influence. In terms of personalities that was reflected in the fall of Van den Berg, who resigned as soon as Botha took office, and the rise of Magnus Malan, who became Defence Minister in 1980.

Further, in his search for efficiency, Botha centralized decision making. He refined the cabinet system by creating a cabinet secretariat and replacing numerous 'ad hoc' committees with a number of permanent committees. A centre-piece of the new structure was the State Security Council (SSC) which Botha himself chaired. It included a mixture of senior ministers and members of the forces and security services; it was serviced by a military secretariat; and had a status different from and above other committees. While in formal terms the SSC was subordinate to the cabinet, in security matters, which were widely defined, it was in practice the top decision-making body. It soon extended its tentacles across the whole country with the introduction of the National Security Management Scheme (NSMS) in 1979 (Frankel 1984: Grundy 1986). Another key area of Botha's government was his own office, first as Prime Minister and later as State President. In broader terms Botha tried to energize the civil service, but with limited success. Dr Piet Koornhof, one of Botha's ministers, compared the service to a tortoise, which if left alone plodded on remorselessly, but if pushed stopped and withdrew its head. Botha pushed, the head was withdrawn, and little progress made.

Botha was fully committed to the concepts of the 'total onslaught' and 'total strategy'. From these he developed a dogmatic view of the world in military-strategic terms, in which South Africa was standing against communist aggression while the ANC was 'the next best thing to the devil' (Seegers 1996: 176). Behind the drive for efficiency was the conviction that a total strategy must be developed to counter the total onslaught. 'I will,' said Botha, 'do everything I deem necessary for our survival.' It was in this spirit that he approached reform. He reached his decisions not from ideological doubts about the principles of apartheid but from practical concerns about security and the survival of the white state. In 1979 he bluntly told his followers to 'adapt or die'. In doing so he claimed not to be deviating from the principles of the NP but simply adjusting methods to suit the times. The greatest danger for Afrikaners, he said, was to cling to policies which were no longer effective. The choice was between 'the path of confrontation, bloodshed, nameless suffering, and the downfall of [white] civilisation in the country – or that of consultation and joint decision making with due regard for [racial] self determination' (O'Meara 1996: 256).

Botha was prepared to challenge previous economic assumptions. He even expressed doubts about the viability of Bantustans, stating that they would never 'become economically viable on their own or . . . satisfy the material aspirations of their people within their geographical borders' (Giliomee 1982: 125). Instead of standing alone Botha envisaged the homelands being absorbed into economic development regions embracing white and black areas. Botha's reforms were based on the assumption that with efficiency and economic growth not only would whites continue to support the government, but a substantial number of blacks would come to accept their lot. In his view, if reform were successful it would expose the extreme and subversive elements, by bringing together moderates of all races behind a common cause. To demonstrate his commitment to reform Botha visited Soweto in 1979 – the first Prime Minister to do so – and, at the other end of the economic spectrum, he was the first Nationalist PM to court English-speaking capitalists. He urged them to participate in politics, appointed them to government commissions and met them at large conferences. The first conference was held at the Carlton Hotel in Johannesburg in 1979, when the businessmen, perhaps overawed by the occasion, said little. However, when a second conference was held in November 1981, at Cape Town, they raised issues which they said needed urgent attention. Harry Oppenheimer, Chairman of Anglo-American, referred to a 'sense of disillusionment' over the results of the previous conference. He accused the government of being unwilling or unable to act on the facts of the situation except in the field of industrial relations. He added that unless the government devised an acceptable political dispensation for blacks, their growing industrial power would be used for political purposes with disruptive effects on the economy. He and others also referred to the need for labour mobility, improved African education and housing.

The Twelve-Point Plan and African Development

In August 1979 Botha presented his reform programme as a twelve-point plan. He avoided using the word 'reform' and although he presented his plan as 'a reafirmation of the basic principles of the National Party,' no mention was made of 'Afrikaners' as a distinctive people (HA 29 April 1980). The plan fell into three sections: economic and social changes for Africans; relations in southern Africa; and new constitutional proposals.

Botha recognized that the Verwoerdian assumptions about the flow of Africans back to the homelands and separate racial economic futures had proved false. 'We have learned from experience,' he said, 'that the scope for decentralising of economic activity is limited. To ignore the high degree of economic interdependence throughout South Africa would be foolish' (Cocker 1981: 236). Botha accepted the reality that Africans were a permanent feature of urban life, but he clung to the idea of a multi-national South Africa. For him, as for his predecessors, there was not a single South African identity but separate racial/national/tribal groups – a plurality of peoples and minority groups. His plans therefore offered no political change for Africans. The Bantustan homelands would remain, and it was to them that Africans must look for their identity and political rights. Based on that assumption Botha encouraged more Bantustan leaders to seek independence. He had some success. In September 1979 Venda, and in December 1981 the Ciskei joined the Transkei and Bophuthatswana as 'independent' homelands. However, the going was never easy. The majority of people in the Ciskei opposed the change of status; there was still no international recognition; accusations of corruption and nepotism continued, and some homeland leaders refused to follow the government's line.

Although Pretoria insisted that all Africans must look to the homelands for their identity, that still left open questions about urban Africans. The government calculated that about half the African population lived in the homelands, 20 per cent in white rural areas, and another 20 per cent in townships that were predominantly inhabited by members of the same tribe and linked to a particular homeland. On that calculation only 10 per cent of Africans were left in mixed tribal townships like Soweto. For a time Pretoria played with the idea of giving these large, mixed towns the status of city-states (the equivalent of urban homelands) to fit into the patchwork of separate political units. However, that remained speculation. Instead Botha supported increased local autonomy based on urban councils. In 1981 he said, 'they will be allowed to a certain extent to control their own law and order and their own health services', and some towns would be given full municiple status (Botha 1983: 17). Despite that there proved to be little support in the townships. When council elections were held in 1983 only 16 per cent of the electorate voted.

The main thrust of Botha's policy for urban Africans was to try to build a stable, reasonably prosperous middle class with a stake in the existing structure through their employment and ownership of property. Alongside increased powers for the councils an attempt was made to enhance the quality of life – by improved housing, education and employment. These were linked to the commissions which were set up in Vorster's time but reported under Botha. Two of them – Wiehahn and Riekert – were concerned with African labour. Wiehan's proposals led to the 1981 Labour Relations Act which attempted to provide both greater job security and control of an increasingly skilled African work force. Statutory job reservation was abolished in manufacturing industry and improvements made in training facilities. In an attempt to regulate and depoliticize the work place, African trade unions were legalized. At the same time the state took less direct responsibility for labour relations and put more trust in private companies to settle issues. Although some black union leaders interpreted the proposals as part of a plot between the government and capitalism, the reforms brought unions into the open as important political players. For its part the Riekert Manpower Commission reached similar conclusions to those of the Fagan Commission back in 1948; namely that Africans were a permanent, not temporary element of urban life. Its proposals included the need to relax the pass laws and ease influx controls. In practice it divided the African population between urban 'insiders' and rural 'outsiders' (O'Meara 1996: 273).

In October 1981 the report of the de Lange commission on education was tabled. Some of its recommendations challenged previous government policy by rejecting race as the determining factor in the allocation of resources. It spoke of equality of educational opportunity, and suggested a single Ministry of Education for all. While Pretoria accepted some of de Lange's recommendations it rejected a single ministry. Instead education was identified as an 'own affair' for the different racial groups, with separate schools and departments. The commitment to Christian National Education was reaffirmed. Finally the Theron Commission, in examining the position of Coloureds, set the tone for later constitutional change. Previously Pretoria had spent its energies trying to widen the gap between whites and Coloureds; now Theron advised that although the Coloureds 'were an identifiable group, they should not be considered as a distinct nation and the lines of their parallel development with whites should be gradually narrowed' (Austin 1985: 11).

*   *   *

Signs of a reaction against Botha's reforms among Afrikaners were revealed when an election was called in 1981. The opposition was especially strong among those whose economic interests were infringed, and/or were committed to rigid apartheid. Within the NP itself there was a strengthening of the right wing, particularly in the Transvaal, where Treurnicht was the leader. At the same time the HNP increased its national vote from 3.3 per cent in 1977 to 14.1 per cent in 1981, and Connie Mulder's short-lived National Conservative Party (NCP) received 2.5 per cent of the vote. The swing to 'the right' was especially discernible in traditionally safe NP seats. In straight contests between the NP and HNP the latter's share of the vote rose from 8 per cent in 1977 to 29 per cent in 1981. There was no danger of the government losing its parliamentary majority – indeed it retained 131 of the 165 elected seats – but it lost votes: 191,249 votes were cast for the HNP in 1981, compared with only 36,161 in 1977. Piet Cillier, a newspaper editor and Botha supporter, commented: 'This is a party [HNP] that has no press support at all, and no real organisation', and yet it has made inroads into the NP's traditional electorate. The situation 'is not yet catastrophic, but it is very ominous' (*Financial Times*, 1 May 1981). However, despite their level of support, neither the HNP nor the NCP succeeded in winning any seats.

At the same election the NP also lost ground to the liberal PFP, which increased its seats from 17 to 26, taking votes both from the NP and the small New Republican Party (NRP). The PFP's gains were not only ascribed to English speakers' concern about the economy and reaction to the divisions in the NP's ranks, but, liberal dissatisfaction about the slow pace of reform.

The Southern African Region

Pretoria's regional policy was another example of parallel policies, combining reform with security. At first the carrot of reform was offered, but that soon gave way to the stick of security. Initially (and despite the military intervention in Angola) Botha said that his aim was to form 'a peaceful constellation of southern African states, with respect for each other's cultures, traditions and ideals'. Although it had aims similar to Vorster's détente, the constellation idea had distinctive qualities, in that it assumed that a bloc of 'moderate' states could be built around South Africa, including 'the nation states inside South Africa's borders' (as Botha described the Bantustans). He further assumed that 'acceptable' settlements could be achieved in South West Africa/Namibia and in Rhodesia. He spoke optimistically of common economic interests, and of political co-operation against communism. He told businessmen of the 'unavoidable linking of our destinies' with the region; of South Africa's 'traditional sphere of influence'; and the need to raise the economic performance of black states through co-operation with South Africa. He explained that the constellation did not denote a formal organization, but 'rather a grouping of states with common interests and developing mutual relationships' (SA Govt 1980).

The early optimism soon gave way to consternation. In 1979, instead of responding to Botha's constellation initiative, the black neighbours formed themselves into the Southern Africa Development Coordination Conference (SADCC), with the stated objectives of greater self-reliance, reduction of dependence on South Africa, and of gaining international support for economic liberation. It was an agenda designed to keep South Africa at a distance. From Pretoria's viewpoint worse followed, when the hard-line Robert Mugabe and his ZANU party won the 1980 election which transformed Rhodesia into Zimbabwe. Mugabe defeated not only Muzorewa (the favoured Pretoria candidate) but the ANC's old ally Joshua Nkomo and his ZAPU party. It was the worst of results for Pretoria, and crippled the constellation initiative. An emasculated version limped on for a couple years, but it consisted only of South Africa and the 'independent' Bantustans. The failure demonstrated again that African states would not support a Pretoria-inspired organization, and that was further confirmed when the black states which had previously committed themselves as 'Frontline States' against Rhodesia, now identified South Africa as their new frontline.

The Southern African Battlefield

In Pretoria the vision of a South African led regional bloc was replaced by that of a battleground in which the white state was fighting for its very existence. From Angola the South West Africa Peoples' Organisation (SWAPO) launched raids into South West Africa. On the other side of the continent MK established bases and its headquarters in Mozambique, where it was on good terms with Samora Machel's government. The high point of that relationship came in 1982 when the Mozambique Government stated that South Africa was in an undeclared war and named the ANC as the main liberation movement. However, the ANC's relations with its host governments was not always straightforward. In Zimbabwe it was distinctly uneasy. In the struggle for Zimbabwe's independence the ANC had associated itself with Nkomo's ZAPU, and at one stage had dismissed Mugabe's ZANU as a 'splinter group' and 'tool of the imperialists' (Thomas 1996: 146). Mugabe, although a bitter opponent of South Africa, was not a man to forgive easily.

From Mozambique MK infiltrated guerillas into South Africa. In the early 1980s it intensified its efforts with attacks on high-profile targets. These included the coal to oil Sasol plant in June 1980; the main Soweto-Johannesburg railway line in October 1980; power stations in the Eastern Transvaal in July 1981; and a military base outside Pretoria in August 1981. Between December 1981 and November 1982 there were at least 26 sabotage incidents, with police posts, power stations, railways and government buildings as the main targets. Even so, claimed Tom Lodge, the ANC realized that it did not have the resources to undermine the economy or challenge the security forces in direct conflict, and so its intention was 'armed propaganda' – 'to inspire confidence among the dominated population rather than terror in the white community' (IRR 1982: 230). However, the ANC was not above exercising its own form of terror. Africans who were deemed to be informers or traitors were singled out, sometimes by petrol bomb attacks on their homes, sometimes by assassination. In August 1981 Tambo announced a change of tactics when he stated that apartheid officials would be attacked and there could arise 'combat situations in which civilians might be killed' (Brewer 1986: 135). A few days later a bomb went off in Port Elizabeth killing civilians. The pattern continued. In May 1983 a bomb placed near the Air Force Headquarters in Pretoria killed 19 and injured 217 people, including blacks as well as whites.

The government's response was strong. The space created by the collapse of the constellation initiative was filled by those who favoured the big stick. Already in presenting the twelve-point plan Botha had underlined the Republic's willingness to use its strength. 'We are better able to defend South Africa militarily than ever before in the country's history,' he declared. 'And I want to warn those who think that we practise our politics from a position of weakness: we are not speaking from a position of weakness . . . If they want to test us, our strength, we will hit back' (Geldenhuys 1981: 62). That was precisely what happened. Pretoria set out to assert its dominance. In his New Year message for 1983 Botha said he was not prepared to allow neighbours to act as springboards for attacks on South Africa. There would be a rude awakening for anyone who underestimated the national will to defend itself.

A combination of methods was used to demonstrate Pretoria's strength: including direct military action, the use of proxy forces, and economic pressures – such as holding up supplies for those land-locked states that relied on SA railways. The military action ranged from major campaigns to commando raids. The campaigns were mainly in Angola, where seven full-scale operations were undertaken between 1978 and 1984; while commando raids were employed against all the neighbours (Seegers 1996: 226). A couple of examples must serve for all. On 10 December 1982 an attack was made on twelve houses in Lesotho where ANC members were alleged to be living. Forty-two people were killed of whom eight were Lesotho citizens. General Constand Viljoen, Chief of Defence Staff, described it as 'a pre-emptive strike aimed at forestalling attacks on SA during the festive season' (IRR 1982: 195). In May 1993, following the MK bomb incident in Pretoria, South African forces attacked Maputo, both from the air and on the ground. Pretoria claimed that 64 'terrorists' were killed, and added that such actions were 'a warning that terrorists and their organisations in neighbouring states . . . would be sought out and destroyed'. The Mozambique authorities disputed the reports, claiming that six civilians had been killed (IRR 1983: 595). The chief example of the use of proxy forces was also in Mozambique, where the SADF took over from the Rhodesians, the Mozambique National Resistance Movement (MNRM) – also known as Renamo – which waged a terror campaign inside the country and fought the Mozambique government forces.

Pretoria's regional policy, which became known as 'destabilization', was designed to demonstrate its own strength, to punish and weaken neighbouring states that aided the liberation movements, and to drive the guerilla forces away from the borders. The aim was to keep potential enemies so weak that they could not threaten the Republic or afford to support the guerilla fighters. Delegates of the Frontline states meeting in March 1982 accused South Africa of 'waging a non-declared war against the free and independent states of the region'. They agreed to reinforce their mutual co-operation and called on the western powers to give them support (IRR 1982: 193). Botha, who described these neighbours as 'politically immature', accused them of trying to undermine South Africa by supporting terrorist organizations, and instead offered them non-aggression treaties prohibiting the use of either country for attacks (IRR 1983: 585).

To an extent destabilization succeeded. Although the black neighbours constantly complained about Pretoria's aggressive policy, they could not break their reliance on her and several concluded that while they would not turn away refugees they would not allow the liberation armies to operate from their territories. In 1982 Swaziland secretly signed a non-aggression treaty with Pretoria. Two years later came the policy's greatest success when Mozambique was pressured into signing the Nkomati Accord. Under the Accord the two governments undertook to respect each other's independence, not to interfere in each other's internal affairs, nor to let their territories be used by groups planning 'to commit acts of violence, terrorism or aggression' – an undertaking Pretoria failed to honour. The Mozambique authorities followed up by raiding ANC and MK houses and camps, temporarily detaining some members, seizing arms and forcing several hundred MK cadre to leave the country. The ANC's reaction was bitter. Privately Tambo described Mozambique as little better than a Bantustan. In public he said the Accord was a sign of Pretoria's panicky but fruitless efforts to isolate the ANC and compel neighbours to act as its agents.

While Nkomati was the policy's greatest success, other neighbours, even when they had not signed agreements, were cautious about housing MK camps. As a result the MK's offensive capacity was restricted and morale problems arose in the camps. Frustration at lack of action, poor conditions and harsh discipline led to mutiny in Angola late in 1983. In an attempt to counter the frustration the MK High Command had decided to employ troops in support of the Angolan government against its internal rival, Unita. In the fighting that ensued the MK acquitted themselves well, but they were disillusioned by the lack of fighting spirit among the Angolan troops and the unpopularity of the government among local people. Asking themselves why they should risk their lives for an unpopular government whose own troops were reluctant to fight, a body of MK troops marched to a camp near Luanda. There they demanded better conditions, an investigation into camp discipline, and a policy review to focus the struggle directly against South Africa. The mutiny – known as 'Mkatashingo' – was resolved by Chris Hani, a respected MK leader, who personally met the mutineers and persuaded them to lay down their arms. A second mutiny in May was put down by force (Ellis and Sehaba 1992: 136).

The New Constitution

Inside the country Botha's greatest challenge was the introduction of a new constitution. It was done step by step. It started in 1977 when Vorster had set up a cabinet committee under Botha's chairmanship. Botha himself was Premier when its recommendations came before parliament in 1979. The next step was to take the matter further by setting up another committee, chaired by Alwyn Schlebusch, the Minister of the Interior. The Schlebusch committee proposed that the Senate (the existing second chamber) should be abolished and replaced by a President's Council, of 60 members drawn from the white, Coloured and Indian communities, but with a white majority. Although the Coloureds and Indians were in a minority in the Council their presence drove a horse and coaches through previous apartheid principles by sharing decision making across the races. The Council's two main tasks were first to comment on legislation, and second to draw up new constitutional proposals. Under the first heading the Council recommended, among other things, the repeal of the Immorality and Mixed Marriages Acts. That shocked the 'verkramptes', but they were even more distressed by the constitutional proposals which followed.

The drafting of proposals was undertaken by a committee of the Council led by Dennis Worrall, a prominent English-speaking member of the NP. Among its recommendations Worrall's committee proposed centralizing power under an executive State President. That caused dispute, but even more controversial was the recommendation to bring Coloureds and Indians into the structure of central government. The committee dressed its proposals in the clothes of 'consociational democracy' – an approach founded on the old assumption that South Africa was composed of separate, distinctive groups. Each group would be allowed to manage its 'own affairs', whereas decisions on 'common affairs' would be reached by consensus. However, the report contained one major and decisive exception. It asserted that 'a single political system in South Africa which includes blacks [Africans] on an unqualified majoritarian or consociational basis could not function as a successful democracy in current or foreseeable circumstances' (SA Govt 1982). Africans were, therefore, excluded and the principle of separate homelands was retained.

In giving a structure to its proposals the committee recommended that the Westminster model should be abandoned in favour of a three-chamber parliament, an Executive State President, a cabinet selected by the President, and a President's Council. The three chambers of parliament would be racially based – one each for whites, Coloureds and Indians. Each chamber was to be responsible for 'own affairs' (i.e. matters, such as education, which were limited to the community it represented). For 'common affairs' all three were to be consulted and joint standing committees were to play a linking role. The State President, elected for five years, was to combine the existing offices of non Executive President and Prime Minister, and would be given extensive powers including choosing and chairing the cabinet. Although he had to consult the cabinet he did not necessarily have to follow its directions. These recommendations formed the basis of the new constitution which was enacted in 1983.

When he introduced the new constitution to parliament Heunis said that it marked a major step forward. The government, he declared, was not prepared to 'walk the path of Africa', nor would it apologize for presenting a constitution which would maintain the security of whites. It was, he stated, a 'unity in diversity' model, which recognized the country's 'multinational heritage'. He spoke of the spirit of the constitution bringing people together in a working partnership by changing the political style from the polarization of the Westminster model to reconciliation. Participants would, he said, 'refrain from continually opposing and reviling one another for the sake of petty, sectional political gain'. He went on to explain the absence of Africans by claiming that their 'constitutional development has gained momentum towards different and separate structures for black nations'. In contrast government ministers continually emphasized the safeguards for whites. There was no intention, stated Botha, of abandoning separation or differentiation. 'No one,' he said, 'is being asked to accept integration. The way of life for whites depended ultimately not on laws, but on their will to be themselves' (IRR 1983: 11).

The constitution immediately ran into opposition. Liberal critics argued that it was an attempt to co-opt the Coloureds and Indians to support a state in which they would participate but whites would retain the power. It was, wrote Dennis Austin, 'apartheid tempered by necessity' (Austin 1985: 22). Liberals also criticized the concentration of power in the hands of the State President. However, the main opposition came from right-wing whites, and black political groups.

The Emergence of the Conservative Party

Despite the NP's traditional deference to the leader, Botha could never rely on the party's whole-hearted support. There were a number of reasons for this. He inherited a party which was already divided between 'verkrampte' and 'verligte' wings and had been badly shaken by the 'Muldergate' scandal; but overriding all that was dispute about the government's ultimate aims. The Verwoerdian certainties had gone and with them the confident assertions of building nations and states on agreed principles. In their place was talk of reform and a journey to an unknown destination. Faction flourished. Botha himself, despite his hard-line on security, became identified with the reformers. They were constantly challenged by a group clustered around Treurnicht, who were committed to strict apartheid. 'If petty apartheid is completely eliminated,' said Treurnicht, 'big apartheid becomes stupid, superfluous and unnecessary . . . You can't make apartheid big, if you kill it little by little' (*Sunday Express*, Johannesburg, 24 April 1977).

Although Treurnicht was NP leader in the Transvaal (the largest province with the most MPs) Botha at first kept him out of the cabinet and then gave him the junior post of Minister of State Administration. Yet, despite these efforts to undermine him, Treurnicht appeared to benefit from the 1981 election. His warnings that the party would lose electoral support if it deviated from the narrow path of apartheid seemed to be confirmed by the support for the HNP among Afrikaners. Following the election there was speculation that Treurnicht's position would be enhanced and Botha would slow down or even abandon his reforms. That did not happen. Botha went ahead and split the NP apart. The rift came even before the introduction of the new constitution, over the concept of 'power sharing'. 'For us,' said Botha, 'the concept of consultation and co-responsibility is a healthy form of power sharing without undermining the principle of self determination' (Davenport 1987: 452). He went on to announce that all the members of cabinet (which included Treurnicht) had accepted power sharing when they agreed to the 1977 proposals. Treurnicht dismissed that as 'blatant and infamous lies'. He told a packed meeting of his rapturous supporters 'that power sharing is a sickness' (*Rand Daily Mail*, 6 February 1982). The dispute reached a crisis in March 1982 at a caucus meeting of National Party MPs. Botha's followers called for a vote of confidence in the Prime Minister. Treurnicht and his supporters refused to give such unqualified support and when the vote went against them they walked out. Treurnicht still hoped to hold onto his power base in the Transvaal, but Botha undermined him there by attending a meeting of the provincial congress unannounced and winning a decisive vote.

There was no going back after that. Treurnicht was expelled as Transvaal leader to be replaced by F. W. de Klerk. Treurnicht then led sixteen like-minded MPs out of the NP to form the Conservative Party (CP). The split was bitter and deep. At its heart was a difference of principle between Botha's belief that white control could only be preserved by accepting change, and Treurnicht's conviction that reform would lead to the collapse of the whole structure with fatal consequences for whites. The essential difference was not about the basic goal of defending the white-controlled state, but about the best way of doing it. 'The CP wanted the state to be openly biased in favour of Afrikaners and whites as a whole; the NP by contrast considered Afrikaner survival to be best secured by making the state more neutral and drawing "responsible" blacks into the state bureaucracy and political system' (Giliomee 1992: 355).

Treurnicht vehemently denounced the new constitution. It was, he said, 'treason against nationalism' and especially Afrikaner nationalism. He insisted that Africans, Coloureds and Indians should move along separate roads; and that whites were not prepared to relinquish exclusive power. If one shared power, he stated, one lost it. If, as the government said, Coloureds and Indians had rights to a direct voice because they lived in the same state as whites, how could the same rights be denied to urban Africans? If the constitution required tolerance, why not tolerate them? In fact, argued Treurnicht, it was not tolerance that the whites were being asked to exercise but the abandonment of their state and their nation. Afrikaners (and Treurnicht often equated 'Afrikaners' and 'whites') were being told that they 'must now be ashamed of being white . . . that to be white is an injustice to non-whites'. The constitution introduced integration, by which 'different ethnic and racial groups with conflicting ideals . . . are being amalgamated in one parliament'. Ahead he saw only disaster because people were being brought into government 'who have already said that racial classification, separate group areas, separate residential areas and separate representation must be abolished' (HA 16 May 1983).

Although the new constitution became the main battle ground other factors compounded NP/CP divisions. One was provincial differences. The CP drew its main support in the Transvaal. As the Coloureds were mainly in the Cape and the Indians in Natal, they seemed peripheral to many Transvaalers. Now, however, the walls of apartheid were being breached by allowing them into parliament, opening up the even greater danger of Africans following them in future. A further dimension to the dispute was the continued hardening of class divisions among Afrikaners. The insistence on unity had become muted as Afrikaners continued to enjoy the economic and social fruits of their political dominance, and their increased role in commerce and finance. The CP concentrated on attracting support from the traditional professions, the lower middle class and government employees. It claimed that if the NP had support from the top 10 per cent of civil servants it had the rest. In crude terms, therefore, Afrikaner political allegiances could be seen in terms of three social layers – with the NP at the top, CP in the middle and HNP at the bottom. Added to class differences were personal antagonisms. Several of the NP old guard resented Botha's behaviour. They included John Vorster and Connie Mulder, who believed they had been victimized in the Muldergate scandal; Jimmy Kruger, who had accepted the Presidency of the Senate without knowing that Botha intended to dissolve it; Louwrens Muller who accused Botha of blocking his appointment as State President; and the Verwoerd family who saw Botha as the betrayer of apartheid.

For those outside the white society it was difficult to appreciate the depth of feeling and the bitterness that was aroused. From the outside it was possible to argue that nothing fundamental was changed by the new constitution. To use a card game analogy: the cards may have been reshuffled and new players allowed at the table, but the aim of the game – the retention of white rule – had not. But that was not how it was seen by many whites and the CP in particular. For them the future of the Afrikaners/ whites was at stake. Professor Carel Boshoff, Verwoerd's son-in-law and a former Broederbond chairman, resigned from the NP saying: 'We have come to the parting of the ways, between those who want to follow the path of mixed government, and those who want a separate self determination for all South Africa's people' (*The Guardian*, 1 November 1983).

The Constitutional Referendum

With its large parliamentary majority the government could simply have pushed the new constitution through. But Botha decided on a referendum to settle internal party concerns, and to demonstrate that the government was acting with the support of the white electorate. In contrast Pretoria decided not to have referenda for Coloureds and Indians, because it feared violence during the campaigns, and only a derisory turn out of voters. But in public the government said that Coloureds and Indians would be able to show their support when elections were held.

The government decided on a long referendum campaign – stretching from the announcement on 24 August to voting on 2 November 1983 – because it feared that the complexity and novelty of the new constitution, plus the ambiguity of the concept of 'power sharing', would be difficult to sell. Within the confines of the campaign itself the government – backed by its information machine, and drawing considerable English-speaking support – scored a notable victory. In reply to the question: 'Are you in favour of the implementation of the constitution approved by parliament?', 66 per cent of the white electorate voted 'yes'. However, the long campaign created problems for Pretoria. As it dragged on it served to underline the diversity and confusion in white political thinking; the depths of division in Afrikanerdom; and, most important it stimulated strong African opposition to the government's plans. The campaign acted as a catalyst activating the tensions in the society.

Among whites the apparently straightforward 'Yes' or 'No' response to the referendum question masked a variety of attitudes. Those who voted 'Yes' extended from people who saw the new constitution as a final act of appeasement to non-whites, to those who hoped it would be a toe in the door of reform which would then be opened wider and wider. Others gave their support from loyalty to the government. The 'No' vote was made up of a strange combination of the most conservative and the most liberal whites. The CP, led by Treurnicht (popularly known as 'Dr No'), declared that the constitution would destroy the structure of society, threaten Christian standards by allowing Hindus and Muslims into a mixed government, and put the country on the slippery slope to majority rule. Alongside them voting 'No' was the PFP. Dr F. van Zyl Slabbert, its leader, argued that far from bringing the races together the constitution would increase racial tension by excluding Africans and place the Coloureds and Indians in a permanently subordinate position. He also asserted that instead of sharing power the constitution would concentrate it firmly in the hands of the white ruling party. The NP would not only control the white chamber, but choose the President, who would then exercise his powers of patronage to the party's advantage. Political control by one party, said Slabbert, 'has deliberately been compounded, nourished, and entrenched'. Instead of sharing power the constitution moved towards white dictatorial rule (HA 16 May 1983).

With the referendum success behind it the government organized elections in August 1984 for Coloureds and Indians for their respective parliamentary chambers – House of Representatives (Coloureds) and House of Delegates (Indians). Both communities faced dilemmas in responding to the situation. Since 1948 the Coloureds had been harshly treated – with forced removals, discrimination, disenfranchisement and the humiliation of racial classification. In their political response to that situation most Coloureds had given their support to the Labour Party, which was led by Sonny Leon, Rev Allan Hendrickse and David Curry; but small radical groups of Marxists and Trotskyites had also been formed. The Labour Party had dominated the Coloured Council, set up by Vorster in 1968, but its powers were limited, its history undistinguished, and its appeal in decline. While in 1969, 38 per cent of the electorate voted for it, by 1975 that support fell to 28 per cent. Then, in 1980, when the Labour Party had challenged government policy, the council was suspended. Soon, however, Labour faced the question of whether or not to participate in Botha's tricameral parliament, and to gain the rewards of improved social facilities and services – such as housing and education – if they did. In crude terms they were being offered sectional advantage for backing the government. After an agonizing and divisive internal debate the majority of Labour decided to do so.

The Indian community faced similar dilemmas. They were fewer in numbers than the Coloureds, they had usually been treated as aliens, and in Natal they were subject not only to government discrimination, but pressure from Africans. For Indians, who often saw themselves as scapegoats, the Durban riots of 1949 remained a vivid memory. Again there was internal division about participation in the new parliament. However, the Indian Council, which was dominated by the National Peoples Party (led by Armichand Rajbansi), eventually decided to 'give it a try'. Far from settling matters, the decision only exacerbated fears when Inkatha issued a statement denouncing it as 'a treacherous betrayal of black liberation' (Lipton 1985: 335). The uncertainties and divisions in both the Indian and Coloured communities were reflected in the low turn out at the polls – 30 per cent for the Coloured and 20 per cent for the Indians. This is partly explained by the rise of the UDF (see below), but probably more by a combination of apprehension and uncertainty.

Following the elections the new – three chamber – parliament was established and P. W. Botha was unanimously elected as South Africa's first executive State President.

When Botha addressed the new parliament he claimed that all reasonable South Africans would enjoy peace, safety and development, for the new constitution reflected 'the acceptance that one part of our population cannot on its own pursue our goals and cannot on its own protect our common fatherland against threats'. The government, he continued, was committed to co-operation which could only be achieved 'if the diversity of our society is recognised', avoiding the dominance of one population group over another. To that end the government had been engaged 'in a programme of reform in every sphere of life'. In the final instance, he stated, 'the security of our country depends on the willingness of all our people, despite the considerable diversity, to accept that we have common interests and goals'. The aim was to give 'all people a say in decision making that affects their interests'.

Despite the call for unity, Botha reiterated that it was neither desirable nor practical to accommodate all communities in the same way. He was, of course, referring to Africans. He claimed that structures would be created for them which were neither inferior nor less effective than those for other groups. Independence, he said, remained the goal for 'self-governing national states', but they would not be forced into it. There would be increasing co-operation between Pretoria and the self-governing states within collective structures. He went on to say that the government accepted the permanence of Africans inside [white] South Africa – describing them as 'communities who find themselves outside the national states'. It had decided to treat them as 'entities in their own right'. Arrangements would be made for them to decide their own affairs, and the question of citizenship was being examined. He stressed the need to improve their daily lives, through housing, orderly urbanization and the modification of influx control. He finished by calling for mutual trust, but warned that those who sought to attack the peace and prosperity of the country by unconstitutional means would be confronted by everything at the government's disposal (SA Govt 1985).

The United Democratic Front (UDF) and the National Forum (NF)

Botha's warning to those who sought to challenge the government by unconstitutional means was a recognition by him of an unforeseen consequence of the new constitution. For all the tumult and shouting among whites its greatest long-term result was the revival of black political activity. Central to this was the establishment in 1983 of two umbrella movements – the United Democratic Front (UDF) and the National Forum (NF). They set out to challenge the constitution and to co-ordinate the activities of the protest groups that had emerged since Soweto. While they both opposed Pretoria they were rivals. The NF was an Africanist movement composed of groups orientated to black consciousness and the PAC, of which the Azanian People's Organization (Azapo) was the most prominent. Azapo criticized the UDF – which was linked to the ANC, and brought together Coloured, Indian, African and even white groups – as a 'conglomerate of ethnically orientated groups; [whereas] the oppressed should be rallied together in a single organization which is not structured on ethnic lines' (*SA Review* 1984: 10).

Despite Azapo's criticism, the UDF turned out to be much the larger and more effective body. It was formed following a call for a united front against the tricameral parliament from Allan Boesak, a dynamic Coloured clergyman from the Cape. 'There is,' said Boesak, 'no reason why the churches, civic associations, trade unions, student organisations and sports bodies should not pool our resources, inform the people of the fraud that is being perpetuated in their name and on the day of the election, expose the plans for what they are' (*SA Review* 1984: 9). The formal launch of the UDF came at a mass rally of about 12,000 people representing more than 500 organizations. Archie Gumede, an ANC veteran, was elected President, with a committee which included other ANC supporters – Terror Lekota as Secretary, Popo Malefe from Soweto, Oscar Mpetha from the trade unions, and Albertina Sisulu, whose husband Walter was a prisoner on Robben Island. With the declared aim of uniting the opponents of apartheid, irrespective of race, the UDF opposed the forthcoming elections, condemned British and US imperialism, declared solidarity with the workers, attacked the migratory labour system, and adopted the Freedom Charter.

Yet, for all its grand ambitions the UDF had an uneven and shaky start. It suffered from the characteristic problems of opposition groups – of organization, communication, finance, provincial differences and overstretch. In terms of provinces it had more impact in its early days in the Cape than in the Transvaal. As an example of over-reaching itself, its 'Million Signature Campaign', launched in January 1984, may have helped in taking the message to the people, but the campaign petered out when 130,000 signatures had been collected. Added to these was early uncertainty of its focus. It took time for the UDF to come to terms with its own diversity. For the Coloureds and Indians the main priority was to undermine the elections for the new constitution. That was less relevant for Africans. For them the constitution simply pointed up their exclusion; while their immediate concerns often focused on local issues such as education and schooling. In terms of Africans Popo Molefe said the UDF came 'trailing behind the masses' (Seekings 1991: 113). And always there was unrelenting opposition from the government in the form of arrests, bans and detentions.

Despite the difficulties and organizational problems the UDF became a major political force. Although it passed resolutions it was not a decision-making body laying down policy. The emphasis was to bring groups and people together. At its meetings each organization had a say, irrespective of size. That was unwieldy and led to unpredictable behaviour, but there were compensations. One was that of sheer size. It was estimated that over two million people were members of the groups which composed the UDF, and their diversity meant that they operated at all levels – from the parish pump to high constitutional affairs. It was here, there and everywhere so that Pretoria had great difficulty in tying it down. Symbolically it was prominent – for example at political funerals. In May 1984 an estimated 6,000 supporters – many wearing ANC colours – attended a funeral of an MK fighter who had been killed by the police. At the ceremony a message was read out from 'Uncle Oliver' in Lusaka. Yet the UDF had to be cautious in its public attitude to violence. Its message was that it did not advocate it, but as violence was instigated by Pretoria, it was not surprising that opponents responded in kind.

Overall the UDF's achievements were to organize opposition to the tricameral parliament; to mobilize and co-ordinate a variety of groups and races; and to ensure that the ANC – under the banner of the Freedom Charter – gained prominence among the internal resistance movements.

Inkatha

Within the context of black politics the UDF's main rival was not the NF but Inkatha. The rivalry was built upon policy differences, competition for support, and the relationship with the ANC – to which must be added an element of personal animosity. Buthelezi described the UDF as 'Johnny come lately', and accused it of concentrating its attacks upon Inkatha instead of the government. In 1984 he said that the UDF had been established by the ANC to destroy Inkatha, and accused the ANC of 'Inkatha bashing' abroad. From the UDF side Archie Gumede stated that Inkatha viewed the liberation struggle as its sole preserve and treated others as interlopers; while Motlana described Buthelezi as 'a traitor'. Almost inevitably the verbal abuse led to physical violence; although initially it consisted of isolated incidents. In October 1983, for example, a UDF meeting at Hammersdale was disrupted by Inkatha members who burnt a bus and damaged cars. In May 1984 Archie Gumede was knocked unconscious, allegedly by Inkatha supporters; and in September of that year UDF members were accused of shooting at Mrs Abbie Mchunu, an Inkatha leader (IRR 1984: 15).

Like all parties Inkatha shaped its message according to its audience. That resulted in a persistent dichotomy. Among Zulus, who were always its main followers, it appealed to their national pride as Zulus, and asserted Zulu distinctiveness. That had great appeal in rural areas and traditional circles, especially in KwaZulu itself where Inkatha formed the government and disposed of considerable patronage. However, Inkatha claimed to be much more than a Zulu party. It presented itself as a national organization, appealing to all Africans and indeed all races. It stated that it was eager to recruit those 'who work for the eradication of all forms of colonialism, injustice and discrimination, and to strive for the attainment of African unity' (Brewer 1986: 356). In July 1979 it replaced most references to 'Zulus' in its constitution with 'Africans'. By the end of 1983 Inkatha claimed to have grown remarkably – to 750,000 members – and to have 2,000 branches.

Despite its commitment and its size Inkatha always ran into difficulties with more militant groups. Among other things there was suspicion about the diversity of its contacts. It had an association with the government through KwaZulu; Buthelezi developed links with conservative leaders abroad; and in November 1978 he had met members of the Broederbond, at which he said: 'Your people [Afrikaners] and my people [Zulus] are South Africans . . . We will fail in our leadership if we cannot bring them together' (Brewer 1986: 372). However, the contacts did not always go smoothly. In January 1984 Buthelezi refused an invitation from Botha because their previous meeting in 1980 had ended in angry exchanges. However, a meeting was eventually arranged in December at Stellenbosch, which was described as an open discussion covering a wide range of issues. Such diverse contacts might seem admirable in an open liberal society but in the deeply divided Republic it was seen as treachery by African radicals. They openly displayed their antagonism to Buthelezi at the funeral of Robert Sobukwe in March 1978. Buthelezi had been invited to address the gathering, but before he could do so militant youths demanded that he (plus white and Coloured 'collaborators') should leave. As Buthelezi withdrew he was jostled and stoned. A bodyguard fired blank rounds to save him from the crowd. Afterwards Buthelezi condemned the 'political thuggery', and claimed the black consciousness movement 'had decided to stage an attack on him and was creating black disunity by attacking Inkatha' (IRR 1978: 33).

Although Inkatha's position was challenged Buthelezi actively promoted discussion about the future of the state. His main image for the future was of a non-racial South Africa based on co-operation between distinct groups, leading to a federal or confederal outcome. He even discussed with Botha the prospects of KwaZulu joining the constellation of states, but took it no further. The major contribution to constitutional ideas came through the Buthelezi Commission – to which Buthelezi gave his name but did not participate directly. The Commission, which reported in 1982, was a mixed-race group, chaired by Professor G. D. L. Schreiner. Although its brief was specific to Natal and KwaZulu, its recommendations had implications for the whole country. In its proposals the commission rejected separate development and the homelands policy, and instead saw KwaZulu and Natal as a single unit. It stressed that the province must always be part of South Africa and contribute to the central government, but it opposed a unitary government and a universal franchise. Instead it supported 'consociational government' based on groups and proportional representation. The powers of the central government and the provinces would be legally delimited and subject to a Bill of Right. Buthelezi commented that the commission's work demonstrated that whites and blacks could work together, and that most people were reasonable in their demands and were prepared to compromise. Inkatha accepted the report as the basis for negotiations, but reserved its position on universal suffrage (IRR 1982: 398). In contrast the government immediately brushed aside the commission's proposals, dismissing them as irrelevant.

The government's response to the Buthelezi Commission's report was not surprising for Inkatha had opposed Pretoria's constitutional plans from the beginning. When the President's Council was formed Inkatha's central committee stated that 'power sharing by forming an extended laager of whites, Indians and Coloureds to the total exclusion of the black masses will only lead to a political cul-de-sac' (IRR 1982: 36). In the run up to the white referendum Buthelezi personally launched a vigorous 'No' campaign – via the media, mass rallies and public meetings. He said that he understood white fears and favoured effective safeguards for minorities, but a 'Yes' vote would be interpreted as rejecting Africans. It would be 'a political death sentence' to twenty-two million fellow South Africans, and was bound to increase bitterness and anger (IRR 1983: 82). He told a white audience: 'Your fate is interwoven with the fate of the rest of South Africa. You will be outnumbered by Africans; you will need African leadership acceptable to Africans.' He added that if Indians and Coloureds participated in the constitution they also would be guilty of betraying Africans (*Rand Daily Mail*, 8 September 1983).

Often, to Botha's chagrin, Buthelezi shared a platform with Dr Slabbert, the PFP leader. Four days before the referendum, at a joint meeting, Slabbert called for a 'No' vote because support for the constitution would be support for apartheid with its pass laws, its removal of people and its break-up of families; while Buthelezi declared that no amount of sabre-rattling by Botha would frighten them (IRR 1983: 17). Botha was equally incensed when Buthelezi took a stand against the constitution with fellow Bantustan leaders. Six of them – including Matanzima and Buthelezi – issued a statement in which they rejected not only the constitution but the homelands policy. They called for a national convention to agree a constitution acceptable to all South Africans. Pretoria's new constitution, they said, would entrench white supremacy by excluding the majority of the population and dividing the country into racially antagonistic camps, which could only lead to violence. The constitution was based on 'the false assumption that the homelands system can be realised in practice'. They pledged to work for the reintegration of their territories into 'a greater South Africa' based on non-racialism, democracy and equal distribution of land and wealth (*The Times* 6 October 1983).

Following the referendum Buthelezi suggested to the ANC and PAC a marriage of convenience with Inkatha, 'even if we differ on strategy'. However, although Inkatha claimed to share the same goals as the liberation movements, relations continued to deteriorate. When, late in 1983, arms caches were found at Ulundi, the KwaZulu capital, Buthelezi accused the ANC of planning to use the arms against Inkatha. The KwaZulu Assembly declared that the ANC was trying 'to eliminate Inkatha by violent means'. Buthelezi further criticized the ANC for pursuing the chimera of the armed struggle. It could never succeed, he said, and only played into the hands of 'the warmongers of Pretoria'. As Inkatha knew that the armed struggle would fail other methods had to be found. In that, as in other matters, Buthelezi accused the ANC in exile of being out of touch with the situation inside the country. The exiles' function, he declared should not be 'to dictate to us from capitals of the world', but to listen to what Africans in the country wanted (IRR 1983: 50).

The Congress of South African Trade Unions (COSATU)

If Inkatha was a rival the UDF soon gained a powerful new ally in the Congress of South African Trade Unions (COSATU). Trade union activity among Africans, which had not been encouraged by Pretoria (at least until Botha's reforms), had increased steadily since the 1960s. It had grown from two unions with 16,000 members in 1969, to 25 unions with 70,000 members in 1977, and (following the implementation of Wiehahn's proposals) there were 35 unions with about 400,000 members by 1984. Black unions had always faced a number of predicaments: Should they confine themselves to shop floor issues or become involved in broader political matters? Should they seek multi-racial or racially exclusive unions? Should they form 'all in' unions or concentrate on a particular industry or group of workers? Late in 1985 a decisive step was taken in answering such questions with the formation of COSATU. It immediately became the largest federation of unions within the country absorbing previous groups, which were mainly but not exclusively black. In all it embraced unions with about 500,000 members, the largest being the National Union of Miners (NUM) with 100,000.

In political terms two features stood out for COSATU. First, it was closely associated with the ANC; and second, it openly espoused political action. In his opening address to the initial congress Cyril Ramaphosa, who was General Secretary of the NUM and had convened the COSATU congress, stated that 'the struggle of workers on the shop floor cannot be separated from the wider struggle for liberty'. He called for worker unity, and for COSATU 'to give firm political direction to the workers'. We must ensure, he continued, that COSATU has 'a strong shop floor base not only to take on employers, but the state as well. Our role in the political struggle will depend on our organisational strength' (IRR 1985: 180).

The congress went on to elect Elijah Barayi (Vice President of the NUM) as COSATU's President, and to agree a set of principles and resolutions. The principles included non-racialism, one union for each industry, and worker control of the organization. The resolutions were concerned with current political and security concerns – with calls for the lifting of the state of emergency, the removal of troops from the township, and the release of all detainees. Support was voiced for international action, including sanctions and disinvestment. On the negative side, the Bantustans were rejected, and a federal constitution for a future South Africa was dismissed as 'a total fraud'. Shortly after the congress Barayi called on a workers' rally at Durban to support nationalization of the mines and major business organizations.

With the UDM, COSATU and Inkatha in place inside South Africa, and the liberation movements outside, the scene was set for a major confrontation.

18

The Black Rising:
and Answering Fire with Fire

Although Botha's constitutional proposals had met strong African opposition, by mid-1984 his reforms appeared to be gaining their ends. The constitutional referendum had been a personal triumph; Chester Crocker of the US State Department described it as 'a step in the right direction'; Botha had signed the Nkomati Accord with Mozambique; in March he undertook a tour of Europe in which he met the leaders of Britain, Germany, Italy and Portugal; in August elections were held for the Coloured and Indian chambers of parliament, and, despite a poor turn out, members were returned; in September, when the new constitution was introduced, Botha was unanimously elected State President; and he went on to appoint a Coloured (Rev Allan Hendrickse) and an Indian (Armichand Rajbansi) to the cabinet. On the eve of his election as State President, Botha confidently predicted that 1984 would be a 'watershed year in the affairs of South Africa and southern Africa'. He spoke of 'hopes for a better and prosperous country' and his 'confidence in the future' (SAIIA, September 1984). Then things fell apart.

The Black Rising

Within days of the introduction of the new constitution a ferocious and sustained black rising erupted. Symbolically it started in Sharpeville, where residents, protesting against the imposition of new council charges, attacked and killed the Deputy Mayor. The rising spread rapidly across the country, often linked to local grievances. By early 1985 'unrest' had become a euphemism for a land in turmoil. Black resistance reached unprecedented levels of intensity. The country was on fire. In part it was caused by economic problems with increasing unemployment, inflation and declining manufacturing industries; but more important was a fury among Africans against discrimination and their continued political exclusion. The rising was fiercer and more prolonged than Soweto, and, unlike Soweto, there were now organizations in place (UDF and Azapo) and members of the liberation movements were infiltrated into the country to give shape to the protests and articulate the grievances. Louis le Grange, the Minister of Police, admitted: 'We are dealing with a revolutionary climate not previously so obvious and not organised in so sophisticated a way' (IRR 1985: 531).

The scale of the disturbances and the associated suffering can be gauged from the government's own figures, which erred on the side of caution. During 1984, 175 people were reported to have been killed in political violence. In 1985 the figure rose to 879; it reached a peak in 1986 with 1,298 deaths; and in 1987, 661 were killed. It was not until late in 1987 that the government regained its security grip. Even then Pretoria was not complacent. Security chiefs spoke of a revolutionary climate, and claimed that the UDF, Azapo and the Congress of South African Trade Unions had become more dangerous than the exiled movements. In the early stages of the rising the police and army were reported to have caused more than half the deaths, but as the conflict persisted Pretoria claimed that most were caused by what became known as 'black on black' violence. That claim must be treated with great caution, because, while 'black of black' violence certainly existed, Pretoria used it for its own purposes. Eugene de Kock, a leading figure in police covert operations, later admitted: 'The black on black violence . . . was a handy propaganda tool because the outside world could be told . . . that the barbaric natives . . . started murdering each other at every opportunity. We contributed to this violence for a number of years both passively (by failing to take steps) and actively (by sponsoring training and protecting violent gangs)' (De Kock 1998: 100). It is safe to assume that many more casualties were the result of security force action than were officially admitted.

The tide of revolt which started in the black townships spread to the Bantustans, turning them into new battlefields, with substantial unrest in Bophuthatswana, Lebowa and KwaNdebele. Enos Mabuza, the Chief Minister of KaNgwane, warned Pretoria that 'the homelands are just as much potential powder kegs . . . as any black residential areas' (IRR 1986: 641). The disturbances, in townships and homelands, took diverse forms. There was mass action short of violence – including boycotts, strikes at work and school, refusal to pay taxes and service charges. In some cases the action escalated into attacks on property: council offices, schools and the homes of councillors, homeland officials and policemen. The government, with some justification, accused the organizers of using intimidation. Within a month of the start of the rising there were reports of UDF members ordering children out of schools, and youths building barricades to stop people going to work. In November 1984 a black newspaper wrote of people being dragged 'screaming into the struggle', and there were reports of men who refused the 'stayaway' call being flogged and some having their ears cut off (Kane–Berman 1993: 33–4).

Further steps up the ladder of violence were attacks upon individuals. The targets included policemen, councillors, homeland leaders, suspected police informers and members of rival black groups. There were attacks by mobs, summary decisions by 'peoples' courts', killings by assassination squads and battles between rival groups. Le Grange announced that in 1985, 26 policemen were killed and 500 of their houses burnt down. In 1986, 63 members of the security forces were killed. Some black townships became virtually 'no go' areas for the authorities, other than for troops and police in heavily armed vehicles. In a number of townships control fell into the hands of young militants, known as 'comrades', who on occasion clashed with older 'vigilantes' (some of whom were supported by the police, but others had no political agenda and were simply tired of intimidation). In 1986 a major clash on the Cape Flats between 'comrades' and 'vigilantes' left 60 people dead and 70,000 homeless (IRR 1986: xx).

Among those implicated in the brutality was Mrs Winnie Madikizela-Mandela – known as 'the mother of the nation' – for her courageous stand against apartheid during her husband's imprisonment. There was, however, a darker side to her personality and actions. According to later findings of the controversial Truth and Reconciliation Commission (TRC) she was responsible for the behaviour of the Mandela United Football Club (MUFC) – a gang of thugs who were involved in at least 18 murders, and a series of assaults, torture and arson. Winnie Mandela knew what was happening and authorized some of the activities. Those who opposed her were 'branded as informers, hunted down and killed'. The Commission found that Mrs Mandela was 'accountable politically and morally for gross violations of human rights committed by MUFC'. She was directly and personally responsible for some crimes, including the abduction and death of a 14-year-old boy, Stomphie Moeketsi. The TRC went on to criticize the ANC as a whole for not accepting responsibility and opposing Mrs Mandela, and for obstructing the course of justice by removing witnesses (*The Guardian*, 30 October, 1998).

On occasion great brutality was employed in the streets, including the notorious 'necklacing' of victims. Necklacing, so ran an account, started with the victim's hands being chopped off or tied with barbed wire to prevent a struggle. Then a tyre was placed around the victim's neck, filled with petrol and set alight. 'It can take up to 20 minutes before the victim dies . . . The victim's relatives are often encouraged to try to help him – which is impossible because of the tyre's enormous heat. The melted rubber is like boiling tar and cannot be removed from the scorched tissue' (IRR 1986: 516). Some black leaders vigorously opposed such methods, including Bishop Desmond Tutu, who argued that a just cause would be ruined by using barbaric methods. The ANC was at first slow to condemn the practice, and even when Tambo came out strongly against it, other leaders, notably Winnie Mandela, endorsed it.

Some of the violence was related to continuing rivalry between black organizations. Azapo students, in criticizing the UDF, repeated the old complaint against the Freedom Charter by disputing its claim that South Africa belongs to all who live in it black and white. 'It is an historical fallacy,' claimed the students, 'to say South Africa belongs to everybody, oppressor and oppressed, robber and robbed. Azania is not a prostitute that belongs to everybody all the time.' The rivalry between the UDF and Azapo was publicly demonstrated when US Senator Robert Kennedy visited South Africa in January 1985, at the invitation of the UDF. In objecting to the visit, Azapo's Vice President, George Wauchope, said that Kennedy was 'promoting imperialism and international capitalism. He is using us as a stepping-stone for the American Presidential campaign in 1988'. In Cape Town an Azapo affiliated organization said that the imperialists throughout the world were becoming worried because the workers were demanding a socialist outcome. The workers did not want 'liberalised capitalism, mere civil rights or American style democracy'. Demonstrations were held against Kennedy and some meetings were disrupted (IRR 1985: 12–13).

More serious than the disruption of meetings was fighting between black groups, as they competed for control of people and territories. It was persistent and bloody, and over the years led to many casualties – killed and wounded. Once the cycle had started it was difficult to contain as local groups took matters into their own hands as they set out to gain retribution for previous wrongs. That helps to explain why, despite a number of 'peace meetings', conflict persisted between the UDF and Azapo (mainly in the Eastern Cape and Soweto) and between Inkatha and the UDF (mainly in KwaZulu/Natal). Again youths were prominent. For example, when the 1987 academic year opened in Soweto and Alexandra fierce rivalry broke out between those schools dominated by Azapo and those by UDF followers. Schools with a dominant group were often renamed after heroes of the movement. Other schools were divided so that rival factions fought it out for control.

The rivalry and conflict was even greater between Inkatha on one hand and the ANC cum UDF on the other. By the end of 1987 a virtual state of war existed between them in parts of KwaZulu/Natal, especially in the Midlands near Pietermaritzburg. During 1987 at least 387 people were killed in Natal. The Inkatha/UDF rivalry does not explain all the conflict, for local warlords and criminals used the situation for their own ends. However, the rivalry was a major factor. Behind the Inkatha/UDF clashes were the old antagonisms, peppered by accusations and counter-accusations about responsibility for initiating the new troubles. Speaking in Lusaka in January 1986, Tambo accused Inkatha and Buthelezi of being Pretoria's instruments. 'We do not accept,' he added, 'that they [the people] agree with these ravings [by Buthelezi] against the ANC.' Buthelezi was accused of attacking those who were fighting for liberation. In November 1986 the ANC's Radio Freedom stated: 'It is clear the puppet Gatsha [Buthelezi] is being groomed by the West and the racist regime . . . The onus is on the people to neutralise the Gatsha snake, which is poisoning the people of South Africa. It needs to be hit on the head' (Kane-Berman 1993: 55). To these attacks Buthelezi replied that the ANC leaders strutted around the international scene claiming to be the sole representatives of the people. Yet 'they tolerate no opposition'. If Africans enter town councils 'they murder them brutally by hacking them to pieces or incarcerating them alive. That is democracy for the ANC mission in exile' (IRR 1986: 541–2).

There was substance in the ANC's accusations. In addition to Inkatha's position as the ruling group in the KwaZulu homeland, where it used intimidation to recruit members and to ensure that they complied with its demands, it also received covert support from the government's security services – in training, the supply of arms and turning a blind eye to its illegal activities. The TRC later found that speeches by Inkatha leaders, including Buthelezi, 'had the effect of inciting supporters to commit acts of violence'. The organization had entered a pact with the government forces 'to create a paramilitary force which was intended to, and did cause death and injury' to opponents. The Commission also noted that Buthelezi had served as Minister of Police, as well as Chief Minister in KwaZuluand, and as such, was 'accountable for the human rights abuses committed by those agencies' (*The Guardian* 30 October, 1998).

The ANC's Response and the Kabwe Conference

The ANC benefited from the 1980s rising. In a sense, as with Soweto, it was again clinging to the coat tails of an unplanned rising over which it had no direct control; but this time its response was more effective. It succeeded in projecting itself through the agency of the UDF, and by infiltrating MK and ANC members into the country. The UDF, which had adopted Nelson Mandela as its patron and the Freedom Charter as its programme, was led by men and women who were either ANC members or sympathizers. They promoted Congress as the vanguard and embodiment of the liberation movement. At the same time, from exile, Tambo spoke of the revolutionary struggle going ahead 'more vigorously than ever before'. He saw the rising as the 'combination of revolutionary factors maturing before our eyes', and, as in the past, he linked together the internal situation with the continuation of the armed struggle (*SA Review* 1986: 226). There was, he repeated, no alternative to the armed struggle, because all peaceful efforts had failed. Why, he asked, are 'we who are victims of violence expected to abandon our violence when the regime presses on with worse violence?' (IRR 1985: 7).

In terms of the armed struggle, the MK demonstrated that it could sustain a small armed presence in the country. Basic military training was provided internally, and the guerilla fighters were encouraged to use their initiative in response to local developments. An ANC official claimed that 'our guerrilla presence inside South Africa is organic in that our fighters are self sustaining' (Kane-Berman 1993: 42). Tom Lodge commented at the time: 'Today a revolutionary movement of considerable proportions exists in the black townships . . . and the ability of the ANC cadres to exercise a commanding influence over it can only be a matter of time'. 1985 was declared 'Year of the Cadre' (*SA Review* 1986: 232).

In June 1985 Tambo called an ANC conference at Kabwe in Zambia. Six months earlier the SACP had secretly held its own Sixth Congress in Moscow. There the SACP decided to extend its activities inside South Africa, by recruiting more members and promoting internal conflict. At the same time it reaffirmed its commitment to the armed struggle, which came as no surprise for virtually all the non-African members of the MK were SACP comrades. In the Politburo elections which followed Chris Hani received the largest number of votes – while others selected to serve on that body included Jack Simons, Mac Maharaj, Joe Slovo and Thabo Mbeki (although Mbeki was recognized more as a social democrat than a communist).

The ANC's Kabwe conference was much larger than its predecessor at Morogoro in 1969: 250 delegates attended, some from inside South Africa and others representing the twenty-one missions abroad. The mood was optimistic and positive. So confident were the leaders that they declared they would not seek a settlement with Pretoria, other than to negotiate a transfer of power when the white regime was defeated. To that end the conference (influenced by the 1978 policy review) decided to put greater emphasis on the power of 'the struggling masses', both to use their economic muscle and to promote an internal rising – 'the people's war' – and so make the country ungovernable. This time, instead of encouraging people to leave the country, as after Soweto, they were urged to stay and fight. Thabo Mbeki speaking on Radio Freedom urged people to attack on all fronts – in factories, mines, farms, schools and villages. 'We will,' he said, 'reply to its [Pretoria's] reactionary violence with revolutionary violence' (Kane-Berman 1993: 41). At the same time the conference agreed that the MK should intensify its activities inside South Africa to cover 'soft' as well as 'hard' targets – 'soft' included civilians such as prominent government supporters, anti-union officials, state witnesses and border farmers; and attacking targets when civilians might be accidentally involved. The people were urged to help the MK, so that 'the doors of the houses of our people should be open to our cadres. Everybody has a role to play' (*SA Review* 1986: 239). 'Let us go to war', proclaimed the delegates.

As well as the resolutions related directly to the struggle other decisions at Kabwe included working more closely with the trade unions – COSATU – inside the country; and both enlarging the ANC's National Executive and opening up membership to all races – thus reflecting the form of society sought by Congress. In the subsequent elections Tambo was reinstated as President, and five non-Africans were voted onto the enlarged executive. The executive members included Alfred Nzo (Secretary General), Thabo Mbeki (youth section), Moses Mabhida (SACP General Secretary), Gertrude Shope (women's section), and Joe Modise (Head of MK).

While the mood at Kabwe was optimistic, away from the euphoria of the meeting Tambo recognized the limitations under which the exiled ANC operated. Before the conference he said that previously too much had been expected of MK and of support from Mozambique. Those hopes had proved false and more emphasis would have to be given to the people's efforts. Yet, Tambo realized that the shift of emphasis to a people's war, involving the masses in revolutionary action, reshaped the nature of the struggle. As noted above it became both wider and more brutal. 'Disciplined violence', wrote John Kane-Berman, was 'replaced by random violence', because the people's war had no command structure to control or curtail it. Casualties greatly increased as action by one group provoked a backlash from another which set off a vicious circle of attack and counter attack (Kane-Berman 1993: 45). Tambo also knew of the persistent debate within the ANC about the nature of targets to be attacked. The decision to include 'soft' targets did nothing to dispel that, for how 'soft' was 'soft'? The debate continued among the leadership, but the actual decisions often had to be left to small units on the ground. Later the TRC condemned, as gross violations of human rights, attacks in which 'the distinction between civilian and military targets was blurred . . . such as the 1983 Church Street bombing of the South African Air Force headquarters' (*The Guardian* 30 October, 1998).

Shortly after Kabwe Tambo stated that although he supported the drive to make the country ungovernable, he had 'no wish to celebrate liberation day surrounded by a desolate landscape of destroyed buildings and machines reduced to scrap metal' (IRR 1985: 10). Tambo also knew that, despite the brave words, the MK was nowhere near to a military victory. Although it had succeeded in infiltrating more fighters into the country, where they could support the rising, they were not a major strategic threat to Pretoria.

Negotiations with Mandela

Running in parallel with ANC and UDF activities were secret contacts between the imprisoned Mandela and the government. Far from disappearing from memory, as Pretoria had hoped, Mandela had become a symbol of the liberation struggle. In prison his personal qualities gained general respect and singled him out as a natural leader; while across the country and abroad there were regular 'Release Mandela' campaigns. This situation created both problems and opportunities for Pretoria. The problems were not only the failure to suppress his name and influence, but also the fear that he might die in prison to become a martyr to the cause. The opportunities were to reach a personal agreement with Mandela which could emasculate the ANC's efforts and gain endorsement for the government's reform programme. Nevertheless the discussions that took place were extraordinary in that the imprisoned Mandela was the symbolic, if not the formal leader of a revolutionary movement which the government was using all its efforts to defeat.

The contacts were intermittent and stretched over years. Even before the 1980s Pretoria had sent out 'feelers', such as an offer to release Mandela provided he restricted himself to the Transkei. Mandela had rejected them all as attempts to isolate him from the ANC. The contacts became easier when in March 1982 he was moved from Robben Island to Pollsmoor prison on the mainland. There, in January 1985, with the rising in full swing, Botha announced to parliament that he was prepared to release Mandela if he 'unconditionally rejected violence as a political instrument'. Botha added: 'It is therefore not the government which now stands in the way of Mr Mandela's freedom. It is he himself'. Mandela's response, which was dramatically read out for him by his daughter Zindzi at a UDF meeting, rejected the offer. Instead Mandela called on Botha to renounce violence, to dismantle apartheid, to unban the ANC and to release political prisoners. Although, said Mandela, he cherished his freedom, too many people had died and suffered for him to give up the struggle now. What freedom, he asked, was he being offered while the ANC was banned, while he could be arrested for a pass offence, while his wife was under a restriction order, and while he was not even regarded as a South African citizen? 'Only free men can negotiate', he declared, 'Prisoners cannot enter into contracts' (Mandela 1994: 509–11).

Despite that rejection contacts were renewed later that year when Kobie Coetsee, the Minister of Justice, called to see Mandela while he was in hospital recovering from an operation. Following that visit Mandela took the initiative himself. He decided that the time had come for talks, while an intense struggle gripped the country and the government ruled via a state of emergency. It was a personal decision which was not cleared with the ANC leaders in Lusaka, and he made it clear to Pretoria that he spoke only as an individual. Indeed, when the ANC in exile heard of the talks some members suspected that Mandela might be selling out to the government. Mandela later explained that sometimes a leader must go ahead of the flock; and further he reasoned that while the ANC had right on its side it did not have might. 'It was clear to me', he wrote, 'that a military victory was a distant if not impossible dream' (Mandela 1994: 513). Early in 1986 Mandela was allowed to meet a visiting group of Commonwealth dignitaries – the Eminent Persons Group (EPG). That meeting covered issues – violence, relations with communists, nationalization and minority rights – which were later raised when Mandela had prolonged discussions with a government group, headed by Kobie Coetsee.

Mandela's position on violence was that it was 'not the oppressed who dictate the form of the struggle. If the oppressor uses violence, the oppressed have no alternative but to respond violently'. For the oppressed it was a form of self-defence. In explaining the ANC's relations with the SACP he said that they were separate organizations, with different long-term aims, but the ANC had no thought of jettisoning 'a long-term ally in the interests of pleasing an antagonist'. What person of honour, he asked, would desert a life-long friend at the insistence of an opponent and retain credibility with his people? With regard to nationalization, Mandela claimed that the aim was not to nationalize the whole economy, but rather to gain a more even distribution of rewards and to counter monopoly industries. Then, when he spoke of minority rights, he explained that no other organization could challenge the ANC's attempts to unite all people and races. He saw the government's rejection of majority rule as an attempt to preserve minority white power. For Mandela majority rule and peace were two sides of the same coin. Finally he summarized his position for the EPG: 'I told them I was a South African nationalist, not a communist, that nationalists came in every hue and colour, and that I was firmly committed to a non racial society . . . that I believed in the Freedom Charter, that the charter embodied principles of democracy and human rights and was not a blue print for socialism. I spoke of my concern that the white minority should feel a sense of security in any new South Africa' (Mandela 1994: 517).

International Reaction

Although the meetings with Mandela were unknown outside a tight circle, the black risings captured massive international attention. Television pictures vividly brought the struggle into people's living rooms, stimulating sympathy for the black masses and criticism of Pretoria's repressive measures. Public awareness of South Africa was further enhanced in November 1984, when Bishop Desmond Tutu followed in Chief Luthuli's footsteps, when he was awarded the Nobel Peace Prize. The exiled movements and western anti-apartheid groups took full advantage of the situation to increase pressure on western governments. In the US the campaign was spearheaded by TransAfrica, a black organization, led by Randall Robinson. From November 1984, demonstrations were held outside the South African Embassy in Washington. By March 1985, 2,000 protesters had been arrested, many of them prominent public figures. In Britain the Anti-Apartheid Movement, with Bishop Trevor Huddleston among its leaders, played a similar role. In London a permanent vigil was mounted outside the South African Embassy in Trafalgar Square.

Under such pressure, combined with their own concern about the situation, western governments felt obliged 'to do something'. They responded by imposing further economic sanctions, extending boycotts, intensifying diplomatic pressure and proclaiming their support for further reforms. Despite President Reagan's opposition, the US Congress passed the Comprehensive Anti Apartheid Act (CAAA) of 1986. That forbade the import of a wide range of South African goods, withdrew landing rights from South African Airways, stopped new investments and the export of oil. The Act also allocated $40m. of aid for the victims of apartheid, but, at the same time, it required the administration to conduct an enquiry into the ANC's use of violence and its connections with communism. Nor was the application of sanctions confined to governments. Acting from a combination of conviction, pressure from the public and shareholders, and because South African connections made them unpopular at home, diverse bodies both public and private – banks, churches, local authorities, universities, sporting organizations – imposed their own measures. The impact of non-government sanctions was especially serious for Pretoria, when banks and companies decided to disinvest, refused further loans and broke their links with the Republic.

Similarly renewed attention was paid to South Africa at international gatherings. At the UN pressure mounted not only against apartheid but for Pretoria to settle the long-running SWA/Namibia dispute, to withdraw from Angola and to stop destabilizing her neighbours. It was also a major preoccupation in the Commonwealth. When Commonwealth leaders met at Nassau in October 1985 a familiar scene was played out, with South Africa the dominant topic and a clash between the majority of members and the British government, led by Margaret Thatcher. She opposed economic sanctions on the grounds that they would stiffen white resistance, and blacks would suffer most. Eventually a compromise was hammered out in which a few additional sanctions were agreed. They were few, but they represented a further half turn of the sanctions screw, with the threat of more to come.

The Commonwealth leaders also decided to appoint a group of senior figures – the Eminent Persons Group (EPG) – who would seek 'to encourage through all practicable ways the evolution of political dialogue', whereby apartheid could be dismantled and the structures of democracy erected (EPG 1986: 142–3). The initial ANC response was one of disappointment because it wanted action not investigation, but it agreed to meet the EPG, which, as noted above, also met Mandela. A similar pattern emerged in Pretoria, where at first the idea was greeted with scepticism, as it was assumed that Botha would not tolerate such external interference and that the group did not have sufficient clout to influence him. However, in the circumstances Pretoria could not afford to be obstinate as further sanctions were a continuing threat, and Thatcher put her weight behind the EPG via a personal appeal to Botha.

The ANC benefited from the renewed international activity. Governments and organizations, eager to demonstrate their opposition to apartheid and Pretoria's repressive policies, paid court to the ANC as the main liberation movement. Tambo realized that an opportunity had opened up. 'It boils down,' he said, 'to the question of how to win, how to compel the support of the United States, Great Britain and the Federal Republic of Germany for the cause of the victims of apartheid' (Thomas 1996: 204). Doors were opened which previously had been closed. In September 1986 Tambo met Geoffrey Howe, the British Foreign Secretary, while previously the British Government had refused to make contact with what Thatcher described as 'a terrorist organization'. In January 1987 Tambo had what he described as a 'very useful exchange' with George Shultz, the US Secretary of State – with agreement on the 'objectives of our struggle and what we want to put in place of apartheid' (IRR 1997/8: 704). Tambo also visited Australia, New Zealand, Japan and Canada. Although these meetings and visits did not produce dramatic changes in western policies, they boosted the ANC's status, brought encouragement to its supporters, and gave it an edge over its black rivals. At the same time Tambo did not neglect the established links with the eastern bloc. In between the western meetings he made another visit to Moscow, where he was promised continued support.

The Government's Response: Fighting Fire with Fire

The government perceived the black rising as part of the total onslaught. 'The UDF', stated Le Grange, 'is pursuing the same revolutionary goals as the banned ANC and is actively promoting a climate of revolution' (SA Review 1986: 260). In its efforts to regain control Pretoria used a variety of methods both overt and covert. It declared states of emergency, banned meetings, arrested leaders and made massive sweeps through the black townships. Regulations were introduced which indemnified the security forces against criminal or civil prosecution, and extended further their powers of arrest and detention. Pitched battles were fought between militant blacks – some of whom had firearms but most of whom used sticks, stones and home-made petrol bombs – and police and troops, using tear gas, firearms and armoured vehicles. In 1986 more than 4,000 people were detained under the Internal Security Act, and an estimated 25,000 were temporarily arrested in sweeps under emergency regulations. The army was called in to support the police. By late 1985 more than 35,000 troops were deployed in townships across the country. 'Part of the country is under military occupation', commented The Sowetan (IRR 1985: 423).

While in their overt operations the security forces were often responding to violence in an attempt to regain order, on other occasions they initiated the violence. The EPG reported; 'Claims that the security forces provoke violence are confirmed by our experience. On our very first visit to . . . Soweto we were confronted by the spectacle of a policeman chasing and shooting at an apparently unarmed person'. The EPG 'became persuaded that there was, in fact a systematic and seemingly orchestrated campaign of intimidation directed at activities in the democratic cause' (EPG 1986: 60/1). One clear case of police violence came at Langa township, Uitenhage on 21 March 1985 (Sharpeville Day) when the police fired on a peaceful procession killing 20 people. The killing did not stop there. In disturbances which followed 10 more people were killed by the police, and in a form of retaliation the locals turned to violence by killing a hated local councillor, Tamsanqa Kinikini, and four of his family. Similar incidents were repeated throughout the period. On 26 August 1986, for example, the police shot and killed 21 people in Soweto. In parliament the PFP, calling for an enquiry into the incident, stated that there was no evidence of stones or petrol bombs being thrown, and that the police had fired into a meeting of residents without warning.

As well as such specific cases apartheid was maintained by a culture of violence, which had become so ingrained that it was either unnoticed or regarded as the norm by members of the government and security forces. The police were trigger-happy. The figures speak for themselves. In 1986 they shot dead 716 people, of whom 252 were said to have been attempting to escape arrest. In more general terms Bishop Tutu spoke of the culture when he addressed a UN committee in October 1985. 'South Africa,' he said, 'is a violent country [and] the primary violence is apartheid.' He went on to give examples of the brute force and humiliation meeted out by the police to Africans. He told of three youngsters lured into a police trap and shot dead; of a three-year-old killed by a plastic bullet; of an eleven-year-old who was beaten to death by the police; of Tutu's own son who was imprisoned for fourteen days as a danger to the state because he swore at a policeman; of his wife and daughters who had been strip-searched at road blocks. 'Your dignity,' said Tutu, 'is not just rubbed in the dust. It is trodden underfoot and spat on. Our people are being killed as if they were flies' (Tutu 1995: 98–9).

While the incidents about which Tutu complained and the shootings were public knowledge, and, in some cases led to formal investigations, other forms of state violence were covert. These included the activities of special units and death squads; the routine torture of prisoners sometimes leading to deaths. Some torturers had fearsome reputations. Among these was Brigadier Theuns Swanepoel, who gained notoriety as early as the 1960s. Among Swanepoel's victims was Mac Maharaj (who later became a government minister). Maharaj told how he had been tortured by having his penis beaten by a stick with rusty nails, and was hung by his ankles from a seventh-floor window. Maharaj said that Swanepoel learnt that the most effective torture was a 'steady, intermittent use of force, both physical and psychological, where, for the victims, fear dominates the mind' (*The Times*, 14 July 1998). Shadowy groups also operated – later known as 'the third force' – whose activities included indiscriminate terror; bomb attacks on anti-apartheid organizations, including the headquarters of COSATU and the South African Council of Churches (Khotso House); support for 'black on black' violence; and disguising themselves as members of rival black gangs to promote further fear and killing. Although there were suspicions about such activities at the time, the government totally denied them. It was only in the 1990s, through court hearings and the work of the Truth and Reconciliation Commission (TRC), that the detailed horror and the full extent of the activities became clearer.

Two examples which came before the TRC in February 1998 will serve to illustrate the nature of the measures employed. The first case took place in June 1985, when according to a former policeman, Johan Martin van Zyl, it was decided 'to eliminate' Matthew Goniwe, a school teacher from Cradock in the Eastern Cape. The decision was taken because the police had lost control of parts of Cradock to street committees, of which Goniwe was a leading figure. 'We had,' said van Zyl, 'to chop off the head of the destabilizing force of the area.' A death squad did that by ambushing a car in which Goniwe and three companions – Fort Calata, Sparrow Mkonto and Sicelo Mhlauli – were travelling. The 'Cradock Four', as they became known, were handcuffed, taken to a remote spot, where they were killed by stabbing and shooting. The bodies were then burnt in an attempt to make the killings appear the work of Azapo or of vigilantes. Another of the policemen involved explained police behaviour in terms of the pressure they were under from political leaders to succeed in countering the black rising. He quoted Botha and Malan who had declared 'we must fight fire with fire' (*Star*, Johannesburg, 24 and 26 February 1998).

The second case took place in June 1988 when Stanza Bopape died in police custody. Bopape was the General Secretary of the Mamelodi Civic Association – a UDF affiliate. According to the policemen who were seeking amnesty Bopape was arrested under the Internal Security Act on suspicion of belonging to a group called 'Maponya' which had made bomb attacks. One of the policemen, Adriaan van Niekerk, told the TRC that when Bopape refused to co-operate it was decided 'to give him a bit of a fright' by subjecting him to electric shocks. Charles Zeelie, another policeman, explained that most members of the force, including the most senior, knew of the electric shock treatment and regarded it as a legitimate way to fight the ANC/UDF. Another, Jacobus Englebrecht, who claimed to be 'only doing my job', admitted that torture and electric shocks were often used. However, in Bopape's case, things went wrong; for after three or four shocks, he slumped forward and died. Because they realized that a death in custody could have serious political and international consequences the police decided to dispose of the body while announcing that Bopape had escaped. Information about Bopape was formally circulated to help with his supposed rearrest. Meanwhile, his body was blown up, and the remains thrown into a crocodile infested river. Englebrecht stated he believed he was helping to keep the government in power. 'The security branch of the police,' he declared, 'was an extension of the government' (*Star*, Johannesburg, 25 and 26 February 1998).

Another extraordinary development which the TRC uncovered was a programme for chemical and biological warfare (named 'Project Coast'). It was led by a scientist, Dr Wouter Basson, who held the rank of Colonel in a special unit in the defence forces. With the support of leading police and military figures, like General Lothar Neethling, Basson recruited a group of eminent white scientists who worked under the cover of the Roodeplaat Research Laboratory. Their experiments ranged widely and were designed to be used against large groups as well as individuals. They included attempts to develop anthrax and cholera as offensive weapons, Mandrax grenades as a means of controlling crowds, anti-fertility drugs to reduce the black birth rate, plus lethal poisons to attack individuals. Later the Army Intelligence Chief, General Joffel van der Westhuizen, stated that the aim was to give 'the SADF an offensive and defensive capability in chemical and biological warfare'. The weapons were for use inside and outside South Africa, and large quantities were developed, but just how widely they were employed is obscure. According to the evidence given to the TRC some attempts succeeded, including the murder of an ANC Russian adviser in Lusaka whose food was laced with anthrax, whereas others failed including an attempt to kill Rev Frank Chikane by contaminating his clothes with para-oxon. A proposal to poison Mandela with a brain-damaging substance was not carried out. The scientists who participated in these fearsome experiments rationalized their behaviour to the TRC in terms of the defence of the state. Their mind set was that of the government in its drive to fight terrorism. 'I had no problem working on this cause for "volk en vaderland"', stated Dr Daan Goosen of the University of Pretoria. After speaking of his experience in treating the wounded after the ANC's Pretoria bomb, he said: 'We were in a climate of war, the politicians spoke all the time about the total onslaught'. When Goosen had asked Basson about his motives Basson had replied: 'I have a daughter. We know that one day the blacks will take over the country. But when my daughter asks me, "Daddy, what did you do to prevent this", my conscience will be clear' (*The Star and SA Times*, 17 June 1998).

As noted above, the government's covert actions were not confined to the Republic. For some years Pretoria's agents and spies had operated abroad. Among the more effective was Craig Williamson, who succeeded in penetrating a number of anti-apartheid groups, set up a network of spies and provided evidence which was used in arrests and prosecutions. He eventually rose to the rank of Colonel in the police service, and was decorated for his efforts. In the early 1980s the actions of such agents had included a bomb attack on the ANC's London headquarters, and the assassination of Ruth First (Joe Slovo's wife) by a parcel bomb in Maputo. These activities were intensified in the late 1980s, and included the assassination in March 1988 of Ms Dulcie September, the ANC's representative in France, and several failed assassination attempts – including those on Albie Sachs, Alfred Nzo and Thomas Nkobi.

The severity of the government's response reflected its perception of the dangers it faced. For Pretoria the total onslaught had developed into a low-intensity revolutionary war. In the dual policy of reform and security, security was always predominant. While in the early 1980s the government had argued that reform would lead to security; now, faced by the black rising, it became convinced that security must precede reform: that it was a precondition for further changes. Moreover, in the mind set of the total strategy, it was assumed that revolutionaries could only be defeated by countering them with their own methods – that fire must be met by fire – that 'only extreme and unconventional measures could prevent political and military demise' (Seegers 1996: 186). It was further assumed that if the core revolutionaries could be smashed the hearts and minds of the rest of the black population could then be won over by reform. But first the enemy had to be defeated. This brutal, no holds barred approach, had been nurtured in Angola and the Namibian borders, where government forces, like the notorious 'Koevoet' (Crowbar), and SWAPO guerillas developed vicious, merciless methods in fighting each other. De Kock, commented that 'on both sides mercy was neither given nor expected. One's emotions soon became blunted' (De Kock 1998: 79). That same attitude was found inside South Africa. Survival was the name of the game and the ends justified the means.

Botha and his followers were convinced that they were fighting against the evil of international communism, as represented by the liberation movements; and in defence of a just cause – western Christian civilization – as represented by the white controlled state. Outside that context such convictions might appear extraordinary and misguided, but they were firmly held within the government, and the security forces. They provided a powerful legitimizing myth. The brutal methods used may have attracted perverts and sadists to the special police units and death squads, but many were driven on by a conviction of right. In 1988 a police statement said: 'It is common knowledge that SA is today the target of the most serious revolutionary onslaught in our entire history. It is only malicious and pathetic people who do not want to realise or accept this fact' (Seegers 1996: 187). 'We were told the enemy was everywhere,' wrote de Kock, 'in universities, trade unions and cultural organisations. They all harboured enemies of the state who were waging psychological and economic warfare against us' (De Kock 1998: 91).

Added to the mind set was the organizational framework that Botha had put in place. The ANC's 'people's war' which helped to change the nature of the conflict was matched by Pretoria's security structure – the State Security Council and the National Security Management Scheme – which was now fully employed. 'What Botha did,' wrote de Kock, 'was to militarise the state and politicise the military and the police. There was in fact a dual state. One part of the [white] government based on the parliamentary process; the other rooted in the security establishment' (De Kock 1998: 91). As the security structure was based upon a clear hierarchy, those at the top, the members of the State Security Council (SSC), must bear a direct responsibility for what happened within the system. They may not have known the details of all the covert security actions, but they must have known the general thrust of affairs, or at least have been prepared to turn a blind eye to them. Those at the top gave general directives, often using ambiguous language – such as ordering the 'removal' of individuals or groups – the consequences of which would be known but would be difficult to pin on them. Those lower down the ladder of authority, although personally responsible for their actions, could claim later that they believed they were working for the good of the state and carrying out the orders of their political masters.

The leading political master was P. W. Botha. The TRC (which Botha dismissed as a circus) concluded that as government leader he was 'responsible for gross violations of human rights'. As chairman of the SSC, whose 'meetings and recommendations were highly ambiguous and were interpreted . . . as authorising the killing of people', he gave support for covert operations 'aimed at opposing and destabilizing the governments of neighbouring countries', and he specifically ordered the bombing of two Johannesburg office blocks housing anti-apartheid organizations. In summary the TRC concluded that 'Botha contributed to and facilitated a climate in which . . . gross violations of human rights could and did occur, and as such is accountable for such actions' (*The Guardian* 30 October 1998).

Government violence, terror and torture were not simply the work of rogue elephants, or ill-disciplined individuals and small groups. Rather they were part of an institutionalized, systematic set of policies, which helped to brutalize the whole society.

19

Retreat from the Rubicon:
The Failure of Reform

In May 1987 Botha called an election for the House of Assembly. It was the first white election since the formation of the Conservative Party (CP) and the introduction of the new constitution. The economic circumstances at the time were unfavourable, with sanctions biting, a recession in place and high inflation. However, the voters' attention was less focused on the economy than on racial, security and political issues. One of Botha's reasons for calling the election was to counter the CP's criticism that the government had pressed ahead with reforms without gaining a mandate from the white electorate. Another reason was to win support for the government's continued tough security approach. Emergency regulations were still in place and troops were in the townships, but Pretoria was steadily regaining its grip.

In the bluster of the campaign the slogans employed by the parties encapsulated their broad approaches. The NP proclaimed 'Reform Yes – Surrender No'; the CP insisted on 'Self Determination Yes – Power Sharing No'; for the PFP it was 'Security through Racial Harmony'; while the HNP bluntly stated 'Reform is Surrender'. The NP asked for a mandate to press on with its dual reform and security approach. Botha attacked foreign interference and US sanctions in particular, and called for 'unity against the spirit of revolution incited from abroad'. Adriaan Vlok, the Minister of Law and Order, stated that three steps were needed to defend the state against 'the revolutionary storm': strong security, strong government and a constitution acceptable to all. The CP continued to argue that partition, based on Verwoerdian lines, was the key to ensure that Afrikaners, and those English speakers who identified with Afrikaners, 'will have a fatherland in which they will be ruled by their own people alone' (Van Vuren 1987: 73). The CP and HNP again discussed the possibility of co-operation and again failed to agree. The PFP called for an end to discrimination, a new constitution based on negotiation between all groups, and a genuine sharing of power 'without the domination of one group over another' (IRR 1987: 762).

When the election results were declared the NP had won 123 seats with 52 per cent of the vote. The remainder were split to the 'right' and 'left' – the CP gaining 23 seats (26 per cent) and the PFP 20 seats (15 per cent). The NP's victory was based upon a combination of traditional loyalty; its position in the centre of white politics; the belief that its tough policy was working; and the hope that it could negotiate an acceptable future. But among Afrikaners it had clearly lost more ground to the CP. It was the CP's first election and yet it had become the main parliamentary opposition. Increasingly the NP was an Afrikaner led party, which looked to English speakers for much of its support. The depth of bitterness between the NP and CP was captured after the election, when Treurnicht, the CP leader, refused to co-operate with the government in planning the celebrations for the 150th anniversary of the Great Trek. You cannot celebrate, said Treurnicht, with those who were 'busy every day destroying everything the Volk had built up' (IRR 1987/8: 22). It was a far cry from the heady days of the 1938 centenary.

On the other wing of white politics the PFP lost some electoral support, but of concern for the government was the breakaway of three prominent NP members – Wynand Malan, Dennis Worrall and Ester Lategan – who accused the government of abandoning its reforming zeal. They formed a temporary coalition, the Independent Movement, which set out to challenge the NP by supporting a vigorous reform programme. Only Malan was elected, but Worrall came within a whisker of unseating Heunis in a previously rock-safe NP seat. They reflected an unease which lay beneath the NP's façade of confidence – an unease that the party had lost its sense of purpose. Even the cautious F. W. de Klerk admitted during the campaign that 'our theory is on the rocks'. Such doubts were part of a broader uncertainty among Afrikaners which surfaced in the Dutch Reformed Churches. In 1985, for example, the NGK Cape Synod reversed its earlier position whereby it had claimed biblical justification for apartheid. Now it denied that. Church members were urged 'to confess their participation in apartheid with humility and sorrow' (O'Meara 1996: 336).

The Failure of Reform

Although the government continued to speak of reform, the voice of security became ever louder. Support for reform was never abandoned entirely, and an internal government debate continued. In 1987, for example, Heunis's Department of Development and Constitutional Planning circulated a confidential and controversial document entitled 'We Are Not Afraid of Anything', which argued that both the detention of political leaders and the reaction of the security forces to violence were counter-productive. By banning and removing established political leaders, so the argument ran, the field was left open for more radical elements to move in, and tough security measures only alienated the mass of people. The report therefore recommended unbanning some political organizations, and removing laws which had become unenforceable, like the Group Areas Act. However, the document made no progress as it immediately ran into opposition from the securocrats and the President's office (Seegers 1996: 248).

Yet, by the standards of previous government policies and previous white attitudes, Botha's reforms were remarkable. Under his leadership many restrictive labour laws were swept aside; the Mixed Marriages and Immorality Acts were repealed; Africans gained permanent property rights in urban areas; more resources were put into African housing, health and education; central business districts were opened up to all races; the machinery of government was reorganized; regional economic structures were created to embrace the non-independent homelands; a new constitution was introduced which abandoned the white monopoly of central government; Coloureds and Indians were included in the cabinet; some political prisoners were released, including Govan Mbeki; undertakings were given to seek political solutions by dialogue; and secret discussions continued with Mandela. They were remarkable. But they failed: failed in the sense that they did not bring peace, order and prosperity to the country; and failed in that the government did not gain the support, or even acquiescence of the bulk of Africans and most Coloureds and Indians. 'At every level of social life,' wrote Dan O'Meara, 'the South African state confronted a crisis whose severity went far beyond that which P. W. Botha had come to office determined to resolve' (O'Meara 1996: 338).

Why did Botha's reforms fail? It may have been that the very act of introducing reforms encouraged the opponents of the state to keep up the pressure because they believed they had the government on the run. Yet, irrespective of that, a situation had probably been reached whereby no reform programme short of political revolution — the transfer of power from the white minority to the majority — would have satisfied the liberation movements. Reform other than that was inadequate for them. Thus, while for whites Botha's reforms invoked heart-searching dilemmas they had little impact on Africans. For example, the decision to revoke the Mixed Marriages and Immorality Acts was seen as a major step by whites, but not so for Africans. Mandela disparagingly described it as a 'pinprick', saying that he had no ambition to marry a white woman or swim in a white pool. 'It is political equality that we want' (Mandela 1994: 508). Motlana was equally adamant. 'We are not interested,' he said, 'in the repeal of these laws; we want effective participation in the running of the country' (IRR 1985: 491).

The reactions of Mandela and Motlana underlined a central paradox in Botha's approach to reform. For Botha and his supporters, the prime purpose was not to change the state but to defend it; and in particular the position of whites. Change was the price that had to be paid to secure the core. The result was a basic misunderstanding between the government and those who saw the main aim of reform as the creation of a new social and political order. The Commonwealth Eminent Persons Group encountered this. For them Pretoria's position defied 'succinct summary'. It had, they stated, 'perfected a specialised political vocabulary which, while saying one thing, means quite another'. While, stated the EPG, the government had declared apartheid 'outmoded', 'finished' and 'dead', it continued to base its policies on the apartheid foundation of ethnic groups, not on individual rights; while it claimed a commitment to a united South Africa it excluded the 'independent homelands' and reaffirmed its goal of independence for the 'self governing homelands'; and while it declared itself against violence, it failed to recognize 'that apartheid itself was sustained through violence and that the inequities and injustice it perpetuated fostered violence' (EPG 1986: 81–2). Because of these different approaches the late 1980s was characterized by apparently contradictory developments. At times it appeared that reform was dominant, at others that tough security was in the driving seat. For those seeking fundamental social change it was a roller-coaster ride of high expectations followed by disillusionment. The explanation was that the hopes were built on a false premise.

The paradox was also evident at a personal level, as Botha sought to combine the roles of a reformer intent on removing the sources of conflict, and a man of steel eager for the fray. For him reform was a top-down process, which he would mould, aided by an inner circle of securocrats, technicians and a few ministers. He concentrated power around himself, partly by reorganization of central government, and partly by his dominant personality. Within the white political system he steadily sidelined the party, parliament and even the cabinet. Although, within his agenda of reform, he dispensed with some of the superstructure of apartheid he maintained its main framework. Botha's South Africa was still shaped by racial groups: by the Population (Race) Classification Act, which designated the status of every individual; by separate residential areas, as embodied in the Group Areas Act; by the provision of separate racial services; and by white control of the state. In most respects he was supported at the time by his senior cabinet colleagues. In February 1986 F. W. de Klerk endorsed the NP's emphasis on the importance of groups; not, he said, because it was discriminatory but because it was necessary for peaceful coexistence. Each group must have its own residential areas, said de Klerk, its own schools, its own institutions and the right to preserve its own culture and identity (IRR 1986: 161).

The result was an apparent contradiction. While on the one hand reform went ahead, on the other apartheid was implemented as vigorously as ever. In the years between 1981 and 1986 more than 200,000 Africans were 'resettled' from white areas, usually by forced removals and often on to inhospitable sites. In 1986 alone Heunis announced that 64,180 people were moved (IRR 1986: xxiii). And this human misery was inflicted directly to fulfil the imperatives of grand apartheid's racial land division. Also services, like health and education, continued to be divided rigorously by race; as did social facilities, such as beaches and cinemas, and always the best were reserved for whites. The bizarre practice of reclassifying individuals by race continued apace. In 1987, for example, 918 people applied to be reclassified: 722 were successful – including 269 Africans who were redesignated as Coloureds; 244 Coloureds as whites; 33 Coloureds as Indians; and 4 whites as Coloureds (IRR 1988/9: 151). Nor did Botha change his perception of Africans as divided into separate tribal nations. Interviewed in 1988 he said that everybody knows 'that the Black man himself does not look upon himself as being part of a big Black majority. They come here as Zulus; they come here as Xhosa. You will find that the Transkeians won't merge with Ciskeians, and you can use all the police forces you have; they simply won't do it' (Pottinger 1988: 238).

Whenever Botha was faced by a clash between reform and security he gave priority to security. That was demonstrated in three prominent cases: the Rubicon speech in 1985; the treatment of the Eminent Persons Group (EPG) in 1986; and the attempts to negotiate with Africans in the late 1980s.

The Primacy of Security: The Rubicon Speech

On 15 August 1985 Botha addressed the annual conference of the Natal National Party. Had it been a routine party affair probably nothing would have been heard of it. But it was not. It was built up as signalling an epoch-making change in South Africa's political future – of crossing the Rubicon with no way back. Botha himself described it as 'a manifesto for the future of our country'. Pik Botha and his Department of Foreign Affairs were especially zealous in spreading the message. As a result the speech generated enormous international attention, with live television coverage in the US, Britain and Germany. In the event it was a disaster. It was not only what Botha said but the way he said it. It was the declaration of an angry, defiant man, who spoke not as a statesman searching for a solution to his country's problems, but as a party boss warning others off his patch.

Botha claimed to have shown great personal patience. 'But don't push me too far', he told his world audience. He was not, he asserted, prepared to 'lead white South Africans and other minority groups on a road to abdication and suicide'. We are, he stated, 'a proud and independent people', but he claimed to be seeking a negotiated settlement for all South Africans, and in doing so said he would not prescribe or set down demands. Then he did precisely that. To start with he rejected the 'simplistic and racist approach that South Africa consists of a white minority and a black majority' and insisted that it was 'a country of minorities'. The population, he said, was multi-cultural and multi-ethnic'. Thus 'horizontal differentiation which amounts to one nation or group . . . dominating another' was inappropriate. He accepted economic interdependence, but said that the constitution must be based on groups participating in matters of common concern, not on individuals in a single political system. He saw independence for some African homelands as part of the solution, but recognized that other Africans would have to be accommodated within the political institutions of the Republic. However, he dismissed the possibility of a separate chamber of parliament for Africans. 'I know for a fact,' he added, 'that most black leaders, and most reasonable South Africans will not accept the principle of one man one vote in a unitary state. That would lead to 'domination of one over others . . . and to chaos. Consequently I reject it as a solution' (*Business Day*, Johannesburg, 16 August 1985).

The Rubicon speech had an immediate and adverse impact. Even many government supporters threw up their hands in despair. Internationally the cry for further sanctions was intensified; foreign banks refused to renew short-term loans; the Rand lost a third of its value in a week; and Pretoria was obliged to suspend repayments and reintroduce exchange controls. Internally the speech intensified African anger, and within the white community it undermined support for Botha. Business people lost faith in the government's ability to revive the economy and break the shackles of sanctions. Therefore they looked elsewhere, to the advantage of the ANC.

In the month following the speech a group of leading business people (mainly English speaking), flew to Lusaka to hold discussions with the ANC, under the chairmanship of Zambia's President Kaunda. The businessmen were led by Gavin

Relly of the powerful Anglo American Corporation. Relly explained that they were less concerned with who governed, black or white, than that South Africa 'will be a viable country and not destroyed by violence and strife' (Meredith 1997: 361). Botha was furious. Yet that meeting marked a path which was soon followed by other whites.

In July 1987 Frederick van Zyl Slabbert, now leading the Institute for Democratic Alternatives for South Africa (IDASA), arranged for a large group of Afrikaners – academics, clergy, businessmen, politicians and journalists – to meet an ANC delegation led by Thabo Mbeki at Dakar in Senegal. At the conclusion of the meeting, a joint communique was issued supporting negotiations, the release of political prisoners, the unbanning of the ANC, and stating that 'the source of violence in South Africa derives from the fact that the use of violence is funda-mental to the existence and practice of racial discrimination' (IRR 1987/8: 707). Botha again bitterly objected to what he said was cheap ANC propaganda. Yet he knew of some of the meetings which took place through Niel Barnard, head of the National Intelligence Service. These included a set of discussions at Mells Park House, near Bath in England, between an ANC delegation led by Thabo Mbeki and Jacob Zuma, and prominent non-government Afrikaners. Among the Afrikaners was Willie Esterhuyse, an academic, who agreed to act as a conduit between Barnard and the ANC, provided he was allowed to inform Mbeki about the arrangement. Mbeki agreed (Sparks 1995: 82).

The Commonwealth Eminent Persons Group

In December 1985, Botha, having agreed to their visit, wrote to the Eminent Persons Group, saying he would approach their initiative constructively. 'Our political programme,' he wrote, 'provides for power sharing, subject only to the protection of the rights of all minorities.' He spoke of all communities having a fair say in government, and of ending racial discrimination, not only from the statute book but also from society as a whole. Then he went a step further than anything he had said in public. 'We are reconciled,' he wrote, 'to the eventual disappearance of white domination' (EPG 1986: 148). It was, in the event, another example of different interpretations – this time of what was implied by 'white domination' – and in EPG terms was contradicted by Botha's previous and subsequent behaviour. Yet, despite the ambiguity, it was a heartening start for the EPG as it began its visits in February 1986. At first its efforts appeared to prosper, as it consulted a wide range of people and organizations: from the government to the liberation movements, and including, with Pretoria's permission, Nelson Mandela.

In March 1986, following the discussions, the EPG presented a 'negotiating concept'. On Pretoria's side that called for steps to end apartheid, the removal of troops from the townships, the restoration of black political activity by lifting bans on political parties and releasing political prisoners. On their part the liberation movements were required to suspend violence and commit themselves to negoti-ation. Early signs were favourable. Pretoria had already lifted the state of emergency and announced the ending of 'pass laws'. Now it said it was not opposed in principle to releasing political prisoners or unbanning organizations, and was prepared to negotiate on an open agenda. Mandela accepted the concept as a starting point, and the ANC in Lusaka, although more cautious, was ready to consider it. Then the mood in Pretoria changed. Had Botha realized that the EPG was making more progress than he had anticipated; or had his security advisers persuaded him of dangers ahead; or was he reverting to type? Whatever the reasons, on 15 May Botha publicly laid down a list of the government's 'non-negotiables'. These included the need to gain the approval of the existing parliament for any changes; and he set out norms and values which had to be met – including recognition that South Africa is a country of minorities and a multi-cultural society; the need to protect minorities against domination and their right of self-determination; adherence to Christian values and civilized norms; and furtherance of private enterprise. Then ominously Botha warned against interference by outside bodies (EPG 1986: 175/6).

On 19 May the EPG was scheduled to meet the Cabinet's Constitutional Committee, to explore the negotiating concept further. However, before that meeting took place, South Africa launched air strikes against three neighbouring Commonwealth states – Botswana, Zimbabwe and Zambia. Pretoria issued a statement claiming that the attacks were directed against the ANC and PAC, and it reasserted its determination to combat terrorism wherever it was found. Botha bragged to parliament that this was just the first instalment, that 'South Africa has the capacity and will to break the ANC' (Meredith 1997: 365). Botha personally must have approved the operation; whereas other ministers, including Heunis and Pik Botha, claimed to have no prior knowledge of the attacks. Inevitably the assaults on Commonwealth states – the group's sponsors – ended the EPG's efforts. The raids were directed as much against the EPG as the liberation movements. The members concluded: 'It was all too plain that, while talking to the Group about negotiations and peaceful solutions, the government had been planning these armed raids' (EPG 1986: 160). In June 1986 Botha reimposed a state of emergency over the whole country. 'Neither the international community at large,' he proclaimed, 'nor any particular state will dictate to us what the content of our political programme should be . . . We ourselves will find solutions to our problems' (*The Times* 25 July 1986).

Negotiations with Africans

Botha, when donning his reforming clothes, regularly stated that Africans from outside the independent Bantustans must be brought into the constitutional equation. He spoke of making progress by consulting African leaders. Pretoria's efforts in that regard developed along two different lines. One was a set of public proposals to create a formal consultative mechanism; the other was the secret negotiations with Mandela.

When opening parliament in January 1985 Botha spoke of further extensive reforms, including an informal, non-statutory forum to discuss constitutional issues with Africans. At the same time he spoke of offering Africans freehold rights in urban areas; clarification of the question of citizenship; steps to amend influx control and to stop forced removals. Reformers jumped with joy. A leading editor wrote: 'It is no exaggeration to say that it was the most important constructive statement on race policy since Dr Verwoerd codified hardline apartheid in the late 1950s and sent South Africa down a dead end street that imperilled security at home and wrecked our reputation abroad' (*The Sunday Times*, Johannesburg 27 July 1985). However, there was a very different reaction from Africans. Azapo stated that it would not be satisfied with anything short of repossession of the land. A UDF spokesperson said that 'only a constitution based on the will and full participation of all South Africans can be the basis of lasting peace'; and Dr Motlana added that Botha 'didn't commit himself to anything; there was still no real declaration of intent on which African leaders would be ready to negotiate' (*The Observer*, London 27 July 1985).

With Pretoria's main attention focused on countering the black rising, it was a full year before Botha returned to the idea of a forum for Africans. Then he said he accepted the notion of an undivided South Africa – excluding the 'independent' Bantustans – and a single citizenship, although he did not spell out the political implications of citizenship. He went on to repeat that group aspirations must be accommodated, and all South Africans should be able to participate in government through elected representatives. Once again, therefore, reformist aspirations were roused and once again they were thwarted. In May 1986 a Bill was published proposing the formation of a National Council for Africans: to advise the State President on matters of common concern and on the creation of constitutional structures for Africans. Any hopes that the proposal would attract widespread African support were dashed when the suggested composition of the Council was announced. It was to be chaired by the State President himself, and consist of the six Chief Ministers of the non-independent homelands; ten representatives (chosen by the State President) of Africans settled permanently in white areas; a number of cabinet members nominated by the State President; three chairmen of ministerial councils; and ten other members again nominated by the State President.

The composition of the proposed council indicated Botha's determination to retain control, and his view of Africans as divided into separate national groups. Colin Eglin, the PFP leader, said that no major African leader would take part in negotiations designed to promote the modernization of apartheid. And he was right. Although Heunis later said that the government would be sympathetic if Africans outside the homelands wished to elect their representatives to the council; and although F. W. de Klerk explained to a Swiss audience that the proposal was an interim measure which would lead to high-level authorities with decision-making powers, the council was rejected by Africans. Buthelezi repudiated it, saying that the prerequisites for negotiations were the release of Mandela and the abandonment of the tricameral parliament. Even Africans, dismissed by the militants as 'puppets', rejected it. Among them was the Reverend Sam Buti, who had been Mayor of Alexandra township. Buti urged those who might be invited to serve on the council to refuse; 'to avoid falling into the trap of consciously or unconsciously propagating the policy of apartheid presented by the State President as reform' (Pottinger 1988: 128).

Following the early set backs the council proposal went through further stages until a new draft emerged in June 1988, but that was no improvement. It was equally dominated by homeland leaders, ministers, officials and members nominated by the President. Therefore while protesting support for the principle of African participation in decision making and power sharing, Botha ran the idea into the sand because he was not prepared to let control slip from the government's hands.

A similar pattern of unfulfilled expectations characterized the secret meetings with Mandela. The government's negotiating group had regular meetings with him from May 1988. At the same time Mandela was given improved living conditions, and was allowed accompanied trips outside prison – presumably on the assumption that he would in time be released. In July 1989 Mandela was taken to see Botha himself at the Tuynhuys – the State President's residence. Mandela later described it as mainly a social visit during which Botha was 'unfailingly courteous, deferential and friendly'. The only point of tension was when Mandela, leaving the social chat aside, asked Botha to release all political prisoners. Botha said that he was afraid he could not do that (Mandela 1994: 539). Botha's aim was not to negotiate with Mandela on points of political substance, but was limited to exploring how Mandela could be released without the government losing face. Botha did not want to show signs of weakness and therefore his aim was to persuade Mandela to renounce violence in return for freedom. There was no follow-up to that meeting, as shortly afterwards Botha stood down as State President.

More characteristic of the final years of Botha's presidency than the meeting with Mandela and the search for constitutional arrangements was the continuing struggle with the African organizations. In February 1988 the government banned seventeen more organizations and their leading figures – including Azapo and the UDF – and issued elaborate regulations in an attempt to restrict the activities of COSATU. Yet African resistance was irrepressible. From the ashes of the UDF arose the phoenix of the Mass Democratic Movement (MDM), made up of a number of organizations including the UDF and COSATU. Titus Mafolo, an MDM leader, explained that the new movement was designed to unite the masses and the working classes in the struggle for liberation. In August 1989 the MDM issued a statement saying that it considered all restricted organizations to be unbanned, and announcing a widespread defiance campaign against apartheid laws.

The Changing Scene on the Frontiers

There was little relief for Pretoria on the borders. It continued to try to bend the neighbouring states to its will by a combination of economic and military measures, but it was circumscribed by changing international circumstances. At the Commonwealth Vancouver Conference in 1987, at which Mozambique was represented, not only did the leaders describe Pretoria's rejection of the EPG's efforts as 'nothing less than a tragedy', the majority of them agreed to impose further sanctions. The exception was Britain, but London applied a different form of pressure on Pretoria, by strengthening its commitment to the southern African region. It did this through development aid, which included military training for the Zimbabwe, Mozambique and Swaziland forces. German and French regional involvement was also enhanced in 1987, by visits to Mozambique from the German Chancellor, Helmut Kohl, and the French Foreign Minister. In the following year the US State Department issued a report strongly condemning the atrocities of Renamo, the South African backed dissident movement, which used terror tactics in its conflict with the Mozambique government. Against this background of western involvement Pretoria sought to improve its relations with Mozambique, now led by President Joaquam Chissano, who had succeeded to the presidency following the death of Samora Machel in an air crash. Pretoria reaffirmed the Nkomati Accord, and this time with better intentions.

In one respect, however, Botha's aggression on the borders paid dividends. Many of the MK's ambitions were frustrated. In this Pretoria gained an unexpected ally as, in the late 1980s, the Soviet Union under Mikhail Gorbachev, steadily withdrew its support for the armed struggle and instead preached peaceful negotiation. That meant that from Pretoria's viewpoint the MK was kept mainly at arm's length. While some guerilla fighters were infiltrated into the country their activities were not a major military threat. In 1986 there were more attacks than ever before – 228 of them – but most were on a small scale and 160 MK personnel were killed or captured, which represented one-third of the losses since 1977. An ANC document of October 1986 admitted that: 'Despite all our efforts we have not come anywhere near the achievement of the objectives we set ourselves'. Tom Lodge concluded that eighteen months after Kabwe the expectations of the conference had not been realized. The MK campaign, he wrote, 'falls well short of representing a major threat to the physical security of apartheid's beneficiaries, of the operations of government outside the townships, or the day to day functioning of the economy' (*SA Review* 1987: 8–10). Yet some members of Pretoria's security services were perceptive enough to recognize that MK should be judged more broadly than its military achievements. Craig Williamson challenged the view that MK was a failure. 'If,' he stated, 'one defines Umkhonto as an organisation of "political fighters", which aims to increase the degree of popular participation in the "struggle" to the level which ANC revolutionary aims become general aims, then Umkhonto has not yet failed' (IRR 1987/8: 700).

The ANC's 1988 New Year message mirrored Williamson's views. It acknowledged setbacks, but also identified a number of advances, including broadening its support base within the country, and obliging the government to rely increasingly on force. However, the message had changed from Kabwe – now there was talk of negotiation as well as continuing the armed struggle. In July the ANC released a document, 'Constitutional Guidelines for a Democratic South Africa', which called for a multi-party democracy in a unitary state; universal suffrage based on one person one vote; a bill of rights; protection of cultural and language rights; a ban on all forms of racism; independent trade unions; and a mixed economy. A further major step along the road towards negotiation was taken when in 1989 the Harare Declaration was agreed by the OAU, and accepted by the ANC. 'We believe,' it stated rather ponderously, 'that a conjunction of circumstances exists, which, if there is a demonstrable readiness on the part of the Pretoria regime to engage in negotiations genuinely and seriously, could create the possibility to end apartheid through negotiations'. The Declaration went on to detail the nature of the society supported by the ANC as well as its preconditions and the guidelines for negotiation. But it was not all plain sailing, for militant ANC members opposed the Declaration and continued to put their faith in the armed struggle. The problem of reconciling these internal differences was compounded late in 1989 when Tambo was incapacitated by a stroke.

The greatest regional change, however, came not on South Africa's immediate borders, but to the West, in Angola, which had a direct impact on SWA/Namibia. Pretoria had based its military presence in Angola on two premises – first it was necessary to counter the communist threat to the whole region, and second to defend South West Africa against SWAPO. In November 1987 Magnus Malan was still making the same point. Without South Africa, he claimed, 'the whole of Southern Africa would be destabilised and subject to Russian domination' (*Citizen*, Johannesburg, 13 November 1987). Yet by early 1988 the situation in Angola had turned against Pretoria following the battle of Cuito Cuanavale, when South African troops clashed directly with Cuban forces. The battle itself was closely contested, but it was Pretoria which suffered the strategic defeat. It was forced to absorb two hard lessons; first that it had lost control of the air, because its ageing Mirages were no match for the Cuban Migs; and second that the loss of white lives was politically unsustainable in defence of a territory which was remote for most white South Africans.

As a result Pretoria abandoned the Angolan battle field for the negotiating table. After tortuous discussions an agreement, brokered by Chester Crocker of the US State Department, was reached whereby Cuban and South African forces would withdraw from Angola; and whereby Pretoria would implement UN resolution 435 to transform South West Africa into an independent Namibia in 1990. In the broad scheme of things the Namibian settlement illustrated the impact of prolonged international pressure on Pretoria. The territory that Louis Botha had conquered, that Smuts had negotiated as a mandate, and that successive white governments had hoped to incorporate into the South African state, was abandoned. Yet it was abandoned in the same spirit as Botha introduced his reforms – it was a worthwhile sacrifice to preserve the core white state.

Part VI

Forging the New South Africa

20

In Search of a New South Africa

On 19 January 1989 Botha had a stroke which temporarily incapacitated him. Heunis became acting State President. A month later, Botha, without consulting his cabinet colleagues, wrote from his sick bed to the chairman of the NP caucus to say that the offices of party leader and State President should be separated. Botha stated that he would remain President as 'a special force for cohesion in our country', but the NP should elect a new party leader. Despite disquiet among members about the constitutional propriety of dividing the two offices, and the arbitrary way in which Botha had behaved, the NP caucus went ahead to elect a new leader. Four candidates stood: Heunis, de Klerk, Pik Botha and Barend du Plessis (the Minister of Finance). Heunis and Pik Botha, ever the bridesmaids, were soon eliminated leaving the field to de Klerk, who was regarded as the conservative candidate, and du Plessis from the party's 'verligte' wing. When the final votes were counted de Klerk scraped home by 69 votes to 61.

The separation of the two offices, with their rival poles of power, inevitably led to tension. De Klerk, determined to resolve the situation, gained the agreement of the NP's National Council that the interests of the country were best served when the party leader was also State President. Under pressure Botha agreed to call a white election for September, after which he said he would resign. But he did not go quietly or graciously, nor did he wait. Following furious rows with de Klerk and the cabinet, he announced his immediate resignation from office in an angry, confused television broadcast on 14 August 1989. De Klerk was elected the new State President.

De Klerk, who had led the Transvaal NP since the overthrow of Treurnicht, was different in style, temperament and experience to his predecessor. He was usually courteous, and a team man with a reputation for cautious pragmatism. He had not been a member of Botha's inner circle, nor did he have strong links with the security establishment, but, as Transvaal leader, he had sat on the State Security Council. Although not close to Botha he was a National Party man through and through. His grandfather had been a friend of Paul Kruger, his father had served in NP cabinets under three Prime Ministers, and his uncle, by marriage, was Jan Strijdom. De Klerk's own cabinet experience had not been in high-profile roles, but had included Home Affairs and Education. In these posts he had pursued conservative policies. For example, as Minister of Education he had opposed the entry of black students into white universities, and acted harshly against radical students. Now, as party leader and State President he faced multiple tasks: to rally a divided party behind him; to establish the primacy of the political arm of government over the security establishment; to respond to the continued challenge of black resistance; and to revive the economy despite international sanctions.

De Klerk hardly had time to draw breath before he faced the September 1989 election. With so little time to prepare, the campaign followed a predictable pattern, with no signs of fundamental change, and certainly no indication that this would be the last exclusively white election. With minor variations it was fought along similar lines to the recent past. The NP proclaimed its commitment to negotiations involving all, but based on separate groups which would handle their own affairs and come together on common affairs. De Klerk denounced those who had made contact with the ANC abroad. The CP attacked the government for mismanagement, for selling out to blacks inside the country and to the UN in Namibia. Instead it preached the Verwoerdian verities of separate races, nations and states. The 'liberal' elements of white politics had reordered themselves into the Democratic Party (DP), which was led by a triumvirate of Zach de Beer, Dennis Worrall and Wynand Malan. The DP sought a non-racial South Africa – it favoured negotiation, universal suffrage and a single country governed on federal lines. When the votes were counted the result reflected an uncertain, divided white society. The NP had again lost support on both sides. NP candidates were returned in 93 of the 166 seats, with 48 per cent of the vote. The party had lost 17 seats to the CP which had 39 seats from 31 per cent of the vote; and 12 to the DP which had 33 seats from 21 per cent. It was the first time since 1958 that the NP had less than half the total votes.

The loss of white votes was not the government's only worry. Outside the white political system it was faced by renewed black protests. At the time of the election the MDM organized demonstrations, strikes, marches and school boycotts. In Lenasia, on the West Rand, an effigy of de Klerk was burned, along with others of J. N. Reddy and Allan Hendrickse, the leaders of the Indian and Coloured chambers. Four days before the election a protest march in Cape Town was broken up by police, using tear gas, whips, water cannon and purple dye; and they arrested more than 500 people, including Allan Boesak. Undeterred the MDM called a two-day strike over the election period, which gained a mass response, and led to even more serious clashes with the police in which 23 people were reported killed. It was another tragedy, and another public relations disaster for the government (IRR 1989/90: 225).

A stalemate had been reached in which the repressive capacity of the state could deny a clear victory to the mass movement and counter the military threat of MK; while the mass movement was powerful enough to create turmoil, deny legitimacy to the government and disrupt the economy. Most people assumed that the stalemate would persist. The government, argued Glenn Moss and Ingred Obery in 1989, 'could persist and maintain military power for a very long time, even though this could mean international isolation, economic decline, and continued warfare'. They asked 'whether popular mass mobilisation can overthrow a regime in the absence of internal breakdown of the state' (*SA Review* 1989: 7).

Yet, even if the government could not be overthrown, the black protests, the white election results and the continued international economic pressure persuaded it that it could not just drift, that a new initiative was needed. Adriaan Vlok, the tough Minister of Law and Order, admitted that 'everyone – including the Police, the government and the country – realise that the status quo cannot continue' (O'Meara 1996: 402). De Klerk showed early signs of easing the tension when he relaxed the restrictions on peaceful protest marches, and went on to release eight prominent political prisoners, including Walter Sisulu. In January 1990, de Klerk told a police conference that in the past they had been asked to undertake two main tasks. One, he said, was 'to handle typical criminal type situations'; but you also had 'a control function connected with a specific political party . . . You will no longer be required to prevent people gathering to canvass support for their views. We don't want to use you any more as instruments to reach certain political goals' (Amnesty 1992: 11).

Uncertainty was not confined to the government. As noted earlier a reassessment was taking place inside the ANC driven by those who were prepared to consider negotiation. It was far from a united position, but Tambo, in commending the Harare Declaration, called on all South Africans to enter discussions 'and make proposals so that finally a position emerges which reflects the broadest national consensus' (Thomas 1996: 212). A similar theme emerged at the SACP's 7th Congress held in Cuba in 1989. A new programme was approved – 'The Path to Power' – which, while reaffirming the 'national struggle' as a stage towards socialism, addressed the possibility of negotiations. The delegates agreed that armed struggle was not a counter to 'dialogue, negotiation and justified compromise, as if they were mutually exclusive categories'; and that all struggles end in negotiation (Liebenberg and Spies 1994: 45).

Taking the Tide at the Full: De Klerk and Mandela

It is one thing to discuss fundamental change; it is another to act on it. F. W. de Klerk did just that on 2 February 1990. He transformed South Africa. In his first address to parliament as State President he announced the lifting of bans on all political parties, the end of apartheid, and the start of negotiations for a new political dispensation to embrace everybody. He called on South Africans to take 'the road of drastic change', to put aside divisions and 'build a broad consensus about the fundamentals of a new, realistic and democratic dispensation'. 'Our country,' he said, 'and all its people have been embroiled in conflict, tension and violent struggle for decades. It is time for us to break out of the cycle of violence and break through to peace and reconciliation' (De Klerk 1991: 34–46). De Klerk and his cabinet colleagues had taken the momentous decision to fly in the face of South Africa's previous history by bringing an end to white domination of the state. Reforming steps had been taken before, and, with the wisdom of retrospect, it is easy to identify the circumstances that led to the decision, but at the time it came as a surprise to almost everybody. It was de Klerk and his cabinet who made the crucial break.

Although a man of strong religious conviction, de Klerk initiated radical change not because of a sudden moral conversion but for practical reasons which led to a moral conclusion. True to his long commitment to the NP, de Klerk argued that initially the concept of apartheid had an ethical purpose in that it aimed to provide justice and opportunities for all through the development of separate nation states. However, he said he now realized that it had failed as a policy, and therefore as a moral cause. De Klerk told parliament that it was clear that 'our efforts over a period of 40 years to find moral grounds for the whites of South Africa to seek their own fatherland have not succeeded' (HA 9 February 1990). Later he confessed that we 'came to the conclusion that we had dismally failed in bringing justice to all South Africans through the establishment of nation states . . . it had just resulted in racial discrimination and minority domination. It was a matter of conscience to say we were wrong' (Waldmeir 1997: 115). Nor had apartheid brought security for whites at home or acceptance abroad. 'We had to escape from a corner where everything had stagnated in confrontation'. Consequently the state had to be rebuilt on different principles, including the abandonment of the concept of separate nationalisms.

Three factors determined the timing of de Klerk's action. First was the chronic problem of internal order. Although in security terms the government was not defeated, the black urban risings of the mid-1980s and the continued penetration by the MK steadily increased the cost – in terms of resources and people – of retaining white power. The alternative to a negotiated settlement, declared de Klerk, was 'growing violence, tension and conflict' (De Klerk 1991: 44). Second, internal disorder and international pressure had created economic stagnation which could only be resolved by a political settlement. During the 1980s economic problems had become acute, with increasing unemployment, high inflation and a fall in the standard of living for most South Africans. Third, the end of the cold war and the collapse of communism had transformed the global scene, removing white fears of a total onslaught, and weakening the ANC because its communist backers were neither willing nor able to continue supporting a liberation struggle. 'It was as if God had taken a hand', said de Klerk, '[it is] a new turn in world history.' He calculated that in these circumstances the ANC would be ready to compromise, and therefore he seized the initiative while the NP was still strong, and the ANC confused. 'We have not waited,' he said, 'until the position of power turned against us before we decided to negotiate a peaceful settlement' (SA Govt 1993). 'The biggest risk today is to take no risks at all', wrote Pieter de Lange (Waldmeir 1997: 53).

Ten days after de Klerk's speech Nelson Mandela was released from prison. His first public action was to address a crowd from the balcony of the Town Hall in Cape Town. It was a narrowly focused speech directed mainly at the party, to reassure it. Although he spoke of de Klerk as 'a man of integrity', Mandela was at pains to emphasize his loyalty to Congress. He had not, he stated, made secret personal arrangements with the government and he called for an intensification of the struggle on all fronts. There was nothing in the speech of a broad vision for a future South Africa. However, when he met journalists on the following day it was a different Mandela – the remarkable man who after twenty-seven years in jail came out preaching reconciliation not revenge. He spoke of understanding white fears, the need to reassure them, to recognize them as fellow South Africans, and to encourage them to help build a new South Africa. While still in prison he had affirmed time after time that although the ANC had been forced to take up arms, violence could never be the ultimate solution; that a settlement must be negotiated. Like de Klerk he now called on all South Africans to work together to reach that settlement. In the affairs of men Mandela and de Klerk had taken a tide at the flood.

For its part the ANC never lost faith in final victory, but there was no immediate prospect of overthrowing the government. It had support from Africans at home, and sympathy within the international community, but in military terms it had lost its communist backers and had been forced to withdraw from many of its southern African bases. Slovo, when asked whether there was an alternative to negotiation, answered: 'In a way the answer is yes. We could have gone on with a combination of armed struggle and political assault. And in the end, inevitably, after five, ten or fifteen years we would have won. But this victory is speculative . . . we must never forget that we are engaged in negotiations with a revolutionary purpose.' We could, he said, have inherited a devastated country. 'We could have won the war, but we might have lost the revolution' (*SA Communist* no.4 1993). De Klerk's put further pressure on the ANC, through the international sympathy his initiative received. To counter that the ANC quickly organized overseas tours for Mandela in which he urged continued support for sanctions and the liberation struggle. Wherever he went he was greeted as a hero. In the US he received an enthusiastic reception and was only the third private person to address Congress. Yet there was a nagging doubt for the ANC that the visits achieved more in symbolism than substance, as de Klerk continued to gain support. Suspicion also remained in the West, certainly among conservatives, about the ANC's old sponsors, and that was brought home again when Mandela spoke in favour of Fidel Castro of Cuba and Colonel Gaddafi of Libya during his US tour. In July 1991 President George Bush ended sanctions against South Africa with hardly a whimper from Congress.

Visions of the Future

Following de Klerk's initiative all the party leaders faced a set of demanding questions. Should they join the negotiations? If so on what terms? On what principles should they stand firm and on what compromise? Should they pull out of the negotiations if they were not gaining their ends? Could they carry their followers with them? Whatever the answers to such questions they were all determined to maximize their position, to gain as much ground as possible. The early messages were therefore full of bravado that their particular viewpoint would prevail. Yet, above all the tactical considerations was a central question: What was their vision of the future, post apartheid South Africa? Each party had a distinctive response to that central question, which reflected not only their values and principles but power considerations. The ANC was keen on majority rule, not simply because it thought it right, but because it was confident it could gain an electoral majority. Inkatha favoured regionalism because its main strength was in one region – KwaZulu/Natal.

The NP supported groups because it wanted the white group to retain substantial influence within the new state. The white right was opposed to the whole endeavour because change could only weaken its position. A diversity of visions therefore emerged as the political parties staked out their claims.

The National Party

The NP now accepted that all people living in the Republic must be recognized as citizens and enjoy political rights. In short they were all 'South Africans'. De Klerk told parliament that the aim was to create a situation in which 'every inhabitant will enjoy equal rights, treatment and opportunity'. Yet, at the same time, he stressed that South Africa was a complex society consisting of distinct groups, with different cultures, languages and histories. Group identity should therefore be reflected in the structure of the new state. There was no point, he argued, in abandoning the domination of a white minority only to replace it with the domination of an African majority. The politics of 'winner takes all' was inappropriate for South Africa. De Klerk put the NP's position in a nutshell when he stated that 'a party which wins 51 per cent of the vote should not get 100 per cent of the power' (Meredith 1997: 453). Instead the state should be based on 'power sharing'. There was, said de Klerk, no escaping the fact that all South Africans shared a common destiny, that different groups and races had to live together in the same borders, and that whites had to co-exist with other peoples. He appealed for a democratic consensus built on acceptance of a universal franchise, but an absence of domination of one group over others. It was not, he said, the government's intention 'that any group – however defined – shall be favoured in relation to others'. Within this context the 'self-governing' Bantustans would be part of the new state, while the 'independent' Bantustans would be free to decide their own future.

The NP's position was spelt out in greater detail by Dr Gerrit Viljoen, Minister of Constitutional Development. He told parliament that the most important shift in the government's thinking was 'the acceptance of the concept of one nation in an undivided South Africa'. Nation building, he said, had been a long and often painful process. Previously it had been exclusive now it would be inclusive. It was time 'to complete the broadening of our nationhood to comprise all South Africans irrespective of race or ethnic origin'. He envisaged a new South Africa which 'binds together all its people into one nation composed of a diversity of recognized minorities, with common patriotism and loyalty to our nation, but without prejudicing the protection of the rights of minorities against discrimination': one nation with cultural diversity (HA 5 February 1990).

Viljoen argued that the new state should be built on a set of common principles: including the promotion of shared values, the elimination of discrimination, the entrenchment of individual justice and freedom of association. However, he was at pains to stress that the building blocks for the state must be 'groups'. The NP would insist, he said, on 'the protection of groups and minorities within . . . one nationhood'. Individuals, insisted Viljoen, would be able to select their own group, but consciously or unconsciously, he assumed they would be drawn along racial lines.

He spoke of the needs of 'the white population group for security against domination and for guarantees of a significant share in political decision making'. There had to be give and take, but, he said, there were matters which were unacceptable to the NP. These included 'a unitary system with a black majority', because that would imply that whites and others groups would 'virtually be reduced to political impotence' (HA 5 February 1990).

When Viljoen translated those points into constitutional proposals, he included universal adult franchise but not a common voters' roll, because, he argued, that would 'inevitably lead to majority domination over minorities'. An arithmetical majority was 'not the alpha and omega' of democracy. It would not fulfil the democratic purpose and would lead to renewed conflict. The essence of democracy, he said, lay in accountability, confidence in elected representatives and the ability to change governments. In hetrogeneous societies these could only be achieved by recognizing the rights of groups. Each group would therefore have its own voters' roll, and function as a constitutionally defined political unit. Further the group principle would be the basis of power sharing and lead to checks and balances in the government. To achieve that Viljoen proposed that the structure of government should include a mixed party cabinet; a rotating Presidency (which would change annually between the leaders of three main parties); and a two-chamber parliament – a House of Representatives elected by universal franchise, and a Senate drawn from groups and regions. Viljoen denied that this was apartheid in disguise. The proposals should, he stated, be judged in terms of the future not the past, with the emphasis on 'one nation and nation building', the end of discrimination and political rights for all (HA 12 February 1990).

Viewed overall the NP had made a clear break with the past – abandoning exclusive white rule, preaching a single nation, opening up political processes, and recognizing that every citizen had political rights. Opponents who accused it of trying to preserve the exclusive white control of apartheid were mistaken. However, in another sense the NP remained wedded to the past, to the concept of a divided society. It was to be a 'multi-group' if not a 'multi-national' state. There was an element of ambiguity about the proposed groups, but the government's thinking was captured when Viljoen spoke of 'the National Party as representative and mandate holder for the whites'. The intention was that whites would negotiate themselves into a powerful if not a dominant position, and be able to exercise a veto over aspects of government. At the same time they would be able to preserve their life-style, culture, language and property rights. In line with this thinking the NP proposed that the new constitution should be drawn up by a body composed of the representatives of major established parties. The buzz term, wrote Dan O'Meara, was 'elite pacting' by which, through bargaining, trade-offs and compromises, group leaders would shape political activity (O'Meara 1996: 405).

The African National Congress

Initially the ANC was caught off guard by the speed and scope of de Klerk's proposals, and was ill prepared for negotiations. Most members had anticipated a continued struggle. 'We defined the struggle,' said an ANC leader, 'as a protracted people's war in which partial and general uprisings would play an important role. This was to culminate in the seizure of power in which the armed elements would be crucial' (*Mayibuye*, December 1990). While its concentration had been on fighting the apartheid regime the ANC had been bound together more by what it opposed than a clear picture of what it proposed; it had broad aspirations rather than detailed plans. In Slovo's words: 'We've had to devote the bulk of our energies to getting here not to what we're going to do when we arrive' (Waldmeir 1997: 163). Added to that it could not match the efficiency of the government's bureaucracy or the NP's party machine. The ANC therefore had to transform itself while negotiating to transform the state. Much of its energy was spent in internal concerns – in building a mass political party from a banned liberation movement, and creating an effective organization.

The enterprise was complicated by the fact that as an illegal body it had not been able to register members inside South Africa; and by the need to forge a single movement from diverse elements with very different experiences – the exiles returning from abroad, the guerilla fighters in their camps, the prisoners released from long years of detention, together with those who had struggled at home in the UDF, COSATU, the street committees, student and civic associations. Many leaders were meeting for the first time. Further the movement was an alliance of the ANC, SACP and COSATU, each with its own structure and viewpoint, plus a degree of autonomy enjoyed by MK. In the year following Mandela's release there was hectic internal activity – registering and recruiting members, creating an administration and reaching accommodation within the alliance. In its initial contacts with the government the ANC concentrated less on long-term constitutional issues than immediate concerns, such as the release of political prisoners and the return of exiles.

However, despite the uncertainty, the ANC's general position had been known from the time of the Freedom Charter, and had been reaffirmed in July 1988 in the party's 'Constitutional Guidelines for a Democratic South Africa'. That document called for a single South African nation and state led by a powerful central government. The state would pursue policies 'to promote the growth of a single national identity and loyalty binding on all South Africans', while recognizing 'linguistic and cultural diversity'. Support was given for a unitary, democratic, non racial state, in which sovereignty would lie with the people as a whole through a universal franchise based on the principle of one person, one vote. The central government would delegate powers to subordinate authorities; it would introduce a Bill of Rights – guaranteeing individual rights irrespective of race, colour, sex, and creed; and 'ensure that the economy serves the interests and well being of the entire population' (Johns and Davis 1991: 302–3).

In his earlier contacts with the government Mandela had identified challenges that lay ahead. He had told both Botha and de Klerk that two issues had to be resolved: 'First the demand for majority rule in a unitary state; secondly, the concern of white South Africa over this demand, as well as the insistence of whites on structural guarantees that majority rule will not mean domination of the white minority by blacks.' Although he recognized the dilemma Mandela never abandoned his belief that the democratic state must rest on the pillar of majority rule. There could, he claimed, never be peace and stability unless that were accepted. He dismissed the idea of democracy via group rights. He argued that despite the NP's claim that it was a way of protecting minorities, it seemed to be an attempt to ensure that white control would be preserved – to ensure that the loser takes all. Mandela told de Klerk that 'it gave the impression that he [de Klerk] wanted to modernise apartheid without abandoning it', and that was damaging for the whites, because it would do more to increase black fears than allay white ones. 'The ANC,' he said, 'had not struggled against apartheid for seventy-five years only to yield to a disguised form of it' (Mandela 1994: 536/544).

The ANC also demanded that the new constitution should be drawn up by a popularly elected assembly: that those who created the constitution should be the choice of the people as a whole and not the representatives of separate groups. In demanding that the ANC presented itself not as a sectional political party; but rather as 'the guardian of national goals and interests', seeking not 'an ANC constitution but a South African constitution'. It was, in the words of Oliver Tambo, poised 'to fulfil its historic mission of liberating the overwhelming majority of our people' (*Mayibuye*, December 1990/February 1991). To achieve that it would be dangerous to sit back and let the government dictate the negotiating process, and the procedure for making a new constitution. In ANC eyes the government could not be both the referee and a player. Mandela stated: 'The point which must be clearly understood is that the struggle is not over, and negotiations themselves are a theatre of struggle, subject to advances and reverses as any other form of struggle' (Mandela 1994: 584).

Inkatha

In July 1990, in the light of changed circumstances, the Inkatha movement converted itself into a political party – the Inkatha Freedom Party (IFP). Buthelezi stated that because of persistent opposition to apartheid from Inkatha the time had never been better for negotiations. In approaching the negotiations the IFP, like the ANC and the government, spoke of a common South African nationalism. 'There is,' said Buthelezi, 'one South Africa; there is one body politic; there shall be one Parliament and it shall be guided by the majority' (Buthelezi 1990: 2). However, Inkatha shared the NP's opposition to simple majority rule. Buthelezi declared: 'There is nothing that justifies the thought that a one man one vote system of government in a unitary state employing winner takes all politics is the only democracy fit for mankind' (IRR 1991/2: 33). He stressed the need for a multi-party process and rejected the ANC's claim to be the sole legitimate voice of the African majority. In Buthelezi's eyes the lines were now drawn between those like the IFP, who favoured a multi-party, federal state built on free-market principles, and those, like the ANC, who wanted a one-party, socialist, unitary state. National unity, argued Buthelezi, could not be based on a single dominant party. Inkatha did not claim that for itself, and saw the ANC as just one among many parties. He dismissed ANC claims that the NP had been brought to negotiations by the armed struggle. Buthelezi pointed out that the politics of violence – of mass insurrection, guerilla fighters and bombing – had failed to overthrow the government, and claimed that continued violence could only divide Africans further. He presented himself as the true inheritor of the ANC's past by seeking justice through non-violent means.

Although Buthelezi's main concern was the ANC, he was also suspicious of the government. He pointed out that he had always refused 'independence' for KwaZulu because he believed it was part of a single South Africa, and he was distrustful of the NP's 'group' proposals. Like the ANC he feared they could be apartheid in another guise. Yet ironically Inkatha's principal concern was the future of a particular people/group – the Zulus, with their distinctive identity, history, culture, traditional rulers and political structure. The IFP's position was not that Zulus would opt out of South Africa, rather they would be a major force in the new state, while at the same time enjoying a large degree of self rule within KwaZulu. 'Zulus are here to stay as Zulus,' said Buthelezi. 'We are proud South Africans because we are also proud Zulus. We will be part of the new South Africa as KwaZulu.'

Inkatha's emphasis on Zulu interests, and the concentration of its supporters in KwaZulu, increasingly led it to favour a federal form of government. Federalism implies a formal division of powers between the centre and the provinces, but to describe a government as 'federal' or 'unitary' is to make a relative judgement. Governments are ranged along a continuum with 'strong unitary' at one end and 'strong federal' at the other. Inkatha favoured the strong federal end, while the ANC wanted a strong unitary state. Buthelezi spoke of his opposition to oppressive centralized government, and gave as an example the Soviet Union (IRR 1991/2: 32). In that spirit the KwaZulu legislature approved a constitution in December 1992 which was a declaration of provincial autonomy. It envisaged KwaZulu/Natal as a member state of the Federal Republic of South Africa – with authority to conscript its own militia, while federal forces could not be stationed there; in which no central law could override KwaZulu law; and no central taxes could be levied without KwaZulu approval. Buthelezi claimed that when the constitution was ratified by the KwaZulu legislature it would become 'the supreme law of the land . . . in spite of whatever course the negotiations at central level happen to take' (IRR 1992/3: 40).

That constitution was never implemented, but tension steadily increased between the ANC and IFP. In 1992 at Shaka Day celebrations (in honour of the founder of the Zulu nation) Buthelezi said that such Zulu ceremonies 'remind us of who we are, where we came from, and where our history has decreed we should end'. He challenged the rights of others to determine the future of the Zulus. He spoke of ANC plots to eliminate KwaZulu entirely. 'There is a campaign,' he said, 'to smash the Zulu sense of identity in a desperate attempt to make you obedient to those who want to destroy KwaZulu. We were born Zulu South Africans and will die Zulu South Africans and we have an historic responsibility to make our contribution to the emergence of a new, just, free and prosperous South Africa'.

Yet for all Buthelezi's rhetoric Zulus themselves were deeply divided. Many were ANC supporters, opposed to the KwaZulu government. In broad terms Inkatha's main strength lay in the rural areas and among traditionally-minded Zulus – chiefs, councillors, KwaZulu civil servants, and migrant workers living in hostels away from home; while the ANC's main support came from the professional classes and permanent urban dwellers.

The White Right

The 'white right' was not a single movement. It was mainly but not entirely composed of Afrikaners, and combined racial concerns with those of preserving an Afrikaner/white identity and power. Despite its differences, the right wing did have common themes – notably that South Africa was not a single nation, but composed of separate nations. To ignore that would, the right wing argued, lead to conflict and disaster. In particular Afrikaners/whites had a right to be masters of their own nation-state. Power sharing was a government lie. You do not share power: you either have it or not. For the future as in the past, argued the right, the way forward lay in separation, in developing distinctive nation states for the benefit of all races. The assumptions made by Verwoerd were sound and should be the foundation for the future as in the past.

Although it shared those common themes the white right was often character-ized more by division than unity. One source of dispute was the form and size of the future white state. Some favoured retaining the existing position, by hiving off the African homelands and retaining the rest of the country under white control. Others were more concerned with establishing a distinctive 'volkstaat', exclusive to whites, but there was uncertainty about its extent and nature. Some advocated building it around the old Transvaal and Orange Free State republics. Others had more modest territorial ambitions, and one group (Afrikaner Vryheidstigting) purchased a small area in the northern Cape, Orania, where they set out to estab-lish an exclusively white society. Others favoured a federal solution, in which one or more provinces would be white controlled, but they too faced the geographical and demographic problems. Whites were spread across the country and however the volkstaat advocates twisted and turned they could not identify an area in which Afrikaners/whites formed a majority. Further differences existed in the methods right wingers were prepared to use in pursuit of their aims. The CP operated through parliament, whereas the militaristic AWB, led by the bombastic Eugene TerreBlanche, constantly threatened to use force. The differences were also apparent in attitudes towards the negotiations. Some, like the AWB, were completely opposed to them. The CP floated in and out but eventually refused to participate in the 1994 election; whereas the 'Freedom Front', formed towards the end of the process, opted in.

The major right-wing party was the CP, which was led by Treurnicht until his death in April 1993, when he was replaced by Dr Ferdi Hartzenberg. The CP was fiercely opposed to de Klerk's initiative. Treurnicht described his speech of 2 February 1990 as 'the most revolutionary' ever heard in parliament. It flew, said Treurnicht, in the face of 350 years of South Africa's history. He accused de Klerk of behaving as though a new nation could be created at the drop of a hat. It could not, declared Treurnicht. He reaffirmed his faith in exclusive Afrikaner/white nationalism. 'The nationalism by which we are fired,' he said, 'will not be

dampened . . . it is nationalism against which the government will smash its head'
(HA 5 February 1990). The CP was committed to the 'continued existence of our
own people and our own fatherland' – for 'a free people is only free within its own
living space, under its own government'. Because of that the CP would offer to
other nations what it asked for itself – separation in its own fatherland.

Treurnicht argued that it was nonsense to speak of non-racialism. 'We do not,'
he said, 'have a common tie which binds us so tightly together when we can speak
of one community. It is absolute nonsense to speak of a non racial community' (HA
29 March 1990). The government's efforts to bring all nations into one would lead
to a Tower of Babel, similar to the chaos in Nigeria. Treurnicht accused de Klerk
of abandoning his own people. Instead of defending them the State President was
now reducing the rightful rulers of South Africa to a minority group. 'We as a
people', proclaimed Treurnicht, 'do not want to be ruled by any other people or
combination of people' (HA 29 March 1990). Yet the government had legalized
terrorist organizations, and had released terrorist and communist, who had been
convicted of the equivalent of high treason. De Klerk was putting the country on
the road to conflict and ruin. His action had awakened the tiger in the Afrikaner
and the crocodile in the African. He had created conditions for a black takeover of
South Africa, but the CP, supported by the majority of the Afrikaner people, would
resist that to the end.

The Pan Africanist Congress and the Democratic Party

Finally, two very different reactions to de Klerk's initiative were provided by the
PAC and the DP. From the beginning the PAC was sceptical about negotiations.
In August 1989 Zephania Mothopeng ruled out the possibility of talks with the
government until the balance of forces was in favour of the African people. It would
be foolish he said to talk while Pretoria had the upper hand. The PAC also distanced
itself from the Harare Declaration, and criticized the ANC for being prepared to
enter negotiations on that basis. The terms on which the PAC would be prepared
to talk included the return of land to the indigenous people, and the removal of the
pillars of apartheid (the Population Registration Act; the Land Acts of 1913 and
1936; the Group Areas Act; the tricameral parliament; the Bantu Education Act;
and the Bantustans). Some PAC members were convinced that those aims could
never be achieved by negotiation. Clarence Makewetu stated that the white-
dominated system could not be changed by negotiation but only on the battlefield
(IRR 1989/90: 741).

In contrast the DP – the party of liberal whites – embraced the government's
initiative. On behalf of the DP Colin Eglin welcomed de Klerk to the ranks of those
who were committed both to negotiation, and to nation building around a set of
democratic principles. Eglin pointed out that the DP had always supported the principles of non-racialism, individual rights, the rule of law based on equality of status,
and a common citizenship. 'For the DP,' he said 'it is not the party, it is the values
that are relevant' (IRR 1990/1: 29). Those values did not include the NP's insistence on group rights. Whites should not claim special privilege. Dennis Worrall

made that clear in March 1990 when he rejected the idea of a special constitutional niche for whites. 'It is not white numbers,' he said, 'that must be represented in government, it is rather the values and interests which whites have claimed for themselves and must be built into the new system of government' – including support for a private enterprise economy – 'and we believe the way to influence the economy is to be part of the political majority' (IRR 1989/90: 705).

Finally the DP was on common ground with Inkatha in supporting federalism, but its reasoning was different. The DP had long favoured it on 'liberal' principles: to restrict the powers of central government; to reflect the diversity of South Africa's peoples; and to bring decision making closer to local people. Zach de Beer stated that the DP's view bore no relationship to proposals for a 'race federation', but reflected federal ideas and principles found in the US, Australia and Canada.

21

Reaching Agreement:
Negotiation, Tension and Violence

It took more than four years from de Klerk's 2 February speech to achieve the birth of the new South Africa – years of negotiations, tension and violence. Often de Klerk must have felt that he had opened Pandora's Box rather than cleared the ground for a new South Africa. Formal multi-party talks did not start for almost two years. There were several reasons for the delay. Not only did the parties start from very different positions, other difficulties arose. First, the leaders had to rally their followers behind them, to persuade them to support the idea of negotiation and then to hold them together through the long process. Both Mandela and de Klerk had problems in that respect. Second, violence increased rather than decreased. De Klerk had hoped that his bold action would damp down the conflict. It did not. Conflict escalated. Third, exacerbated by the violence, friction arose between the leaders of the main parties, resulting in a lack of trust and in mutual suspicion. Fourth, there were disputes about the form the negotiations should take, and arrangements for governing the country during the interim period.

From the beginning the government and the ANC were the main participants in the process, and the relationship between them determined its progress. The binding element between the two was the conviction of leading figures that negotiation was the way forward. An encouraging start was made in May 1990 when government and ANC representatives met and signed the 'Groote Schuur Minute', which was based on a common commitment to eliminate violence and intimidation so that peaceful negotiations could proceed. It was agreed to establish a working group to open up lines of communication and iron out differences, and the government promised to consider lifting the State of Emergency. De Klerk spoke of 'an important breakthrough in the peaceful process we want to take place in South Africa' (IRR 1989/90: 732). However, differences soon surfaced. How could it be otherwise when they had fought each other for decades; when suspicion of each other's motives persisted; when they had such different hopes for the future; and when they both sought to gain maximum advantage for themselves from the negotiations?

The ANC never trusted Pretoria, stating that it could not be both a player and the referee of the process. The government argued that the ANC should abandon the armed struggle before discussions began. At first the ANC simply refused. An ANC spokesman retorted: 'We have always said the notion of unilaterally abandoning the armed struggle is out of the question. Any cessation of hostilities will have to be negotiated and will arise out of a mutually binding ceasefire' (IRR 1989/90: 681). However, in August 1990 it agreed to 'suspend' not abandon the armed struggle when it signed what became known as 'the Pretoria Minute'. In February 1991 the ANC and the government agreed that MK need not be disbanded until the transition to democracy was complete (Sparks 1995: 131). The ANC also wanted the release of all political prisoners, but there were conflicting definitions of who were 'political' prisoners – the ANC wanting a much broader definition than the government was initially prepared to concede. Dispute also arose about the body that would draft the constitution; the government favouring an assembly made up of the representatives of established parties, whereas the ANC wanted a popularly elected body. And so it went on with both sides blaming the other for slow progress.

The disputes were fought out on the international as well as the South African stage. Both Mandela and de Klerk undertook extensive international tours. They saw the international dimension as an extension of the negotiations at home. Their aim was to rally foreign support for their cause – in diplomatic and material terms – to gain legitimacy, and to encourage their party supporters. The difference in their aims and approaches was captured in their attitudes to sanctions. De Klerk was eager to see them lifted, as a reward for his initiative, as a means of reviving the economy and as a way of reassuring his followers that he had taken the right road. In contrast Mandela urged the international community to maintain pressure on Pretoria through sanctions, arguing that apartheid was still in place, and it was essential to continue the struggle until the racist regime was removed. The international reaction to these pleas was mixed, as some, but not all, Western states and business organizations steadily lifted sanctions. At the same time both Mandela and de Klerk were fêted overseas, and granted honours, including the joint award of the Nobel Peace Prize. Standing on the podium together to receive their prizes they captured the paradox of the peace process – they were at the same time the two major architects of the process and the two main political rivals.

The international dimension persisted. For instance, following the breakdown of negotiations in June 1992, the United Nations Security Council discussed the situation in South Africa. Appearing before the Council, Mandela accused the state of criminal intent in promoting violence. He spoke of a 'cold blooded strategy of state terror', and said that the ANC would only resume talks if the government was prepared to accept majority rule. In response Pik Botha accused the ANC/SACP alliance of building up arms caches in the northern Transvaal. He offered immediate talks with the ANC on the disputed issues. After hearing the evidence the Security Council trod a narrow path between the two parties. It adopted a resolution backing the government's call on the ANC to resume negotiations, and the ANC's demand to investigate the violence. With regard to the latter, it decided to investigate the situation by sending Cyrus Vance, a former US Secretary of State, to recommend measures to bring an end to the violence. The Council's response characterized external reactions throughout the period of negotiations. The thrust of the international community – as represented by the United Nations, the Organisation of African Unity, the European Community and the Commonwealth – was to urge an end to violence, and for the parties to push forward with negotiations. And the international dimension persisted until the end, when groups of foreign observers monitored the election of April 1994.

Reorganizing the ANC

Although the ANC accused the government of delaying formal negotiations so that the euphoria of Mandela's release would subside and divisions appear in ANC ranks, the ANC itself was in no state to face up immediately to complex, prolonged negotiations. For a time it was in disarray, with a gap between those who believed in the process and those who wanted to continue the armed struggle. Even Mandela could not resolve that. He had been a compelling symbol in prison but was an unknown to most members. Now that the symbol had become flesh they were unsure what to make of it. He was a man of a different generation and experience to most activists – far removed from the children of Soweto or the youths of mid-1980s rising – and without the experience of the UDF and MDM, or those who had served in exile or in the armed wing. Further it became known that he had conducted personal discussions with the government. Mandela's early impact was therefore mixed. The more militant elements were suspicious. Mac Maharaj stated: 'The word was that Madiba [Mandela] was wearing a three-piece suit, drinking wine, you name it – he was a sell out' (Meredith 1997: 411). Yet others were soon won over by him. They included the tough MK leader, Chris Hani. Hani stated: 'I think we're going to learn from him that we need to be better South Africans; to forgive and forget and to look forward to building a new South Africa' (Meredith 1997: 412). Steadily, the Mandela 'magic' – a combination of a powerful person-ality; plus charm, wisdom and tolerance; and combined with iron determination in seeking his ends – made him the ANC's undisputed leader. He still faced criticism but he had no rivals.

The ANC needed time to improve its weak organization and bureaucracy, to recruit and register members, to educate them to the new situation, to sustain pres-sure for the release of prisoners and to hasten the return of exiles. At the same time it was trying to transform itself from a liberation movement waging an armed struggle to a political party ready to negotiate and eventually to take over the reins of government. This was undertaken at a time when Tambo had been incapaci-tated by a stroke. In moments of self-confession the leaders admitted that they were 'snowed under' by the challenges (*Mayibuye*, March 1991). One of the challenges was internal co-ordination of the ANC, SACP and COSATU alliance. Slovo explained its workings. Each of the three sections, he said, had its own organ-ization, which co-ordinated their efforts through a committee which met every two months and a full executive which met at least once a year. Common de-cisions were reached and there was always consultation – formal and informal – but each organization retained its independence. They need not agree on all policy matters, and each could develop separate bilateral relations (*Mayibuye* April 1991).

Added to those organizational concerns the ANC continued to operate along twin tracks – one of negotiation, the other of armed struggle. In July 1990 the government uncovered 'Operation Vula' an MK initiative, which was kept secret even from Mandela. It had started in 1988 when Mac Maharaj, Siphiwe Nyanda and Ronnie Kasrils had been infiltrated back into the country on Tambo's orders, to strengthen the internal wing and provide intelligence appraisals of the internal situation. They had established themselves so successfully that even after de Klerk's initiative it was decided to keep them in place, as an insurance policy in case negotiations failed or Pretoria sprang a trap (Sparks 1995: 123). When the security forces exposed 'Vula' they assumed that it was preparing to stage a 'coup d'état'. At the same time active MK recruiting continued and according to Annette Seegers numbers increased substantially, from about 6,000 in 1990 to over 16,000 in 1994. Seegers suggested this had three aims: to enhance the ANC's bargaining position; to have a greater say in the formation of the future armed forces; and to control the energies of the township youth and ensure their support for the ANC (Seegers 1996: 277). To that may be added the continuing belief among many members that ultimately the issue could only be resolved by force.

The powerful image of the armed struggle was demonstrated when Slovo and Mandela proposed its suspension as the best way forward and a means of seizing the moral initiative from de Klerk. They decided that Slovo should introduce the idea because his revolutionary credentials were impeccable. Even so it met strong opposition before it was carried in the executive; and then it provoked a furore in the movement, with Slovo himself admitting that 90 per cent of ANC members saw it as a 'sell out'. The practical affect of suspension was negligible, but 'the rhetoric of revolution was deeply rooted among the mass of ANC supporters' (Meredith 1997: 417). Despite that the armed struggle was suspended in August, when the ANC and the government agreed the Pretoria Minute, but Mandela had to tread warily. On occasion he was shouted down when he called for an end to violence. Within the party he never succeeded in restraining such people as Peter Mokoba, the Youth Leader, who raised the cry 'Kill the Boer: Kill the farmer'; Harry Gwala, the vicious leader in Natal, who called for an end to negotiation and the resumption of armed struggle; and Winnie Mandela who, to the delight of militants but the distress of her estranged husband, accused the leaders of climbing into bed with the NP.

Such was the early disarray in the ANC camp that its first full conference inside South Africa since 1959 had to be postponed. Meanwhile a 'consultative conference' was held in December 1990, when the leaders came under more pressure. Mandela was criticized for his autocratic style; his failure to consult in the manner of the UDF; and for working too closely with de Klerk. The leadership was overruled when it suggested a moderation of the sanctions policy, and the conference called for greater efforts to release prisoners and dismantle the Bantustans. In July the full conference met. It was a massive affair with more than 2,000 delegates and 350 observers. The average age of the delegates was 34, with strong representation of the militant element. The conference decided to remain as a liberation movement rather than convert formally to a political party. It voted in favour of mass action, international sanctions, and the retention of an underground structure. It declared 1991 'a year of mass action for the transfer of power to the people'. In the elections Mandela became President, but several of the old guard failed to gain executive seats, while the youthful Cyril Ramaphosa, with a strong trade union background, became Secretary General.

The Resurgence of Violence

Disputes about the process of negotiation were frustrating, but they could be anticipated. More sinister was the violence that developed. It involved not only the ANC and the government, but Inkatha, the PAC, right-wing whites and some homeland governments. While the leaders of the major parties proclaimed their commitment to achieving change by peaceful means there were elements within or associated with all the parties who were determined to pursue their ends by force. Far from dousing it down de Klerk's initiative produced an outburst of violence, which rivalled anything that had gone before. While in 1989, 1,403 people were reported killed in political violence, in the following two years the figures rose to 3,699 and 2,760 respectively (IRR 1991/2: 27).

As in the past the violence took various forms, with overlap between 'political' and 'criminal' activity. The MK and the security forces continued their struggle; in the Cape the ANC and the PAC clashed in the black townships; and right-wing whites employed violence through organizations like the AWB. Elements of the government forces acted as a covert 'Third Force', employing both indiscriminate slaughter to cause panic, and hit squads with precise targets. Several ANC leaders were assassinated. In the townships ANC and PAC youths revived the practice of control by terror, including arbitrary 'people's courts' and 'necklacing'. The MK was also active. In the first seven months of 1990 more than 400 attacks were made on police and councillors, with an increasing use of guns; 42 policemen were killed. However, the bloodiest clashes came between Inkatha and the ANC, both in KwaZulu/Natal – where rural warlords fought to dominate people and territory in the name of their parties – and in townships along the Rand where IFP hostel workers fought ANC comrades. With justification the ANC accused the police of supporting Inkatha. Among this general violence certain cases stood out. They included the attack at Sebokeng in July 1990 (which started the 'Reef' war) when Inkatha followers killed more than thirty ANC supporters. Mandela complained bitterly that the government had ignored repeated ANC prior warnings of the raid Then, in September 1990, came the first commuter train massacre when 26 black people were killed on a Johannesburg commuter train. The ANC accused the 'Third Force'.

The explanations given for the violence were as numerous as its forms – reactionary whites trying to hold onto power; security forces used as instruments of oppression; a black struggle for power; black socio-economic conditions; recalcitrants on all sides trying to undermine negotiations by destabilizing society; and an in-built culture of violence fuelled by political intolerance, youths brought up in a mood of defiance, plus the rhetoric of the armed struggle and the total strategy. Whatever the reasons the violence was appalling, and led to bitter accusation and counter-accusation. One report favourable to the ANC claimed that in a twelve-month period along the Reef, Inkatha was responsible for 51 per cent of the violence, the police 23 per cent, other groups also 23 per cent, and the ANC only 6 per cent. Over the same period the police attributed 56 per cent of violence to the ANC, 40 per cent to Inkatha and the rest to the PAC and Azapo (IRR 1991/2: xxxv). In April 1991 Mandela declared that the security forces were the main sources of violence in the black townships. 'What we are witnessing,' he said, 'is an attempt to bludgeon African communities into submission . . . to install a psychosis of mistrust and uncertainty.' De Klerk, on his side, attacked the ANC. The people, he said, 'are sick and tired of violence and destabilisation. Yet the ANC and its allies persist in planning mass action and gratuitous violence' (IRR 1991/2: 1iii, 18).

As distrust increased acrimonious public outbursts soured the atmosphere for negotiation. Mandela and de Klerk were soon at loggerheads, both exaggerating the degree of control the other could exercise within his organization. Mandela came to regret his description of de Klerk as 'a man of integrity', and instead accused the State President of following a double agenda – of advocating negotiation while promoting violence; of being unable or unwilling to control the government forces, and being indifferent to the loss of black lives. In October 1991 he accused elements of the police of 'turning themselves into killing machines' (IRR 1991/2: xxxviii). On his side de Klerk accused Mandela of making vicious and unwarranted attacks upon him personally. He also criticized the ANC for refusing to abandon the armed struggle, for failing to control township youths and for mass action based on intimidation.

The lack of trust was equally apparent between Mandela and Buthelezi. Dealing with Buthelezi was never easy, but during his long imprisonment Mandela had kept contact with the Inkatha leader; while Buthelezi had consistently advocated Mandela's release. Shortly after his release Mandela reminded an ANC rally of this and Inkatha's refusal to join negotiations while the ANC was banned. Mandela stated that despite the differences Inkatha 'has contributed in no small measure to making it difficult for the regime to implement successive schemes designed to perpetuate minority rule' (IRR 1991/2: 720). Then Mandela began to accept the ANC line drawn by those opposed to Inkatha. The most extreme of these was Harry Gwala who urged his followers to gain peace not by negotiation but by destroying Inkatha. In March 1990 the ANC backed out of a joint peace rally at which Mandela and Buthelezi were scheduled to speak. Buthelezi was astonished at the ANC's explanation that the situation was too tense and there was too much fighting to go ahead. As he pointed out the very purpose was to deal with those issues. Buthelezi was also offended by Mandela's failure to make personal contact. When eventually the two leaders met in January 1991 the atmosphere was sullen and little progress was made. A tripartite meeting between de Klerk, Buthelezi and Mandela in September was equally unfruitful.

As the violence increased so did disputes about the degree of responsibility of the leaders. Did they actively promote the violence, or turn a blind eye, or did it flourish despite their best efforts? Fingers were pointed at all the leading figures, but de Klerk was the most exposed, because not only was he party leader, he had final responsibility for the state and the security forces. He had served on the SSC during Botha's time, and although not an insider he must at least have had a general idea of the scope and methods used by the forces. On taking up office he set out to curb the powers of the security establishment and to bring it under cabinet control. Within weeks he dispensed with the National Security Management System and replaced it with a National Co-ordinating Mechanism, which placed greater emphasis on socio-economic development. He went on to lift the state of emergency; to reduce security expenditure; and when reports of security malpractice were received, he set up commissions to investigate them.

However, de Klerk had at best only partial success. He had altered the system but the same personnel were in their posts. Some of the more sophisticated members of the security services, like Niel Barnard and Mike Louw of the National Intelligence Service, recognized the necessity of a negotiated outcome, but others remained wedded to the total strategy, in which their mission was to fight the ANC. De Klerk could never be sure of their loyalty and so he trod warily. Further the forces, and particularly special units like the notorious Civil Co-operation Bureau (CCB), often operated on their own initiative and could call on substantial resources. Nor could de Klerk count on full loyalty in the party or even the cabinet, where ministers like Magnus Malan and Adriaan Vlok were wedded to the old ways. The right wing regarded de Klerk as a traitor, and he was constrained by the need to ensure that the white community as a whole did not lurch to the right. Yet in the end he had responsibility.

De Klerk was trying to reshape a system which was not fully under his control, but at the same time he was reluctant to face harsh truths. When he received complaints about security forces malpractice, he tended to explain it away as the behaviour of a few rogue individuals. That view was largely supported by the early reports of the commissions he set up to look into the situation. One, under Justice Louis Harms, established in February 1990 to investigate allegations of hit-squad activities, concluded that although the CCB was something of a law unto itself, there was no evidence of police hit-squads, and it cleared Magnus Malan of responsibility for any wrongdoing. Commenting on the evidence he and his colleagues gave to Harms, Eugene de Kock simply said: 'We lied' (De Kock 1998: 185). A more thorough investigation was undertaken by Justice Richard Goldstone. In his April 1992 report Goldstone concluded that the causes of violence were many and complicated – including the use of security forces as instruments of oppression; the sudden unbanning of political organizations; the climate of intolerance and economic hardship among blacks; and the failure of the government, ANC and IFP to discipline their forces. Yet, even he concluded that there was no evidence of an organized 'Third Force', and that the primary cause of violence was not the security forces, but Inkatha/ANC rivalry (IRR 1992/3: 125).

However, the tide of revelations turned steadily against the security forces. 'Hundreds of armed men, among them police,' reported an Amnesty International investigation in 1992, 'swept through a squatter camp outside Durban attacking and killing residents. The victims are apparently targetted because they support the ANC. In the middle of the night policemen in plain clothes, with their faces disguised raid the home of Sipho Cela a trade union official in northern Natal . . . A trade union activist, Jonas Kgosietside, falls to his death from a second-floor window of Phokeng police station where he was being interrogated. A former political prisoner, Tsepo Lengwati, dies from multiple gunshot wounds in the middle of the night while in police custody in Sharpeville'; and so the list continued (Amnesty 1992: 6). In June 1992 an army intelligence officer revealed (in what became known as 'Inkathagate') that Inkatha had been given substantial funds and arms to use against the ANC.

These were followed by more Goldstone Commission revelations. In November it exposed a 'dirty tricks' operation by military intelligence employing 'prostitutes, homosexuals, shebeen owners and drug dealers' to compromise ANC and MK leaders. A further internal army report uncovered military intelligence's involvement in the train massacres, assassinations, and gun running (Meredith 1997: 479). Later Goldstone revealed 'a horrible network of criminal activity' among senior police officers, including the second in command (General Baise Smit) and the chief of counter intelligence (General Krappies Engelbrecht). Based on the reports de Klerk took some action. He moved Malan and Vlok from their security portfolios, but not from the cabinet; and he went on to remove 23 officers, including two generals, but let them retain their pensions. His actions, while incensing the right wing, did not satisfy the ANC, and the revelations weakened his negotiating position. It had become clear that the illegal practices were not the work of a few mavericks but the outcome of an elaborate, covert system, involving senior figures, set up in P. W. Botha's day. 'I had not acted out of some kind of depraved personal motive,' stated de Kock later. 'My orders had come from the highest levels' (De Kock 1998: 270).

The Convention for a Democratic South Africa (Codesa)

While the violence and investigations were continuing the formal negotiations eventually started in December 1991. The breakthrough came when Mandela proposed an all-party congress to negotiate an interim constitution and the creation of a constituent assembly. This offered a compromise, in that it satisfied the NP's call for a multi-party convention, but it also suited the ANC, because the convention would agree only an interim constitution leading to an election for a constituent assembly which would approve the final constitution. Delegates representing nineteen parties attended the start of Codesa (Convention for a Democratic South Africa). But there were significant absentees, including the main parties at the ends of the political spectrum – the CP and PAC. The CP dismissed the negotiations as a 'travesty of democracy because different peoples and different races can never form a single nation'. The PAC said that negotiation would not bring about the emancipation of the dispossessed masses, and accused the ANC and NP of forming a secret pact to rule the country by decree. Clarence Makwetu, the PAC President, said that the government was 'hell bent on vetoing our rights to self determination and the reasons are obvious – they wish to protect white privilege and racist hegemony' (IRR 1991/2: il, li, 44).

Inkatha hesitated. At first its delegates attended but in May 1992 Buthelezi withdrew them because of the failure to gain separate representation for the Zulu monarch. It was the first of a series of walk outs by the IFP, and Buthelezi personally never attended. The ANC suspected that Inkatha and the government were planning to form an anti-ANC pact. Although there was collaboration among security personnel, there was no evidence to suggest co-operation among senior political figures. De Klerk took few steps to mollify Buthelezi or to resolve the misgivings that surrounded Inkatha's position. There was also uncertainty about the response of the four 'independent' Bantustans. In the event they split. Two attended – the Transkei, where General Bantu Holomisa threw in his lot with the ANC, and Venda where the government collapsed in confusion and debt – whereas Lucas Mangope of Bophuthatswana and General Oupa Gqozo of the Ciskei sought to demonstrate their independence by boycotting the talks.

Yet, despite the absentees, it was a remarkable achievement to bring together such a wide range of representatives to shape the country's future. Those who did attend were determined to maximize their claims; and so the early messages were defiant; with much talk of 'bottom lines' and 'non-negotiable' terms. The parties were in a new contest, in which Joe Slovo underlined the link between negotiation and mass action. He claimed that experience had shown that 'negotiations are a terrain of struggle which, at the end of the day, depend upon the balance of forces outside the process' (*Africa Communist*, 1993: 22).

For the government de Klerk stated that whites were not prepared to 'bow out apologetically from the stage of history'. He did not believe he would be South Africa's last white President, and was looking for a system that practically enforces government by coalition (Waldmeir 1997: 147). His aim was not to negotiate whites out of power but to reach a settlement that would preserve their position, values and property. He spoke of compromise not surrender; of change with stability; and of building on existing foundations. He made clear that the NP have never sought a mandate to transfer power to the ANC. In contrast the ANC's public message was that the government was weak, and had been forced into negotiations by the success of mass action, MK raids, and military defeat in Angola. It called for early majority rule, opposed group rights and supported a popularly elected assembly to draw up the constitution. The ANC's language was that of conflict not compromise; of change not stability. Pallo Jordan, the Information Secretary, claimed that the ANC 'had compelled the enemy to seek negotiation'. The intention was to gain power and 'negotiations in such a situation are aimed at the liquidation of the antagonists as a factor in politics' (Adam and Moodley 1993: 42).

On the first day of Codesa things started well. Agreement was reached to establish working groups to handle various aspects of the settlement, and most delegations endorsed a Declaration of Intent, which committed them to an undivided South Africa with constitutional safeguards. However, Inkatha refused to sign because an 'undivided' country might rule out a federation. At the end of the session the delegation leaders made statements. Again all went well. Dr Dawie de Villiers, leading for the NP, even offered an apology for apartheid, saying that his party had hoped that separation would bring peace, but instead it had brought conflict, injustice and misery, which he regretted.

Then the atmosphere changed. As head of government de Klerk spoke last. He used the occasion to attack the ANC, accusing it of failing to keep agreements.

'He began,' wrote Mandela, 'to speak to us like a schoolmaster admonishing a naughty child. He berated the ANC for failing to disclose the location of arms caches and then rebuked us for maintaining a "private army" [MK] in violation of the National Peace Accord of September 1991. In intemperate language he questioned whether the ANC was honourable enough to abide by any agreement it signed.' Mandela was incensed. He immediately returned to the rostrum to berate de Klerk, describing him as 'the head of an illegitimate, discredited minority regime'. He accused the State President of being less than frank, and the government of breaking its word. While the ANC had suspended the armed struggle de Klerk was colluding with those waging war – using the negotiations not to achieve peace but to score political points. If he failed to control or to recognize the duplicity of those surrounding him he was not fit to be head of government. This confrontation took place not only before the delegates but television cameras, exposing to all the deep divisions that had to be bridged. Yet Mandela finished on a more conciliatory note. 'Let us work together openly,' he appealed to de Klerk. 'Let there be no secret agendas . . . I am prepared to work with him in spite of all his mistakes' (Mandela 1994: 588–9). But the clash soured relations further.

Despite the strains negotiations proceeded because the main leaders continued to believe that they were the best way forward. Codesa held together until June 1992. By then considerable progress had been made, with all sides gaining and losing points. Agreement had been reached on some major issues and principles – including a single nationality and common citizenship; equality of race, sex and creed; an independent judiciary; multi-party democracy; a Bill of Rights; and elections based on proportional representation. As favoured by the NP the multi-party conference would agree an interim constitution and principles on which the final constitution would be built; but, as insisted by the ANC, the adoption of the final constitution would be by a popularly elected National Assembly. Seventeen of the parties also supported an undivided South Africa with a single nationality and common citizenship. However, the IFP still refused to accept that because 'an undivided South Africa with one nation would undermine the federal concept' (IRR 1991/2: i1).

Yet, difficulties persisted. These were three-fold: first, the leaders had to hold their parties together; second, the remaining gaps between the parties had to be bridged; and third, the continuing violence had to be countered. As the negotiations proceeded tension arose not only between parties but within them. Both the ANC and the NP had their obdurate hawks, and their flexible doves. A gap also emerged between those who were directly involved in the negotiations – with its learning process on all sides – and those outside who felt excluded and were more aware of pressure from their own constituencies than reaching agreements with opponents. In the government's case this led to cabinet splits, over such matters as working with Inkatha and other homeland parties, which was favoured by the 'old guard', such as Pik Botha, Tertius Delport and Hernus Kriel, and opposed by 'the negotiators', including Roelf Meyer and Dawie de Villiers (Reynolds 1994: 14).

To reassure NP doubters that he was not in Mandela's pocket, and to avoid defections to the CP, de Klerk continued to attack the ANC. Despite that a crisis arose early in 1992 when the CP won a parliamentary by-election in a traditionally safe

NP seat at Potchestroom. Immediately the cry went up that this was a backlash against the negotiations; that de Klerk had lost the confidence of the white electorate. Instead of shying away de Klerk met the challenge head on. In March 1992 he called a white referendum specifically to ask whether or not negotiations should continue. It was a risk because if the answer were 'No' the whole negotiating process would have collapsed. De Klerk was opposed by the CP and other rightwing groups, while the DP supported a 'Yes' vote. In the campaign de Klerk gave as one of the reasons for voting 'Yes' that he could negotiate a settlement without conceding majority rule. 'Vote Yes if you're scared of majority rule' read an NP poster. However, there was a change of emphasis. De Klerk made little mention of groups and instead spoke of constitutional safeguards. He announced that the NP's 'fundamental requirements' included a bill of rights, regional powers, limitations on the power of the President, the protection of private property, the maintenance of standards and law and order. On the day de Klerk won a resounding victory, gaining two-thirds of the white referendum vote.

Then in May 1992 the Codesa negotiations broke down. The immediate issue was an apparently technical matter about the percentage of support which would be required in the National Assembly for the adoption of sections of the final constitution; but behind the figures was a question of power. The NP, perhaps over-confident after its referendum success, wanted to drive the figure up to 75 per cent for reserved matters; whereas the ANC would go no higher than 70 per cent, because it believed that the NP's aim was to exercise a white veto over the constitution – hence the high percentages. Also despite the progress that had been made Mandela noted three further ANC concerns: 'entrenched regional powers'; 'an undemocratic and unelected senate that had veto power over new legislation'; and an attempt 'to make an interim constitution negotiated by the convention into a permanent constitution' (Mandela 1994: 595).

Added to the constitutional differences were continued suspicion and distrust over the continued violence. At first de Klerk and Mandela tried to mask the breakdown in the talks, and may have succeeded had it not been for another major violent incident. On 17 June 1992 forty-six ANC followers, mainly women and children, were killed at Boipatong. The assailants were not identified, but the ANC was convinced that they were an Inkatha gang, and that the government was guilty by omission or commission – at best, by failing to prevent the massacre; at worst, by the direct involvement of the security forces. Mandela exploded. 'I can no longer explain to our people,' he declared, 'why we continue to talk to a regime that is murdering our people and conducting war against us' (Waldmeir 1997: 206). When de Klerk tried to show his sympathy by visiting Boipatong 'a crowd turned on him in a chilling display of hostility' (Sparks 1995: 141). Later Mandela angrily concluded: 'It is impossible to defend him [de Klerk]. In his view their [black] lives are cheap. When it comes to blacks he is completely insensitive' (Waldmeir 1997: 187).

The ANC withdrew from negotiations and organized a campaign of 'rolling mass action'. It had a remarkable impact. For three months the country was crippled by demonstrations, strikes, marches, civil disobedience and violence. It culminated in a general strike at the beginning of August when millions of workers stayed at home, and in a vast rally outside the government's Union Buildings in Pretoria when Mandela assured the people that one day they would occupy the buildings as the democratic government. Then in September there was another major clash as ANC militants, led by Ronnie Kasrils, tried to enter Bisho, the capital of 'independent' Ciskei, despite a ban by General Gqozo. It was a rash attempt to topple a Bantustan government by mass action. When the marchers broke through a protective cordon the Ciskei police fired indiscriminately, killing twenty-nine and injuring many more. According to the ANC they were shot down in cold blood by an illegitimate regime while exercising their democratic rights to march anywhere in South Africa; according to the Ciskei authorities the ANC deliberately set out to challenge a legitimate government by ignoring its authority and provoking its forces to fire in defence of the state.

The Return to Negotiation

While violence had helped to drive Mandela and de Klerk apart, ironically it was now responsible for bringing them together again. They both realized that the chance of gaining a negotiated settlement was fast disappearing beneath the bloodshed, and they knew that if it continued control would slip away from them to the men of violence. De Klerk stated: 'The simple truth is that devastating war will ensue if negotiation does not succeed'. Added to that were economic concerns. Following Bisho the Finance Minister Derek Keys told Trevor Manuel, the ANC's Financial Director, that the economic position was grim and would become disastrous unless negotiations were resumed (Reynolds 1994: 11).

Mandela and de Klerk had poor personal relations but they were tied together into a process to which each had committed his political life. They needed each other. 'My worst nightmare,' said Mandela, 'is that I wake up one night and de Klerk isn't there. I need him. Whether I like him or not is irrelevant' (Waldmeir 1997: 231). For both of them there was no real option. De Klerk had pledged himself to gaining a solution by negotiation. He had summoned up an image of the future based on co-operation and sharing. There could be no retreat from that; no going back to white dominance based on the sword. The mandate he had gained at the referendum was to negotiate a settlement not to renew the battle; the new international status he had achieved for South Africa was on the understanding that apartheid and white oppression were dead. Equally Mandela had never believed that the white regime could be driven into submission by force alone. He was committed to negotiation, and now he saw more clearly than ever that a devastated country, divided into warring factions lay ahead if a settlement were not reached. And he too was conscious of the international pressure, whereby the UN Security Council had endorsed the government's call to the ANC to return to the negotiating table, and had appointed Cyrus Vance, a former US Secretary of State, as a special envoy to seek an end to the conflict. No longer was the government treated as an international pariah, particularly in the West. The message now was to seek a settlement.

★ ★ ★

Even after the breakdown of negotiations informal contacts had been retained between the ANC and government. The main channel of contact was between their chief negotiators Cyril Ramaphosa for the ANC, and Roelf Meyer, who was made Minister of Constitutional Development shortly after the Codesa breakdown. They were both young, able, pragmatic men who established an effective working relationship – 'the Roelf and Cyril Show' (Sparks 1995: 179). One outcome of their efforts came in September 1992 when the government and the ANC signed a 'Record of Understanding'. Initially the ANC had drawn up a list of fourteen conditions before it would agree to resume talks. However, it finally boiled them down to three which the government accepted – the release of political prisoners (on which Mandela stood firm against de Klerk), the fencing of Inkatha workers' hostels, and the banning of traditional weapons carried by the IFP. Inevitably, as two of the conditions were directed against Inkatha, the Record of Understanding infuriated Buthelezi, and it sacrificed whatever chance the government had of working with the IFP. However, it reopened ANC/Pretoria relations. It was a recognition that the government had nowhere else to go. Circumstances had moved against it as the ANC had demonstrated its enormous strength through mass action short of civil war. The violence and disruption associated with this had an adverse impact on the economy. When de Klerk launched his initiative in 1990 he had hoped for an economic revival. It did not come. In that year and the three that followed the Gross National Product fell. Part of the explanation for this lay in a prolonged drought which hit agriculture severely, but at least as important was the continued imposition of some sanctions and the failure to attract overseas investment and trade because of the political uncertainty. It was clear that economic fortunes were directly tied to the political outcome.

The government could not handle the situation other than by a return to repression or negotiation. De Klerk had chosen the path of negotiation. When asked what the government gained by the Record of Understanding Roelf Meyer simply replied 'the resumption of negotiations'. The interplay of hope and despair once again characterized the process. That was illustrated in April 1993. The month started in hope when it was agreed that multi-party negotiations would be resumed, but then came crisis when a white extremist assassinated Chris Hani. There were real fears of racial civil war. That was avoided because those who supported negotiation, again realized the dangers. Joe Slovo said the SACP would not call for suspension of negotiations following Hani's death, because that 'would be playing into the hands of the murderers' (IRR 1993/4: 541). The aftermath of Hani's death also demonstrated a clear shift in the balance of power away from de Klerk to Mandela, from the government to the ANC. Following the murder it was Mandela who broadcast to the nation calling for calm and his voice was heeded. 'Now is the time', he declared, 'for all South Africans to stand together against those who . . . wish to destroy what Chris Hani gave his life for – the freedom of us all' (Waldmeir 1997: 223).

Yet, even after the negotiators reassembled at Kempton Park the right-wing white challenge continued. In June 1993 about 3,000 AWB supporters assaulted the centre where the negotiations were being held. After they had smashed down the main doors with an armoured vehicle, the AWB flooded in, forcing the delegates to flee to cries of: 'We don't want Kaffirs in here. Kaffirs, we are going to shoot you dead today' (Sparks 1995: 191). However, even that ugly incident only served to make the negotiators all the more determined to make progress.

At the resumption of talks the CP, IFP and PAC initially decided to attend, but they did not stay. In June the IFP and the CP, together with the representatives of Bophuthatswana and the Ciskei, walked out, because of change in working arrangements and the mood of the talks. While at Codesa the participants had concentrated on achieving specific objectives (even if compromises had to be made), now the emphasis shifted, most noticeably on the government's side, towards achieving a settlement, even if the terms were less than ideal. That did not imply that any outcome was acceptable, but the drive was to gain an overall settlement rather than specific ends. One of the ways this was facilitated was to make progress on the basis of 'sufficient consensus', which in practice, came to mean the ANC and the NP. This approach infuriated those who had specific aims in mind, including the CP with its search for a Volkstaat, and the IFP with its belief in federalism and a constitution negotiated by multi party agreement. Dr Ziba Jiyane of the IFP accused the ANC, aided by a weak government, of aiming not at peace and democracy but party dominance. He said that the ANC opposed a multi-party approach because 'they seek a centralised state in which the regions will toe Pretoria's line'. In contrast the IFP was eager to avoid conflict by 'inclusive consensus not bilateral consensus', and that implied a federation (*Barometer*, vol. 5, no. 7, November 1993).

In October 1993 most of those who had walked out of the talks – the IFP, CP, other small white parties and the homeland separatists – formed themselves into the Freedom Alliance (FA). They issued a manifesto which opposed strong central powers and favoured the rights of distinct peoples rather than a single nation/state. Instead it envisaged a number of separate states which would express people's rights to self-determination, and whose boundaries would be determined by the people of the states rather than the central government. It was a recipe for the Balkanization of South Africa. Despite such opposition the momentum of the negotiation was sustained and it was agreed by 'sufficient consensus' that national elections would be held on 27 April 1994. The timetable having been set the ANC and the government were determined to keep to it and that established deadlines for everything else. By November 1993 agreement had been hammered out on the interim constitutional arrangements, and the principles on which the final constitution would be established.

22

Towards the Promised Land

During the negotiations both the major parties had absorbed lessons. On the ANC side came the realization that to build a single South African nation it had to gain the confidence of those it had previously ignored or fought in the liberation struggle. An article in *Mayibuye* stressed that the needs and fears of ethnic and racial communities must be addressed. It asked whether adequate attention had been paid to ethnicity as a social force. It further argued, with reference to Africans, that notice must be paid to rural communities where activists had often scorned traditional leaders and structures. As a result, said the article, the ANC is seen as 'elitist', looking down on elderly and unsophisticated Africans. 'Pride in people's history and traditions has not been sufficiently harnessed . . . Ultimately the solution to the national question lies in the united struggle which affects people both urban and rural' (*Mayibuye*, June 1991).

The ANC leadership recognized that to build an effective new state it had to gain the confidence of a substantial number of whites, especially in the administrative and business sectors. Mandela, confident as he was of winning an election, stated that 'to take power is easy', but added 'the most difficult thing is to retain that power'. Within this context an important initiative was taken by Slovo, when he proposed a set of 'sunset clauses', designed specifically to gain white trust in the transition to a democratic state. Slovo proposed a two-stage arrangement. The first, to be based on a five-year interim constitution which would include power sharing; and alongside that a guarantee to government officials that their posts would be protected for a set period. Power would be shared by forming a government of national unity drawn from the main parties; and the security of tenure would cover civil servants and the armed forces. During this interim period a final constitution would be agreed to form the base of the second stage, which would achieve the ANC's aim of majority rule. As with all compromises Slovo's proposals ran into opposition, but with Mandela's support they were eventually accepted by the ANC executive.

The NP government also absorbed lessons. It quietly dropped its insistence on group identities. Although it continued to advocate power sharing, it did so on the basis of political parties not ethnic groups; and its claim for 'rights' focused on individuals. It now concentrated on achieving an ordered society in which constitutional safeguards would protect rights and limit the powers of government; in which the constitution rather than parliament would be sovereign; and in which whites would retain leadership roles through their skills, experience and education in business and administration. When Meyer reported to parliament in February 1993, he stressed that although negotiation involved co-operation with the ANC no alliance had been struck; the co-operation was confined to the negotiating process. The NP's aims, he said, were to achieve a constitution based on order not revolution, which would guarantee citizens against abuse of power and offer a power-sharing democracy, and in which civic communities (in sport, culture, religion, education and trade unions) would be protected from state intervention. Meyer made no mention of 'groups', but spoke of 'unity in diversity', and argued that as decision making should be close to the people the regions must be given adequate powers and resources. The NP, said Meyer, was eager to build a single nation, but it would take time and would not be realized if existing diversity was not respected.

Another shift for the NP was to abandon the pretence that the 'independent' Bantustans could stand outside the new South Africa. In December 1993 a bill was approved for their reincorporation into South Africa and the return of citizenship to their residents. Although Mangope in Bophuthatswana and Gqozo in the Ciskei initially refused to accept the change, the NP proposed that the homelands should be incorporated into a new provincial structure. However, it did not support the degree of federalism advocated by the IFP. The NP sat somewhat uneasily between the strong central government advocated by the ANC and the powerful provinces favoured by the IFP. It feared a state dominated by the ANC, but in office it too had centralized power, and found it difficult to abandon that approach. Also, unlike the IFP, it did not have the incentive of a province where most of its supporters were concentrated.

The Interim Constitution

The outcome of the negotiations was agreement on: (a) A one person one vote election to be held on 27 April 1994; (b) transitional arrangements to operate until then; (c) a five-year interim constitution to come into force immediately after the election; (d) a process under the interim constitution for agreeing the final constitution; (e) a three-tier structure of government – centre, provinces and local; and (f) a set of principles on which to base the final constitution.

In terms of the structure of government the interim constitution provided for a National Assembly of 400 members – elected by proportional representation, based on party lists and not individual constituencies. There would also be a Senate of 90 members – ten from each of the new provinces into which the country was to be divided. The dual functions of these two bodies was law-making and drawing up a permanent constitution. Power sharing in the interim constitution was to be achieved through a Government of National Unity (GNU) – a mixed party body with memberships dependent on the support a party received at the election. For every 5 per cent it received of the national vote a party would be entitled to a cabinet seat. The President would allocate the posts to a party while the party would choose the individuals to fill them. The President was to be elected by a majority vote of the Assembly, but there was to be an element of power sharing in the arrangements for Deputy President. Two Deputies could be appointed, drawn from the largest parties, provided those parties had gained 20 per cent of the vote.

A set of principles (thirty-four in all) were also approved for incorporation into the final constitution. They were the stuff of a liberal democratic state, and in part reflected the influential role played by the DP in the negotiations. The hour of the 'liberals' had come. Previously they had been pushed into the sidelines of South African politics but when it came to laying down constitutional principles and structures people like Colin Eglin had a real and lasting impact on the negotiations. The principles laid the ground for an open, representative, multi-party democracy. They included the recognition of the constitution as the supreme law of the land; the separation of legislature, executive and judiciary; guarantees of multi-party democracy; and individual rights backed by a Human Rights Commission.

The principles also included guidelines for relations between central and provincial governments. Yet, despite the guidelines, and the attention that had been devoted to the 'federal question', it remained open to dispute. The ANC showed some signs of movement. Influenced by a visit to Germany (where the centre and the parts have concurrent powers, but the final say goes to the centre) the ANC

Nelson Mandela, Thabo Mbeki and F. W. de Klerk (courtesy of the South African High Commission)

negotiators accepted that provinces would have their own structure and powers. These fell far short of the aspirations of Inkatha or right-wing whites for a volkstaat, and they left the future balance uncertain. 'Contrary to IFP rhetoric,' wrote Richard Humphries and Thabo Rapoo, 'the interim constitution was not a charter for a unitary state. It created provinces with elected governments and powers, and left it to the political process and courts to determine how much autonomy they would have. Whatever the intentions of ANC strategists, the future of regional government was left unresolved' (Friedman 1994: 177).

Following the agreements there was a rush to put things into place – a Transitional Executive Council was formed; an Independent Electoral Commission (IEC) was appointed to organize the election; and country-wide voter education began. The IEC, under the direction of Judge Johann Kriegler, faced a formidable task. It had to devise and supervise a completely new system for an unregistered electorate. That involved employing 300,000 people, establishing 9,000 voting stations and 900 counting centres; and it had to do so without direct help from the government which was seen as one of the competing parties. To add to the problems circumstances were constantly changing (such as the Boputhatswana crisis and Inkatha's change of heart; described below). And, the prospect of an election intensified rivalry and tension, and the activities of opponents of the settlement, leading to more violence. In 1993 3,794 people were killed in political violence and the rate of killings increased in the period following the agreement and before the election. In March 1994, 537 people were killed and in April, the month of the election, the death toll was 436 (IRR 1994/5: 438). Intimidation was rife. 'Perhaps,' wrote Steven Friedman, 'the key feature of the campaign was a pattern in which parties were prevented from gaining access to voters in hostile parts of the country'. Thus the NP, DP and IFP were driven out of townships controlled by the ANC or PAC, and thus the ANC was unable to campaign in areas dominated by the IFP or right-wing whites (Friedman 1994: 310).

To Fight or not to Fight the Election

A major uncertainty was the attitude of parties which had boycotted or been in and out of the negotiations. Would they contest the election? One of these was the PAC which, throughout the period of negotiation had been divided and uneasy. Although it had decided to join the resumed negotiations in 1993, it was never comfortable. It was 'in' the process but not 'of' it: convinced that, as the voice of the oppressed black masses, it should play a major part in shaping the new state, but uneasy to be doing so through multi party/racial negotiations. Many PAC members continued to advocate force not talk – contemptuously rejecting compromise; convinced that the racist regime could be destroyed only by armed struggle; calling for 'one settler, one bullet'. The aim, said Maxwell Nemadzivhanani, the national organizer, was not to share power but to get the land back from the settlers. Of white farmers he said: 'The more you kill them, the more you come closer to liberation' (Meredith 1994: 156). The result was a dual policy, of arm's length participation, without ever fully abandoning the armed struggle. Early in 1993 the APLA commander, Sabelo Phama, announced that the struggle would continue, and he went on to fudge the distinction between hard and soft targets, simply stating that APLA's main targets were the 'pillars of racist regime and its support structures', including white farmers (IRR 1993/4: 645). In March 1993 the Goldstone Commission linked APLA to 34 vicious attacks in which 26 people died including policemen, farmers, and whites who were attacked in church, a golf club and a restaurant.

The PAC's internal tension and dual policy persisted. In December 1993 the party conference decided both to fight the election, and to continue the armed struggle – declaring 1994 to be 'The Year of the Bullet and the Ballot'. However, under pressure from the government, Clarence Makwetu, the President, announced that the armed struggle would be suspended because of the forthcoming election, but he warned that it would take time to inform all units. To underline that qualification an APLA commander stated that his section would continue to fight, although 'the leadership had suddenly developed "cold feet"' (IRR 1994/5: 428). Other sections of the party, including the student and youth wings, opposed involvement in the election. Yet, despite these tensions and inadequate preparation the PAC mounted a campaign of sorts – based more 'on appeal to African emotions rather than coherent arguments' (Davenport 1998: 43). It opposed power sharing and promised power to the people; it proposed to change the country's name to 'Azania' (a name used by early Greek cartographers); but the main message was that all land would be seized by the state and distributed to the people. 'We promise you the return of the land of our forefathers which was taken away by force', said Makwetu (Meredith 1994: 157).

At the other end of the political spectrum was a mixture of black and white parties, including Inkatha, parties from the Ciskei and Bophuthatswana, the CP and the Afrikaner Volksfront (AVF). They were products of the separate nationalisms of the old fragmented South Africa. In the changed political conditions they were vulnerable not only because they opposed the process, but because they had narrow support bases. The ANC and the NP, already the largest parties, made general appeals across the electorate, whereas these parties were limited to discrete social groups. With the exception of Inkatha they could expect to gain only a small percentage of the votes in a general election. In an attempt to strengthen their position they came together in loose alliances – first as Cosag (Concerned South Africans Group), and then, in opposition to the election, they reformed as the Freedom Alliance (FA). However, as the election approached and pressure increased, the alliance fragmented. The split extended to 'right-wing' whites. When de Klerk advised them to look to the constitution 'rather than working for a Volkstaat which is unobtainable', they dismissed his notion of diversity within a single South African nationalism (Star, Johannesburg, 20 April 1994). Ferdi Hertzenberg, the CP leader, claimed that the establishment of an Afrikaner homeland was inevitable and a way would be found to achieve it. In October 1993 he stated that the CP rejected the election because it would mean a return to colonialism. Instead he called for a white-only referendum to decide whether a transitional authority should be established and whether whites wanted a free Afrikaner republic.

The CP did not stand alone, but attempts to bring the right-wing whites together failed. A number of extreme groups – such as the AWB, the Boere Republican Army, the Oos Transvaal Boerekommando, the Pretoria Kommandogroep, and the Wit Wolve – were paramilitary organizations, which despised compromise, asserted that Afrikaners could not live without a homeland and were willing, even eager, to fight for it. The CP was ambivalent towards such militants, and yet it joined the Afrikaner Volksfront (AVF). Among its leaders was General Constand Viljoen, a former defence chief with no previous experience of politics. Although Viljoen recognized that Afrikaners were dispersed across the country, he argued that this did not reduce their national sentiment or their aspirations. He denounced the interim constitution as a takeover by a communist ANC, which ignored the rights of national minorities, such as Zulus, Tswana and Afrikaners. Initially he did not rule out the use of force to achieve white aims, but saw it as a last resort. In an attempt to break the deadlock the AVF held discussions with the ANC, but when the ANC refused to give an undertaking to accept a volkstaat the AVF resolved to boycott the elections. However, contacts continued, during which Viljoen established good relations with Mandela. Mandela spoke of him as 'a very honest man and I would welcome him in the Government of National Unity. It would strengthen the government . . . This is a man with whom we can work and solve problems' (Meredith 1994: 161).

In mid-February Mandela announced a number of concessions, including acceptance of the principle of 'internal' self-determination for groups sharing common language and culture; and the investigation of the volkstaat question by a council of twenty members, to be elected by MPs who wanted to gain a volkstaat by constitutional means. Following those concessions, and the collapse of Boputhatswana (see below) Viljoen broke ranks and decided to fight the election through a new party – the Freedom Front (FF). He concluded that without employing force, which could wreck the country and might be ineffective, it was impossible to gain agreement on a volkstaat before the election. He therefore urged Afrikaners to demonstrate their support for the peaceful formation of a volkstaat by going to the polls and voting FF.

Bophuthatswana Falls

The formation of the FF may have saved the country from widespread white violence, but it did not prevent it entirely. One major incident was tied to the fate of Boputhatswana. There Lucas Mangope opposed reincorporation into South Africa. Hartzenburg rashly claimed that an attempt to impose a decision on Bophuthatswana would be interpreted by the CP as a declaration of war. War was also contemplated by Matthew Phosa, of the ANC, who warned that if any of the homelands refused reincorporation 'the tanks will roll in' (IRR 1993/4: 35). By March 1994 Mangope's regime was in serious trouble, with strikes (backed by the ANC) among its civil service and security forces. In his plight Mangope appealed to Viljoen, who sent a force of 1,500 lightly-armed volunteers to Mmabatho, the capital. They were not the only whites to appear. An AWB contingent arrived, despite pleas from Mangope and Viljoen to stay away. The AWB force consisted of an ill-disciplined set of thugs, who drove through the streets, firing at bystanders in what a newspaper described as a 'nigger shooting picnic' (Waldmeir 1997: 247). In retaliation the Bophuthatswana security forces mutinied, attacked the AWB, killed three of them before television cameras, and drove the rest out. Viljoen withdrew his men without taking any action. The homeland collapsed into rioting, looting and fighting before South African troops moved in to restore order.

The Bophuthatswana affair was a defining point in several respects. First, it spelt the end of attempts by the 'independent' Bantustans to stand outside the settlement. Mangope was deposed and the administration of the homeland taken over by Pretoria. Ten days later Gqozo in the Ciskei, also faced by rebellious police and civil servants, invited Pretoria to take over his homeland. It was the end of the Bantustan myth. Second, the affair undermined the claim by militant whites that they could take matters into their own hands by force of arms. Third, when the army under General Georg Meiring obeyed orders to take control of Bophuthatswana it revealed that the forces were prepared to back the transitional government, and, by implication, the new South Africa. Fourth, it finally persuaded Viljoen that he must follow the election route. Later he explained that on his way back from Mmabatho, he decided: 'We would not be able to maintain a volkstaat financially, and politically it would be completely isolated . . . I decided to go for a negotiated settlement. And that gave me only one choice: to go through with the election'(Waldmeir 1997: 247).

The Bophuthatswana affair was not, however, the end of white violence. Paramilitary groups continued to train and stock pile weapons, and a series of bomb attacks were made until the eve of the election. The targets included taxi ranks (where black people congregated), polling stations, the ANC and COSATU offices in the Orange Free State, and in Johannesburg bombs went off near the ANC head-quarters, and at the main airport. Many lives were lost, but the attacks were more isolated incidents rather than a sustained campaign. In retrospect they can be seen more as the kicks of a dying animal than a vigorous assault. They failed to under-mine the election, and on the eve of the poll thirty-two white extremists were arrested.

KwaZulu and the Inkatha Freedom Party

As South African troops moved in to take control of the Ciskei a delighted Slovo said: 'Two down, one more to go'. The 'one more' he had in mind was KwaZulu. The ANC's attitude towards KwaZulu and Inkatha was a combination of exasperation, bullying and reasonable pleading. Again there was some wild talk of sending in the tanks and Slovo foolishly predicted that, following the election, Buthelezi would be 'merely a smell in history' (Meredith 1994: 88). Until the very last minute the IFP refused to participate in the election, adamantly retaining its commitment to a federal structure, a special position for KwaZulu/Natal, and its belief that the final constitution should be agreed by existing parties not an elected assembly. In January 1994 Buthelezi told his followers that in the face of ANC's refusal to make concessions, 'it is impossible for me to lie to you, and reassure you that the IFP's opposition to fighting the election under the present constitution will not bring casualties and even death. But we must resist the ANC and their communist surrogates' (Meredith 1997: 506). The IFP therefore refused to register for the election, and those who went into KwaZulu to make preparations for it were resisted. In one incident, fifteen ANC supporters were shot and hacked to death after displaying election posters. In the three months prior to the election more than 700 people were killed in ANC/IFP clashes.

Under Buthelezi's leadership, the IFP became increasingly isolated. It had long abandoned any prospect of co-operation with the NP (although links remained with the security forces), and the other members of the Freedom Alliance soon discovered that Buthelezi was a frustrating partner. Yet, even standing alone, Inkatha was a considerable force. An estimated 12 per cent of the total South African electorate lived in KwaZulu; and Buthelezi now brought into play the Zulu King, Zwelithini, to boost Inkatha's traditional support base. The King, angry at an ANC proposal to abolish the name KwaZulu by absorbing it into Natal, reacted by rejecting the interim constitution and demanding that the Zulu kingdom be restored to its 1830 boundaries, embracing all Natal. Mandela came to realize the serious threat posed to the election, and in mid-February announced concessions, including the use of separate provincial and central ballot papers (as requested by the IFP), wider provincial powers, and the renaming of Natal as 'KwaZulu-Natal'. Yet, Buthelezi dismissed these steps as 'cheap politiking', which fell far short of his demands. In a further effort at appeasement Mandela arranged to meet Buthelezi on 1 March, declaring beforehand: 'I will go down on my knees to those who want to drag our country into bloodshed and to persuade them not to do so' (Meredith 1997: 509). Little progress was made, but when Mandela offered to submit the dispute to international mediation Buthelezi agreed to register the IFP 'provisionally' for the election.

The ANC/IFP rivalry was far from over. It reached its nadir on 28 March 1994, when Inkatha staged a protest march in central Johannesburg, which included a demonstration at the ANC's headquarters in Shell House. When the marchers – brandishing knobkerries and spears – reached Shell House, ANC security guards, fearing that the building would be stormed, shot into the crowd, killing eight people and wounding many others. In the ensuing confusion and conflict a further forty-five people were killed. On the following day Mandela refused to allow police into Shell House to investigate the incident; and he later admitted that he had instructed the security guards to shoot at the demonstrators if it were necessary to protect the building. Buthelezi proclaimed that: 'The Shell House massacre shows that we have now entered a final struggle to the finish between the ANC and the Zulu nation' (Meredith 1997: 514). New clashes arose in KwaZulu and along the Rand. In an attempt to counter the danger the government declared a state of emergency and sent a hastily established and ineffective National Peacekeeping Force (composed of a mixture of MK, homeland forces and regular troops) into the townships of the Rand.

Eleven days after 'the Shell House massacre' (as it became known to Inkatha), and only three weeks before the election, Mandela, de Klerk and Buthelezi met in a further attempt to avert disaster. The sparse outcome of a bad-tempered meeting was an agreement to go ahead with international mediation. However, even that was aborted when the two main mediators – Henry Kissinger, the former US Secretary of State, and Lord Carrington, the former British Foreign Secretary – arrived to find that Inkatha and the ANC disagreed on their terms of reference. Buthelezi wanted them to consider a postponement of the election; the ANC refused. Kissinger and Carrington flew out immediately. The situation was desperate, with the prospect either of no election in KwaZulu or a bloodbath if it went ahead. Two weeks before the voters were due to go to the polls, senior army officers, conscious of the threats in KwaZulu and from right-wing whites, advised the IEC to postpone the election. On balance Judge Kriegler decided to ignore the advice.

Then, with a week to go, Buthelezi changed his mind and decided that the IFP would fight the election. The change came in part from the renewed efforts of Professor Washington Okumu from Kenya, who had been involved in the mediation effort and remained behind when Carrington and Kissinger left. Okumu, with strong support from private companies, like Anglo American, pleaded with Buthelezi to recognize the dangers ahead and subordinate his interests to those of the general good. At the same time the ANC led Buthelezi to understand that shortly after the election the international mediators would be asked to return (an undertaking that was not honoured). These matters played their part, but so did Buthelezi's realization that he had become isolated, and that the situation in KwaZulu might develop into another Bophuthatswana, only on a grander and more prolonged scale. There were rumblings of discontent among KwaZulu officials, and even King Zwelithini was discussing terms with the ANC. With these hopes and dangers in mind Buthelezi accepted the offer of a constitutional role for the Zulu King, but dropped his other demands and agreed to fight the election. There were seven days to go. Two days before the election the white-dominated parliament met for the last time, in special session, to give constitutional recognition to the Zulu King. Inkatha was finally in the election.

The Democratic Party (DP)

In contrast with the IFP the Democratic Party (DP) played a positive part in the negotiations, and had no doubts about fighting the election. In its campaign the DP preached support for federalism, limitations on the powers of central government, the market economy and the private sector, and it raised issues concerning human rights and civil liberties. In its more optimistic moments the DP predicted that it could gain between 10 and 15 per cent of the vote. Yet, despite its credentials, the party faced problems. First, the record of support for 'liberal' parties in white politics was weak, nor was there a strong liberal tradition in black politics. Second, to increase its vote substantially the DP would need considerable black support, but its image was associated with affluent, urban whites and capitalists. Among blacks it was little known, and militants attacked it as a party which had offered tea and sympathy to blacks while participating fully in the apartheid structure. Third, the DP lacked the party organization and resources (both people and money) to be effective country-wide. The result was a patchy campaign. In some areas leaders like the energetic, articulate Tony Leon, made an impact; in others the DP lacked drive and people to forward its cause. Finally, the DP leader, Zach de Beer, could not match de Klerk or Mandela either in the resources at their command or the media attention paid to them.

Allies and Rivals: the ANC and NP

Both the ANC and the NP claimed success from the negotiations. In doing so they selected issues which suited them, and interpreted areas of uncertainty in the best light. The NP emphasized the checks and balances on government, the sharing of power in the interim constitution, proportional representations and the constitutional principles. To reassure its Afrikaner followers it pointed to the principle which stated that: 'The diversity of language and culture shall be acknowledged and protected'; and the agreement that as far as practicable education would be in the language of choice (Davenport 1998: 60). However, while there had been compromise on both sides, the balance had swung in favour of the ANC. The NP had been forced to change its ground while the ANC achieved most of its aims. Slovo had no doubts. He spoke of a 'famous victory', and concluded that 'we got pretty much what we wanted' – including a central, not a federal system, with 'the purse strings in the hands of the central government'. The new state would 'not remotely be a federation . . . We've managed to give them devolution, without losing control' (Waldmeir 1997: 242). Further, he boasted, the final constitution would be approved by an elected assembly, which meant that 'apart from the constitutional principles (which we support) everything in the interim constitution can be rewritten by the democratically elected representatives of the people' (*African Communist*, no. 135). Slovo recognized, however, that the struggle was far from over. The next task was to gain an electoral victory.

The election campaign served to confirm that the ANC and the NP were, at the same time, both the main political collaborators and the main rivals. They had collaborated in the negotiations, and now they were both committed to implementing the new political system, starting with the election. It was no easy walk to democracy. They faced chronic violence, the resistance of right-wing groups, the vacillations of Inkatha, and the problems of mounting an election in a large country in which most people were voting for the first time and in which new problems arose on a daily basis. Had the NP government and the ANC not held firm the settlement would have fallen apart.

Yet on the other side of the coin they were rivals. They had competed in the negotiations, now they competed in the election. They offered different policies, appealed to different interests, and strongly criticized each other. But, even in the heat of the contest, they never lost their determination to maintain the settlement. That was dramatically illustrated in a television debate between de Klerk and

Mandela. During the programme de Klerk, while making some criticism of the ANC, was at ease and constructive in putting forward the NP's case; whereas Mandela was tense, and spent his time attacking the NP and its past record. Then, at the very end, Mandela transformed the scene. Leaning towards de Klerk he said that their differences should not obscure the fact that 'we are a shining example to the entire world of people drawn from different racial groups who have a common loyalty, a common love of their country that is the dominant issue'. Taking de Klerk's hand, he said: 'Sir, you are one of those I rely on . . . We are going to face the problems of the country together. I am proud to hold your hand for us to go forward' (Meredith 1994: 168). It made public their mutual dependence. It was also a brilliant piece of electioneering.

The Election Campaigns: NP and ANC

The NP launched its election campaign claiming it would attract more than 30 per cent of the vote. Yet, as Mandela had stressed in the television programme, the NP carried the luggage of the past. If it were to fulfil its ambitions it had to leave behind apartheid, exclusive white nationalism and racial dominance. In short it had to re-invent itself. De Klerk had already started to do that, but the real test came with the election. A new NP was presented which had consciously abandoned apartheid for a democratic future; which was eager to work with others in a Christian democratic alliance; which emphasized 'standards' and 'order'; which had put South Africa on a fresh international course, opening it up to the world – to trade, commerce, finance, sport and tourism – and offering a western market economy. De Klerk's personal leadership was emphasized. The election manifesto claimed that he was universally recognized as the person who had liberated South Africa. Yet, in other ways de Klerk had to move cautiously if he was to retain support within his party. Although he distanced the NP from the past he did so in terms of it having 'committed an error of judgement, rather than a gigantic wrong' (Davenport 1998: 40).

In other respects too the NP looked to the past. On the positive side it emphasized the experience it would bring to government, which, it argued, would lead to a prosperous South Africa, based on a market economy, efficient economic management and sound monetary policies. On the negative side the NP attacked the ANC for its lack of experience, its violence, its communist links and claimed that an ANC government would bring the country to its economic knees. Over and over again, said the NP, socialism had destroyed economies – in the Soviet Union, eastern Europe and Africa. The ANC was a dangerous party, controlled by communists who would be dominant if the ANC gained power. Added to which the ANC employed violence, strikes, disruption in education and intimidation – even in the election. When de Klerk had visited an African squatter camp near Witbank he had been surrounded by aggressive ANC youths claiming their 'democratic right' to drive him away, and threatening the lives of Africans who welcomed him. The NP also attacked the more extreme ANC leaders. An NP advertisement had a photograph of Winnie Mandela, with details of her crimes, including her part in the disappearance and death of Stomphie Moeketsi. It concluded: 'Mrs Mandela could be your new Minister of Law and Order, or even the Minister of Child Welfare . . . Only your vote can stop this' (Meredith 1994: 173).

Another respect in which the NP looked to the past was in anticipating support from the majority of whites. Although it had abandoned hopes of a constitution based on ethnic groups; it assumed that most whites would vote for it, and it further assumed that this would give it leverage in the new state because of the importance of whites in the civil service and armed forces. However, if the NP was to fulfil its electoral ambitions it needed support from other races. Among Africans it made little progress, despite placing 22 Africans among the top 80 names on the party's national list, and despite de Klerk's campaigning.

Among Coloureds and Indians, however, the NP had greater success. They too had suffered under apartheid, but now looking to the future they feared 'positive discrimination' against them by an African government. The NP was not above fuelling those fears by playing the race card. To an extent it worked, especially among Coloureds in the Cape, where, since the removal of the apartheid barriers, Africans had settled in great numbers, competing for jobs and housing. In the years since the introduction of the tricameral parliament the Coloureds had gained in terms of housing, education and medical facilities, giving them a stake to defend against African newcomers. (Between 1984 and 1993 more than 100,000 houses had been built for Coloureds.) Added to that many Coloureds had cultural and linguistic ties with Afrikaners; 80 per cent speaking Afrikaans as their home language. Anwar Ismael, a Coloured NP supporter, reasoned: 'We speak Afrikaans, we live as conservatives, attend church and raise our children on traditional values, hence we are National Party. The Xhosa of the Transkei and the ANC are the real settlers here. The ANC with its black profile and Communist cloak repels us' (Giliomee 1995: 225). Coloured support was crucial in the Western Cape where they formed a majority of the electorate, and it was in Cape Town that de Klerk held his major eve of election rally, with a predominantly Coloured audience. At the election about 1.5 million blacks (mainly Coloureds and Indians) voted for the NP, making up a third of its total (Lodge 1995: 475).

The African National Congress

In fighting its first ever national election the ANC faced the dual task of building a campaign organization and preparing policies. Responsibility for the campaign was given to Popo Malefe and Kheto Gordon. They were backed by substantial external funding (the ANC probably had four times the NP's financial resources); and by advisers, including Stanley Greenberg and Frank Greer (who had advised US President Bill Clinton). The policy issues were dealt with by working groups. Conscious that the party stood on the edge of power, their efforts were a further stage in the ANC's journey from liberation movement to government. The reports were a mixture of idealism blended with an increasing recognition of the constraints and pressures that came with office. For example, idealism was prominent in the foreign policy paper. 'South Africa's foreign policy,' wrote Mandela, 'will be based on our belief that human rights should be the core concern of international relations.' The new state would not join any military bloc and would settle all matters peacefully. In southern Africa it would help to rebuild the region 'not in the spirit of paternalism or dominance but with mutual co-operation and respect' (Mandela 1993).

While the ANC could look to the past with much greater pride and confidence than the NP, it too inherited problems – none more so than in shaping economic policy. The importance given to the economy was reflected in the title of its manifesto – 'A Better Life for All' – and one of its major appeals to Africans was to hold out the prospect of a better material life. Many of the problems were not of the ANC's making, for the economy had been distorted by apartheid, the privileges given to whites, the impact of sanctions, the high expenditure on security and Pretoria's protectionist policies. However, other problems were derived from the ANC's past. During the years of struggle – working with the SACP, socialist states and COSATU – the ANC's economic orientation had become increasingly socialist. Now, however, the communist bloc had disintegrated, socialist policies were discredited and the international scene was dominated by the West. Some argued that socialism had not failed it simply had not been tried. 'We have not,' declared Slovo, 'abandoned our long-term aim of winning a future in which all the means of production are socialised to serve the interests of the whole society.' But such views did not go unchallenged inside the ANC. Pallo Jordan pointed out that socialism had given rise to oppression in the USSR and he accused the SACP of nurturing a culture which had 'resulted in a spirit of intolerance, petty intellectual thuggery and political dissembling' (Meredith 1994: 131–2).

The result was a fierce internal debate about future economic policy, based on different interests and ideologies and central to which was a growth versus redistribution dispute. All sides wanted both, but in crude terms those who emphasized growth put their faith in western market values. They saw the government's main role as providing the right conditions for investment and enterprise, which, they said, would benefit everybody; whereas 'over rapid redistribution would guarantee economic collapse' (Nattrass 1994: 351). Those who were mainly concerned with redistribution were more wedded to socialist ideas. Their slogan was 'Growth through Redistribution'. They argued that market forces had created injustice and would continue to do so. In their view the state should play a major role in economic and social engineering, and so they advocated nationalization of capitalist enterprises – such as financial institutions and the mines – which, they said, had generated great wealth for a few whites at the expense of many blacks.

The outcome of the debate was the ANC's Reconstruction and Development Programme (RDP), drawn up under the guidance of Jay Naidoo. The RDP went through an extensive consultation process with six drafts before it was published. Initially it had read like a socialist blueprint – including a wealth tax, a reconstruction levy, minimum wage legislation, a programme of nationalization and state intervention – but at each stage it was modified. Eventually Mandela could point out that it contained no mention of nationalization or a single Marxist slogan; that it stressed fiscal and monetary discipline and the need for private and public sectors to work together; and that he had discussed it with Harry

Oppenheimer, the doyen of South Africa's capitalists, and with World Bank officials. Mandela presented the RDP as a means of avoiding the sins of a centralized command economy or an unfettered market system. He saw it furthering the democratic cause; by rectifying past inequalities and building a better future; it provided the path towards a more just society and national unity. 'Democracy,' stated the RDP, 'is not confined to periodic elections. It is rather an active process enabling everybody to contribute to reconstruction and development' (Nattrass 1994: 358).

The RDP was translated into the ANC's election manifesto as a set of ambitious targets, based on major public works – including a million new houses within five years; running water and flush lavatories for another million; electrification for two and a half million; plus roads, clinics and schools. Within ten years the aim was to offer free schooling to all children, and create new jobs for two and a half million people. The growth target was 5 per cent per annum. The sources of funding were not given. Inevitably, conflicting views arose within and between the parties about the RDP. Was it a bold agenda for a better future, or an unrealizable wish list?

While policies and manifestos played their part in the election a greater impact was made by broad party images. These images were derived from the past, from the social groups identified with the parties and from their present leadership. In all these respects the ANC had advantages. It presented itself as a party whose time had come: that had stood firm against apartheid and yet had never abandoned its commitment to a united non-racial South Africa. Across the country it could count on support from most of the organizations that had struggled against apartheid: black trade unions, civic associations, and youths. While its greatest appeal was to Africans, it also had support from other racial groups – not in large numbers but people of strong convictions and often great ability. The ANC was also blessed with impressive leaders. Above all stood Mandela. Alongside his other virtues he proved to be an excellent election campaigner. He was not a great orator, but wherever he went he drew large enthusiastic crowds; he related well to journalists and reporters; and he responded to diverse settings – apparently at ease whether at a mass rally in Soweto, or meeting tribal elders in rural areas, or addressing grey-suited businessmen. Wherever he went his humanity stood out. His message was of hope for a new South Africa based on a common nationalism. Yet he was not afraid to underline home truths: whether it was telling Africans to work harder and to drink less; or chastizing whites for criticizing the ANC's links with communists. He pointed out that while most whites, including the Dutch Reform Church, had supported apartheid the SACP had opposed it. 'Why', he asked, 'should we listen to you about our comrades in the Communist Party?' (Meredith 1997: 503). And, while Mandela was the dominant figure, the ANC was blessed with other impressive leaders – such as Walter and Albertina Sisulu from the older generation; a middle-aged band including Thabo Mbeki, Jacob Zuma, Jay Naidoo and Tokyo Sexwale; and younger leaders like Cyril Ramaphosa, Cheryl Carolus and Frank Chikane. There was no doubt that the ANC would be the largest party in the new parliament – the question was by how much.

Liberation Through the Ballot Box

'I cherish the idea of a new South Africa', said Mandela as he cast his vote. It was a sentiment shared by the majority of his fellow citizens, and especially Africans who saw the act of voting as their personal contribution to converting the 'apartheid regime' into 'our government'. It was a liberating experience for most whites as well, for by voting many turned their backs on the past and embraced the new state. The election itself was remarkable. The turn out was very high, with more than nineteen million people (87 per cent of the estimated electorate) casting their vote. It was remarkable also in the commitment of individual voters who often waited long hours at polling stations; in the relative absence of violence over the voting period; and in the outcome whereby the three main parties – ANC, NP and IFP – finished with a sense of achievement.

As expected the main victory went to the ANC, which gained majorities in the national poll and in seven of the nine provinces. However, its national vote did not reach the two-thirds that would have enabled it to ride roughshod over other parties in future constitutional negotiations. The FF, DP and PAC were disappointed with their results; but the NP and IFP were reasonably pleased both with their shares of the national vote and the majority each gained in one province – the Western Cape for the NP and KwaZulu/Natal for the IFP. At the centre of government the pattern of power sharing gave the ANC 18 cabinet seats, Mandela the Presidency, and Thabo Mbeki became First Deputy President; the NP had 6 seats, with de Klerk as Second Deputy President; while the IFP gained 3 cabinet seats. Who would have predicted, even in 1990, that Mandela, de Klerk and Buthelezi would sit together in the same cabinet?

Table 22.1   General election results, 1994

Party	Percentage of National votes	Assembly seats
ANC	62.62	252
NP	20.39	82
IFP	10.54	43
FF	2.17	9
DP	1.73	7
PAC	1.25	5
ACDP	0.45	2

Note: ACDP = The African Christian Democratic Party

The overall judgement was that, given the circumstances, the election had been 'substantially free and fair'. Yet, inevitably, because of the formidable task which faced the IEC, there were major organizational problems, and at times the arrangements came near to breaking point. There were also electoral malpractices, especially in KwaZulu 'with reports of pirate polling stations, the stuffing of ballot boxes, and presiding officers using their position to encourage, and sometimes force, voters to cast their ballots for the IFP'. As a consequence the result in KwaZulu owed a great deal to political expediency and 'horse trading' behind closed doors. The IEC, after investigating the cheating in KwaZulu, reduced the IFP's regional total by 250,000 votes. The IEC also reported that there had been 165 'no go' areas across the country where the dominant party refused to allow others to campaign. Of these 39 per cent were in ANC areas, 27 per cent in IFP and 12 per cent in right-wing white areas (Lodge 1995: 473/497).

A further concern, especially for the hopes of building a single nation, was the voting along racial lines. Perhaps that too was inevitable, given South Africa's past, and party support was mainly based on race and tribe. The ANC made its appeal across the races, but its majority was built on African votes. James Hamill and Jack Spence saw its success more as a 'pan tribal' than a multi-racial victory (Hamill and Spence 1994: 130). The NP also boasted of drawing support across the races, but that was true only of the minority races – whites, Coloureds and Indians. It had minimal backing from Africans. The IFP's support was even more restricted. Although it gained more than 50 per cent of the vote in KwaZulu Natal it attracted only 0.9 per cent outside the province. Votes for the FF and DP came from whites; and the PAC's from Africans.

Losing and Gaining a Nation

On 10 May 1994 princes, presidents and prime ministers assembled at the Union Buildings in Pretoria to celebrate the birth of the new South Africa and to greet the new President, Nelson Mandela. While the world leaders paid their personal respects, television cameras beamed the ceremony around the globe. The world rejoiced. On the platform with Mandela stood his predecessor F. W. de Klerk. The transfer of power was achieved in an atmosphere of good will. 'Mr Mandela,' said de Klerk, 'has walked a long road and now stands at the top of the hill. A man of destiny knows that beyond this hill stands another and another. The journey is never complete. As he contemplates the next hill I hold out my hand to Mr Mandela in friendship and co-operation' (Meredith 1997: 518). The new President was equally gracious towards de Klerk, recognizing their past differences, but now able to shake hands and join together in working for the future.

Together they could look to the immediate past with pride for they had steered South Africa through a political revolution. A new state had been born. Although it was accompanied by violence the driving force had been negotiation and not force, and although there was pressure from below which created the setting for change the process had been top-down: the product of conference halls, smoke filled rooms and press conferences. Because it had been driven forward by men in dark suits and not those in battle-dress there was much talk of 'transformation' but little of 'revolution'. Yet to describe the outcome as anything less than a 'revolution' would be to undervalue it. South Africa had been changed, irredeemably changed. However, a revolution is not a fixed point; rather it is a process that stretches over time; a journey over hills, as de Klerk had said, and there is no shortage of hills in South Africa. The political revolution would certainly be followed by economic and social changes, but what forms would they take? Although apartheid was dead could racism be killed? Will the tolerance shown at the election persist? Will tribal divisions tear the country apart? Can economic growth and redistribution be achieved? Can a society that has suffered so much violence settle down in peace? Will corruption undermine the state?

The two leaders were also conscious of what had been gained and lost. In that respect de Klerk was vulnerable. When he had presented the final negotiated agreement to the cabinet an outraged minister (Tertius Delport) had shouted at him 'What have you done? Why have you given South Africa away?' (Waldmeir 1997: 232). Later Hermann Giliomee outlined the changes in de Klerk's negotiating position. In 1990 de Klerk had anticipated an 'Afrikaner-led multi-racial oligarchy', and had claimed that the NP would 'have its hand on the tiller for many years to come'. Yet negotiations had produced an outcome which 'very few had expected and many feared: largely untrammeled majority rule in a unitary state'. According to Giliomee the NP had 'failed to secure any of its major political and cultural objectives', and he put it down to a lack of strategic thinking on the part of the leadership. In January 1997 de Klerk himself admitted that: 'A decision to surrender the right to national sovereignty is certainly one of the most painful that any leader can take. Most nations are prepared to risk total war and catastrophe rather than surrender that right. Yet this was the decision we had to take. We had to accept the necessity of giving up the ideal on which we have been nurtured and the dream for which so many generations of our forefathers had struggled and for which many of our people had died' (Giliomee 1997).

De Klerk acted with great courage. He saw clearly what had to be sacrificed for the future of the country, but once he had been forced to abandon the idea of 'group alliance' he had no clear vision of what should replace it. He simply made the best bargain he could. He proved to be a pragmatist. Had he harboured the ideological convictions of a Verwoerd, or been afraid to split Afrikanerdom like Vorster, or baulked at the consequences of change as had P. W. Botha, a negotiated settlement could not have been achieved. The outcome was a failure only in the sense that his proposed version of nationalism (and the associated structure of the state) had proved to be inadequate and unjust – as had Milner's imperialism; Smuts's white nationalism; Malan's Afrikanerdom; Verwoerd's apartheid; P. W. Botha's power sharing. The outcome of negotiation was to launch South Africa along the road towards a new nationalism and a new state. Shortly before he was installed as President, Mandela told a church congregation in Soweto: 'The day we have been fighting for has come. Let us forget the past. Let us hold hands and unite. The time has come for men and women, Africans, Coloureds, Indians, whites, Afrikaners and English speakers to say we are one country; we are one people' (Meredith 1997: 519). That is the vision and challenge for South Africans in the twenty-first century.

References

Adam, Heribert and Giliomee, Herman, *The Rise and Crisis of Afrikaner Power*, David Philip, 1979a.
—— and —— *Ethnic Power Mobilized: Can South Africa Change?*, Yale University Press, 1979b.
—— and Kogila Moodley, *The Negotiated Revolution*, Jonathan Ball, 1993.
Amnesty International, *South Africa: State of Fear*, Amnesty, 1992.
ANC, *ANC Speaks: Documents and Statements of the African National Congress*, no publisher, no date.
Arnold, Millard, *The Testimony of Steve Biko: Black Consciousness in South Africa*, Graton Books, 1979.
Austin, Dennis, *South Africa 1984*, Routledge and Kegan Paul, 1985.
——, *The Commonwealth and Britain*, Routledge and Kegan Paul, 1988.
Barber, James, *Is There a South African Nation?* South African Institute of International Affairs, 1987.
—— and Barratt, John, *South Africa's Foreign Policy: The Search for Status and Security 1945–1988*, Cambridge University Press, 1990.
Barrett, Howard, 'The Turn to the Masses: the ANC's Strategic Review of 1978/9'. Journal of Southern African Studies (JSAS) vol. 18, no. 1, 1991.
Beinart, William and Dubow, Paul (eds), *Segregation and Apartheid*, Routledge, 1995.
—— and Bundy Colin, *Hidden Struggles in Rural South Africa*, James Currey, 1987.
Biko Steve, *I Write What I Like* (ed. Aelred Stubbs) Heinemann, 1978.
Botha, Jan, *Verwoerd is Dead*, Books of Africa, 1967.
Brewer, John D., *After Soweto: An Unfinished Journey*, Oxford University Press, 1986.
Brits J. P., *South Africa in the Twentieth Century: 1919–1934* (in Liebenberg and Spies, 1993).
Bundy, Colin, *The Rise and Fall of the South African Peasantry*, Heinemann, 1979.
——, 'Land and liberation: popular rural protest and the national liberation movements in South Africa, 1920–1960' (in Marks and Trapido, 1987).
Buthulezi, Mangosuthu G., *South Africa: My Vision of the Future*, Weidenfeld and Nicolson, 1990.
Campbell, Keith, *ANC: A Soviet Task Force?*, Institute for the Study of Terrorism, London, 1986
Carter, Gwendolen, *The Politics of Inequality: South Africa since 1948*, Thames and Hudson, 1962.
Clark, Steve (ed.), *Mandela Speaks*, Pathfinder, 1993.
Cocker, Christopher, 'The South African Election and Neo Apartheid'. *The World Today*, June 1981.

Davenport, T. R. H., *The Afrikaner Bond 1880–1911*, Oxford University Press, 1966.

——, *South Africa: A Modern History*, Macmillan, 1987.

——, *The Birth of a New Nation: South Africa*, University of Toronto Press, 1998.

De Kiewiet, C. W. A., *History of South Africa: Social and Economic*, Oxford University Press, 1957.

De Klerk, Willem, *F. W. de Klerk: The Man In His Times*, Jonathan Ball, 1991.

De Kock, Eugene, *A Long Night's Damage: Working for the Apartheid State*, Contra Press, 1998.

Dengenaar, Johan, *The Myth of the South African Nation*, Mowbry, IDASA Occasional Paper no. 40.

D'Oliveira, John, *John Vorster – The Man*, Ernest Stanton, 1977.

Doyle, Conan A., *The Great Boer War*, Smith and Elder, 1902.

Dubow, Saul, 'Race, Civilisation and Culture: the Elaboration of Segregation Discourse in the Inter-war Years' (in Marks and Trapido, 1987).

Ellis, Stephen and Sechaba, Tsepo, *Comrades Against Apartheid: The ANC and the South African Communist Party in Exile*, James Currey, 1992.

EPG, *Mission to South Africa: Findings of the Commonwealth Eminent Persons Group on Southern Africa*, Penguin, 1986.

Everatt, David, 'Alliance Politics of a Special Type: The Roots of the ANC/SACP Alliance'. *JSAS*, vol. 18, no. 1, 1991.

Fisher, John, *Paul Kruger: His Life and Times*, Secker and Warburg, 1975.

Frankel, Philip H., *Pretoria's Praetorians: Civil–Military Relations in South Africa*, Cambridge University Press, 1984.

Fraser, Peter, *Joseph Chamberlain: Radicalism and Empire 1868–1914*, Cassell, 1966.

Friedman, Steven (ed.), *The Long Journey: South Africa's Quest for a Negotiated Settlement*, Ravan Press, 1993.

—— and Atkinson Doreen (eds), *The Small Miracle: South Africa's Negotiated Settlement*, Ravan Press, 1994.

Garson, N. G., 'South Africa and World War I'. *Journal of Imperial and Commonwealth History*, vol. III, no.1, 1979.

Geldenhuys, Deon, 'The Effects of South Africa's Racial Policy on Anglo-South African Relations: 1945–1961' Cambridge University, Ph.D. dissertation, 1977.

——, *Foreign Policy Implications of South Africa's 'Total National Onslaught' Strategy*, South African Institute of International Affairs, Johannesburg, 1981.

Gerhart, Gail, *Black Power in South Africa: the Evolution of an Ideology*, University of California Press, 1978.

Geyser O. (ed.), *B. J. Vorster: Select Speeches*, Institute of Contemporary History, Bloemfontein, 1977.

Giliomee, Hermann, *The Parting of the Ways: SA Politics 1976–1982*, David Philip, 1982.

—— 'The beginning of Afrikaner Nationalism 1870–1915'. *South African Historical Journal*, vol. 19, 1987.

—— '"Broedertwis": Intra Afrikaner Conflicts in the Transition from Apartheid 1969–1991'. *African Affairs*, vol. 91, no. 364, July 1992.

—— 'The Non Racial Franchise and Afrikaner and Coloured Identities, 1910–1994'. *African Affairs*, vol. 94, no. 375, April 1995.

—— 'Surrender Without Defeat: Afrikaners and the South African "Miracle"'. *Daedalus*, vol. 126, no. 2, Spring 1997.

Greenberg, Stanley B., 'Ideological Struggles within the South African State' (in Marks and Trapido, 1987).

Grundlingh A. M., *South Africa in the Twentieth Century: 1938–1948*, (in Liebenberg and Spies, 1993).

Grundy, Kenneth W., *The Militarization of South African Politics*, I.B. Tauris, 1986.

HA. (Hansard), South African Parliamentary Debates.

Hamill, James and Spence, J. E., 'South Africa's Watershed Election'. *The World Today*, vol. 50, no. 7, July 1994.

Hancock, W. K., *Smuts: The Sanguine Years: 1870–1919*, Cambridge University Press, 1962.

———, *Smuts: The Fields of Force: 1919–1950*, Cambridge University Press, 1968.

Heard, Kenneth A., *General Elections in South Africa: 1943–1970*, Oxford University Press, 1974.

Hepple, Aleander, *Verwoerd*, Penguin, 1967.

Hill, Christopher R., *Bantustans: The Fragmentation of South Africa*, Oxford University Press, 1964

Hill, Robert A. and Pirio, Gregory, '"Africa for the Africans": the Garvey Movement in South Africa, 1920–1940' (in Marks and Trapido, 1987).

Hofmeyr, Isobel, 'Building a Nation from Words: Afrikaans Language, Literature and Ethnic Identity, 1902–1924' (in Marks and Trapido, 1987).

Horne, Alistair, *Macmillan 1957–1986*, vol. II, Macmillan, 1989.

Hyslop, Jonathan, 'Problems of Explanation in the Case Study of Afrikaner Nationalism'. *JSAS*, vol 22, no. 3, 1996.

IDAAF, *International Defence and Aid Fund* – International Service, London.

IRR, South African Institute of Race Relations *Race Relations Survey* – annual.

Jenkins, Simon, 'Destabilisation in Southern Africa'. *The Economist* 16 July 1983.

Jay, Richard, *Joseph Chamberlain: a Political Study*, Oxford University Press, 1981.

Johns, Sheridan, 'Obstacles to Guerrilla Warfare: A South African Case Study'. *Journal of Modern African Studies*, vol. 11, no. 2, 1973.

——— and Davis R. Hunt Jr (eds), *Mandela, Tambo, and the African National Congress: The Struggle Against Apartheid 1948–1990*, Oxford University Press, 1991.

Judd, Denis, *Radical Joe: a Life of Joseph Chamberlain*, Hamish Hamilton, 1977.

Kane-Berman, John, *Political Violence in South Africa*, South African Institute of Race Relations, 1993.

Karis, Thomas and Carter, Gwendolen (eds), *From Protest to Challenge: A Documentary History of African Politics in South Africa 1882–1964*, Hoover Institute Press. Vol. 1 *Protest and Hope: 1882–1934*, 1972; Vol. 2 *Hope and Challenge: 1935–1952* 1973; Vol. 3 *Challenge and Violence: 1953–1964*, 1977.

Kenny, Henry, *Architect of Apartheid: H. F. Verwoerd – An Appraisal*, Jonathan Ball, 1980.

Kohn, Hans, *Nationalism: Its Meaning and History*, Anvil Books, 1965

Kruger, D. W., *The Making of a Nation: A History of the Union of South Africa 1910–1961*, Macmillan, 1969.

Kruger, Rayne, *Good-Bye Dolly Gray: the Story of the Boer War*, Four Square, 1964.

Lavin, Deborah, *From Empire to International Commonwealth: A Biography of Lionel Curtis*, Oxford University Press, 1995.

Leatt James, Kneifel Theo, Nurnberger Klaus (eds), *Contending Ideologies in South Africa*, David Philip, 1986.

Legassick, Martin, 'British Hegemony and the Origins of Segregation in South Africa: 1901–14' (in Beinart and Dubow, 1995).

Lehmann, Joseph, *The First Boer War*, Buchan and Enright, 1985.

Le May G. H. L., *British Supremacy in South Africa 1899–1907*, Oxford University Press, 1965.

———, *The Afrikaners: An Historical Interpretation*, Blackwell, 1995.

Liebenberg, B. J. and Spies, S. B. (eds), *South Africa in the 20th Century*, J. L. van Schaik, 1993.

Liebenberg, I. et al. (eds), *The Long March: the Story of the Struggle for Liberation in South Africa*, HAUM, 1994

Lipton, Merle, *Capitalism and Apartheid: South Africa, 1910–84*, Gower/Temple Smith, 1985.

Lodge, Tom, *Black Politics in South Africa Since 1945*, Longman, 1983.

——, 'Political Mobilisation in the 1950s: an East London case study' (in Marks and Trapido, 1987).

——, 'The South African General Election April 1994: Results, Analysis and Implications'. *African Affairs*, vol. 94, no. 377, October 1995.

Mandela, Nelson, *The Struggle is My Life*, International Defence and Aid Fund, London, 1978.

——, *Long Walk to Freedom: The Autobiography of Nelson Mandela*, Little, Brown and Co., 1994.

——, 'South Africa's Future Foreign Policy'. *Foreign Affairs*, vol. 72, no. 5, 1993.

Mansergh, Nicholas, *Documents and Speeches on British Commonwealth Affairs 1952–1962*, Oxford University Press, 1963.

Marais, J. S., *The Fall of Kruger's Republic*, Oxford University Press, 1961.

Marks, Shula, *The Ambiguities of Dependence in South Africa: Class, Nationalism and the State in Natal*, Ravan Press, 1986.

—— and Trapido, Stanley (eds), *The Politics of Race, Class and Nationalism in Twentieth Century South Africa*, Longman, 1987.

Martin, David and Johnson, Phyllis, *The Struggle for Zimbabwe*, Faber, 1981.

Meredith, Martin, *The Past is Another Country: Rhodesia UDI to Zimbabwe*, Pan Books, 1980.

——, *South Africa's New Era: The 1994 Election* Mandarin, 1994.

——, *Nelson Mandela: a Biography*, Hamish Hamilton, 1997.

Meli, Francis, *A History of the ANC: South Africa Belongs to Us*, James Currey, 1988.

Midlane, Matthew, 'The South Africa General Election of 1977'. *African Affairs*, vol. 78, no. 311. April 1979.

Moodie, Dunbar, *The Rise of Afrikanerdom: Power, Apartheid and the Afrikaner Civil Religion*, University of California Press, 1975.

Motlhabi, Mokgethi, *The Theory and Practice of Black Resistance to Apartheid*, Skotaville Publishers, 1984.

Muller, C. F. J. (ed.), *500 Years: A History of South Africa*, Academica 1969.

Nasson, Bill, *Abraham Esau's War: A Black South African War in the Cape, 1899–1902*, Cambridge University Press, 1991.

Nattrass, Nicoli, 'Politics and Economics in ANC Economic Policy', *African Affairs*, vol. 93, no. 372, July 1994.

Nimocks, Walter, *Milner's Young Men*, Duke University Press, 1970.

Nutting, Anthony, *Scramble for Africa: the Great Trek to the Boer War*, Constable, 1970.

O'Brien, Terence H., *Milner* Constable, 1979.

O'Meara, Dan, Volkskapitalisme: Class, Capital and Ideology in *Afrikaner Nationalism 1934–1948*, Cambridge University Press, 1983.

——, *Forty Lost Years: The Apartheid State and the Politics of the National Party, 1948–1994*, Ravan Press, 1996.

Pakenham, Thomas, *The Boer War*, Futura, 1982.

Paton, Alan, *Hofmeyr*, Oxford University Press, 1964.

Pirow, Oswald, *James Barry Munnick Hertzog*, Howard Timmins, Cape Town (undated).

Plaatje, Sol T., *Native Life in South Africa*, Ravan Press, 1982.

Poel, Jean van der, *Selections from Smuts' Papers*, vol. VII, Cambridge University Press, 1973.

Pogrund, Benjamin, *How Can Man Die Better: Sobukwe and Apartheid*, Peter Halban, 1990.

Pottinger, Brian, *The Imperial Presidency: P. W. Botha the First 10 Years*, Southern, 1988.

Powell, Enoch, *Joseph Chamberlain*, Thames and Hudson, 1977.

Pyrah, G. B., *Imperial Policy and South Africa 1902–1910*, Oxford University Press, 1955.

Reddy, E. S., *Oliver Tambo and the Struggle Against Apartheid*, Sterling Publishers, 1987.

Reynolds, Andrew, *Election 94: South Africa*, David Philip, 1994.

Rich, Paul B., *State Power and Black Politics in South Africa 1912–1951*, Macmillan 1996.

Roberts, Michael and Trollip, A. E. G., *The South African Opposition 1939–1945*, Longman Green, 1947.

Robinson, Ronald and Gallagher, John, *Africa and the Victorians*, Macmillan, 1961.

Rotburg, Robert, *The Founder: Cecil Rhodes and the Pursuit of Power*, Oxford University Press, 1988.

SA Government. Government Press Releases and 'Hand Outs'.

SAIIA. South African Institute of International Affairs.

SA Review. *South Africa Review: I–V*, Ravan Press, 1983–9.

Scher, D. M., *South Africa in the Twentieth Century: 1948–1966* (in Liebenberg and Spies 1993).

Seegers, Annette, *The Military in the Making of Modern South Africa*, Taurus Academic Studies, 1996.

Seekings, Jeremy, 'Trailing Behind the Masses: The UDF and Township Politics'. *JSAS*, vol. 18, no.11, 1991.

South Africa Year Book. Government Printers, Pretoria

Smith, Iain R., *The Origins of the South African War 1899–1902*, Longman, 1996.

Smith, Ian, *The Great Betrayal*, Blake Publishing, 1997.

Smuts, J. C., *Plans for a Better World*, Hodder and Stoughton, 1942.

Sparks, Allister, *The Mind of South Africa*, Heinemann, 1990.

——, *Tomorrow is Another Country: The Inside Story of South Africa's Negotiated Revolution*, Heinemann, 1995.

Steward, Alexander, *The World the West and Pretoria*, David McKay, 1977.

Stultz, Newell M., *Afrikaner Politics in South Africa: 1934–1948*, University of California Press, 1974.

Taylor, A. J. P., *From the Boer War to the Cold War*, Penguin, 1996.

Thomas, Scott, *The Diplomacy of Liberation: The Foreign Policy of the ANC since 1960*, Tauris Academic Studies, 1996.

Thompson, Leonard, *The Unification of South Africa 1902–1910*, Oxford University Press, 1960.

——, *The Political Mythology of Apatheid*, Yale University Press, 1985.

——, *A History of South Africa*, Yale University Press, 1990.

Thornton, A. P., *The Imperial Idea and Its Enemies: A Study in British Power*, Macmillan, 1966.

Tudor, Henry, *Political Myth*, Pall Mall, 1972.

Tutu, Desmond, *The Rainbow People of God: South Africa's Victory over Apartheid*, Bantam Books, 1995.

Van Diepen, Maria (ed.), *The National Question in South Africa*, Zed Books, 1989.

Vandenbosch, A., *South Africa and the World: The Foreign Policy of Apartheid*, University Press of Kentucky, 1970.

Van der Merwe P., 'What Middle Road for the Coloureds?'. *New Nation*, Pretoria, 1971.

Van Onselen, Charles, *Studies in the Social and Economic History of the Witwatersrand: 1886–1914. 1 New Babylon; 2 New Nineveh*, Longman, 1982.

Van Vuuren D. J., Latakgomo J., Marais, H. C. and Schlemmer, L. (eds), *South African Election 1987*, Owen Burgess, 1987.

Waldmeir, Patti, *Anatomy of a Miracle: The End of Apartheid and the Birth of the New South Africa*, Viking, 1997.

Walker, E., *A History of South Africa*, Longman, 1968

Walshe, Peter, *The Rise of African Nationalism in South Africa*, Ad Donker Ltd., 1987.

Warwick, Peter, *Black People and the South African War 1899–1902*, Cambridge University Press, 1983.

Wheatcroft, Geoffrey, *The Randlords: The Men Who Made South Africa*, Weidenfeld, 1993.

Willan, Brian, *Sol Plaatje: South African Nationalist 1876–1932*, Heinemann, 1984.

Worden, Nigel, *The Making of Modern South Africa*, Blackwell, 1995.

Worsfold, W. Basil, *Lord Milner's Work in South Africa*, John Murray, 1906.

Index